The Philosophy of Food

The Philosophy of Food

Edited by

David M. Kaplan

UNIVERSITY OF CALIFORNIA PRESS

Berkeley   Los Angeles   London

University of California Press, one of the most distinguished university presses in the United States, enriches lives around the world by advancing scholarship in the humanities, social sciences, and natural sciences. Its activities are supported by the UC Press Foundation and by philanthropic contributions from individuals and institutions. For more information, visit www.ucpress.edu.

University of California Press
Berkeley and Los Angeles, California

University of California Press, Ltd.
London, England

Library of Congress Cataloging-in-Publication Data

The philosophy of food / edited by David M. Kaplan.
   p.   cm.
  Includes bibliographical references and index.
  ISBN 978-0-520-26933-0 (cloth : alk. paper)
  ISBN 978-0-520-26934-7 (pbk. : alk. paper)
  1. Food.   I. Kaplan, David M.
  TX357.P53 2011
  641.3–dc23

                2011032946

Manufactured in the United States of America

20   19   18   17   16   15   14   13   12   11
10   9   8   7   6   5   4   3   2   1

In keeping with a commitment to support environmentally responsible and sustainable printing practices, UC Press has printed this book on Rolland Enviro100, a 100% post-consumer fiber paper that is FSC certified, deinked, processed chlorine-free, and manufactured with renewable biogas energy. It is acid-free and EcoLogo certified.

Matt Margolin
(September 13, 1966–September 24, 2010)

TABLE OF CONTENTS

Introduction

The Philosophy of Food

David M. Kaplan

Philosophers have a long but scattered history of analyzing food. Plato famously details an appropriate diet in Book II of the *Republic*. The Roman Stoics, Epicurus and Seneca, as well as Enlightenment philosophers such as Locke, Rousseau, Voltaire, Marx, and Nietzsche, all discuss various aspects of food production and consumption. In the twentieth century, philosophers considered such issues as vegetarianism, agricultural ethics, food rights, biotechnology, and gustatory aesthetics. In the twenty-first century, philosophers continue to address these issues and new ones concerning the globalization of food, the role of technology, and the rights and responsibilities of consumers and producers. Typically, these philosophers call their work "food ethics" or "agricultural ethics." But I think they sell themselves short. Philosophers do more than treat food as a branch of ethical theory. They also examine how it relates to the fundamental areas of philosophical inquiry: metaphysics, epistemology, aesthetics, political theory, and, of course, ethics. The phrase "philosophy of food" is more accurate. We might eventually come to think of the philosophy of food as a perfectly ordinary "philosophy of" if more philosophers address food issues and more colleges offer courses on the subject—or at least that is my hope.

But why is this subject—a footnote to Plato just like the rest of the philosophy— not yet fully entrenched as a standard philosophical subject? Why do philosophers only occasionally address questions concerning food? The subject is obviously important and the scholarship on food has real pedigree. So why does "philosophy of food" have a novel ring? Some have argued that food is eschewed because of the perception that it is too physical and transient to deserve serious consideration.[1] Others have argued that food production and preparation have conventionally been regarded as women's work and, therefore, viewed as an unworthy topic for a male-dominated profession.[2] Still others argue that the senses and activities associated with food (taste, eating, and drinking) have traditionally been seen as "lower senses" and are too primitive and instinctual to be analyzed philosophically.[3] These are all plausible explanations.

But perhaps the real reason why relatively few philosophers analyze food is because it is too difficult. Food is vexing. It is not even clear what it is. It belongs simultaneously to the worlds of economics, ecology, and culture. It involves vegetables, chemists, and wholesalers; livestock, refrigerators, and cooks; fertilizer, fish, and grocers. The subject quickly becomes tied up in countless empirical and practical matters that frustrate attempts to think about its essential properties. It is very difficult to disentangle food from its web of production, distribution, and consumption. Or when it is considered in its various use and meaning contexts, it is too often stripped of its unique food qualities and instead seen as, for example, *any* contextualized object, social good, or part of nature. It is much easier to treat food as a mere case study of applied ethics than to analyze it as something that poses unique philosophical challenges.

But things are starting to change. The level of public discourse about diet, health, and agriculture in the United States is remarkably more sophisticated than it was only ten years ago. Food books are best sellers, cooking shows are ubiquitous, and the public is more informed about food safety and food politics. The mainstream media no longer tend to blame malnutrition and food insecurity on overpopulation but on poverty and poor governance. And most people, I suspect, regardless of one's take on animal ethics, would be sickened to learn that a staggering fifty-six billion land animals are slaughtered each year for food.[4] Philosophers are not immune from these facts and trends. We are increasingly joining other academics, journalists, and citizens who take food very seriously. More philosophical work has been done on food and agriculture in the last five years than the previous thirty.[5] Hopefully, we are not just following a trend but helping to steer it in a more intelligent and responsible direction.

The role of philosophy is to cut through the morass of contingent facts and conceptual muddle to tackle the most basic questions about food: What is it exactly? What should we eat? How do we know it is safe? How should food be distributed? What is good food? These are simple yet difficult questions because they involve philosophical questions about metaphysics, epistemology, ethics, politics, and aesthetics. Other disciplinary approaches may touch on these questions concerning food but only philosophy addresses them explicitly. Once we have a clear understanding of philosophy's unique role, we will all be in a better position to engage in dialogue aimed at improving our knowledge, practices, and laws. We should also gain a renewed appreciation for the scope and relevance of the discipline of philosophy itself.

FOOD METAPHYSICS

We presuppose some conception—however vague—of what food is whenever we eat or identify something as food. Different conceptions can have real consequences for our health, the environment, and the economy. Metaphysics makes these implicit assumptions explicit by examining the very notion of what food is and what property or properties make something food. The answers to questions concerning the nature of food are not at all obvious. Nor are the answers to other metaphysical questions about the difference between natural and artificial food, the identity of food over time (from raw to cooked to spoiled), the difference between food and an animal, or the difference between food and other edible things (such as water, minerals, or drugs). Predictably, there is no consensus among philosophers about the nature of food, but there are several good candidates.

Food as nutrition.   Food is a substance or material that originates in the environment in plants, animals, or water. It is made up of naturally occurring nutrients metabolized by an organism to sustain, grow, and repair vital life processes. The primary function of food is to provide nourishment to an organism. Nourishment is furnished by nutrients: carbohydrates, fats, fibers, protein, vitamins, and minerals. These and other chemical compounds are essential for basic bodily functioning. Food on this model has objective properties (that are really present) that are not open to interpretation.

Food as nature.   Nature is not only objective but also normative. It is often perceived to have intrinsic value distinct from its instrumental value satisfying human ends. In this sense, food not only comes from nature but it is good when it does and bad when it does not. The more natural food is, the better it is. When viewed holistically as a part of a food chain, food production and consumption are seen as belonging to interdependent ecological relationships. The more we live in accordance with natural processes, the more healthy and "balanced" our lives will be. Harmony with nature is good; disharmony, bad.

Food as culture.   Food has social meaning and significance beyond its nutritive function; it is also expressive. Each society determines what is food, what is permissible to eat, and how and when particular things are consumed. Food laws, for example, specify what is intended to be, and can reasonably be expected to be, ingested by humans. There are good and bad foods, legal and illegal foods, appropriate and inappropriate foods, basic and celebratory foods, ritualistic and symbolic foods, and so on. Food preparation and consumption are bound to the beliefs, practices, and laws of nations and cultures. Food and culture define one another.

Food as social good.   Food is a basic thing that humans want and need in order to live together in societies. As such, it is the subject of social justice. Governments play a role in the distribution of food according to some conception of justice (e.g., free market, religious tradition, the principle of utility, the difference principle, and so on). Food, on this model, is something people can use, allocate, and exchange in a way that is consistent with the meanings societies give to it. Food distribution concerns the basic institutions of society and the principles of justice that regulate how this social good is allocated.

Food as spirituality.   Food is central to religious traditions throughout the world. Religions typically prescribe which foods should be eaten and which should be avoided; they assign significance to food production, preparation, and consumption; and they connect dietary regimentation with moral conduct and spiritual salvation. Food on this model has a *meta*physical—nonmaterial—dimension that is realized only in religious practice. This spiritual dimension of food connects us to religious communities and to the supernatural when consumed appropriately.

Food as desideratum.   Food is the object of hunger and desire. It is the focus of what we want when we feel the urge to eat. This desire, or appetite, is tied primarily to the physical sensation of hunger caused by complex physiological reactions. A "food craving" is a desire to eat a specific food generated by something other than hunger, such as a memory, psychological motivation, or pregnancy. When food is viewed as the object of desire we are led into murky depths of the unconscious and bodily urges—often coupled with a social realm that influences our desires.

Food as aesthetic object.   Food is aesthetic in two senses. First, as the object of aesthetic experience it has a taste and it appeals to the senses. We describe food as, for example, delicious, satisfying, or disgusting; overcooked, fresh, or crunchy. Second, food is artful. We describe it in terms of its visual presentation and sensual composition. We attribute aesthetic properties such as "elegant," "hearty," or "simple." Food on this model is primarily the subject of aesthetic judgment about its taste and appearance and only secondarily about nature and nutrition.

This list is far from exhaustive. Other metaphysical conceptions of food include food as diet (inevitably connected with a lifestyle and often a tradition); food as fuel (like nutrition but more narrowly construed as primarily energy producing); food as commodity (an economic good with value relative to the market); food as veganism (no animal flesh or animal products); and, less commonly, food as technology (a manufactured and processed social reality, more akin to a drug than to nature). Food can plausibly be any of these things, often more than one at the same time.[6]

FOOD EPISTEMOLOGY

The metaphysics of food is always bound up with epistemology: different conceptions of food are connected to our different beliefs about it. Obviously, *what* one thinks food is depends upon *how* one perceives and judges it. This claim applies to any object and to the metaphysics-epistemology relationship in general. But food epistemology is somewhat different. It is not only concerned with typical epistemic questions about knowledge, justification, and truth because food is not merely an object of experience. It is also an object of consumption. We do not just perceive it; we also prepare it and eat it. We have different interests, rely on different sources of knowledge, and justify our beliefs differently. We perceive food as something that might taste good, make us sick, have symbolic significance, spoil unless refrigerated, and spark other various concerns that are unique to food perception. In addition to typical epistemological questions concerning the reasons and conditions that warrant beliefs, food epistemology is also about risk and trust, practical reason, and the effects of physiology and psychology on perception.

Risk.   Food consumption (as well as production and distribution) always involves uncertainty. Risk refers to situations where there is uncertainty as to whether an undesirable event will occur. It involves partial, incomplete knowledge: enough is known about a situation to know that not enough is known about its probable outcome. With food the risks usually involve safety. The absence of reliable knowledge means that there is always a chance that our food is unsafe to eat or drink. Every day, public health officials deal with practical questions about acceptable food risks. Often the standards come from the Codex Alimentarius Commission, the international body developed in 1963 by the Food and Agriculture Organization of the United Nations and the World Health Organization. The commission is responsible for standardizing the Codex Alimentarius, the international food code, designed to protect consumers and ensure fair trade practices.[7]

The Codex defines food risk analysis as a process of assessment, management, and communication. First, regulators identify and assess food hazards and the likelihood of adverse effects. Then, food control agencies weigh policy alternatives and take steps for prevention or control. At the same time, information is communicated among governments, industry, NGOs, and consumers. Food risk epistemology on this model involves not only science but also decision making and public policy. Risk analysis takes place through vast networks of actors and institutions.

Trust.   Risk and trust form a pair. Risk refers to uncertainties and hazards; trust refers to situations where, in the absence of assurances, one must rely upon or place confidence in someone or something. Risk taking often requires trust in others; trust always involves the risk of dangers. Although people sometimes knowingly take risks about food (like eating something you suspect could be spoiled), most of the time we simply trust that others have made our food safe to eat and have labeled it properly. It is questionable as to whether our trust in food is truly justifiable or even avoidable. And if trust is unavoidable, is it even a rational choice or is it instead more like an act of faith—something we just commit ourselves to in the absence of evidence? Food consumption is an exercise in the epistemology of trust. We typically have no choice but to trust the safety of our food in the absence of reasonable assurance. And, unlike risk assessment, "trust assessment" is typically a solitary activity.[8]

Practical reason.   Food is also the object of practical knowledge, or skills. We not only *know that* but we have food *know-how.* We know, for example, how to farm and fish, process and package, cook and dispose. Knowledge with respect to action is called "practical reason." We learn it from others and hone it through practice. The standards are historical and highly sensitive to context. In academic food studies this knowledge is part of what is called "foodways." Like folkways, foodways refers to the study of food production and consumption—the culinary practices of what a group eats and what it means. These tradition-bound activities and beliefs largely determine how a group organizes and understands its food-related practices. We typically rely on practical wisdom to address questions concerning food risk and trust—that is, if questions even arise. Practical reason (and its cousins, common sense, custom, and habit) usually determines what kinds of things are even candidates for epistemic justification. Everyday life usually determines if and when something food related becomes questionable, and it usually determines the answer—not some impartial risk assessment or other set of rational criteria.[9]

The involuntary and the unconscious.   Sometimes our experience of food is inexplicable. There is often no apparent reason why we have an urge or repulsion. We just do. Some of these basic (yet enigmatic) experiences are caused by involuntary bodily processes, some by unconscious motives and desires. Food epistemology is complicated by physiology and psychology. The usual stock of epistemological concepts (such as "belief," "justification," and "truth") are primarily concerned with propositional knowledge and are ill equipped to deal with something as visceral as the sensation of a craving or the feeling of disgust. When it comes to food, the traditional epistemic task of evaluating the reasons for beliefs in order to convert them into knowledge is challenged by physiological causes and unconscious motives. Eating disorders (such as anorexia, bulimia, and binge eating) are extreme cases of perception that has been distorted by the body and unconscious mind. But even ordinary experiences, like a food preference or desire, point to limits in our knowledge. We have to go beyond our immediate, desire-influenced experience in order to explain it. Perhaps philosophical reflection needs to be supplemented by empirical sciences and psychoanalytic psychology in order to make sense of the experience of eating food.

FOOD AESTHETICS

Of the five senses involved in eating, taste is the most important. It is our most direct, embodied encounter with food; it affords pleasure and disgust; and it is the one sense we cannot help but use. Yet taste is more than something that just happens in the mouth: it is also the leading metaphor in aesthetics. Taste refers to our discrimination regarding art objects and our standards for artistic judgments. To have taste means the ability to discern aesthetic qualities in things. It is a particular kind of knowledge especially appropriate for artworks—one that bridges epistemology and philosophy of art.

When we direct aesthetic attention to food and drink, however, we find that the parallel to artworks is tested. Judgments about tastes in food are more difficult to justify. Although most of us believe there is a difference between good food and bad food, we also acknowledge that tastes are highly subjective, or at least cultural. The sense of the taste itself—what happens in the mouth—is one of the least reliable senses. It is difficult to describe how something tastes because it is less differentiated and less sensitive than vision or hearing. The relationship of gustatory to art-centered aesthetics is further strained by the questionable status of food as an art form. Should culinary art be considered high art? Does it require the same skill to produce? Faculties to appreciate? Should salads be displayed in museums alongside of paintings? The aesthetics of food, drink, and cooking pose unique challenges to aesthetic theory and philosophy of art.

Taste as judgment.   When philosophers speak of a judgment of taste, we typically mean the ability to identify the aesthetic qualities of artworks and nature. This kind of judgment has traditionally been understood to be both subjective and universal. It is subjective because it is based on a feeling or sensation; universal because "subjective" does not mean that we cannot all potentially agree on feelings and shared pleasures. Historically, the problem for philosophers has been to acknowledge the subjective character of taste while avoiding a slide into a relativism of incommensurable personal preferences. They want to affirm critical standards for judging artworks in the face of the highly subjective pleasures that underlie our tastes.[10]

One of the ways aesthetic theorists have traditionally achieved these two competing goals is to disentangle aesthetic taste from literal taste. Actual taste is seen as low in the hierarchy of the senses, even antithetical to the rational character of genuine aesthetic experience. The experience of beauty requires reason, imagination, and other cognitive activities that accompany aesthetic pleasure. Philosophers from Plato to Hegel to the present insist on this distinction between mere physical enjoyment and the reasoned (even spiritual) pleasure of beauty. Genuine aesthetic taste requires cognitive content so that we might discern and evaluate a work in terms of a common language—and literal taste is hardly the right tool for the job. An aesthetic theory of artworks and objects needs cognition or at least one of the more reliable senses, like vision or hearing, so that our judgments are substantive and meaningful. The aesthetics of food and drink is somewhat different. We must embrace the sense of taste: there is no other way to know what something tastes like! Gustatory aesthetics begins with the immediate, direct, even pleasurable experience of eating and drinking but does not try to explain it away, nor treat taste as a mere metaphor for "higher" forms of judgment. Instead philosophers today are likely to affirm both the cognitive and sensual experience of food. Taste experience might be subjective but that does not rule out the possibility that there is something objective in food that our sense of taste detects, rather than invents. It is what permits standards of judgment and discrimination. People disagree about tastes because there is actually something about their *food*—not just their *experiences*—to disagree about. (If we only quarreled about subjective experience and not what the experience is about there would be no way to disagree: each person's claims about his or her experience would always be right!) Furthermore, philosophers today typically recognize some kind of cognitive or symbolic dimension to food in a way our Enlightenment predecessors did not. Food has meaning. It does not represent or depict as well as art but it does, nevertheless, tell us something about the world. Food expresses its culture and history (pizza, jambalaya, sushi), ceremonial function (Eucharist, horseradish on a seder plate), and customary consumption (hot dogs rather than beef Wellington at a baseball game, champagne rather than milk for a toast). Gustatory aesthetics directs attention to both the sensual and meaningful qualities of food and drink.

Food as art.   The status of food as art is debatable. Their differences might be more relevant than their similarities. Granted, in judgments about both food and art we pick out significant aesthetic qualities, discern attentively, enjoy pleasurable experiences (or react negatively), refer to the judgments of experts, and dispute using reasons with the intention of convincing others. The activity of judging the aesthetic properties of food and drink is quite similar to that involved with works of visual arts, music, dance, and other art forms. Certainly the culinary arts require high-level skill and artistry—but does that make culinary objects fine art? Most would agree that food and artworks overlap but each does something the other cannot. Artworks can say more than food; they relate to broader, more articulated histories and meanings; they enjoy a very different social status; and art can depict food and eating with far more sophistication than food can depict art. Of course, food, by virtue of the very sensual character that likens it to art, does things that fine art could never do, such as nourish, sate hunger, spoil, decay teeth, cause allergies, pose health risks, and do other things that distinguish the materials and embodied experience of food from fine art. Food and art may both be meaningful and moving (even profound) but in entirely different ways, perhaps enough to distinguish culinary from fine art—or even to make the comparison moot.[11]

FOOD ETHICS

Food is about life as well as luxury. It is about serious things like hunger and malnutrition, diabetes and heart disease, eating and being eaten. It is a profoundly moral issue. It always has been. Even ordinary, everyday acts of cooking and eating are forms of ethical conduct. Cultural and religious traditions since antiquity have prescribed what we should and should not eat. In fact, ethical choices about food used to be considered as important as other more recognizably moral issues. Today people in the industrialized North tend to be less concerned about the relationship between diet and moral-religious conduct than we are about more mundane matters of health and, to a lesser extent, animals and the environment. Most of us are familiar with the standard ethical questions concerning food. They are becoming increasingly commonplace. What should we eat? Is it wrong to eat meat? What should we do about world hunger? Do my food choices even make a difference? Although debatable and unsettled, these issues are at least on the radar. Ethical issues about food and eating are dizzying in scope and difficult to catalog much less resolve. Nevertheless, there are several broad sets of concerns.

Responsibilities to self and others.   Part of the landscape of ethical theory is the discourse of obligation and responsibility, also known as duty. On this model, there are some things people have to do simply because they are the right thing to do. As Kant famously argues, an action must be performed out of duty to have any moral worth. Actions motivated by self-interest, or love, or anticipated consequence are, of course, permissible but not moral in this narrow sense. Kant distinguishes between "perfect" (strong) and "imperfect" (weak) duties. Perfect duties are those that are always required of us; imperfect duties are those that are contingent and only sometimes required of us. He further divides duties between those we have to others and those one has for oneself. For example, the perfect duty to myself is to refrain from suicide; the imperfect duty is to develop my talents. The perfect duty to others is to refrain from acts of violence and coercion; the imperfect duty is to help others. Obviously, there is more to say about responsibility than Kant's schema of duties, but it is a helpful place to start in considering how food figures into the moral landscape.[12]

What are our duties to others concerning food? Minimally, we should neither eat people nor deprive them of food. We probably have an obligation to prevent starvation and to feed the hungry, although it is not clear who "we" are. Doctors have obligations to feed patients in hospitals, sometimes intravenously or forcibly for those who cannot eat. Food manufacturers, farmers, restaurateurs, and other sellers have a moral (not just legal) responsibility to provide safe food. Our imperfect food duties to others are to alleviate suffering and to be hospitable, although the latter is probably a virtue not a duty.

What are one's duties to oneself? Minimally, neither to starve nor to endanger oneself by food deprivation (although a hunger strike is a morally justifiable form of protest). If eating is a necessary condition to realize our autonomy and human dignity, then each has the duty to eat a healthy and nourishing diet. A person who dines on only cheese doodles and vodka, for example, fails to respect himself—he has "let himself go." The imperfect food duty to oneself is to eat in a way that helps to realize one's potential. We should eat not only to survive but to flourish and enhance ourselves. Perhaps an athlete has a responsibility to eat a specialized diet to improve performance, while the rest of us should strive to improve our well-being through diet, not simply to maintain it.

This brief list of food duties is far from determinate but is representative of the kinds of arguments that can be made. Each claim, of course, needs to be justified and further clarified to specify who is responsible, to whom, and under what conditions. The very notion of a food duty raises more questions than it answers: How many people am I responsible for feeding? At what cost to myself? What kind of food do I owe to others? How much of it? It is less important to settle these questions than to note how effectively they can be addressed within the framework of rights, duties, and self-development. This moral language is not only commonplace but exceptionally strong rhetorically.[13]

Food virtues.   Another part of the landscape of ethical theory is the discourse of moral virtue. Virtue ethics is less concerned with moral rules and principles than character traits and dispositions. The key question to ask is not "what should I do?" but "what kind of person should I become?" The answer is given in terms of virtues a person should aspire to, such as integrity, courage, magnanimity, wisdom, and so on. The heart of our ethical life is rooted in character traits, relationships, and communities. Virtue ethics (and care ethics alike) challenge uninspiring, improperly legalistic moral frameworks. Ethical life is about being a good citizen, not following rigid rules.

Philosophers have focused their attention on three food virtues: hospitality, temperance, and table manners. The virtue of hospitality, or hospitableness, is the virtue of sharing one's accommodations, food, and drink with friends, strangers, and guests. In so doing, we recognize in another our common vulnerabilities and needs. A good host provides warmth and community and, above all, something to eat and drink. By contrast, the virtue of temperance is less concerned with how one feeds others but rather how one moderates one's own pleasures of eating and drinking. It is best understood in terms of its vice: gluttony. A glutton eats and drinks excessively: too much, too soon, too quickly, and too voraciously. A glutton is weak willed, self-indulgent, and lacking restraint. An overly temperate person finds no enjoyment in food or drink. That person is abstemious and ascetic.

Like temperance, table manners are about appropriate eating and drinking behaviors. They regulate a wide range of conduct—down to the minutiae—when eating, especially when dining with others. Manners are fundamentally social traits that aim to foster health, enjoyment, and community. The list of do's and don'ts is not trivial. Manners regulate the appearance of the table, the cleanliness of the diners, the placement of the hands and feet, the usage of utensils, the manner of eating (including chewing, licking, and swallowing), regulation of the eyes, conversation topics, and belching. All cultures have rules that govern eating practices even if tables and utensils are not used. Even within a culture, different contexts and settings involve different virtues (for example, when eating in a restaurant or at home). The discourse of moral virtue is particularly well suited for food ethics given the vast and nuanced range of activities involved in eating and drinking.[14]

Vegetarianism and animals.   Humans have moral obligations to animals. Even proud meat eaters appreciate that there are some things humans should never do to animals, like torture them for fun or eat their neighbor's pets. Raising animals for food is, of course, more debatable. There are two main philosophical approaches to this issue: deontological (rights-based) and utilitarian (consequence-based). Deontological approaches affirm the rights of animals, hence the obligations of humans to respect those rights. Animals, like humans, have inherent value and interest in self-preservation and thus enjoy the same fundamental right as we do not to be treated as mere things. That implies the obligation not to eat animals or to disregard their interests. Other rights theorists maintain that the legal ownership of animals is unjust and, therefore, any use of animals is unjust regardless of how humanely they are treated. This abolitionist theory of animal rights affirms veganism, not just a vegetarian diet. Other rights theorists contend that only humans have rights because only humans have obligations. Animals cannot tell the difference between their interests and what is the right thing to do. Without that distinction it makes no sense to say that an action is performed on the basis of duty; there has to be a choice between acting out of obligation and acting from desire. Those who argue against animal rights do not necessarily endorse eating meat; they merely challenge a rights-based justification for vegetarianism.[15]

Utilitarian (or consequentialist) approaches argue that animals (like humans) have no fundamental rights. Rather, they have the capacity to experience pleasure and to suffer and are thus no less morally significant than we are. Utilitarian approaches require that we give equal consideration to the interests of humans and animals alike. Equality of consideration is prescriptive, not descriptive. It is a moral idea, not an assertion of fact. The strength of the animal welfarist appeal is, however, the obvious fact of animal suffering and animal cruelty. Most arguments for *ethical* vegetarianism and veganism are based on animal welfare and the need to give animals moral consideration. Another set of arguments focus on different consequences, such as the vast amounts of fuel and water used in ranching, the greenhouse gases produced, wasted food on feeding animals rather than people, and increased risk of heart disease from eating meat. These are among the many good reasons for not eating meat. Consequentialist arguments can, of course, be marshaled in defense of meat eating. Some typical arguments include that the suffering of animals is offset by the economic benefits to people whose prosperity would be destroyed were we all to stop eating meat; the special dietary needs of pregnant and breast-feeding women require more protein than a vegetarian diet can supply (and that poor people cannot afford or do not have access to dietary supplements); or that long-standing customs and rituals trump animal suffering.[16]

Arguments from the moral virtues are less common but make a similar appeal to animal suffering and to the character traits of those who either condone or oppose it. For example, an uncaring person turns a blind eye to animal cruelty; a compassionate person does not. The traditional virtues oppose things like the consumerism and insensitivity to animals that drives factory farming. Kant makes a similar claim when he argues that it reflects a poor character to treat animals poorly. We diminish ourselves in our acts of cruelty and become more likely to harm other humans. In other words, we should treat animals well less for their sake than for ours. Virtue ethics can also be marshaled in defense of meat eating. This class of arguments typically finds support in the rich heritage of cultural or religious traditions that involve eating animals: ceremonial feasts, symbolic meanings, the virtues of respect and appreciation for nature's bounty, culinary virtues, perhaps even the virtues of preparing and eating an animal stalked and hunted.[17]

Agricultural and environmental ethics.   Agricultural ethics deals with issues related to the farming of food, ranching and processing livestock, and the cultivation of crops for food, fiber, and fuel. Industrial agriculture (farming based on the use of machinery, chemicals, and monocrops), although highly productive, raises moral questions about appropriate use of the land, pollution, and animals. The ethical concerns are typically consequentialist. Industrial agriculture produces a litany of harms, such as topsoil erosion, loss of biodiversity, water contamination, and health risks to farmworkers and consumers. Sometimes the moral appeal is made in the name of future generations, who would be adversely affected by actions in the present. By contrast, sustainable agriculture and ranching is designed to avoid these problems while at the same time satisfying the world's food needs. Sustainable production practices should enhance environmental quality, use resources more effectively, integrate natural biological cycles and controls, and improve the quality of life for farmers, ranchers, and societies as a whole. Sustainable practices are putatively more practically and morally defensible than industrialized farming and ranching.[18] Advocates of industrial agriculture contend that sustainable practices cannot meet the world's food needs and are, therefore, practically and morally indefensible.

Another approach to questions concerning agriculture and the environment is to call into question the *anthropocentric* (human-centered) bias of philosophical perspectives, which have traditionally devalued the moral standing of the natural environment and its members. Since the early 1970s, the literature in environmental ethics has challenged the view that only humans have *intrinsic value* while nonhuman things have *extrinsic value* as means to human ends. Some environmental philosophers argue for new, nonanthropocentric theories of natural environments and animals. Aldo Leopold's "land ethic" represents an attempt to argue that the biosphere as a whole has an integrity and beauty that deserves moral consideration. Nonanthropocentric, holistic (rather than individualist) approaches are best suited to make sense of our moral relations with the land.[19]

A related approach to a land ethic is found in the American agrarian tradition. An agrarian philosophy stresses the role of farming and ranching in the formation of moral character and in preserving culture and traditions. By living a rural lifestyle connected to the climate and soil, we acquire a sense of identity and place that can only come about by direct contact with the land. Agrarian philosophy is critical of the social and environmental impacts of industrial agriculture. Wendell Berry, for example, argues that modern agriculture and exodus from farms to cities harms the environment, destroys communities, and eclipses the basic human dignity that comes from an agrarian lifestyle. "Eating," he famously says, "is an agricultural act."[20] We are all involved in agriculture and our food choices affect how land is treated.[21]

FOOD TECHNOLOGY

Everything humans eat has been grown, raised, or processed in some way. Even the most ecologically attuned organic farming and ranching uses technologies to transform plants or animals into food. We use simple technologies for cooking, drying, fermenting, and slicing; complex ones for pasteurizing, freezing, irradiating, and flavoring. Some processing involves food additives and dietary supplements; other forms, genetic modification and nutrient enhancement. Everything we eat under-goes varying amounts of technological processing before reaching our mouths. Raw food (especially organically grown) is the least processed, then whole food (some-times cooked), then natural food (no artificial ingredients), then conventional food (with artificial ingredients). Perhaps the very idea of a "natural food" is dubious if all food requires the intervention of humans. Of course, food processing in itself is not such a terrible thing. The benefits are apparent: safety, availability, nutrient fortification, and convenience. But some technologically processed foods pose real risks and raise philosophical questions. The main issues concerning food technol-ogy—other than industrial agriculture itself—are genetic modification, animal biotechnology, and functional foods. These matters not only raise concerns about health and environmental consequences but also questions concerning consumer choice, food labeling, and animal rights, as well as the very metaphysical status of what we eat.

Genetically modified food.   Genetically modified (GM) foods are plants and animals that have been altered using recombinant DNA technology, a tech-nique that combines DNA molecules from different sources into a single mol-ecule. The purpose of genetic modification is to produce new and useful traits otherwise unattainable through conventional techniques. Most often foods are genetically modified to contain their own pesticides or to be herbicide resistant, although a small percentage of crops are engineered to be nutritionally enhanced or drought resistant.[22] Advocates of GM foods maintain that they pose neither health nor environmental risks. They promise to increase yields, increase food security, and protect the environment. Critics warn of unknown health risks and environmental damage. Since labeling is not required in the United States, there is no way for most consumers to choose to avoid or to purchase GM foods. Critics also worry about the abuse of intellectual property rights laws that permit the privatization and patenting of life forms. For example, it is illegal for farmers to save and store GM seeds without paying royalty fees. Food security is then threatened, as seeds become private property. At the very least, the priva-tization of GM seeds increases food dependence on industrialized nations by developing nations.[23]

Animal biotechnology.   Animal biotechnology applies recombinant DNA tech-niques to animals. The largest class of genetically engineered (GE) animals are designed to produce pharmaceuticals (also known as "agriceuticals"); another class is designed for industrial purposes; another for food. Livestock and fish are engi-neered to be disease resistant, have improved nutritional value, increased growth rates, decreased pollutants in their manure, or to produce antimicrobials that target *E. coli* and *Salmonella*. We have already encountered many of the arguments for and against animal biotechnology in the discussion of animal rights and GM food. Advocates cite the benefits of increased resistance to disease, productivity, and hardiness; GE animals yield more meat, eggs, and milk; and they provide more healthy food. Critics contend that genetic manipulation violates an animal's intrinsic value (or its *telos,* its natural function) and that mixing the genes of different species tampers with the natural order. Others maintain the more defensible position that we should not engage in practices (using biotechnology or otherwise) that make food animals worse off than they are now.[24]

Functional foods.   A functional food, or "nutraceutical," is a food-based product that has added ingredients believed to provide health benefits. Such foods are designed to assist in the prevention or treatment of disease, or to enhance and improve human capacities. They include products like vitamin-fortified grains, energy bars, low-fat or low-sodium foods, and sports drinks. Functional foods eliminate properties from the food to make it more nutritious—even to replace medicine. The key moral issue is these foods' claim to function as medicine, blurring the boundaries between food and drugs. Manufacturers can produce food items that make *general* health claims (to promote health) so long as they make no *specific* claims (to treat diseases). There is no legal definition for functional foods in the United States, and neither premarket approval for safety nor proof of general health claims is required. The lack of regulation raises questions about the proper role of governments in regulating food and protecting public health.[25]

FOOD POLITICS

Food choices are inevitably political. Even our simple acts of eating have public consequences when aggregated. The choices consumers make ripple through the realms of food production, distribution, and consumption, shaping the character of our food system. But perhaps even more important than individual choices are the political and economic realities that affect national and international food systems. Governments have tremendous power to make decisions over entire nations (and entire species). So do transnational corporations. We have already encountered several issues that have political dimensions, such as food safety, hunger, animal rights, and genetically modified food. (Any issue where there are "advocates" and "critics" is already politically charged). These issues are both economic and political. Some additional food issues that deserve to be mentioned are food security, global trade, marketing, and labeling.

Food security.   Food security exists when people have access to sufficient, safe, and nutritious food to live healthy lives. The Food and Agriculture Organization estimates that one billion people suffer from hunger; another billion from under-nourishment.[26] There are a number of reasons for chronic and temporary food insecurity. They include poverty, economic crises, poor governance, and poor agricultural infrastructure. People cope with food insecurity by eating less, selling assets, and forgoing health care and education. Women are affected worse than men; girls more than boys. Food insecurity traps people in poverty and poor health and it compromises basic daily activities. It is a matter of social and international justice.

In order to prevent food shortages, nations need to invest in agriculture and infrastructure and expand safety nets for short-term, acute situations. They need to create jobs and increase agriculture and local value-added food production. Small farmers need access to resources and technologies that allow them to increase productivity. Nations need vibrant agricultural systems and strong food security governance to increase production, distribute food to those in need, and protect citizens from both natural and economic crises.

As if the practical challenges are not enough, the philosophical challenge is to justify the claim that governments have the obligation to protect food security. If they have food duties, is it because citizens have food rights? Do noncitizens? What do nations owe to each other? What role should markets and the financial system play in protecting food security? What about NGOs and consumer choice? In other words, what should we do about massive, remediable, undeserved suffering regarding food and to improve the lives of as many as possible using means that are just, fair, and culturally appropriate?[27]

Global trade.   Trade and the globalization of agriculture are increasingly internationalizing the politics of food. Producers and consumers are often vulnerable to events that take place far away and subject to decisions over which they have little control. Transnational agribusiness and global financial institutions exercise tremendous influence over national and international food policies. It is debatable whether the current global trade system helps or harms nations. The transfer of technology for the most part helps, although industrial agriculture often reduces employment and drives farmers into cities and slums. Trade liberalization is good for farmers in industrialized nations, but it too often creates poverty in poor countries as subsidized commodities drive crop prices down. Local farmers cannot produce food as cheaply as the imports, forcing poor nations to become dependent on wealthier nations for food. Developing countries need to have the ability to raise tariffs on agricultural products to protect national food security and employment. A further consequence of globalization is that traditional, local diets are being replaced by a "Western diet" and lifestyle: energy-dense, nutrient-poor foods with high levels of sugar and saturated fats, combined with reduced physical activity. Not surprisingly, global rates of obesity, diabetes, and heart disease continue to increase in both rich and poor countries.[28]

The local food movement in wealthy nations is, in part, a response to the globalization of food. A "locavore" is someone who aims to eat only food grown or produced within a relatively short radius of where one lives, typically within 100 miles. Local networks of small farms, community-supported agriculture, co-ops, and farmers' markets are said to enhance relationships among producers and communities while also leaving a smaller carbon footprint. Another response to globalized food production is the slow food movement started in Italy by Carlos Petrini in the late 1980s as a reaction to the spread of fast food. Slow food is premised on the conviction that locally grown food and traditional farming and food production methods protect regional culinary practices and lifestyles. Slow food proponents claim that such food regionalism not only enhances relationships among farmers, communities, and environments but also produces better-tasting food.

Critics argue that farmers in the developing nations are harmed when consumers in wealthy nations eat locally. Our moral obligation to alleviate suffering abroad (probably) has priority over our obligation to mitigate environmental degradation. In addition, the environmental impact of transportation is often exaggerated. A more thorough environmental assessment also takes into account the amount of energy used in food production. Often the energy use in food transported great distances is less than that produced locally. Some suggest that a better alternative to food provincialism is to support "fair trade" products. These are food items produced sustainably on farms and ranches that respect worker rights and worker safety and that pay living wages. To receive a fair trade designation, the entire supply chain must be in compliance—from production to distribution.[29]

Labeling and marketing.   Consumers need information in order to make decisions about what to purchase and what to eat. We get this information from food labels and advertising. Arguably, we have a right to know about the ingredients and perhaps even the processing and packaging of our food. The risks of false information can be harmful—even lethal. Or, less gravely, false information compromises our ability to make informed choices. How can a person, for example, avoid sodium, support fair trade, or eat kosher foods unless products are labeled? Even if we deny that consumers have the right to information (and producers an obligation to provide it), a market economy is premised on the freedom to make informed choices. The most reasonable way for consumers to be informed is through food labels and advertising. And the only way that information is going to be made available is if producers disclose it. Granted, it is far from clear how much information is enough to inform consumers; what the limits of marketing and advertising are beyond not lying; or what kind of product liability is appropriate for food and drinks. These are legal as much as moral-political questions.[30]

FOOD AND IDENTITY

Food and drink figure into our everyday lives in countless ways. A diet expresses ethnic, religious, and class identification; it prescribes gender roles; it is embodied in rituals and manners; and it relates directly to our aspirations to perfect ourselves. Food and drink tap our pleasures and anxieties, memories and desires, and pride in or alienation from our heritage. This connection between diet and identity raises a number of philosophical questions. Nothing we eat (short of poison) *determines* an identity. And yet dietary preferences are indeed a part of who I am individually and who we are collectively. Sometimes the role of food is trivial (e.g., one's idiosyncratic tastes and food memories); sometimes significant (e.g., sugar and the Atlantic slave trade, or Ireland and the potato in the 1840s). Either way, food is a marker of identity.

Gender is a particularly good example. Men and woman act out their identities, roles, and relationships through their very different relationships with food: different division of labor, access, and meaning attributed to eating. By mapping gender onto each stage of food production, distribution, and consumption, we have a powerful lens through which to explain gender relations. Do the same with race or class and, again, we get a window into one realm of activities that manifests social relations. We get answers to the "who?" questions: who farms, who trades, who eats, who cooks, who manages waste, who profits, and so on. Why is this philosophically interesting? Because diet nicely manifests two basic philosophical topics: identity and justice. Any thorough analysis of these concepts cannot ignore diet. To put it noncontroversially, any personal or collective identity is formed in a (social and environmental) context. Food and eating are a crucial part of that context. Food does not make an identity, nor does it exhaust questions of justice, but it is a key part of each story.[31]

CONCLUSION

Of course, there is much more to the philosophy of food than the issues sketched above. I probably left out more than I included. I am certain some readers are shaking their heads in disbelief: What, no mention of food packaging? Nothing about climate change or developments in nutrigenomics? What about cannibalism? (You're right! Good points.) Some probably think that I skirt deeper questions on the metaphysics of natural and artificial foods; or ignore biocultural and ecological issues; or fail to recognize that the multiple meanings food has complicates food ethics and politics. (True.) Some might note that I simply apply traditional areas of philosophy to food issues rather than using the occasion to stretch the boundaries of the discipline itself.[32] (Yes, that's the approach I take.) And some readers probably expected at least some cloying food idioms, like "something to chew on" or "food for thought." (Frankly, I thought I was sparing you.)

Fortunately, the contributors to this volume more than make up for my errors and omissions. They are an exceptionally well-regarded and accomplished group. They address themselves to a wide range of questions concerning food, from different philosophical backgrounds and perspectives. We have philosophers who identify with the Anglo-American tradition, the Continental tradition, American pragmatism, feminism, and various combinations of the above and none of the above. The contributors are as motley as the subject matter itself. Each of their chapters deserves a detailed introduction, which space does not permit. So I will be brief.

The first two chapters examine the social role of eating. Roger Scruton, in "Real Men Have Manners," argues that seemingly small things like table manners and politeness are important because they express what kind of people we are for others. His plea for "life enhancing courtesies" is to restore the virtues of gentleness, intimacy, and decency. Lisa Heldke, in "Down-Home Global Cooking," argues that our attitudes toward food do not map on neatly to the dichotomy in social-political theory between cosmopolitanism and localism. She suggests a third option that might help to change how we think about and create food systems that are neither entirely local nor cosmopolitan.

The next three chapters turn from identity to aesthetics and examine questions concerning taste in food and the status of food as art. Kevin Sweeney, in "Hunger Is the Best Sauce," analyzes Kant's and Brillat-Savarin's ideas about food and drink in order to construct a notion of "gustatory imagination," which, in conjunction with appetite, characterizes the pleasures of eating and drinking. Emily Brady, in "Smells, Tastes, and Everyday Aesthetics," argues that smells and tastes should not only be considered as among our ordinary aesthetic responses but also satisfy the conditions of inclusion in the aesthetic domain as set out by traditional aesthetic theory. And Carolyn Korsmeyer, in "Ethical Gourmandism," argues that if one truly enjoys a dish, one must acknowledge the appropriateness of what is eaten: a positive aesthetic assessment is a positive moral assessment when it comes to tastes.

We then move from aesthetic to moral and political judgments. The next three chapters examine a range of topics concerning the normative dimension of food, eating, and food policy. Michiel Korthals, in "Two Evils in Food Country," argues that the misrepresentation of "food styles" (like a lifestyle) is a form of moral-political misrepresentation: the fact that some groups have a disproportionate voice in the food sector while others have none privileges some food styles over others. Gary Comstock, in "Ethics and Genetically Modified Food," asks if it is ethically justifiable to pursue GM crops and food. His answer is yes, provided we proceed responsibly and with appropriate caution. Jeffery Burkhardt, in "The Ethics of Food Safety in the Twenty-First Century," argues that the national (not local) government has the responsibility to ensure food safety and security given the concentration of agricultural production and manufacturing, the globalization of the food trade, and the threat of agri-food bioterrorism.

The next three chapters turn from food ethics and politics in general to questions concerning vegetarianism and the ethical standing of animals produced for food. Richard Haynes, in "The Myth of Happy Meat," argues that the disagreement between animal welfarists and animal liberationists hinges on flawed conceptualizations of happiness applied to animals; if correctly conceptualized, the difference between welfarists and liberationists would disappear. Gary Francione, in "The Problem of 'Happy Meat' and the Importance of Vegan Education," argues that when animals are seen as property, it is impossible for animal welfare reform to fully protect animal interests. The only position that is consistent with the recognition that animals have a right not to be treated as mere means to human ends is veganism. And David Fraser, in "Animal Ethics and Food Production in the Twenty-First Century," details the complexity of animal ethics issues, addresses the shortcomings of animal ethics philosophy of the recent past, and indicates how animal ethics philosophy must change in order to be applied effectively to food production in the twenty-first century.

We then consider the relationship of agriculture and aquaculture to questions concerning our relationship to natural environments. Paul Thompson, in "Nature Politics and the Philosophy of Agriculture," examines the divide between industrial and agrarian philosophies of agriculture in order to assess both political and environmental issues in contemporary farming practice and food system organization. Matthias Kaiser, in "The Ethics and Sustainability of Aquaculture," analyzes intensive aquaculture and expands on existing decision-making matrices to argue that current practices could be far more ethical and sustainable without compromising the ability to meet food production demands. And David Castle, Keith Culver, and William Hannah, in "Scenarios for Food Security," use scenario building to develop plausible stories about the possible role of aquaculture for the planet and for global food security. The authors are optimistic about the potential for aquaculture to alleviate malnutrition and hunger in the face of ecological crises.

We conclude with two chapters on food technologies. Gyorgy Scrinis, in "Nutritionism and Functional Foods," analyzes the "ideology of nutritionism" (the phrase he coined and that Michael Pollan has popularized) as a reductive understanding of nutrients and their relationship to bodily health, in order to examine the ways in which nutritionally reductive scientific knowledge has been translated into technological practices and marketing strategies. Finally, Stellan Welin, Julie Gold, and Johanna Berlin, in "In Vitro Meat," examine the ethical issues related to the new in vitro meat technology and argue that it may contribute to the solution of some pressing problems caused by conventional meat production, while at the same time generating a different set of ethical problems.

The contributors join me in the hope that their reflections on the philosophy of food will help you to think more clearly and more responsibly about what we eat and drink, how we provide for ourselves, and the reasons why we do so.

NOTES

1. Elizabeth Telfer, *Food for Thought* (New York: Routledge, 1996).

2. Lisa Heldke and Deane Curtis, eds., *Cooking, Eating, Thinking: Transformative Philosophies of Food* (Bloomington: Indiana University Press, 1992).

3. Carolyn Korsmeyer, *Making Sense of Taste: Food and Philosophy* (Ithaca, NY: Cornell University Press, 2002).

4. Food and Agriculture Organization of the United Nations, http://faostat.fao.org.

5. *Philosopher's Index* (Bowling Green, OH: Philosopher's Information Center, 2010).

6. For more conceptions of what food is, see Solomon H Katz and William Weavers, eds., *Encyclopedia of Food and Culture* (New York: Charles Scribners, 2002).

7. Codex Alimentarius Commission. www.codexalimentarius.net.

8. For more on food risk and trust see, Karsten Klint Jensen, "Conflict over Risks in Food Production: A Challenge for Democracy," *Journal of Agricultural and Environmental Ethics* 19, no. 3 (2006): 269–83; and Franck L. B Meijboom, "Trust, Food, and Health. Questions of Trust at the Interface Between Food and Health," *Journal of Agricultural and Environmental Ethics* 20 (2007): 231–45.

9. For more on food and practical reason, see Pierre Bourdieu, *A Social Critique of the Judgment of Taste,* trans. Richard Nice (Cambridge, MA: Harvard University Press, 1984).

10. Hume describes a judgment of taste in terms of pleasurable feelings of "approbation" (of the beautiful and agreeable) and unpleasurable feelings of "disapprobation" (of the ugly and disagreeable). Experienced critics with refined palates and sensibilities set the standards of good taste. David Hume, "Of the Standard of Taste," in *The Philosophical Works of David Hume,* vol. 3. (Boston: Little, Brown and Company, 2004).

Kant similarly describes a judgment of taste in terms of a feeling of pleasure, but he insists that it be a *disinterested* feeling in order to distinguish it from ordinary desires and moral feelings. A truly disinterested (i.e., impartial) feeling of pleasure demands universal agreement: everyone *ought* to share my pleasure and agree with my judgment. Immanuel Kant, *Critique of Judgment,* trans. Werner Pluhar (Indianapolis, IN: Hackett, 1987).

11. For more on gustatory aesthetics, see Korsmeyer, *Making Sense of Taste.*

12. Immanuel Kant, *Grounding for the Metaphysics of Morals,* trans. James W. Ellington (Indianapolis, IN: Hackett, 1981). Most philosophical discussions about responsibility are less concerned with obligation and duty than with problems associated with attributing praise and blame to someone for an action, the criteria for being a moral agent, and the objects of responsibility (actions, inactions,

intentions, character traits, etc.). This literature begins with Aristotle, who was the first to develop a theory of moral responsibility.

13. For more on food justice, see William Aiken and Hugh LaFollette, *World Hunger and Morality*, 2nd ed. (Upper Saddle River, NJ: Prentice Hall, 1996).

14. For more on virtue ethics and eating, see Telfer, *Food for Thought*; Leon Kass, *The Hungry Soul: Eating and the Perfecting of our Nature* (Chicago: University of Chicago Press, 1994).

15. For more on rights theory and vegetarianism, see Tom Reagan, *The Case for Animal Rights* (Berkeley: University of California Press, 1983); for property rights and animals, see Gary L. Francione, *Animals, Property, and Law* (Philadelphia: Temple University Press, 1995); for rights arguments against vegetarianism, see Roger Scruton, *Animal Rights and Wrongs* (New York: Continuum, 2007).

16. For more on consequentialism and vegetarianism, see Peter Singer and Jim Mason, *The Way We Eat: Why Our Food Choices Matter* (New York: Rodale, 2006); for consequentialist arguments against vegetarianism, see R. G. Frey, *Rights, Killing, and Suffering: Moral Vegetarianism and Applied Ethics* (Oxford: Blackwell, 1983).

17. For more on virtue ethics and vegetarianism, see Steven R. L. Clarke, *The Moral Status of Animals* (Oxford: Oxford University Press, 1977).

18. For more on sustainable agriculture, see "Sustainable Agriculture: Information Access Tools," USDA National Agricultural Library, www.nal.usda.gov/afsic/pubs/agnic/susag.shtml.

19. For more on land ethics, see J. Baird Callicott, *In Defense of the Land Ethic: Essays in Environmental Philosophy* (Albany: SUNY Press, 1989).

20. Wendell Berry, "The Pleasures of Eating," in *What Are People For?* (New York: Counterpoint, 1991), 145.

21. For more on agrarianism, see Paul B. Thompson, *The Agrarian Vision: Sustainability and Environmental Ethics* (Lexington: University of Kentucky Press, 2010).

22. For a fairly neutral assessment of the ethical, legal, and social issues of GM food, see the website for the US Human Genome Project, www.ornl.gov/sci/techresources/Human_Genome/elsi/gmfood .shtml.

23. For more on GM food, see Michael Ruse and David Castle, eds., *Genetically Modified Food: Debating Biotechnology* (New York: Prometheus, 2002).

24. For more on animal biotechnology, see Paul B. Thompson, *Food Biotechnology in Ethical Perspective*, 2nd ed. (Dordrecht, the Netherlands: Springer, 2007).

25. For more on functional foods, see David M. Kaplan, "What's Wrong with Functional Foods?" *Ethical Issues in the Life Sciences*, ed. Frederick Adams (Charlottesville, NC: Philosophy Documentation Center, 2006).

26. Food and Agriculture Organization of the United Nations (FAO) and World Food Programme, *The State of Food Insecurity in the World 2009* (Rome: FAO, 2009), www.fao.org.

27. For more on the ethics and politics of food security, see Per Pinstrup-Andersen and Peter Sandøe, eds., *Ethics, Hunger, and Globalization: In Search of Appropriate Policies* (New York: Springer, 2007).

28. The World Health Organization reports that there are over one billion overweight adults globally. "While genes are important in determining a person's susceptibility to weight gain, energy balance is determined by calorie intake and physical activity. Thus societal changes and worldwide nutrition transition are driving the obesity epidemic. Economic growth, modernization, urbanization and globalization of food markets are just some of the forces thought to underlie the epidemic." "Global Strategy on Diet, Physical Activity and Health," World Health Organization, 2004, www.who.int/hpr/gs.fs.obesity.shtml.

29. For a critique of local food, see James McWilliams, *Just Food: Where Locavores Get It Wrong and How We Can Eat Truly Responsibly* (Boston: Back Bay Books, 2009). For a defense of fair trade, see, Singer and Mason, *The Way We Eat*, 151–70.

30. For more on food labeling, see Robert Wachbroit, "Understanding the Consumer's Right to Know," *Philosophy and Public Policy Quarterly* 21, no. 4 (2001): 25–31.

31. For more on food and gender, see Greta Gaard, "Vegetarian Ecofeminism: A Review Essay," *Frontiers: A Journal of Women Studies* 23, no. 2 (2002): 117–46.

32. See, for example, Lisa Heldke, "The Unexamined Meal Is Not Worth Eating, or Why and How Philosophers (Might/Could) Study Food," *Food, Culture and Society* 9 (2006): 201–19.

Real Men Have Manners

Roger Scruton

"Manners makyth man"—the old adage reminds us of an important truth: that people are made, not born, and that they are made by their relation to others. Of course, a human being might exist in a state of nature—savage, speechless, solitary. But he would not have our distinctive form of life; in an important sense, he would not be a person.

Manners were once described as *la petite morale,* meaning all those aspects of morality left unspoken by the judges and preachers but without which the preachers would have no one to speak to. The Ten Commandments are not addressed to savages: they presuppose an already existing community of listeners, people already in relation to their "neighbors," whom they might rob, kill, cuckold, or offend. Manners, properly understood, are the instruments whereby we negotiate our passage through the world, earn the respect and support of others, and form communities, which are something more than the sum of their members. But in a world where people hasten from goal to goal, with scant regard for the forms that secure the respect and endorsement of their fellows, these truths are increasingly obscured.

In the scramble for profit, the polite person is at a seeming disadvantage. He does not jump queues; he does not shout and push and fight his way to the goods; he loses precious moments giving way to slower, more defenseless people; he sits down to meals with family and friends, instead of scarfing a sandwich on the hoof; he listens patiently to bores and makes time for people whose only claim on his time is that they need it; he allows relationships to develop slowly and in an atmosphere of mutual respect; if he has a goal in getting to know you, he will reveal it only at the proper time and when he has ascertained that you will feel neither used nor offended. He is, in short, a loser: or so many people seem to think, viewing politeness as an obstacle to personal success. In a world of cutthroat competition, the rude person will be first at the winning post. So why be polite?

This reasoning looks especially persuasive when everyone can obtain so much without the cooperation of others. Once, people needed someone to cook for them, talk with them while eating, relax with them over a card game. Neighbors depended on one another for entertainment, transport, nursing, shopping, a thousand daily needs. Today, this dependency is dwindling—at least on the surface, where most people live. Television has removed the need for cooperative forms of entertainment; fast food and take-out have made cooking obsolete; the supermarket teems with solitary solipsists who forage silently for their one-person families. In some workplaces, certainly, people need the acceptance and endorsement of others to get through the day, but many offices are places of solitude, in which the only object of study is a computer screen and the only vehicle of communication a telephone.

The fact that we can survive without manners, however, does not show that human nature doesn't need them in some deeper way. After all, we can survive without love, without children, without peace or comfort or friendship. But all those things are human needs, since we need them for our happiness. Without them, we are unfulfilled. And the same is true of manners.

It is children who most vividly remind us of this truth. Because there is a deep-down need (a species need) to love and protect them, there is a deep-down need to make them lovable. In teaching them manners, we are putting the finishing touches on potential members of society, adding the polish that makes them agreeable. (Etymologically, "polite" and "polished" are connected; they sound identical in French.) From the very outset, therefore, we strive to smooth away selfishness. We teach children to be considerate by compelling them to behave in considerate ways. The unruly, bullying, or smart-aleck child is at a great disadvantage in the world, cut off from the lasting sources of human fulfillment. His mother may love him, but others will fear or dislike him.

The teaching of manners to children goes beyond just controlling their behavior. It also involves a kind of shaping, which lifts the human form above the level of animal life, so as to become fully human, fully sociable, and fully self-aware. Eating is a prime arena of this transformation. Traditionally it has been a social occasion, in which food is offered and taken as a gift. Through eating, we nourish not only our bodies but also our social relations and therefore our souls. That is why table manners are so important—and the primary lessons in politeness that are given to children. "Please," "thank you," "may I have," and "could you pass the"—even when uttered by Mother, who has no choice but to provide—resound ever after in the consciousness of a child.

How we eat, what kind of consciousness we reveal in our eating—these are the important matters, since they affect what we are for others. Like the animals, we ingest food through the mouth. But the human mouth has another significance. It is the place from which the spirit emerges in the form of speech. It is with the mouth that we scowl, kiss, or smile, and "smiles from reason flow, and are of love the food," as Milton puts it. The mouth is second only to the eye as the visible sign of self and character. Our way of presenting it is therefore of the greatest importance to us. We shield it when we yawn in public; we dab at it with a napkin rather than wiping it with the back of the hand. The mouth is a threshold, and the passage of food across it is a social drama—a movement from outer to inner and from object to subject. Hence we do not put our face in the plate as a dog does; we do not bite off more than we can chew while conversing; we do not spit out what we cannot swallow; and when the food passes our lips, we strive to make it vanish, to make it become unobservably a part of us.

Table manners ensure that the mouth retains its social and spiritual character at the very moment when it is supplying the body's needs. They therefore enable us to combine conversation and consumption. Without manners, the meal loses its social meaning and fragments into a competition for the common store of fodder. Eating then degenerates into feeding—*essen* into *fressen*—and conversation into snorts and grunts.

Different cultures have developed their own methods to prevent this happening. There are few domestic sights more beautiful than a Chinese family sitting around a steaming mullet or sea bass, each adding to the common fund of hilarity while discreetly helping himself to the common dish. The chopstick, which deals in small portions and does no violence to the mouth, helps to guarantee both restraint and conversation. But the gentle reciprocity of such a family meal does not require this artificial mediator between hand and mouth. The African custom of eating with the fingers is just as effective at inducing good manners, when the bowl sits at the center of the family circle and everyone must reach forward ceremonially to partake of it, afterward raising hand to mouth while looking and smiling at his neighbor. All such customs point toward the same end: the maintenance of human kindness.

When manners are forgotten, the meal as a social occasion disappears, as is already happening. People now eat distractedly before a TV screen, replenish their bodies in the street, or walk around the workplace with a sandwich in their hands. When I first taught in America, I was shocked to find students carrying into the lecture hall pizzas and hot dogs, which they proceeded to stuff into their faces while staring in mild curiosity at the dude on the dais. Later, colleagues told me that this behavior didn't spring from the university ethos; it began at school—it began in the home itself. Already the most important moment of social renewal—on which families depend for their inner self-confidence, and out of which serious friendships grow—was becoming marginal for the young. Eating was shrinking into a function, and it is not surprising if a generation of children brought up in this way should find it difficult or alien to settle down in any relationship other than a provisional and temporary one.

The rudeness of the glutton and the face stuffer are obvious. Equally ill-mannered—though it is politically incorrect to say so—is the food faddist, who makes a point of announcing, wherever he goes, that just this or this can pass his lips, and all other things must be rejected, even when offered as a gift. I was taught to eat whatever was placed before me, choosiness being a sin against hospitality and a sign of pride. But vegetarians and vegans have now succeeded in policing the dinner table with their nonnegotiable demands, ensuring that even when invited into company they sit down alone.

Both the faddist and the glutton have lost sight of the ceremonial character of eating, the essence of which is hospitality and gift. For each of them, I and my body occupy center stage, and the meal loses its meaning as a human dialogue. Though the health-food addict is in one sense the opposite of the burger stuffer and the chocaholic, he too is a product of the fridge culture, for whom eating is feeding, and feeding a solipsistic episode, in which others are disregarded. The finicky beak of the health freak and the stretched maw of the junk-food addict are alike signs of a deep self-centeredness. It is probably better that such people eat on their own, since even in company they are really locked in solitude.

Table manners help us to see that politeness is not, after all, a disadvantage. Although the ill-mannered person can grab more of the grub, he will receive less of the affection; and fellowship is the real meaning of the meal. Next time, he will not be invited. Politeness makes you part of things and so gives you an enduring edge over those who never acquired it. And this gives us a clue to the real nature of rudeness: to be rude is not just to be selfish, in the way that children (until taught otherwise) and animals are instinctively selfish; it is to be ostentatiously alone. Even in the most genial gathering, the rude person will betray, by some word or gesture, that he is not really part of it. Of course he is there, a living organism, with wants and needs. But he does not belong in the conversation.

Where this defect most dismayingly shows itself is in sexual relations. Even in these days of hasty seductions and brief affairs, sexual partners have a choice between fully human and merely animal relations. The pornography industry is constantly pushing us toward the second option. But culture, morality, and what is left of piety aim at the first. Their most important weapon in this battle is tenderness. Tender feelings do not exist outside a social context. Tenderness grows out of care and courtesy, out of graceful gestures, and out of a quiet, attentive concern. It is something you learn, and politeness is a way of teaching it. Not for nothing do we use the word "rude" to denote both bad manners and obscene behavior. The person whose sexual strategies involve coarse jokes, explicit gestures, and lascivious embraces, who stampedes toward his goal without taking "no" or "maybe" or "not yet" for an answer, is looking for sex of the wrong kind—sex in which the other is a means to excitement, rather than an object of concern. Entered into in this frame of mind, sex is not an accepting but a discarding of the other, a way of maintaining an iron solitude in the midst of union. That is why it is so deeply offensive and why women, especially, feel violated when men treat them in this way.

Codes of sexual conduct are an obvious example of the way in which we try to raise our conduct to a higher level—the level where the animal sinks away and the human replaces it. And what distinguishes the human is the concern for others, whose sovereignty over their own lives we must respect and whom we are not to treat as though our desires and ambitions take automatic precedence over theirs. This is what Kant had in mind in his second formulation of the categorical imperative: act so as to treat humanity, whether in yourself or in another, always as an end in itself and never as a means only. Kant's way of putting the point shows the truth in the old French description of manners as *la petite morale*. Morals and manners (and law, too) are continuous parts of a single enterprise, which is to forge a society of cooperative and mutually respectful individuals out of the raw material of self-seeking animals.

But, says the cynic, we are self-seeking animals, and all these attempts to disguise the fact are just hypocrisy. This insidious thought takes many forms. La Rochefoucauld described hypocrisy as the tribute that vice pays to virtue—a compliment, in its way. Without hypocrisy, what praise does virtue ever get? But more influential to moralists have been Christ's words: "Woe unto you, scribes and Pharisees, hypocrites!" This is the master thought of the Protestant tradition, which tells us that we establish our title to goodness and salvation by inner obedience, not by outward show. Manners, forms, courtesies, and graces are mere ornaments, designed to distract attention from the moral truth. And much of the boorishness of modern Britain and America can be seen as the last legacy of this Puritan way of thinking.

Manners seem like hypocrisy when they are not second nature to you. You move in them awkwardly, as in a set of borrowed clothes. And then arises the peculiar thought that somehow, somewhere, trapped inside all this constricting artifice, is the real me, crying to be let out and show itself. The real me, when finally it shook off its social integument, stood revealed as nothing but the self-seeking animal that civilization had tried to tame. Indeed, it was not really a me at all. The "I" exists, as Martin Buber poignantly reminds us, only in relation to a possible "you"—a "you" who is the partner in a dialogue and in whose gaze I stand corrected. Manners exist to make this dialogue possible.

Oscar Wilde wrote that, in matters of the greatest importance, it is style and not sincerity that counts. Not that we should learn to be insincere—but that we should learn something else, so that sincerity is worth it. The something else, which Wilde calls style and I call manners, resides in the minute ability to live and act for others, to stand in their gaze and to influence and be influenced by their judgment. It is a discipline at once of the soul and of the body. And if you do not acquire it at an early age, there is a danger that you will never acquire it at all, or never feel at home with it.

Without this discipline, sincerity becomes only rudeness. Who is more sincere, less a hypocrite, than the person who farts and burps as his body suggests; who swears and curses at the smallest irritation; who makes a grab for whatever he immediately desires, be it food or drink or sex; who is "in your face" to everyone and as explicit in his needs as a dog or a horse? And who is a better proof of Wilde's remark? If that is what sincerity amounts to, then let's have more hypocrisy. If sincerity means showing what you really are, it's good to be sincere only if it's good to show what you are.

The modern preference for sincerity over politeness is in part a result of a social and political movement that goes back to the eighteenth century, and in particular to the egalitarianism of the French Revolution. The revolutionaries set themselves against the "inhuman" artifice of aristocratic life, against the elaborate forms and titles and manners of an elite that no longer fully believed in its right to social power, and whose rococo ways seemed merely a last-ditch effort to retain its distinction and prerogatives. The Revolution simplified dress, rejected the confectionery of the toilette, and adopted blunt, uncompromising forms of address in place of the old styles and titles. Everybody was now *citoyen,* a word that very soon acquired the ironical tone of "comrade" in the Soviet empire, when people saw that the destruction of manners was, after all, no more than a prelude to the cutting off of heads.

Despite the moral and political catastrophe that ensued, something of the revolutionary contempt for artifice survived as a permanent feature of European and American civilization. The Americans were particularly loyal followers of the revolutionary ideal. Dickens, after his 1842 American tour, described Americans as rejecting what they called the "withering conventionalities" of the oppressive old world, since they were "nature's noblemen," which they displayed by incessant spitting and grabbing at the communal dish with knives—knives!—that they had already put into their mouths.

We are not merely animals; we are also persons—moral beings, with rights, duties, and a need to bestow and receive respect. The word "person" comes from "persona," the bearer of rights and duties, a term borrowed from the theater, where it means a mask. And in a sense, it is right to compare the person to a mask—one that is created not only for others but also by them. The moral being is the creature of dialogue, and politeness is his way of making a place for himself in the conversation of his kind. Hence clothes too are part of manners. You dress for others, and even if you thereby make yourself more attractive, it is the opinion of others that tells you so.

The young are acutely aware of the social meaning of what they wear and are careful to signal through their dress the kind of social relations that they feel comfortable to engage in. When I first entered an American lecture hall, I was amazed to confront a room in which the young women were all different, clearly making an effort to stand out, and the young men were all alike, devoted to being inconspicuous, part of a crowd. The symbol of this is the baseball cap. Anyone can wear it, whatever his intelligence, culture, or physique. And because it signifies attachment to a team, the cap lays claim only to a vicarious prowess and makes no personal boast on the wearer's behalf.

Is this a new form of politeness, one that cancels the rudeness of wearing a cap indoors? I pondered the question for many weeks before concluding that no, it is not politeness but a way of retreating from the world where politeness counts—the world where you are judged for what you seem. By adopting the outward appearance of a moron, the American college kid hopes to ensure that nothing will be demanded of him. His talents, conversation, looks, and achievements will all seem surprising and creditable, if they emerge from a body rooted in sneakers and crowned by a baseball cap. The cap is his refuge from a world that can be successfully negotiated only by style—only by the manners and graces that he has never been taught. And when, under the cap, a dripping pizza is crammed into a distorted maw at the very moment when you are explaining Kant's distinction between the sublime and the beautiful, how can you avoid the thought that this kid has been badly treated by his parents and mentors, that he has been sent into the adult world in a state of acute vulnerability to a judgment that he can do nothing either to respond to or avert?

Of course, this simple form of rudeness can coexist with a gentle temperament and a real concern for others. The problem is, how do we convert that temperament into a polished personality? For if we do not do so, then we do a great disservice to the young. We deprive them of something they need to win the full trust and cooperation of others—not of their intimates only, but of the many strangers on whom they will be every bit as dependent for their happiness.

A parent facing this problem confronts a seemingly insuperable difficulty: the surrounding culture seems to promote rudeness as a way of life. Young people who set their sights on the world of commerce, for example, see nothing but a mad scramble for profits, in which old and gentlemanly ways of doing business are obsolete and the monsters come away with the goods. Adam Smith's account of the market, in which self-interest produces by an invisible hand a benign, orderly abundance, is immensely appealing; but Smith's era clothed self-interest in politeness, and the market moved more gently and more slowly. In the new world of commerce, things move too fast for manners. Commercial life seems like a buzzing cloud of atoms, in which a myriad of solitary individuals bump and bruise one another in their search for some momentary advantage. The most striking symbol of this new world is the mobile telephone—perhaps the most effective addition to the repertoire of rudeness since take-out. A person with a cell phone is never really with the company he keeps. Even when eating out or visiting, he is secretly attached to his own sphere of action, the sphere of private profit, which can at any moment call him away from his conversation and cause him to shout into the distance, negating his companions and rubbing out their thoughts, with that hint of belligerence characteristic of rudeness.

This happens not just in the world of commerce. I recently saw two young students, boy and girl, walking hand in hand through a narrow and otherwise deserted street in Oxford, the dignified walls of colleges on either side of them, a pale autumn moonlight glinting on the cobbles. Only a year or two ago, such a couple would have paused to whisper and kiss; but these two merely staggered from side to side, shouting into their separate telephones—a vivid symbol of the essential apartness of young people, once grace and courtesy have vanished from their lives. And the worst thing, as with every fault that comes from a lack of education, is that they themselves have no notion of what they lack, since no one has bothered to teach them.

Human beings endlessly create problems for themselves, but they also find solutions. Having abolished one solution, of necessity we create another. Manners were a solution to the problems of social existence. They enabled people to raise one another up to a higher plane—a plane on which they appeared as idealized, spiritual beings, open to intimacy but only toward those who had established a right. Manners enchanted the human world and filled it with a congenial mystery: the mystery of human freedom.

In a world organized and disciplined by manners, therefore, strangers could have confidence in one another. They did not feel threatened in the street or in public gatherings; they negotiated their passage with relaxed, easy gestures. Take manners away, and public space becomes threatening, relations take on a provisional aspect, and people feel naked and exposed.

In such a situation, people begin to arm themselves with law. In every sphere of human relations—work, study, romance, even family—lawsuits begin to wipe away the smile. But litigation, caused by distrust, also causes it: the more people settle their disputes through law, the more do they turn away from one another and lock themselves within an adamantine solitude.

In the absence of manners, law is not the only recourse. You can try to preempt conflict by pretending that you are not living among strangers at all. Thus arises a substitute for manners that, while it generates an inferior ideal of human life, nevertheless enables us to avoid the worst of our frictions. This substitute is informality. Where manners prevail, people stand at a certain distance from one another. They hold themselves in reserve—in just the way that courtship holds sex in reserve. Such reserve does not diminish the value of intimacy but, on the contrary, augments it by raising it to the level of a gift. The loss of manners implies that true intimacy is less and less obtainable, since less and less is there the condition with which intimacy is contrasted and from which it gains its meaning. Instead, a pretense of intimacy has arisen, enabling people to deal with one another not as strangers but as friends.

Familiarity, then, is both an offense to good manners and a substitute for them, a way of getting others to your side with the speed and impersonality of a transaction on the stock exchange. Modern business therefore depends upon familiarity. The person who insists on antique forms and courtesies is on his way to early retirement. Hence in the world of business and the professions, there is much affectation of friendship but very little friendship. Paradoxically, the loss of manners, rather than abolishing hypocrisy, has created a vast realm of pretense.

Where today's presumptuousness has destroyed the sense of shame, we cannot shame ill manners away. But in the young, the sense of shame often vibrates just below the surface. In the young, shame is not an evil but a necessary preparation for social life—a sign of the readiness to be corrected. It is therefore a powerful foundation on which to rebuild the old, life-enhancing courtesies. The fashion among young people for swing dancing, and the popularity of the recent Jane Austen films, re-creating the ceremonious world where manners are a mirror of the soul, show that the young are susceptible to, even hungry for, the enchantment that comes from formality and distance. By precept and example, therefore, parents and teachers could still do for young people what parents and teachers traditionally have done—namely, show them the slow track to an intimacy that the fast track can never reach.

Down-Home Global Cooking

A Third Option between Cosmopolitanism and Localism

Lisa Heldke

A COSMO-LOCAL PHOTO ALBUM

A snapshot: The municipal council of Lucca, Italy, rules that, "with a view to safeguarding culinary traditions and the authenticity of structure, architecture, culture and history, establishments whose activities can be tracked to different ethnicities won't be allowed to operate" in the center of the town (quoted in Krause-Jackson). The ban affects all restaurants serving foods not considered a part of the region's heritage cuisine, which runs to rabbit, salt cod, and beans. A discussion of the ban on the Association for the Study of Food and Society (ASFS) e-mail list finds me initially arguing *for* it, in the interest of what I've elsewhere called strategic authenticity.[1] The ban, I suggest, will give this cuisine a fighting chance to survive the onslaught of multinational fast food establishments—at least on its home territory. Others on the list point out that the ban is more pointedly aimed at the small, independently owned kebab shops that dot the town's center and are operated by immigrants scrambling for a financial foothold in their new community. Responding to this motive, one critic of the ban notes that "kebabs and eggrolls don't really belong in Italy . . . , really? . . . So the choice is between authentic, local, I am assuming long-ago, slow food, or fast food? Nothing in between? [And] how many people of a particular kind must be there for how long to represent a culture?" (Ray). The Lucca ordinance, many posters agree, is a case of culinary racism masquerading as the preservation of an authentic local culture. Many others are not so sure; they argue that there *is* a meaningful way to talk about the relationship between cuisine and place, and we ought to do what we can to preserve such links.

A snapshot: Interest in locally grown foods surges to the point that the word "locavore" is voted the term of the year for 2007 by Oxford University Press ("Oxford Word of the Year"). Responding to the almost-messianic fervor with which advocates promote locally grown food, critics point out that "local" does not always mean "better for the community" or even "better for the environment."[2] Theorists critical of what they perceive to be the "local = good" equation coin the phrase "the local trap" to refer to the way in which the local is "assumed to be desirable. . . . What is desired varies and can include ecological sustainability, social justice, democracy, better nutrition, and food security, freshness, and quality. For example, the local trap assumes that a local-scale food system will be inherently more socially just than a national-scale or global-scale food system" (Purcell and Brown, 280). Criticisms aside, interest in local food grows, and "is it local?" becomes shorthand for "is it (environmentally, culturally, politically) virtuous?"

A snapshot: In Chicago's Union Station, a small boy (six?), dressed in the clothing of the Old Order Amish, walks, beaming, through a crowd waiting for an Amtrak train. He carries a paper McDonald's bag, thrust before him as if it were a pearl of great price. Seeing it, I'm struck by the almost parodically epic quality of the scene. Thinking about this snapshot several years later, in a season that brought us "Whopper Virgins,"[3] it's hard to stop myself from creating a mental McDonald's ad featuring a horse and buggy moving slowly down a dirt road, a Sunday dinner table ready and waiting to be laden with food. Cut to the arriving family, unloading bags of Chicken McNuggets from the buggy, where they've been kept warm with a heated brick and a horse blanket.

Parody, to be sure, but at times I have found myself taking very literally the notion that the world is neatly divided between Things (and People) That Belong Here and Things That Don't.[4] At the time I witnessed the Amish McDonald's tableau, for instance, I wrote a rather maudlin, tear-streaked piece about the ways it embodied the powerful allure of global industrial commodity culture *even* for those who actively choose not to engage with it. (The title of that piece could have been "Exposing Poor Defenseless Amish Children to the Horrors of McDonald's.") I concluded it with a quotation from environmental theorist David Orr, who writes that the largest challenge for those who seek to replace the mind-set of global, industrial agriculture with an agrarian approach is "the vast gap that separates sound agrarian culture from the daily lives most of us live now. Agrarianism simply doesn't compute with the experiences of people whose lives are shaped by malls, highways, television, and cyberspace" (Orr, 97–98). I added, "The Amish child with the McDonald's bag represents a companion challenge, namely that shopping mall culture exerts a terrible attraction, even to those outside it."

So reads the version of the story told by my localist self. Fast forward a few years, throw in a "locavore revolution," and the cosmopolitan me finds that version rather hard to swallow. What if that Amish kid wanted to grow up to be a gay vegetarian and sing in a rock band? I find myself asking. Or what if he just wanted to be a hippie organic farmer instead of an Amish one? A Wiccan, maybe? What support for those life choices would he find in his community?

These three disparate photos cluster together for me not because of the motives of participants or the particular ethical, cultural, or environmental beliefs that underlie them. Rather, what join them are the ways in which examples such as these get conceived as skirmishes in a battle between cosmopolitanism and localism—and the ways they are deployed, defended, challenged, or otherwise used to shore up one side or the other in that battle. I've pasted the three into a conceptual photo album titled "The Cosmopolitanism/Localism Dichotomy," a fat collection of impressions exploring the multifarious ways that I've experienced this dichotomy giving shape to the world.

WHY COSMOPOLITANISM AND LOCALISM?

What can be accomplished by exploring this dichotomy using the medium of food? Cosmopolitanism is a concept with a substantial philosophical profile; it possesses a long and deep history and considerable political and moral significance. Can it be anything other than waggish impertinence to examine so significant a concept using food? On the other hand, considering the topic from the perspective of food studies, one might ask whether it is *valuable* to think about food and agriculture in terms of an arcane philosophical dichotomy, the terms of which are anything but clear and settled. What, precisely, can the study of food gain by thinking about food through the lens of such a dichotomy?

I can identify at least four reasons that such an investigation is useful, both for philosophy and for food studies. The first two are more practical or strategic; the second two more conceptual and substantive. First, as current public debates well illustrate, food and agriculture are subjects of no small moral and political significance (despite the nonchalance with which they have often been treated). It does neither food nor philosophy a disservice to reflect upon some of the most fevered public conversations about food and agriculture in light of this deeply influential, fraught, confusing, multipronged[5] dichotomy. Doing so can shed light on both this dichotomy and contemporary food discussions.

Second, cosmopolitanism is a topic of not only perennial philosophical concern but also considerable contemporary interest; it has received a flurry of attention from high-profile public philosophers like Martha Nussbaum and Kwame Anthony Appiah. For a philosopher of food, there's something both appealing and strategic about showing other philosophers that *food* has a meaningful part to play in such an ongoing philosophical conversation. (It's noteworthy that Appiah actually uses food examples quite often in his book *Cosmopolitanism*.)

My third reason points to the fact that the dichotomy, for all its seeming abstractness, has more than academic significance. I see it operating as a kind of moral/political sorting mechanism in contemporary culture, separating "us" (whoever we are) from "them" (whoever they are) with no remainder, and no overlap. For instance, no small amount of the *heat* generated by debates about the virtues and failures of local food movements can be attributed to the fact that participants, opponents, and commentators alike often discuss these movements in ways that suggest that the food choices available to growers and consumers *always already* neatly, completely, and unambiguously embody one side of the dichotomy or the other—and thereby illustrate the shortcomings of the other side. (Locally grown is seen as environmentally virtuous to its advocates and harmful to third world economies to its critics.) Similarly, cultural debates about cuisines often unfold in ways that presume that it is possible to distinguish clearly between local (authentic, traditional) choices and cosmopolitan (hybrid, trans-planted) ones; evidence is kneaded, sliced, and diced in such a way as to support that presumption.

In short, we often bemoan or celebrate aspects of our food systems and food-ways[6] by reading them as instantiating (or failing to instantiate) our vision (or nightmare) of a robust cosmopolitan or local society. (Apropos this point, Tim Lang argues that "the agro-food system is both a symptom and a symbol of how we organize ourselves and our societies. It is both a vignette and a microcosm of wider social realities" [218].) Making this particular dichotomy and its workings visible is one contribution philosophy can make to the project of understanding food and society.

Related to this point, I believe, fourth, that paying attention to the ways the dichotomy organizes and informs our food lives can have salutary effects both for the dichotomy and for food. To be more forthright, I mean that paying attention to and *transforming* the dichotomy can have such effects. As is no doubt clear from my opening snapshots, I believe that this dichotomy is problematic—for our attitudes to food and more generally as well. In looking at the ways cosmopolitan-ism versus localism shapes how we produce and consume food and how we talk about it, I want to try to glimpse—out of the corner of my eye, as it were—ways of thinking (and, more importantly, ways of *being* and *doing*) that escape both sides of the opposition, that give the lie to its tidiness. The dichotomy is an unhelpful sorting mechanism.

Analyzing this mechanism can contribute to the transformation of our food systems, by making the conceptual space within which to reimagine them. By coming to understand the effects on our food systems of a sorting mecha-nism such as the cosmopolitan/local dichotomy, creators and participants in those systems can, for instance, reconsider elements of them that resist such categorization.

In the remainder of this chapter, I attempt to substantiate my two-part claim: namely, that this dichotomy is problematic both because it is a dichotomy and because of the ways cosmopolitanism and localism have been constituted. Examining the snapshot examples that began the chapter can yield a rich set of characteristics that define (at least some forms of) cosmopolitanism and localism.

COSMOPOLITANISM AND LOCALISM: SOME SKELETAL DEFINITIONS

Localism

Josiah Royce offers a succinct definition of localism (which he approvingly calls provincialism) that can serve as a starting point for this discussion. Provincialism constitutes "the love and pride which leads the inhabitants of a province to cherish as their own [those] traditions, beliefs and aspirations [with which a province is associated]" (61). Understood in its most positive light, the action by the city of Lucca constitutes an effort to cherish a set of culinary traditions that are perceived as at risk from encroachment by other, more powerful traditions.

Royce calls upon a "province to possess its own customs and ideals" (61), a directive that suggests that local places come to be associated with a particular set of traditions, customs, and so on. Wendell Berry suggests a somewhat more elemental sense of connection between custom and place; his agrarian version of localism suggests that literal, physical, earthy place *shapes* culture to a considerable degree. *Deep* and *long* connection to a particular patch of earth, he argues, is the starting point from which to develop both a sound agriculture and a sound *culture,* the two being intimately linked. This understanding of soil-community links underlies religious communities such as the Amish.[7] Concrete connection to an earthy place—not a built environment or cultural group—forms the irreplaceable core of his agrarian localist thinking. Consumer/grower movements for local food explicitly and implicitly draw this link between strong agriculture and strong community. In particular, it is embodied in the concept of "terroir," understood as a complex (sometimes almost mystical) connection between soil, methods of production, and community, all of which must develop over time. "Purity," "integrity," and "authenticity" are words that often get used to describe aspects of agrarian localism, which emphasizes a deep sense of "really" belonging to a place in the way that, say, a plant species is native.

For the agrarian localist, both agriculture and the culture intimately tied to it depend upon longevity in a *physical* place. Why? First, regarding agriculture, Berry argues that good farming can't happen until the third generation on the land; it takes this long to build up a store of memories so that "the land [does] not have to pay the cost of trial-and-error education for every new owner" (193). To farm well, one must have intimate knowledge of this particular, very physical place: its soil and its geographical contours, its plants and its weather. Intimate attention and connection to a physical place (in its most earthy sense) lie at the heart of agrarian localism.

The local food movement has at *its* heart a commitment to the health of local farmland in *every* locale. Consumers (in principle) can invest in stable, long-term farms, because (in principle) these farms serve as repositories of knowledge about how best to grow food in this place. Growers (in principle) can make the choices they believe best for the land, knowing that community members who share their concerns about the soil will support those choices, even if it means higher prices for their food.

Regarding the second goal—good culture—Berry asserts that good community grows up around good farming; it too is the work of the third generation. Such culture "would not be imported from critically approved cultures elsewhere. It would not come from watching certified classics on television. It would begin in work and love" (194). In pursuit of this goal, many agrarian and bioregionalist theorists argue for preserving the rights of people to remain on the lands of their ancestors and to know that their children and grandchildren will retain that right. For some, like Berry, it is more than a right; it is a responsibility, a moral injunction. We have an obligation to dig in for the long haul and make community. If we're unfortunate enough to have been "unsettled" in a recent generation, we're obliged to settle ourselves now, so that our children and grandchildren have a fighting chance at real community.

The local food movement also embodies, for localists, the ways deep and long attachment to place cultivates good community. CSA farms,[8] farmers' markets, farm-to-table programs, and community gardens not only produce good food close to home, they also foster relationships among members of a community— relationships that begin as simple transactions involving vegetables and money. These transactions are economically important but are also important symbols and examples of the kinds of person-to-person, group-to-group connections that spin into the fibers of strong community. Indeed, advocates of these agricultural options have argued strenuously that, while local foods are not always the most sustainable choices, considered purely on environmental grounds, it would be wrong to evaluate them on environmental grounds alone; their cultural/social/political capacity to build sustainable *communities* is itself an enormous benefit of such movements.[9]

Cultivating deep and long connection to a place, the agrarian localist argues, promotes the kinds of justice and democratic faith that can only arise when people are "face-to-face"—when you know the persons on whom you rely, for example, for the production of your food. Such connection also enables deep, specific, contextualized *knowledge* of a place—local knowledge that can address the idiosyncrasies and nuances of a given locale. To preserve (and develop) this knowledge, it is necessary to preserve (and develop) the cultures responsible for its cultivation.

This emphasis on contextuality is again related to the "earthiness" of many forms of localism; the particularities of a physical place are not well tended with knowledge that is so general as to be universal; what is true of "growing corn in general" will not be of much help when it comes to growing corn on this field.

Cosmopolitanism

Anthony Appiah describes cosmopolitanism as constituted by two "intertwined strands"; first, "the idea that we have obligations to others . . . that stretch beyond those to whom we are related by . . . even the more formal ties of a shared citizenship," and second, "that we take seriously the value not just of human life but of particular human lives, which means taking an interest in the practices and beliefs that lend them significance" (*Cosmopolitanism*, xv). Note that these strands not only maintain their independence; they also often refuse to be reconciled. "There will be times when these two ideals—universal concern and respect for legitimate difference—clash" (xv).

If Berry's agrarianism argues for rooting oneself by way of deep and long connections to a particular plot of land, Appiah's cosmopolitanism acknowledges the inevitability of cultural exchange, interchange, and mixing. As he states it, "We have always been a traveling species" (*Ethics*, 215). While many of the world's travelers are on the move only unwillingly, or under great duress, the "interpenetration of societies and forms of life is a very old phenomenon, one that is natural to us" (215).

The cosmopolitan's interest in learning from diversity (as well as the cosmopolitan's desire to uncover what is shared among humans) emerges from the recognition that all cultures are already mixtures. Human societies have always imported food supplies from distant locales. Furthermore, as examples like ketchup, satay, and curry suggest, those "supplies" haven't only been agricultural commodities; cultures have treated each others' cuisines as supplies—borrowing and stealing from them, adulterating and doctoring them up—probably since the discovery of fire. The notion that Lucca, for instance, can identify what is "truly, purely, authentically Luccan" about itself and protect that from "foreign influence" is an attempt to board a train that has already left the station. The best Lucca can do is to welcome the opportunity for cuisines to flourish, influencing and challenging each other culinarily in the process.

The idea of a "before," during which a culture was "pure," "unmixed," or "purely local," is as imaginary as Rousseau's state of nature. Claims to purity are the *consequences* of efforts to sort out or separate Them from Us—to *establish* the boundaries that enable us to distinguish, for example, Their wheat-eating ways from Our rice-eating ones.

The cosmopolitan defense of intermingling involves more than "we've always done it that way," however; there is also a moral value to this mobility and detachment. The cosmopolitan understands cultures' relationships to their "places" and individuals' relations to their cultures as arbitrary. For Martha Nussbaum, whose cosmopolitanism emerges from the Stoic tradition of Diogenes, we are "citizens of the world," whose "first attachment" is to humanity in general (59). True, we must learn one language, not attempt to learn all, but our *attachment* to that language must always preserve the *detached* air that comes from realizing how arbitrary our speaking it is. Appiah translates this detachment into an argument for shared cultural patrimony: "there's something odd, to my mind, about thinking of a Hindu temple sculpture or Michelangelo's and Raphael's frescoes in the Vatican as the contribution of a people. . . . Which *people* exactly made that contribution? The people of the Papal States? The people of Michelangelo's native Caprese? The Italians?" (*Cosmopolitanism*, 127). Appiah observes that mobility also affords us greater exposure to alternative ways of being, doing and thinking: "if we want to preserve a wide range of human conditions because it allows free people the best chance to make their own lives, there is no place for the enforcement of diversity by trapping people within a kind of difference they long to escape" (*Cosmopolitanism*, 105). Appiah is making two claims here: first (implicitly), that free people are best able to make meaningful lives if exposed to many options for constructing those lives; and second, that people must be free to embrace—or cast off—cultures into which they have been born or otherwise inserted. The latter point bears underscoring, given the arguments of the agrarian localists; traditions are not to be preserved in the absence of people who wish to participate in them.[10] They have no inherent value; the freedom of individuals to opt in or out of a culture far outstrips any value that a culture might have in and of itself. The Amish child's right to choose to become a Wiccan is of far more importance than preserving any particular aspects of Amish culture. "There is no place for the enforcement of diversity by trapping people within a kind of difference they long to escape" (105). The virtues of family farms are not so great that they should supplant an individual's choice to flee said farm.[11]

If local food movements represent the clearest food-related manifestations of agrarian localism, then the diversity of ethnic restaurants, and the resultant culinary tourism, fusion cuisine, and other kinds of food borrowings and lendings, best embody the cosmopolitanism Appiah advocates. Urbanites in the United States can meet their ethnic and racial Others via plates heaped with the cuisines of dozens of cultures. Diners can also bear witness to an endless stream of new cuisine hybrids, created when chefs from one culinary tradition learn from traditions far removed from their own. What stronger testament to the virtues of life as "the world traveler, who takes pleasure in conversations [over dinner!] with exotic strangers?" (*Ethics*, 222). Indeed, food can be a nonthreatening medium to initiate dialogue with members of a culture far removed from one's own—a serious entry point into another's culture.[12]

Appiah's cosmopolitanism recognizes not only the reality but also the cultural value of transience and exposure to ways of life other than one's own. Furthermore, his is a *rooted* cosmopolitanism; it seeks to avoid at least one danger of other versions—the drive to an abstract, all-encompassing universalism. Proponents of Stoic cosmopolitanism sometimes see the qualities displayed by their own cultures as *just* the ones that ought to be universalized—a tendency leading Appiah to suggest that such cosmopolitans are themselves provincial. His cosmopolitanism, on the other hand, embraces the particular, the situated, the idiosyncratic. He notes, "Humans live best on a smaller scale," and thus "liberal cosmopolitans should acknowledge the ethical salience of not just the state but the county, the town, the street, the business, the craft, the profession, the family *as* communities" (*Ethics*, 246). Rooted cosmopolitanism values the conversation with the stranger not as a means of confirming and expanding the reach of some set of universal maxims, but as a means of confirming just how different we sometimes are. In celebrating "conversations with exotic strangers," and cultural borrowings, Appiah holds out a vision of a world in which communities of Others are not a problem to be solved, but an opportunity to be embraced.

DICHOTOMIES: A PRAGMATIST'S FIELD GUIDE
FOR THE WARY

I've suggested that cosmopolitanism and localism exist in a dichotomous relationship to each other. What follows from this? Dichotomies and dichotomous thinking lie in the background or on the "garden level" of much of Western culture. Foundational dichotomies such as mind/body, self/other, subject/object, and reason/emotion make their way into everything from religious doctrines to scientific theories to commonsense beliefs, shaping our most treasured institutions and informing how we act. Of course they have also been subject to no small amount of criticism from philosophers and others.

My most important philosophical forebear is the pragmatist philosopher John Dewey, and if there is any pattern of which Dewey was wary, it's the dichotomy, with its tidy, neat two-ness. I've inherited Dewey's wariness. Among the more serious problems I associate with dichotomies, three are particularly important to the cosmopolitan/local dichotomy.

First, dichotomies' tendency to set up not just a contrast but an antagonism between their two poles, such that to be *this* means to be *not that*.[13] Each pole gets defined in such a way that it contains nothing of the other. To be a mind is to be utterly unlike body. To be cosmopolitan is to reject, out of hand, all things "localist"—and vice versa. Fail to maintain this separation, and you risk contamination.

This feature, not surprisingly, leads to the second characteristic of dichotomies: their tendency to erase nuance; to eliminate the possibility of anything's existing in between their poles; to purify, to "clean up" ambiguous cases by shoehorning them into one extreme or the other.[14] Dichotomous thinking requires understanding cases in the middle as ultimately being instances of one of the two polar extremes—or at least identifiable admixtures of the two. The poles are always the conceptual foundations in terms of which other things are defined; they, in contrast, are never explained in terms of anything else.[15] Dichotomous thinking thus encourages rigid partisanship; the belief that only one pole represents the right choice, the virtuous position, the thing worth caring about.

The debate about the merits of local food being vigorously carried out in the mainstream press illustrates this tendency. A recent opinion piece and the comments it engendered are typical of the sharp antagonisms that have arisen over this set of issues. In "A Bitter Reality," Tom Keane argues that "the local food movement is an affectation based on bad logic and bad economics, one that, widely adopted, would actually harm the environment and potentially impoverish millions. Particularly here in New England, it would also turn mealtimes into dull, pallid affairs." Keane dismisses local foods on all counts, including economic, culinary, and environmental ones, and argues unequivocally for the virtues of a globalized food system. Responses posted in the first two days were almost all critical—and almost all equally sweeping in their praise of local foods and their criticism of global food. This example interests me not because of the truth of any individual claims made, but because of the stark way it illustrates the partisanship.[16] A respondent to Keane's "Bitter Reality" illustrates this tendency, even as this person attempts to challenge it. In an effort to nuance the issue, the commenter writes, "It's not always about giving up things outright nor is it about trying to make the whole world filled with only small farms," but in the same paragraph this person suggests that "for those who find the whole philosophy taxing to think about, you can boil it down to a simple A or B choice: if there are 2 apples for sale and one is grown in New England and the other in Washington State or New Zealand . . . choose the local one!"

The third and final relevant feature of dichotomous thinking is this: Particular groups of dichotomies operate together, such that they mutually reinforce each other to create a way of understanding the world that is more plausible because of its cohesiveness. I suggested earlier in footnote 4 that the cosmopolitan and the local operate in such a cluster. Some of the other dichotomies that cluster with it include urban/rural, culture/nature, global/local, industrial/agrarian, transience/rootedness, universalism/contextualism, individualism/communalism.

This clumping tendency magnifies the power of any individual dichotomy, while also often masking any implausibility it would have were it to be examined on its own terms. Consider, for example, how the binaries of mind/body, reason/emotion, and man/woman effectively created a worldview that long seemed more coherent and plausible because each pair relied upon and "stuck up for" the others. The local foods case also illustrates this gathering effect; naming something "the local food movement" collects together a whole set of (perhaps previously only loosely related) practices and principles that partisans then tend to defend or criticize as an entire package. While it can be very useful to understand a set of concepts as related to each other, when doing so prevents us from seeing them as separable the salutary effects of this tendency are decidedly diminished. In the case of the local food movement, for instance, (more casual, less well-informed) defenders of the local resist acknowledging numerous studies that show that the environmental impact of our food is far more complicated than answering the question "how far was it transported?" Once "local" became associated with "environmentally superior," it became very difficult to decouple the two.[17]

Within any cluster of dichotomies, the relationships among dichotomies are complex; wormholes connect particular ones together in ways sometimes evident, sometimes hidden. Arguments that begin from one can slip, without notice, to another. This tendency strengthens the sense that particular dichotomies are in fact integrally connected to each other. In the cluster containing cosmopolitanism and localism, for instance, the path connecting "cosmopolitan" and "urban" is so broad and flat that sometimes the terms are practically understood as synonyms. The connection between "purity" and "localism," on the other hand, is more subtle and indirect and may require a journey through other concepts like "authenticity." (This kind of indirect link can be put to rather crafty uses, saying indirectly what can't/shouldn't be said directly. For instance, given the insidious associations with the concept of "purity," it can be handy to use the word "local" instead, knowing that it will make back-channel connections to purity.)

SHARED TROUBLES

In *Cosmopolitanism*, Kwame Anthony Appiah suggests in various ways that we already occupy a cosmopolitan world; the question to ask is whether or not we are going to do it well. Elsewhere, he suggests that we have always been "a traveling species" (*Ethics*, 215). In response, Wendell Berry might well observe that we are already occupying a world of the local, the provincial, and that we have always been a "nesting species." If we look around us for evidence that the world "is" one way or the other, or that people "are" one way or another, we will find no shortage on either side.

Appiah identifies our travel (willing and unwilling), and our encounters with persons defined as Other, as the preconditions for cultivating that respect for "legitimate difference" that is one of the defining elements of his cosmopolitanism. His illustrations point to the various uses of Coca-Cola and McDonald's, halal goat meat, hot milky tea, sweets from India, and chocolate. Berry points to three generations of agriculture on one plot of land as a necessary condition for the cultivation of a strong, knowledgeable, *rooted* community. In true dichotomous fashion, each side seems quite sure that the other is incapable of offering what it has—and what everyone should agree is necessary. The cosmopolitan—mistakenly, I believe—seems to think that meaningful encounters with legitimate difference are only likely to come as a result of travel (or exposure to travelers). The local—mistakenly, again—sees strength, rootedness as something that is only likely to develop by staying put. Both these mistakes, I believe, emerge as a result of the features of dichotomies I described earlier—particularly the clustering effect, and the tendency to define the sides as diametrically opposed to each other.

Cosmopolitanism is sometimes described in ways that suggest that it, alone, has a corner on difference—that the path of provincialism necessarily leads to a dangerous insularity of which racism is just one insidious form. Certainly this is true—some of the time. But by the same token, the travel advocated by cosmopolitanism as the essential precondition to "respecting legitimate difference" can also turn us into imperialistic cultural elitists, certain that our own way of thinking/doing/being is the only right way.[18] There is no guarantee that cultural exchange "broadens."

Provincialism is sometimes framed in such a way as to suggest that only someone who has spent a long time in a community—and who comes from a long line of persons who have spent a long time in a community—has the kind of insight into that place that enables that someone to know how it differs from the norm, the generalization, the universal. In a way, the local, too believes it has a corner on difference. Localism suggests that only this kind of "depth work" will develop the potential of unique and particular places. It tends to gloss over the fact that "staying put" is *also* no guarantee that one will love a place, will come to know it in the way that enables one to take care of it—something that coming to a place with fresh, eager attention, *can* sometimes do.

ANOTHER PHOTO ALBUM IS POSSIBLE

What if we take seriously the claim that we, as a species, are always traveling *and* staying put—a state of affairs that surely both Berry and Appiah would acknowledge, even if they don't necessarily like all of its implications? What if we moved away from seeing these features of human being as marks of (or arguments for) our being "truly cosmopolitan" or "actually local"—or even some complicated admixture of the two that is nevertheless defined in terms of them? What kind of philosophy can underpin and advance the development of food practices that value both local food and ethnic cuisine swapping? That can acknowledge the legitimate rights of communities to cultivate deep and long connections to the soil, while also recognizing and valuing the insights that come from newcomers? What kind of theoretical underpinnings can manifest the *connections*, rather than the disconnections, between the snapshots that began this chapter, the nuances of shading, rather than the broad contrasts of light and darkness? Where can we begin to glimpse the outlines of a third option, the option of the "nested traveler?"[19] I conclude with some tentative suggestions in this direction.

To be adequate, a third option must achieve several aims. First, it will manifest literal "groundedness," a nonarbitrary, nonoptional, earthy contextuality. I say "nonarbitrary" because, all appearances to the contrary, we are linked, literally, physiologically, to the soil, and we have very good reasons to dig into the *soil closest to us* much more intentionally—to *contextualize* our lives with dirt and its denizens. This digging in should be paired with an intentional interaction with ways of being and thinking that challenge one's own. In contrast to Berry's tendency to suggest that *only* deep and long local knowledge is valuable, the advocate of this third option recognizes that interchange with Other knowledges is *also* irreplaceable. Among the many uses of such interchange is that it cultivates community skepticism about the adequacy of its own understandings of the world.[20]

Second, this alternate option will recognize that no place is too small, local, and homogeneous to escape us/them thinking, nor is any connection between two people too tenuous to preclude the possibility that they will share a sense of being from the same tribe. That is, connections and disconnections are never simple matters of location or dislocation. Any number of factors can create in us the impulse to define someone as Other; so too, any number of factors contribute to our naming someone as One of Us. A nested traveler will be wary of both impulses and will work to identify those contributing factors.

An accompanying snapshot for these first two aims? The St. Paul, Minnesota, farmers' market, where immigrant Hmong growers are now the "old-timers" sharing market space alongside Euro-American "newcomers"—lifelong Minnesotans whose familiarity with the land, and with the sheep, goats, and sixteen varieties of garlic growing on their patch of that land is less than ten years old. Which group constitutes the newcomers? Which group is rooted? The nested traveler is forced to notice that longevity has many layers; a Hmong farmer may be new(ish) to Minnesota, but her long experience with the soil makes her more of an old-timer on a Minnesota farm than the formerly suburban liberal arts college professor who has just bought her first goat.

A third option will also exhibit greater concern with the cultural than displayed by many agrarian forms of localism, and more concern with the agricultural than most versions of cosmopolitanism manifest. Wormholes connecting the cosmopolitan, the urban, and the "cultural," on the one hand, and the provincial, the rural, and the "natural" (or the "uncultured"), on the other, need to be rerouted, and new ones bored, to attend to the fact that the cultural and the agricultural are interdependent, not independent; that cities, too, are "agricultural places,"[21] and "remote" country locations are also cultural crossroads.[22]

The snapshot here: An "American terroirist moment," inspired by Amy Trubek's book *The Taste of Place.* The concept of terroir, as it evolved in France, is a self-conscious interconnection of culture and agriculture; it twines together soil, climate, production method, cultural heritage, and any number of other "natural" and "cultural" elements to give a unique cultural-agricultural "fingerprint" to a food—for example, a wine or a cheese. As it has developed (and been institutionalized) in France, however, the concept has tended toward "a nostalgic interpretation of the past," in which "heritage becomes a fixed institutionalized fact," and "the past . . . functions as the gatekeeper for truly tasting terroir"; and also toward an "essentialist" emphasis on "the importance of 'location, location, location'" (247, 248). In short, French terroir shares much with agrarian localism. Trubek cultivates a new notion of terroir, designed in part to acknowledge America's shorter history, but centered upon an older notion of the word, which simply meant "the earth from the point of view of agriculture" (248). "Tasting terroir means having a sensibility, adopting a set of framing values that inform agricultural practices and shape physiological tastes. . . . This vision of the taste of place certainly embraces Gustavo Esteva and Madhu Suri Prakash's call for a 'grassroots postmodernism,' an orientation that neither clings to the past nor is mired in the present but looks toward the future" (248–49). While Trubek's snapshot is still underdeveloped (more a glimpse than a clear photo), its potential is considerable.

A fourth aim of this third option is that it ought to help us think about how food practices could enable us both to *conceptualize* and to *enact* justice and sustainability—two sociopolitical aims toward which many eaters are attempting to aim our forks. Note that cosmopolitan options tend to emphasize that they alone are capable of safeguarding global justice, while localist options tend to suggest that they alone are concerned about environmental (and other forms of) sustainability. And note further that both of these concepts are the subjects of vigorous, often contentious debate—debate fueled by accusations that very much spring from provincial and cosmopolitan strongholds.

Photographs of committee meetings are notoriously dull, but the snapshot I would select to represent this aim would depict a meeting of a food policy council in a city somewhere in the United States or Canada—Knoxville, Tennessee; Toronto; Portland, Oregon. Food policy councils represent food democracy in action. They convene groups of citizens who represent broad arrays of organizations, interests, and expertise for the purpose of examining the food systems in their area and making policy recommendations about those systems. Members are consumers and producers, government and NGO representatives, and private citizens. Some are partisans of particular movements, while others might represent no one outside themselves. When councils are broadly and deeply representative, the issues they take up might run the economic, social, and environmental gamut, from improving access to fruits and vegetables for people in low-income neighborhoods (by providing bus service, creating affordable farmers' markets, stocking neighborhood convenience stores with produce), to providing nutritionally adequate meals for children in school lunch programs, to creating community gardens where growers can raise and share foodstuffs representative of their own ethnicities that are not readily available in mainstream supermarkets. Most importantly, councils foster cross-fertilization of food issues by convening representatives of such a broad sweep of interests and organizations. It is difficult to fail to see relations between producers' and consumers' concerns, or the concerns of environmentalists and of antipoverty activists, when "their" issues are laid out next to each other in the context of an organization whose focus is food.

The world we inhabit isn't either cosmopolitan or local in its organization and orientation—no matter how our theories might encourage us to think about it. How can campaigns and movements for local food, fair trade, and sustainably grown food, expanding interest in, and knowledge of, ethnic and regional cuisines (both one's own and "Others'"), help us to think beyond cosmopolitanism and localism into a third option for food systems, foodways, individuals, and communities?

NOTES

1. For a definition of strategic authenticity, see my *Exotic Appetites*.

2. An even more recent discussion on the ASFS list prompted a long, lively, and sometimes heated discussion about how to make tough choices among various "virtuous foodstuffs"—local, organic, fair trade, and so on. Even—or perhaps especially—among this learned group of food scholars and food professionals, there was nothing like consensus about which choice is the right one. Interestingly enough, there seemed to be considerable agreement that there *had to be* a right choice—the matter couldn't be in principle irresolvable.

3. The "Whopper Virgin" ads were a series of television advertisements constructed like ethnographic films, in which people from cultures without fast food participated in taste tests comparing Whoppers and Big Macs. The representatives of traditional cultures were decked out in their most "authentic" clothing and were presented as being, for the most part, utterly baffled by the burgers, unsure just what to do with them. But hands down, they preferred the Whopper to the Big Mac. See www.youtube.com/watch?v=fbNoofDM1rM for a full-length video that includes comments from the "documentary filmmakers." One hardly knows when to stop putting words in quotation marks.

4. Later, I discuss the way in which dichotomous concepts cluster into "packs" so as to mutually reinforce each other. Here, I will note that "being from here" is also associated, more or less closely and more or less frequently, with tradition, stability, longevity, rootedness, the earth, the countryside, production, agriculture, preservation, purity and simplicity, homogeneous place-based community, provincialism, and agrarianism. "Not being from here" is variously associated with travel, mobility, leave-taking, consumption, multiplicity, variety, experimentation, the city, globalization, hybridity, and heterogeneous, "rootless" community. My discussion in the remainder of this chapter focuses on the member of the pack that I see as playing the most predominant role: namely, the cosmopolitan/local dichotomy.

5. How can a dichotomy be multipronged? Just this way: There is considerable fluidity with respect to what these terms encompass—and what relationship they bear to other, similar terms. What is the

relationship between globalization and cosmopolitanism, for instance? Between provincialism and localism? Because the referents in this dichotomy are less fixed than they are in, say, the mind/body dichotomy, I refer to it as "multipronged." I chose cosmopolitanism and localism because these concepts seem the most inclusive; they can serve as collectors that gather together instances and ideas that might not seem particularly connected to each other at first glance.

More "iconic" dichotomies like mind/body seem to me characterized by this kind of gathering role; their power lies in part in their capacity to collect disparate instances and give them a shared meaning. The present dichotomy, while less familiar, also functions in just these ways. Part of what I understand myself to be doing in this chapter is explicitly pointing to this dichotomy *as* a dichotomy—as two concepts that exist in oppositional relation to each other. Partisans of both views make their cases against a real, if unstated opponent, lying across a seemingly unbridgeable chasm.

6. In choosing to use both the terms "food systems" and "foodways," I mean to include both production and consumption aspects of food and food studies. While the usage may not be standard, I refer to "food systems" to address matters related to the production side of food and "foodways" when I focus on consumption-related questions.

The categories of production and consumption are themselves set up as a dichotomy and they map, albeit messily, onto the cosmopolitan/local dichotomy. For instance, the most vigorous advocates of localism among food scholars tend to work on questions about production—agricultural production most specifically. Advocates of cosmopolitanism tend to be more involved in questions about consumption. There are deeper reasons for these connections, among them that some of the most important arguments for the local assert that connection to literal soil—through agriculture, most importantly—is the foundation for community, the foundation for all that is powerful and good about the local. Likewise, arguments for cosmopolitanism often focus on culture and cultural change, which are manifested very clearly in patterns of consumption.

7. It should be mentioned that agrarianism was also, in some senses, the "founding philosophy" of the United States. See Thompson and Hilde's *Agrarian Roots of Pragmatism* for essays exploring the agrarianism of early Americans, especially Thomas Jefferson.

8. CSA, or community supported agriculture, is a form of farming in which consumers buy a "share" in the growing season, and share its harvest—and its loss.

9. While I do not pursue the problem here, the theoretical limitations of localist philosophies begin with this matter of community formation.

10. Appiah heaps scorn on liberals who believe others should preserve cultural traditions they would be unwilling to save, in order that they and their children might enjoy them. I share his irritation, even as I worry about the ease with which he seems to distinguish choice from coercion when it comes to preserving or abandoning aspects of one's culture. Is it choice that leads me to abandon some aspect of my culture that everyone around me regards as uncool? That I cannot practice without fear of public ridicule?

11. Appiah notes, matter-of-factly, "So the time of the successful farming family has gone. . . . But . . . we cannot afford to subsidize indefinitely thousands of distinct islands of homogeneity that no longer make economic sense" (104). Appiah's form of cosmopolitanism, at least, seems willing to accommodate economic globalization.

12. I am skating over my own objections to the easy assertion that culinary travel is a fine way to encounter the Other; for an exploration of the ways in which such traveling promotes and reinforces colonialism, see my *Exotic Appetites*. For perspectives on culinary tourism, see Lang.

13. I assign agency to dichotomies, even though clearly it's humans who deploy dichotomies in these ways. Part of what we seem to experience in the presence of a dichotomy, however, is that its two poles seem to suck us toward them; what were Scylla and Charybdis, after all?

14. Notably, in many Western philosophical accountings, just these features of dichotomous thinking are seen as its strengths.

15. One of the clearest illustrations of this feature comes from an arena unconnected to my present inquiry. Bisexuality and transgender are sexual identities that tend to be understood as "combinations" of hetero and homosexuality, or of maleness and femaleness; the latter are the foundational categories in terms of which these "hybrid" identities *must* be understood. I've suggested that it would be quite possible to reverse the order of explanation, to understand bi and trans identities as foundational and to define the others in terms of them. See my "Dear Kate Bornstein."

16. Keane is hardly the strongest spokesperson for the views he espouses. Others—in both the scholarly and popular press—make the critical case much more strongly. I will not review that voluminous and ever-expanding literature here. Suffice it to say that, in the final days of work on this chapter, dozens more articles, blogs, and opinion pieces, both supportive and critical of the local food movement, came through my e-mail inbox.

17. On the matter of carbon footprint, for instance, research has shown that transport represents a relatively small percentage of the energy used in producing food, making the link between "local" and "green" considerably more tenuous. See Edwards-Jones et al. and DeWeerdt for both academic and mainstream explorations of this. For some of the first work on the relation between miles food travels and ecological effects, see the work of Rich Pirog and Iowa State's Leopold Center for Sustainable Agriculture. Regarding the tendency to associate the local with all things positive, see Born and Purcell; and Purcell and Brown. And for instances of the persistent tendency to think "local = less energy intensive," see any newspaper on any day.

18. How, after all, do we decide what a "legitimate difference" is? In a clash between Appiah's two principles—universalism and respect for legitimate difference—when do we decide that this is an instance for universalism, not for appreciation for "Their" different way of doing things? In the face of an unpalatable difference, cosmopolitans can retreat to the comfort of a claim to universality. But this, of course, is just the charge brought against the provincials—that they refuse to engage with and respect difference. The cosmopolitans can find themselves guilty of just such a refusal.

19. Isn't a "nested traveler" just a "rooted cosmopolitan"—Appiah's term—in other language? While there are no doubt similarities, Appiah's rootedness seems to me inadequate because, in the end, its roots do not lodge in any literal dirt—something that I suggest is crucial in a third option beyond the provincial and the cosmopolitan. I do not further explore the similarities and differences between our two positions here.

20. One theorist developing such an approach is art theorist Lucy Lippard, in her book *The Lure of the Local*. Of the work, Lippard writes, "I will continue to be an emotional nomad and a radical (the root of which means 'root'), playing the relatively conservative values of permanence and rootedness off against restlessness and a constructed 'multicenteredness'" (5).

21. Urban agriculture is again receiving considerable attention, thanks to movements like community gardening and guerilla gardening, aided by new and renewed techniques such as gardening on garbage heaps and "green [i.e., vegetal] roofs."

22. Sarah Orne Jewett's collection of stories, *The Country of Pointed Firs,* makes this point abundantly clear. Writing about a remote region of Maine at the turn of the twentieth century, she reveals a culture of people deeply tied to the natural world—particularly the sea—but also deeply knowledgeable about cultures far removed from them (thanks to the sea).

REFERENCES

Appiah, Kwame Anthony. *Cosmopolitanism: Ethics in a World of Strangers.* New York: W. W. Norton, 2006.

———. *The Ethics of Identity.* Princeton, NJ: Princeton University Press, 2005.

Berry, Wendell. *The Art of the Commonplace: The Agrarian Essays of Wendell Berry.* Ed. Norman Wirzba. Washington, DC: Counterpoint, 2002.

Born, Branden, and Mark Purcell. "Avoiding the Local Trap: Scale and Food Systems in Planning Research." *Journal of Planning Education and Research* 26 (2006): 195–207.

Charles, Jeffrey. Posts to Association for the Study of Food and Society e-mail list. January 2006.

DeWeerdt, Sarah. "Is Local Food Better?" *Worldwatch*, May–June 2009. www.worldwatch .org/node/6064. Accessed July 1, 2009.

Edwards-Jones, Gareth, Llorenç Milà i Canals, Natalia Hounsome, Monica Truninger, Georgia Koerber, Barry Hounsome, Paul Cross et al. "Testing the Assertion That 'Local Food Is Best': The Challenges of an Evidence-Based Approach." *Trends in Food Science and Technology* 19 (2008): 265–74.

Heldke, Lisa. "Dear Kate Bornstein." *Radical Philosophy Association Proceedings 3*, ed. Greg Moses (2006): 95–103.

———. *Exotic Appetites: Ruminations of a Food Adventurer.* New York: Routledge, 2004.

Jewett, Sarah Orne. *The Country of Pointed Firs.* New York: Simon and Schuster, 1997.

Keane, Tom. "A Bitter Reality: Choose Local Food for the Taste? Sure, but if You're Convinced You're Saving the World, Think Again." *Boston Globe Sunday Magazine*, June 28, 2009. www.boston.com/bostonglobe/magazine/articles/2009/06/28/a_bitter_ reality/?comments=all. Accessed June 30, 2009.

Krause-Jackson, Flavia. "Tuscan Town Accused of 'Culinary Racism.' For 'Ethnic' Food Ban." *Bloomberg Muse*, January 27, 2009. www.bloomberg.com/apps/news?pid=news archive&sid=a77r35bgJ2NA. Accessed January 28, 2009.

Lang, Tim. "Food Policy for the 21st Century: Can It Be Both Radical and Reasonable?" In *For Hunger-Proof Cities: Sustainable Urban Food Systems*, ed. Mustafa Koc, Rod MacRae, Jennifer Welsh, and Luc J. A. Mougeot, 216–24. Ottawa: International Development Research Center, 1999.

Lippard, Lucy R. *The Lure of the Local: Senses of Place in a Multicentered Society.* New York: New Press, 1997.

Nussbaum, Martha. *Cultivating Humanity: A Classical Defense of Reform in Liberal Education.* Cambridge, MA: Harvard University Press, 1997.

Orr, David. "The Urban Agrarian Mind." In *The New Agrarianism: Land, Culture, and the Community of Life*, ed. Eric T. Freyfogle, 93–110. Washington, DC: Island Press, 2001.

"Oxford Word of the Year: Locavore." *OUP Blog*, November 12, 2007. http://blog.oup .com/2007/11/locavore. Accessed June 26, 2009.

Pirog, Rich. *Food, Fuel, and Freeways: An Iowa Perspective on How Far Food Travels, Fuel Usage, and Greenhouse Gas Emissions.* Ames: Leopold Center for Sustainable Agriculture, Iowa State University, 2001. www.leopold.iastate.edu/pubs/staff/ppp/index.htm. Accessed June 23, 2009.

Purcell, Mark, and J. Christopher Brown. "Against the Local Trap: Scale and the Study of Environment and Development." *Progress in Development Studies* 5, no. 4 (2005): 279–97.

Ray, Krishnendu. Post to Association for the Study of Food and Society e-mail list. January 31, 2009.

Royce, Josiah. "Provincialism." In *Race Questions, Provincialism and Other American Problems*, 55–108. New York: Macmillan, 1908.

Thompson, Paul B., and Thomas C. Hilde, eds. *The Agrarian Roots of Pragmatism*. Nashville, TN: Vanderbilt University Press, 2000.

Trubek, Amy. *The Taste of Place: A Cultural Journey into Terroir*. Berkeley: University of California Press, 2008.

"Whopper Virgins (Full Length Video)." www.youtube.com/watch?v=fbNoofDM1rM. Accessed June 15, 2009.

Hunger Is the Best Sauce

The Aesthetics of Food

Kevin W. Sweeney

We live in a blossoming age of gastronomy. The interest in cuisine, culinary innovation, and regional traditions of cooking has never been greater. Of course, we are
under attack by the forces of fast food and industrial mass production, but those
threats are opposed by a growing slow food movement that champions flavorful,
healthy, and carefully prepared meals. The number of restaurants that offer innovative cuisine keeps expanding. Fine dining is not limited to a few restaurants in
major cities and the three-star restaurants in the *Michelin Red Guide* for France.
Culinary instruction is vigorously supported both by professional institutions such
as the Culinary Institute of America and by less formal means such as specialized
magazines, the many television cooking shows on the Food Channel, and respected
food writers and critics. The ranks of amateur chefs and hungry consumers with
refined palates continue to grow.[1]

Yet, if interest in gastronomy is expanding, philosophical interest in gustatory
aesthetics seems inhibited by traditional theories that reject our experiences with
cuisine as fully authentic aesthetic encounters. There is a long-standing argument
found in Plato and later in Hegel that only our senses of sight and hearing—our
"intellectual" senses—afford us profound aesthetic pleasures. The bodily senses of
taste, smell, and touch lack a spiritual focus that renders them incapable of providing experiences of the beautiful.[2] Later thinkers base their opposition to the critical
appreciation of food not on the senses employed but on the nature of the experience itself. Even though there are eighteenth-century thinkers such as Hume and
Voltaire who accept as critically genuine our appreciation of food and drink, they
do not provide a developed account of appreciative gustatory experience that would
effectively challenge the opponents. It is only in the early nineteenth century, with

innovative thinkers such as Alexandre Grimod de La Reynière and Jean-Anthelme Brillat-Savarin, that the aesthetics of gastronomy begins to be explored.[3]

One of the significant clashes of ideas that led to the development of serious critical interest in gastronomy occurs in Brillat-Savarin's response to Immanuel Kant's views on gustatory appreciation. Kant rejects food and drink as objects of contemplative critical appreciation. In his *Critique of Judgment,* he transforms theorizing about critical appreciation by popularizing the notion of the *aesthetic* and developing an account of imaginative appreciative experience.[4] He claims that authentic aesthetic experience—the hedonic experience that allows one to judge objectively the merits of what one experiences—must be disinterested, contemplative, and reflective. For Kant, gustatory experience fails on all counts and by its very nature only allows for subjective assessment. It exhibits a personal preference that prevents it from serving as the basis for a universal or objective evaluation.

In setting out his aesthetic theory, Kant depends upon several central gustatory examples to support his rejection of food and drink as affording disinterested, contemplative, and reflective aesthetic experience. Although Kant's views on aesthetics are well known, philosophers have only recently started to question his views on food, and some contemporary philosophers still agree with his rejection.[5] Examining his examples and exploring the philosophical position that gives rise to those examples illuminates his reasons for rejecting a gustatory aesthetics. Additional perspective can be achieved by critically examining Kant's views in the light of Brillat-Savarin's counterproposal to advocate our gustatory experience with cuisine as a complex reflective hedonic encounter.

Unlike his contemporary in France, Benjamin Constant, who explicitly challenged Kant's views on ethics, Brillat-Savarin never specifically refers to Kant in his discussion of gastronomy.[6] Nevertheless, he does use some of Kant's terminology when he discusses cuisine as an object of reflective pleasure. In the title of his book, *The Physiology of Taste; or, Meditations on Transcendental Gastronomy,* Brillat-Savarin also makes several veiled allusions to Kant's aesthetic theory. First of all, Brillat-Savarin presents his views on the pleasures of food and drink as a *transcendental* gastronomy. Although he does not offer a "transcendental deduction" in the Kantian sense, by opposing Kant's restrictions on gustatory experience Brillat-Savarin urges that what we taste and smell has an equal right to be the object of a reflective contemplative hedonic experience as what we see and hear. In addition, the term "physiology" in the book's title challenges Kant's view that an individual's gustatory pleasures are personal preferences and do not reflect a "commonsense" or universal basis for critical evaluation. Instead, Brillat-Savarin insists that our common physiology of smelling and tasting serves as the basis for a universal appreciative experience of food and drink and its critical evaluation. By critically discussing both Kant and Brillat-Savarin's ideas about food and drink, I hope to shed some light on this pivotal clash of ideas about gastronomy and set the stage for further exploration into the foundation of gustatory aesthetics.

DISINTERESTEDNESS

Traditionally, at least since the Enlightenment, taking a critical appreciative attitude toward either a natural object or an artifact such as a work of art has required that one be *disinterested*. Ordinarily, we use the term "disinterested" in a moral or legal context, meaning that judges should be impartial or unprejudiced in their opinions, that they shouldn't have a financial interest in the outcome of a trial or have some other personal stake that might sway or bias their opinions. For Kant, "disinterestedness" has a special meaning. He claims that sensory appreciation can only be aesthetic if one's pleasure is disinterested, meaning not connected with the existence, but only directed at the appearance, of the object appreciated.[7] If one admires, for example, a piece of architecture such as a palace, one's pleasure with the building is aesthetic only if one takes pleasure in experiencing the appearance of the building, what Kant calls the "presentation" of the building. If one's enjoyment is produced by the existence of the building instead of solely by its appearance, then one's experience is not aesthetic. An example of pleasure being produced by the existence of the building would be being pleased because one owns the building and is admired by others because of this.

To help explain this distinction between interested and disinterested pleasures, Kant introduces three examples, one of which is about food. Kant says, "Suppose someone asks me whether I consider the palace I see before me beautiful. I might reply that I am not fond of things of that sort, made merely to be gaped at. Or I might reply like that Iroquois *sachem* who said that he liked nothing better in Paris than the eating-houses. I might even go on, as *Rousseau* would, to rebuke the vanity of the great who spend the people's sweat on such superfluous things" (*Critique*, 45–46). In the first and the third examples, the dislike is directly connected with the existence of the buildings. In contrast, the Iroquois *sachem* likes some Parisian buildings, although he is indifferent to what others admire as the city's magnificent architecture. The Native American's pleasure is with the rotisseries of Paris, but he likes them because of the existence of a plentiful supply of roast meat, which would satisfy his hunger, a bodily interest. Kant holds that the *sachem*'s pleasure is not an aesthetic pleasure; he does not appreciate just the appearance or presentation of the rotisseries.

In later passages in the *Critique*, Kant goes on to develop the idea that our enjoyment of food is not aesthetic, because it is primarily based on an interest in the existence of the food, on having the desire to consume the food.[8] Ordinarily, we are interested in the existence of our food because it satisfies our hunger. Eating is not usually an experience in which we are indifferent to the existence of what we eat and concentrate solely on pleasurably sensing the qualities of what we ingest.

In addition to interests based solely on hunger, Kant claims that we can have other interests in the existence of food. We might want to eat—and even enjoy—certain foods because they are nutritious. Or, we might avoid—and hence dislike—certain foods because of their harmful effect on our health or digestion. With this concern in mind, Kant holds that if we did like or dislike certain foods because of their effect on our health, we would enjoy or find them awful *indirectly* (50). An aesthetic encounter, Kant believes, is not an *indirect* but a *direct* appreciation, indulged in not for some indirect reason but solely for the pleasure taken in the object's appearance or presentation.

Nevertheless, there are occasions in which we enjoy food not because it is low in salt or cholesterol or because it is high in fiber and antioxidants but because we simply enjoy its taste. Don't we sometimes enjoy a meal for no other reason than we like the taste of the food? Yet Kant still resists considering such an appreciation an aesthetic encounter, because he believes that in most cases our enjoyment of food or drink is stimulated by our appetite. Our appetite, he believes, determines that our interest is directed toward the existence of what we are ingesting. No enjoyment of the presentation or appearance alone of what we eat would satisfy this desire.

Kant does qualify this position by holding that if one were to approach what one was ingesting without appetite, without an appetite-driven interest in what one tasted, one might possibly have an aesthetic encounter with what was ingested. He poses a situation in which instead of being hungry one is sated or fully satisfied, and he considers if in such a condition one could enjoy, aesthetically, what one was tasting: "Here everyone says: Hunger is the best sauce; and to people with a healthy appetite anything is tasty provided it is edible. Hence if people have a liking of this sort, that does not prove that they are selecting by taste. Only when their need has been satisfied can we tell who in a multitude of people has taste and who does not" (52). The assumption seems to be that if one is hungry—Kant doesn't say that one must be starving, but only that one have a "healthy appetite"—one will be interested only in finding something to satisfy a craving for food. For Kant, the ordinary hunger of a healthy appetite—one's desire—seems to disqualify appreciative engagement with food as being an aesthetic encounter. Enjoying what we eat or drink is an interested pleasure that comes from satisfying our appetite. However, he seems to allow that if one approaches what one ingests without that desire—if one approaches food after "need has been satisfied"—only then might one have an aesthetic encounter with what has been ingested. I say "might" because Kant goes on to develop a "contemplative" account of aesthetic experience that undercuts even this begrudging allowance of an aesthetic encounter with food.

However, before examining Kant's "contemplative" account of aesthetic appreciation, let us examine further his views about the sated encounter with food. Kant seems to be saying that only if one has no desire to eat or drink because one is sated is it possible to engage aesthetically with what one ingests. Thus, he repeats the nostrum that "hunger is the best sauce" and in so saying means that, as long as one is hungry and encounters anything edible, one will be inclined to enjoy it. In his view, hunger is such a strong desire that it indiscriminately makes anything palatable as long as it is edible.

Consider the experience of approaching food with a healthy appetite as opposed to being sated, and compare that experience with listening to music or looking at painting when one is fresh and rested as opposed to fatigued. Both our enjoyment of established art forms such as painting and music as well as our experience with food demand a certain attention and sensitivity, which aids our appreciation. For all appreciative experiences, our powers of discrimination and enjoyment can tire because of long periods of exposure or intense and demanding involvement. "Museum fatigue" is a known phenomenon. It is foolhardy to try to see in one visit everything in the Louvre or the Metropolitan Museum of Art. Instead, visitors are advised to pick a few pieces or select a particular national or period style (e.g., seventeenth-century Dutch genre painting) and see the rest on other occasions. Viewers will enjoy a few works more than they will enjoy trying to see everything in the collection, a project that will leave them bleary-eyed and exhausted. Listening to music for long periods also dulls one's powers of discrimination and capacity for enjoyment. Foregoing sleep and attempting to listen to all of Haydn's symphonies straight through—over a hundred—would be exhausting. Instead, one would be advised to listen to a few at a time. Very long theatrical performances also wear down one's attention and sensitivity.

One might think that eating and enjoying music or painting are different because we do not have an appetite for music and painting comparable to our physical need and biologically induced desire for food. Of course, there is a physical need to eat, and our survival does not depend upon satisfying our aesthetic pursuits. Yet, those who have developed a "taste" for painting and music can certainly feel deprived if for some reason they cannot listen to music or see works of art. Our engagement with the arts or our desire for aesthetic experiences with nature depends upon our having certain emotional, cultural, and personal needs. I think that the value we place on food also reflects very similar emotional, cultural, and personal needs. Most people want something more than a subsistence diet designed to meet their physical needs and maintain their health. As long as one is not starving, simply satisfying the requirements of basic nutrition does not fulfill those same emotional, cultural, and personal interests that form the motivation behind all of our aesthetic pursuits. We want imaginative and delicious meals to savor rather than just to satisfy our hunger. Thus, I think that there is a greater resemblance than Kant recognizes between our gastronomic interests and our other artistic or culturally appreciative interests.

I also think that Kant misinterprets the nostrum "hunger is the best sauce" and misunderstands the role of a "healthy appetite" in our enjoyment of food. Hunger, he seems to say, will make one inclined to enjoy indiscriminatingly what one is eating, as long as what one is consuming is edible. Certainly, if one is starving that is likely to be true. One will just be glad to have something to eat. However, a more charitable interpretation of the nostrum is that a healthy appetite will incline one to have a heightened enjoyment of a meal. If one has had one's fill of even the best food, one won't enjoy what one eats. Under those circumstances, eating will not be a pleasure. In the more charitable interpretation, a healthy appetite will enliven one's palate. It will make one more sensitive to the subtle nuances of what has been ingested, highlighting the qualities that might otherwise be missed if one were sated. Hunger—at least a healthy appetite—increases one's powers of discrimination and prepares one to enjoy the qualities of the food tasted.

Brillat-Savarin weighs in on this debate in the following ways. Although he does not specifically mention the notion of disinterestedness in appreciative alimentation, he does discuss the role of appetite and hunger in appreciating what we ingest. He remarks on how frequently we hear people say, "How wonderful to have a good appetite, when we are sure of enjoying an excellent dinner before long!" (*Physiology of Taste*, 57). He also tells an anecdote about a young Chevalier who so stuffed himself on the first courses of a feast that he had no appetite for the wonderful dishes that followed (362–65). Nevertheless, he cautions that in appreciating what one eats and drinks one should not be ruled by one's appetite.

In making this reservation, he considers gustatory appreciation in the context of what he calls "gourmandism," which he defines as "an impassioned, considered, and habitual preference for whatever pleases the taste" (148). In pointing out the "considered" nature of this interest, Brillat-Savarin holds that gourmands necessarily have "a power of concentration, without which the most delicious dishes can pass them by unnoticed" (159). Appreciative ingesting, for Brillat-Savarin, is not an automatic and unthinking process but one that demands that we pay attention to—and relish—what we consume. He repeatedly stresses that gourmandism is not to be confused, as it sometimes mistakenly is, "with *gluttony* and *voracity*" (147). To appreciate what one eats and drinks requires that one not be so ravenous or so obsessed with consuming that one loses the ability to discern a dish's flavors or enjoy the meal. Gourmandism, he says, "is the enemy of overindulgence; any man who eats too much or grows drunk risks being expelled from its army of disciples" (148).

By distinguishing gourmandist attention to what is consumed from inattentive voracity, Brillat-Savarin acknowledges Kant's concern that the ravenous individual does not exercise critical taste. Brillat-Savarin also recognizes what one could think of as a role for a form of disinterestedness in his account of appreciative alimentation. This form appears in his distinction between what he refers to as the "pleasures of eating" as opposed to the "pleasures of the table." The former are merely pleasures one has in satisfying a need for food. The latter pleasures exhibit "a reflective sensation" (182). Rather than merely experiencing pleasure from satisfying one's hunger, one considers what one ingests and experiences pleasure on encountering the qualities of what one puts in one's mouth. The "pleasures of the table" depend upon the gourmand being actively engaged in employing the "power of concentration" to enjoy her or his meal. In the social context of a special meal, gustatory pleasures heighten other pleasures—the pleasures we experience from what we see, hear, and touch.

Brillat-Savarin contrasts the two pleasures in the following way: "The pleasure of eating demands appetite, if not actual hunger; the pleasures of the table are most often independent of either one or the other" (182). He illustrates the two pleasures in the following example.

> During the first course, and at the beginning of the feast, everyone eats hungrily, without talking, without paying any attention to what may be going on about him, and no matter what his position or rank may be he ignores everything in order to devote himself to the great task at hand. But as these needs are satisfied, the intellect rouses itself, and conversation begins, a new order of behavior asserts itself, and the man who was no more than an eater until then becomes a more or less pleasant companion, according to his natural ability. (182)

With his discussion of the pleasures of the table, Brillat-Savarin is responding to the Kantian concern that critical taste should not be instigated by a desire to satisfy a bodily need. Nevertheless, I think that he is too accommodating to the Kantian concern for disinterestedness. Brillat-Savarin clearly wants to distinguish the gourmandist interest in cuisine from gluttony and voraciousness. Yet, one needs to distinguish the insensitivity and excessiveness of those obsessions from the beneficial effects of a good appetite. Rather than getting in the way of appreciating what one eats, a good appetite can stimulate an interest in the qualities of what one encounters on one's palate. Both Kant and Brillat-Savarin only consider two possible appetitive states that one might be in when sitting down to a meal: one can be ravenous or one's appetite can be under control because one has satisfied an urgent need for sustenance. Neither thinker considers a third possible state: one might want to enjoy the meal but be unable to do so because one lacks an appetite. Consider the following example. It has been a long, hard day at the office, and one would like to relax and enjoy an evening meal with friends or family. However, it has been a stressful day, and one has no appetite. What is needed in such a situation is something to stimulate the appetite—a few light snacks or an aperitif to get the gastric juices flowing. Certainly, trying to enjoy a meal without an appetite will not be as pleasurable as approaching it with an appetite. Thus, having an appetite—even though it involves an interest in the existence of what one ingests and thus violates Kant's requirement of being disinterested—contributes to our gustatory enjoyment.

GASTRONOMIC EXPERIENCE REFLECTS ONLY PERSONAL PREFERENCE

Kant resists accepting our experiences with cuisine as being authentic aesthetic encounters because he believes that our judgments about food cannot be objectively supported. The main reason he thinks that gustatory judgments cannot be objective is that they are not disinterested; they are based on our appetite. Only disinterested pleasures and the judgments based on them are objectively assessable. However, Kant has some additional reasons for resisting the aesthetic character of our experience with cuisine. He believes that gustatory pleasures or revulsions cannot serve as the basis for an objective evaluation because they are tied to idiosyncratic preferences—quirky, personal likes or dislikes for what we eat or drink. Kant distinguishes a subjective preference, which produces a pleasure that he labels as being "agreeable," from more objective valuations in the following gustatory example of "canary wine."

> Hence, if he says that canary wine is agreeable he is quite content if someone else corrects his terms and reminds him to say instead: It is agreeable to *me*. This holds moreover not only for the taste of the tongue, palate, and throat, but also for what may be agreeable to any one's eyes and ears. To one person the color violet is gentle and lovely, to another lifeless and faded. One person loves the sound of wind instruments, another that of string instruments. It would be foolish if we disputed about such differences with the intention of censuring another's judgment as incorrect if it differs from ours, as if the two were opposed logically. (*Critique,* 55)

In this passage, Kant is claiming that I might like a particular wine from the Canary Islands, but you might not like it, and this holds true about everything we ingest. We each have our own individual preferences about what we like to eat and drink, just as we have preferences about the colors we like, and neither one of us is correct or incorrect to have such preferences. However, Kant holds that contemplative aesthetic experience—what he claims will be the basis for an objective judgment commanding universal validity that something is beautiful—depends on grounds other than personal preference. Food is too much a matter of personal taste to serve as an object of a well-grounded aesthetic assessment.

In attempting to distinguish an appreciation based on subjective preference from an aesthetic encounter that can serve as a ground for an objective assessment, Kant inherits some earlier popular ideas and concepts for describing our critical appreciations. Before Kant's popularization of the concept of the *aesthetic*—the concept of the aesthetic was unknown in France and England in the eighteenth century—the predominant way of describing critical appreciation employed the concept of *taste*. Critical taste was metaphorically based on literal taste or gustatory experience. Certain core similarities between gustatory experience and critical appreciation made the concept of taste metaphorically appropriate for describing the pleasures we experience in listening to music or viewing paintings.

First, the role played by individual experience in literally tasting—sensing what one has put in one's mouth and by one's hedonic reaction judging if it is good or not—was seen as similar to the process whereby one reached a critical assessment about other things. In both cases it was thought that the grounds for assessment or valuation must be based on personal experience. One could not appeal to a rule or an authority. No a priori support was available. To have *taste* demanded that one critically assess on the basis of one's own experience. Kant acknowledges this point when he explains that this was "one of the main reasons why this aesthetic power of judging was given that very name: taste. For even if someone lists all the ingredients of a dish, pointing out that I have always found each of them agreeable, and goes on to praise this food—and rightly so—as wholesome, I shall be deaf to all these reasons; I shall try the dish on *my* tongue and palate, and thereby (and not by universal principles) make *my* judgment" (148). The same condition held true for critical assessment. To possess taste, one had to determine on the basis of one's own hedonic experience the appropriate evaluation. One could not appeal to rules or authorities to substantiate one's judgment; instead, one's judgment had to be grounded on one's own personal engagement with what was being evaluated.

A second recognized similarity between gustatory and critical experience was that we judge both on the basis of the stimulated pleasure. Alimentation is fundamentally hedonic: when one puts something in one's mouth to taste, one naturally expects to react somewhere within a hedonic range from extreme pleasure to revulsion. We can react hedonically to sights and sounds but not to the inherent extent that we do with what we taste. Critical appreciation presupposes a similar hedonic reaction; at least people thought so in the eighteenth century. We value our critical experiences with art and nature because they provide us with pleasures. One of the favorite metaphorical terms used in the eighteenth century to describe the pleasurable experience of one's critical encounter was to refer to oneself as "relishing" the object. (See Voltaire's use of the term in the first sentence of the quotation below.)

Third, critical taste and gustatory experience were both held to induce an immediate response as far as evaluation was concerned. Both critical and gustatory tastes were believed to provide a quick hedonic reaction as an assessment of what was being encountered. Voltaire compares critical—or "intellectual taste" as he calls it—with the "quick discernment" of the palate.

> Taste, then, in general is a quick discernment, a sudden perception, which, like the sensation of the palate, anticipates reflection; like the palate, it relishes what is good with an exquisite and voluptuous sensibility, and rejects the contrary with loathing and disgust . . . [Intellectual] taste must not be a vague and confused sensation; but must be attended with a distinct view, a quick and comprehensive discernment of the various qualities, in their several relations and connections, which enter into the composition of the object we contemplate. And in this we see another striking resemblance between the intellectual taste and the sensual one; for as a nice palate perceives immediately the mixture of different wines, so the man of taste will quickly discern the motley mixture of different styles in the same production.[9]

It was thought that literal taste or gustatory experience gives an immediate verdict. As Voltaire says, it "anticipates reflection." In trying a new food, one takes a bite and is expected right away to tell if one likes or doesn't like what one has eaten. Similarly, possessing critical taste was thought to have the power to discern quickly what was good and pleasurable in a work of art and what was faulty and displeasing.

One noticeable drawback to "taste" as a general critical concept for describing appreciative experience was that, in emphasizing individual experience and hedonic immediacy, it left critical appreciation open to being criticized as a subjective activity: how could taste be held to some objective standard if it was based primarily on individual hedonic reaction? Kant sets out to address this problem by splitting critical appreciation into two sorts of taste. First, he articulates what he calls the "taste of sense" as a basic form of appreciation. Adapting some of the problematic characteristics of previous theories of taste, Kant holds that the taste of sense is restricted to a stimulus-produced pleasure, reflecting the specific personal preferences of the sensory perceiver. Its immediate hedonic effect occurs without benefit of input from our higher cognitive faculties. No acts of the imagination or the understanding are involved in this sensory liking or disliking. With the taste of sense, our pleasure or displeasure—Kant refers to them as agreeable or disagreeable—constitute only our personal evaluation about what we have experienced.

For Kant, gustatory experiences conform to this model of the taste of sense. In eating and drinking, we either like what we taste, take the negative view that it is bland and uninteresting, or register our disgust at what we have had the bad fortune to put in our mouths. Kant thinks of gustatory experience as purely sensory. In a telling comment about the limited sensory nature of food as opposed to more authentic aesthetic encounters, Kant says, "For we consider someone's way of thinking to be coarse and ignoble if he has no *feeling* for beautiful nature . . . and sticks to the enjoyments of mere sense that he gets from meals or the bottle" (170). In order for food and drink to be objects of refined appreciation, as opposed to coarse objects of "mere sense," our appreciative experience would have to involve the imagination; and Kant thinks that because we react immediately to what we ingest, there would be no extended temporal opportunity to bring our "higher" powers to bear on our gustatory encounter.

Imaginative engagement is a feature of the second sort of taste that Kant introduces, the "taste of reflection." An initial difference between the two "tastes" is that in the taste of sense the pleasure or displeasure is immediately felt on contact; however, in the taste of reflection the hedonic experience is not immediately felt. Pleasure occurs not "first," as Kant says, but as a "consequence" of our aesthetic engagement (61). Instead of the rather passive sensory reaction of the taste of sense, the taste of reflection describes the perceiver taking some time to engage actively with the focus object. This active engagement, Kant says, does employ some of our cognitive faculties. Because of the time involved, this aesthetic encounter is referred to as a "contemplative" activity: one maintains an engagement with the object, and in so doing one is said to contemplate the object. Kant says this engagement involves a "free play" of the imagination. Since there is no determinate object that we identify and come to know by means of our cognitive faculties, we imaginatively play—and this is a pleasurable activity—with what we experience. It is also *reflective* in the sense that the perceiver takes pleasure in the way our imaginative cognitive faculties engage in various different ways with the object. In a reflection, we register the pleasure of being imaginatively engaged in those particular ways.

Kant distinguishes perceptual knowledge from an imaginative aesthetic experience (the taste of reflection) in the following way. In ordinary perceptual knowledge, Kant claims that our imagination works together with our understanding to supply concepts so that our initial sensory experience is recognized as having a particular *determinate* form (i.e., it is seen as a dog or heard as a train whistle). We come to identify and know what we perceive by means of this application of concepts. However, in aesthetic encounters—at least pure ones—since it is pleasure rather than knowledge that we are interested in, our understanding does not supply a determinate concept or purposive nature to our sensory experience. We don't just identify something as an instance of a particular concept (i.e., a dog or a whistle). Instead, we are content to accept a measure of indeterminacy to what we are experiencing so as to allow our imagination the freedom to play with the presentation. It is not complete indeterminacy because in our imaginative play we do attribute something like a determinacy to the object. We perceive it to have what Kant calls a "purposiveness without a purpose" (65). Our imagination is actively engaged in playing with the presentation. In cases of experiencing something as beautiful, Kant claims that our cognitive experience—our imaginative free play—achieves a harmony (62). This harmony of our cognitive acts of engagement Kant identifies as an experience of something's being beautiful.

Kant claims that experiences afforded by the taste of reflection are amenable to objective assessment. In cases of judging something beautiful, one's judgment is intended to command universal assent. One is not just expressing a personal preference but is judging for everyone. He says that if one "proclaims something to be beautiful, then he requires the same liking from others; he then judges not just for himself but for everyone" (55). There are two basic reasons for this basis of objective assessment. First, in one's appreciation of a presentation, one's liking of the object is "devoid of all interest" (53). In one's disinterested pleasure, one's experience has that impartiality that is held necessary for one's judgment to be objective. Second, the imaginative free play with the presentation and the resulting pleasure is not merely a personal form of engagement. Kant believes that all imaginative engagement with an object and the resulting pleasures indicate a common basis for a critical assessment. The imaginative free play reflects a "common sense," a common cognitive form of engagement, held by all human perceivers, one which could provide everyone with a pleasure. The common sense of our cognitive powers—we all have the same cognitive powers—gives a basis for the universal application of one's hedonic assessment (86–87).

The taste of reflection is contemplative; however, contemplation for Kant is not a rapt, passive, mesmerized attention. As his theory of imaginative free play indicates, contemplation is an active intellectual engagement with the presentation. In a sense, one imaginatively works with the various different aspects of the presentation. To the extent that the presentation affords material for this imaginative free play, there is the possibility of a harmonious integration of one's cognitive processes. The positive hedonic value of harmony indicates that one's imaginative aim is not to concentrate on single elements, however agreeable they may be. Single elements such as a color in a painting or a single tone in a musical composition, Kant says, "only deserve to be called agreeable" (70). For the taste of reflection, he proposes that it is the form of the presentation—what he refers to as the "purposiveness of the form" (69)—that provides in its multiplicity of elements the occasion for a full imaginative engagement (70–72).

Based on the nature of his food examples, Kant believes that our gustatory experiences do not provide opportunities for engaging the taste of reflection. Since he does not offer a sustained specific argument about why this is so, one has to piece together his position. If one were to hold that gustatory experience only afforded an immediate hedonic reaction, there would be no opportunity for an extended contemplative engagement with what one ingests. In immediately and hedonically reacting, one, it would seem, could not defer one's pleasure in order to engage in gustatory imaginative free play. There would be no extended temporal period within which an active imaginative engagement could take place. Since, for Kant, eating is motivated by appetite, our hedonic assessment of what we ingest would not be disinterested; and without benefit of imaginative free play, there would be no "common sense" cognitive basis for a universal or objective judgment about what we eat and drink.

THE "PHYSIOLOGY" OF TASTE

I think that Kant is mistaken in several respects about the nature of gustatory experience and our appreciative encounter with what we consume. Kant's insis-tence on gustatory immediacy overlooks some important features of the process of alimentation, specifically that there is an extended act of tasting, smelling, and other modalities of sensing that occur when we ingest our food. As opposed to Kant, Brillat-Savarin proposes a gustatory aesthetic in which ingestion is a more complex process than Kant recognizes. Instead of provoking an immediate hedonic reaction, eating and drinking, Brillat-Savarin holds, offer extended occasions for reflective aesthetic encounters.

First, Brillat-Savarin insists that gustatory pleasure does not come "first" but occurs during and after the process of ingesting. During the act of eating and drinking, there are occasions for us to have multiple hedonic valuations of what we are tasting rather than being confined to just a single immediate response. In encountering a wide variety of gustatory elements, we have the time to contemplate and consider them reflectively. Brillat-Savarin holds that there are certain basic tastes—such as sweet, sour, and bitter—that are simply sensed in a Kantian way as "agreeable or disagreeable" (*Physiology of Taste,* 38). However, he also maintains that gustatory qualities are not experienced with a single sensory modality—taste. Much of what we experience as a particular taste is in fact sensed through our retro-nasal organs of smell. "When the sense of smell is cut off," he says, "taste itself is paralyzed" (39). He also claims, "I am not only convinced that there is no full act of tasting without the participation of the sense of smell, but I am also tempted to believe that smell and taste form a single sense" (39). Rather than having just a small set of agreeable or disagreeable tastes, taste and smell work together to provide us with a vastly expanded set of flavors and gustatory experiences. He claims there are an infinite number of such "tastes" (38). Because there are such a vastly increased number of tastes, there is a greater opportunity for complex aesthetic combinations.

Second, Brillat-Savarin recognizes that these flavors do not occur as isolated single sensory effects; rather, they usually are conjoined in sequence. This takes place because of the "physiology," as he calls it, of alimentation. Brillat-Savarin emphasizes the physiology of alimentation because he wants to stress the common sensory way that human beings ingest their food. Hunger and the natural course of ingesting are the "common sense" of humanity. This common process of ingesting takes some time from its inception to its completion. First, we react to the visual appearance and aroma of what we are about to put in our mouths. Then there are the initial tastes and flavors we encounter when we take our first bite or sip. Once what we have ingested starts to vaporize and affect our retro-nasal passages, a new set of flavors might develop on our middle palate. Finally, after we swallow there are often aftertastes that make their appearance and linger. Thus, the extended process of ingesting presents us with a complex set of qualities. Because of the temporal period required, we have the opportunity to reflect on and contemplate the gustatory sequence of flavors that has occurred and hedonically respond to them. Rather than food and drink provoking only an immediate hedonic reaction, there is the occasion, especially with fine cuisine, for imaginatively gauging the relationships of sensed elements and the overall structure of what we have ingested.

Brillat-Savarin offers a tripartite model of the extended valuation of gustatory experience in order to show how such experiences can be reflective. He claims that there are three principal sorts of valuation that occur in the process of ingesting. In order, he labels them as "direct," "complete," and "reflective" sensations.

> The *direct* sensation is the first one felt, produced from the immediate operations of the organs of the mouth, while the body under consideration is still on the forepart of the tongue.
>
> The *complete* sensation is the one made up of this first perception plus the impression which arises when the food leaves its original position, passes to the back of the mouth, and attacks the whole organ with its taste and its aroma.
>
> Finally, the *reflective* sensation is the opinion which one's spirit forms from the impressions which have been transmitted to it by the mouth. (40)

In order to emphasize the valuational character of this reflective process, Brillat-Savarin gives several illustrative examples. Here is his example of drinking a glass of red wine and afterwards evaluating it.

> While the wine is in the mouth one is agreeably but not completely appreciative of it; it is not until the moment when he has finished swallowing it that a man can truly taste, consider, and discover the bouquet peculiar to each variety; and there must still be a little lapse of time before a real connoisseur can say, "It is good, or passable, or bad. By Jove, here is a Chambertin!" (40–41)

Instead of having an immediate impression of liking or disliking, the wine connoisseur needs time to reflect on the whole experience in order to determine whether the wine is a great Burgundy, merely a passable table wine, or outright "plonk." The qualities of the wine one is evaluating are not presented all at once. Some occur at different stages of ingesting the wine. Getting a sense of the structure of the wine, how the sensory parts develop and fit together, takes some time and concentration.

In the case of food, we pause and consider whether the cayenne pepper is too assertive in the gumbo.[10] Does the apple pie need a touch more cinnamon or all-spice? Is the soufflé or the puff pastry light enough? In addressing these matters, we have to taste and give some reflective consideration about what we have tasted. This is an extended rather than an immediate process. Brillat-Savarin's tripartite model of gustatory appreciation provides a framework for raising these aesthetic concerns and realizing the reflective aesthetic engagement we have with what we eat and drink.

One should keep in mind that gustatory experience is not merely a single experience of what we are at the moment consuming. Sometimes we do just focus on what we are at that moment ingesting, and we only pay attention to, and judge the merit of, those particular qualities that we are tasting and swallowing. This is a unitary consideration about what we have in our mouths or what we repeatedly put in our mouths when consuming a particular dish. However, we should keep in mind that our appreciative encounter with food is not usually unitary. Yes, we do try a sip of this white wine or a taste of that baba ghanoush. However, in the course of a meal we usually taste and respond to *multiple* things on our plate. In addition, we often compare different dishes, especially in a particular sequence during a meal.

Ordinarily, the basic unit of what we taste and evaluate is the *meal,* not just the single bite, and a meal might be composed of several courses and perhaps different drinks appropriate to specific courses (e.g., coffee with dessert). Even on a single plate, there might be several different preparations. Rarely in eating a meal do we eat just one thing. Usually a main dish will have accompanying starches, vegetables, and condiments. Even the lowly hot dog or burger comes in a bun with a variety of relishes or an accompaniment like lettuce and a slice of tomato. To taste and judge a whole meal sometimes takes considerable time. With an elaborate celebration, we might spend a considerable amount of time comparing all of the various dishes we have eaten. It is well to remember that Brillat-Savarin's ultimate gustatory category is the "pleasures of the table." This is a synthetic appreciation that recognizes all the relevant contributions to the meal and that calls on our concentration and active participation in the evaluation.

Given the variety of tastes that we encounter when eating, can we say that there is an imaginative character to our enjoyment of food and drink? As I indicated earlier, I think that there can be. Although I do not subscribe to Kant's theory of imaginative free play as a harmony of cognitive processes, I do believe that we can imaginatively engage with what we consume, especially with fine cuisine. I certainly would not limit aesthetic involvement to a restricted formalism as Kant does; instead I recognize broad opportunities for an active gustatory imagination. Within the time frame of the process of ingesting or within the time frame of a meal, we sometimes compare and contrast gustatory qualities, identify a qualitative tone to a particular dish or a qualitative overtone to a meal or a series of courses.

We come to discern the culinary style of a chef or the regional character of New Orleans Creole cuisine. This is an imaginative process in the same way that hearing a melody calls on our imagination: each note is separate, but when we hear them together we recognize their mutual identity as a melody. In our active imaginative noting of salient features in what we eat and drink, we come to see harmonies, contrasts, and structure in what we ingest. All of this insight requires an active imaginative participation.

Finally, as an aid to our imaginative efforts with what we eat, I believe that "hunger is the best sauce." Sauces do many things. Sometimes they complement what they are served with; other times they provide a contrast. They can bring together otherwise differing flavors or provide a missing quality that accents a particular dish. They play a creative role in the ultimate character of a dish or meal. Our gustatory imagination, sharpened and aided by our appetite, also seeks to bring out the distinctive flavors or other salient characteristics of what we eat. It is no wonder that the French often wish a diner at the start of a meal, "Bon appétit."

NOTES

1. For an overview of contemporary gastronomy, see Peter Scholliers, "Novelty and Tradition," *Food: The History of Taste,* ed. Paul Freedman (Berkeley: University of California Press, 2007), 333–57.

2. For a discussion of the intellectual versus bodily senses debate, see Carolyn Korsmeyer, *Making Sense of Taste: Food and Philosophy* (Ithaca, NY: Cornell University Press, 1999), 12–26, 60–63; and Emily Brady, "Sniffing and Savoring: The Aesthetics of Smells and Tastes," *The Aesthetics of Everyday Life,* ed. Andrew Light and Jonathan M. Smith (New York: Columbia University Press, 2005), 178–85.

3. For a discussion of Grimod de La Reynière's influence on gastronomy, see Giles MacDonogh, *A Palate in Revolution* (London: Robin Clark, 1987). For a discussion of Brillat-Savarin's influence on gastronomy, see another book by Giles MacDonogh, *Brillat-Savarin: The Judge and His Stomach* (Chicago: Ivan R. Dee, 1992); and Kevin W. Sweeney, "Can a Soup Be Beautiful? The Rise of Gastronomy and the Aesthetics of Food," *Food and Philosophy,* ed. Fritz Allhoff and Dave Monroe (Malden, MA: Blackwell, 2007), 117–32.

4. Immanuel Kant, *The Critique of Judgment* (1790), trans. Werner S. Pluhar (Indianapolis, IN: Hackett, 1987). Further references to this work are to this edition and appear parenthetically in the chapter text.

5. See Monroe C. Beardsley, *Aesthetics: Problems in the Philosophy of Criticism,* 2nd ed. (Indianapolis, IN: Hackett, 1981), 98–99, 111; and Roger Scruton, *The Aesthetics of Architecture* (Princeton, NJ: Princeton University Press, 1979), 113–16, and *Art and Imagination* (Boston: Routledge and Kegan Paul, 1982), 156–57. For an opposing view, see Frank Sibley, "Tastes, Smells and Aesthetics," *Approach to Aesthetics,* ed. J. Benson, B. Redfern, and J. Cox (New York: Oxford University Press, 2006), 207–55.

6. Jean-Anthelme Brillat-Savarin, *The Physiology of Taste; or, Meditations on Transcendental Gastronomy* (1825), trans. M. F. K. Fisher (New York: Harcourt Brace Jovanovich, 1971). Further references to this work are to this edition and appear parenthetically in the chapter text.

7. For further discussion of the role of disinterestedness in the history of aesthetic appreciation, see Jerome Stolnitz, "On the Origin of 'Aesthetic Disinterestedness,'" *Journal of Aesthetics and Art Criticism* 20 (Winter 1961): 131–43. For further analysis of Kant's views on disinterestedness, see Donald W. Crawford, *Kant's Aesthetic Theory* (Madison: University of Wisconsin Press, 1974), 37–54. On Kant's

liking "devoid of all interest," see Paul Guyer, *Kant and the Claims of Taste,* 2nd ed. (New York: Cambridge University Press, 1997), 148–83.

8. Scruton, *Aesthetics of Architecture,* 113–16; Dave Monroe, "Can Food Be Art? The Problem of Consumption," *Food and Philosophy,* 133–44.

9. Voltaire, "An Essay on Taste," translated from Voltaire's article on taste in Diderot and D'Alembert's *Encyclopédie* (1757) in Alexander Gerard, *An Essay on Taste,* 2nd ed. (1764; repr., New York: Garland, 1970), 209–10.

10. It might seem that whether or not the gumbo has enough cayenne is a matter of personal taste. However, this traditional dish of New Orleans cuisine, I think, needs to be judged by recognized regional standards for the cuisine. Of course, there are personal preferences for music and painting as well as types of cooking. One might not like opera but Mozart's *The Magic Flute* can still be credited with being a great opera.

4

Smells, Tastes, and Everyday Aesthetics

Emily Brady

Mr Bloom ate his strips of sandwich, fresh clean bread, with relish of disgust pungent mustard, the feety savour of green cheese. Sips of wine soothed his palate. Not logwood that. Tastes fuller this weather with the chill off.

JAMES JOYCE, *ULYSSES*

Sniffing and savoring are central to human life and the lives of many other animals. Eating, drinking, and navigating environments and the objects within them depend upon these senses. Yet, despite this importance, the study of smells and tastes is neglected in philosophy, more generally, and in aesthetics too, where one might expect to see proper attention paid.[1] This neglect stems at least in part from the belief that smells and tastes are improper objects of aesthetic judgment, a belief traceable to the philosophical distinction between the higher and lower pleasures. A more general reason arises from the predominance of the visual in human experience and thus in the subject matter of aesthetics. In this chapter, I try to put things right by asserting the legitimacy of smells and tastes in aesthetic appreciation. I argue, first, that they can be appreciated as having aesthetic qualities in themselves and meet the conditions of inclusion in the aesthetic domain as set out by traditional aesthetic theory. That domain, normally reserved for high art and the beauty or sublimity of nature, can be expanded to include olfactory and gustatory experiences. Drawing on recent work in everyday aesthetics, I then argue that smells and tastes have a place in our more ordinary aesthetic responses. I confine my discussion to bringing smells and tastes into the domain of aesthetics rather than putting forward arguments concerning the artistic status of food.[2]

ANALYZING SMELLS AND TASTES

Establishing the aesthetic status of smells and tastes depends on a clear understanding of their nature and character. My analysis here takes its lead from Frank Sibley's extended and detailed discussion presented in "Tastes, Smells and Aesthetics."[3] Like Sibley, I concentrate mainly on smells. Much of what we commonly call tasting is, more accurately, smelling. Smell is physically defined by receptors in the nose, combined with the olfactory nerve. Taste is physically defined by receptors in the tongue, or taste buds. By these physical criteria smell has a dominant place because our sensation of what comes into the mouth is perceived also through olfactory receptors. Furthermore, the nose is commonly held to be a more sensitive receptor than the tongue, so all in all smell is doing most of the work. The two senses do work together, though, which leads some writers, such as J. J. Gibson, to define smells and tastes through their function within a perceptual system.[4] Carolyn Korsmeyer points out, too, that smells and tastes have been described as a "mouth sense" that synthesizes "taste, olfaction, chemical sensitivity, temperature, and touch."[5] In practice, we can often discern the difference between the two senses, and one way to do this is according to their function. Smell is the sense that involves sniffing or breathing through the nose, while taste is the sense that involves savoring—eating, drinking, and tasting through the mouth.

There are different kinds of smells and tastes, for example, the taste of milk, the aroma of coffee; but within kinds, Sibley makes a useful distinction between the particular and the general. Particular smells and tastes are particular instances of them, for example, the taste of this particular cup of coffee or the smell of a particular person's sweat. The "general" category refers to the general smell or taste associated with something or the generic category of the particular, for example, the taste of Earl Grey tea, rather than this particular cup; the smell of sweat, as opposed to a particular person's. In many cases it will be hard to distinguish general categories. Against Sibley, one could argue that the general/particular distinction is unfounded. It might be claimed that there are only particulars because there are no common characteristics to create such general categories. Indeed, most of the examples I give here are of particular instances of smells and tastes. Nevertheless, the distinction is a useful one even if it does not hold categorically. We can usually discriminate between different tastes of water in some sort of way and at the same time discern the taste of water generally. One taste of water is chlorinated, another brackish, yet we still recognize the water taste they both belong to and can distinguish that water taste from a milk taste. The use of general categories does not entail that there is some essential taste to water or to milk but only that we can reasonably identify a generic taste. Even if we wanted to develop an essentialism of smells and tastes, it would be very hard to come up with the appropriate descriptions. Like faces, smells and tastes become easily recognizable, yet their essence can be difficult to put into words. In humans, these modes of sensory perception are generally less developed than the other senses, which is one reason why many people do not have a rich vocabulary for describing them.

A second useful distinction made by Sibley is between single and mixed smells and tastes. Single smells or tastes are simple, where only one smell or taste can be discerned and where a smell or taste is not distinguishable into separate or different ones, for example, the taste of salt and the taste of lemon. Mixed smells and tastes involve compounds, where more than a single smell or taste is discerned. This category is interesting for pinning down the complexity of what we experience through the nose and mouth. The flavor of Sprite seems to be a mixture of three tastes—the fresh citrus of lemon and lime with the clean, slightly salty taste of carbonated water. The smell of raspberry yogurt combines the creamy, slightly sour smell of yogurt with the sharpness of raspberry. Although it is sometimes challenging to identify the complex mixture in a smell or taste, I suspect that most are mixed. Certainly it is possible to discriminate the various mixtures there are. Some mammals can discriminate with precision the blend of smells in the scent of a particular person, some humans can distinguish every individual scent in an aroma or fragrance, and even machines can make such distinctions relatively accurately.[6] An admixture of tastes may also create a whole new single taste or flavor altogether, which makes the distinction between single and mixed less sharp.

DEFENDING SMELLS AND TASTES
IN AESTHETIC APPRECIATION

With some idea of the nature of smells and tastes, I now turn to objections raised against them within philosophical aesthetics.[7] Most of these criticisms come from a traditional approach to aesthetic judgment and response, as typified by Kant's aesthetic theory. My strategy here is to argue that smells and tastes can meet the objections of this approach on its own terms even if, ultimately, it too narrowly defines what counts as a proper object of aesthetic appreciation. My overall aim is to show that smells and tastes (especially in relation to food) constitute aesthetic objects that legitimately fall within specialized, connoisseur-type appreciation *and* aesthetic responses in everyday life. They meet the criteria of more traditional aesthetic objects associated with seeing and hearing, while at the same time pervading our more ordinary encounters. In attempting to show how smells and tastes run across these concerns, I am not supporting a high-low dichotomy, as such, in our aesthetic responses. Rather, I want to address the limitations of past approaches and point to the significance of smells and tastes in ordinary experience.

Earlier, I pointed to an underlying reason why smells and tastes are a neglected topic: the predominance of the visual. For most humans eyesight is the predominant sense, so it is not surprising that, along with hearing, visual qualities have historically received the most attention in aesthetics. Emphasis on visual qualities is not, of course, a bad thing in itself, and in many cases these qualities will be the most relevant feature of an aesthetic object (e.g., a painting). But focusing only on visual qualities may be inappropriate and leaves aside a fuller, multisensory experience, resulting in a more limited basis for aesthetic appreciation and judgment. New work in environmental aesthetics, for example, has sought to move attention away from the narrowly visual and scenic to appreciation informed by the range of senses.[8] These discussions are, however, much more recent and do not reflect early neglect of the other senses.

A principal reason for the neglect of smells and tastes in aesthetics stems from their association with the body and nonhuman animals so that, historically, they have been relegated to the realm of the crude, so-called lower pleasures. This first prejudice stems from the long philosophical tradition of making a distinction between the lower and higher pleasures, a distinction closely tied to mind/body dualism, which holds that the mind is distinct from and has more value than the body. The lower pleasures associated with the body include eating, smelling, sex, and other bodily functions such as sweating, while the so-called higher pleasures are associated with the mind and the intellect. One early source of this kind of thinking is Plato. In *Phaedo,* for example, the bodily pleasures are considered an obstacle to achieving truth and a desirable afterlife.[9] This idea is continued famously by John Stuart Mill: "It is better to be a human being dissatisfied than a pig satisfied; better to be Socrates dissatisfied than fool satisfied."[10]

Despite emphasis on the body in phenomenology and in postmodern and post-structuralist thought, the prejudice continues, no doubt supported by the conventions of everyday life. Many societies in Western culture still dictate that smells and tastes are baser pleasures. For example, smelling socks is considered unseemly, perhaps because our behavior is compared to nonhuman animals (another reason is, presumably, that taking interest in *bad* smells is unseemly). Add to this that we mask natural odors such as sweat with perfumed scents. Another convention that supports the prejudice is criticism of excessive eating and drinking, except when raised to an intellectual art or connoisseurship that combines smelling and tasting with thorough and refined knowledge.

The prejudice against smells and tastes has also found its way into the art world. Combined with the fact that sight is our dominant sense, smells and tastes have had little role in the history of art. Still life is a genre of visual art in which the other senses are played on, but it is clearly visual even if some paintings make one's mouth water. It is possible to find olfactory descriptions in literature, and many writers regularly use smell and taste descriptions—Proust, Woolf, and Joyce are prime examples.[11] On the whole, though, the literary imagination tends to be a visual one. An especially interesting exception is Peter Süskind's *Perfume: The*

Story of a Murderer, the story of a perfumer who lacks any personal scent, yet who has an extraordinary sense of smell that eventually leads to his demise.[12] The novel describes a rich olfactory world, using smell to build an image of the central character and the way his nose constructs the environment around him.

Some contemporary artworks have made progress in drawing on our sense of smell by using different scents and organic materials (e.g., soil, vegetables, blood, chocolate, milk, and honey). The Belgian "olfactory artist," Peter de Cupere, creates smell installations, scent paintings, scent concerts and other works. For example, *Spaghetti House* (2007) used nine hundred kilograms of cooked spaghetti to form a small house, which was then scented with basil, oregano, and tomato.[13] There are also many food artists who use food to design all sorts of objects as well as "edible art."

One way to defend smells and tastes against the lower/higher pleasures objection is to argue that the distinction itself is untenable. This argument would begin by challenging mind/body dualism. While I cannot present such an argument here, it is worth noting that, although recent materialist theories of mind have all but defeated the mind/body split, this seems to have had little effect on aesthetic theory in terms of expanding its attention to the other senses. Two more brief points help to make some headway against the entrenched view. Our other senses have also been associated with the "distasteful" aspects of the body; sight, sound, and touch are all also associated with eating, drinking, sex and sweating, so why pick on smells and tastes? Furthermore, that many smells are unpleasant surely contributes to their neglect, but many bodily smells are pleasant: skin smells like milk or honey; hair smells soft and fresh; kisses are described as sweet.

The claim that smells and tastes belong to the baser pleasures also associates them very closely with consumption and desire, which leads some philosophers to argue that these senses cannot be disinterested.[14] When applied to aesthetic appreciation, disinterestedness stipulates contemplation of an object's aesthetic qualities for their own sake, rather than for some interest it might serve. Eating and drinking are practices of consumption, and we often want more of whatever smell or taste we enjoy. But smells and tastes, as well as other sensations, have a qualitative dimension that stands alone. The aroma of ripe Stilton cheese can be appreciated without wishing to consume it (or in the moments before we do in fact consume it in order to satisfy hunger). The same is true in the most sophisticated kinds of olfactory and gustatory appreciation, like wine tasting, where only a sip of wine is savored.

Sniffing and savoring are not, however, always appreciative, that is, many of our sensory responses do not involve making aesthetic judgments, often because we are simply not paying attention. A meal is consumed quickly to satisfy hunger or during conversation, and flavors go completely unnoticed. On the other hand, aesthetic qualities often impose themselves upon us: a smell is so strong we cannot fail to notice it, describe it and judge it as pleasant or unpleasant. The strong scent of eucalyptus slows our gait in a forest, or a peculiar or strange taste interrupts dinner conversation.

The association of tastes and smells with the body supports another objection: that tastes and smells lack the mental component considered essential to aesthetic appreciation. Traditional aesthetic theories argue that aesthetic experience involves immediate sense perception but also, importantly, a reflective or contemplative feature associated with thought and imagination. Lacking this, tastes and smells are relegated to the realm of mere sensory experience.[15] For Kant, tastes and smells belong to the realm of the "agreeable." In his distinction between the beautiful and the agreeable, the beautiful involves disinterested contemplation of an object's form or appearance. The agreeable involves interest and merely what "the senses like in sensation," and so for this reason it is not disinterested and not contemplative.[16] The realm of the agreeable identifies mere preferences, while the beautiful and the sublime identify proper aesthetic judgments. Importantly, too, the agreeable lacks the imaginative engagement that characterizes contemplation of the beautiful.

These claims rest on a particular understanding of the aesthetic object. In Kant's view there must be something more than mere sensation, that is, some form or structure in order for an object to give rise to an aesthetic judgment.[17] This approach becomes more explicit when Kant dismisses color alone as a proper object of aesthetic contemplation, as well as single tones of music. If smells and tastes lack structure, like colors, they can never be included in the category of aesthetic objects.

But smells and tastes are more aesthetically interesting than this account suggests. Let me first address Kant's claim that smells and tastes have no structure. As discussed earlier in this chapter, we find single and mixed smells and tastes, particular and generic ones, and we can discriminate the different strands of mixed or complex smells and tastes. The complexity that typifies many olfactory and gustatory experiences is evidence of their structure, as illustrated by this description of cheddar from a guide to cheese: "The flavour starts off fairly mild and meadowsweet with nutty tones, often with a light salty tang. It matures to a strong, full, wonderfully nutty taste with a real piquancy to it. Older cheeses attack the tongue with their salty acidity."[18] Cheese tasters use a range of descriptions, which attest to the structure of various cheese flavors: rich, mild, aromatic, spicy, sharp, bitter, salty, goaty, bittersweet, farmyard aroma, buttery, milky, creamy, nutty, mushroomy, and "reminiscent of condensed milk, fudge, fresh almonds, wet vegetation."[19]

Smells too can exhibit structure.[20] Perfume, used by many people every day, combines any number of different smells, such as spicy, floral, or fruity. The terminology of perfumery draws on the compositional descriptions and terms of symphonic music, such as "accords," "notes," and "tones," to describe the character of a particular scent: "Boronia absolute is a delightful oil rich in violet notes of betaionone. The top note is fresh, the body notes extraordinarily rich and warm."[21] Further evidence of the complexity and structure of smells and tastes can be found by examining the act of appreciation itself, the best example being in the principles of olfactory and gustatory connoisseurship. Wine, whisky, and cigar tastings proceed through careful judgmental steps that take in various qualities of the thing. For whisky it is color, nose, flavor, then finish, with additional general notes. Cigar tasting begins with the "aesthetics," or look and feel of the cigar, followed by prelight condition, postlight condition, flavor and strength, aftertaste, aroma, and general notes.[22]

In this sort of focused appreciation, discrimination is clearly taking place. But we need not turn smells and tastes into a high art to find cases where aesthetic judgments are made. Our everyday lives are infused with this kind of appreciation, in choosing the best ingredients for tonight's dinner, appreciating our daily route to work, and so on. One aroma is lovely, another stinks, one taste is vibrant, another dull. That we make and defend judgments like these indicates our capacity for aesthetically appreciating different smells and tastes. If we go along with the terms of Hume's famous argument for the standard of taste, the most experienced judges, who have developed their olfactory and gustatory senses and are free of prejudice, are best equipped to make the most refined judgments. But even when these skills are less developed, such appreciation is significant and too often overlooked. In any case, that we do make aesthetic judgments suggests a complexity to smells and tastes that Kant and other philosophers miss.

Another reason behind Kant's classification of smells and tastes as the agreeable is his belief that mere sensations are the subject of an individual rather than intersubjective liking. This claim is a commonly held belief, that is, the view that we are more likely to question or seek justification for a judgment of a work of art than a preference for raspberries over strawberries.[23] However, if my argument for the legitimate status of smells and tastes as objects of aesthetic appreciation is accepted, it should follow that they may also be the subject of aesthetic judgments for which we can provide justification. That is, they do not belong only to the domain of preferences. In making this claim I am not putting forward an argument for objectivity across aesthetic judgments, but simply pointing out that at the very least we can give reasons for these judgments. In the case of smells and tastes we may lack the requisite critical vocabulary that enables that justification. But when there is careful attention and our critical abilities are practiced and sharpened, it is easier to formulate justifications and engage in critical discourse. Proof for this can be found in extensive food and drink criticism (meals, cheese, chocolate, spirits, wine, beer, etc.), perfumery, and other skilled activities that focus on smells and tastes. The activity of aesthetic appreciation itself also shows that Kant is wrong in his second claim, that the appreciative activity of smells and tastes lacks a mental component. In enjoying the taste of a particular kind of ice cream we may be involved in contemplation; we reflect on the taste, making comparisons as we try to approximate where the qualities of the taste fit into our experience, and whether it is pleasant or unpleasant. When we describe the taste of vanilla ice cream as smooth, silky, and mellow, we draw on the concept of smoothness or perhaps make associations to other objects with that aesthetic quality. Imagination comes into play here too, since smells and tastes, like paintings and poems, evoke images and associations. Smells are notorious for bringing to mind particular times, places, or experiences of the past, so memories may also become part of the reflective activity. Many of our associations will be particular and personal, while others will be more generic and communicable.

The more basic feelings of pleasure and displeasure are an obvious part of the aesthetic response to smells and tastes. But emotions, which involve thought, also get a foothold in olfactory and gustatory appreciation. Smells and tastes regularly involve emotional arousal, at least as often and perhaps more so than aesthetic responses to the visual. To someone who enjoys clean, fresh air, the burning, carbon fumes of exhaust evoke feelings of disgust and dismay at the prevalence of car culture. A hot cup of tea makes some people (even a whole nation) feel relaxed and secure. By contrast, the musky odor of a skunk causes fear in humans (if only fear of being enveloped in that awful smell).

A final objection, suggested already in my discussion of Kant, is the claim that smells and tastes are not easily specifiable as aesthetic objects. Compared to the sensory experiences of sight, touch, and hearing, smelling and tasting are considered more unstable and transient experiences. Smells come and go in an instant, and sometimes we cannot easily attach them to any specific source. Tastes leave our palate soon after food is consumed. Both smells and tastes are also not easily "bounded." In contrast, art is more stable and permanent. Paintings sit on the walls of galleries for years, waiting to be appreciated at one's leisure. Musical performances and the moving images of films can be revisited; and, in the age of digital technology, we can slow and pause CDs, iPods, and DVDs to enable more focused attention.

The points already made concerning the place of reflection, imagination, and emotion support the claim that smells and tastes can be the subject of aesthetic appreciation, even if they are unlike the kinds of aesthetic objects that occupy galleries and museums. We can identify, individuate, select, and revisit smells and tastes; they can be localized and specified, even if their nature means they do not always provide as sustained an experience as other objects of aesthetic attention. Besides, other sensory experiences, such as sounds, are fleeting too, yet we consider combinations of them to be worthy objects of aesthetic appreciation. If an aesthetic object cannot be temporary, then in this view it is difficult to see how natural environments could ever be appreciated appropriately. The richness of our experience of nature is related importantly to its temporal quality, such as changes in weather and light, seasons, the effects of growth and decay, and, in a shorter time frame, moving animals and leaves, birdsong beginning and ending.[24] The aesthetic object criticism therefore rests on a limited notion of the character and diversity of aesthetic objects.

Smells and tastes meet the narrower, traditional criteria of what counts as an object of aesthetic appreciation. Moving critically beyond this, some contemporary aestheticians argue that a key feature of aesthetic appreciation is the cognitive element of the aesthetic response, especially because many contemporary art forms demand conceptual reflection. Can smells and tastes meet this condition, given the belief that they lack content, refer to nothing beyond themselves, and thus are devoid of meaning for interpretation?[25] I have shown that emotional and imaginative associations accompany olfactory and gustatory experiences, but can these experiences involve other kinds of meaning? A central argument in Korsmeyer's philosophical study of taste maintains that, rather than being merely sensuous aesthetic objects, smells and tastes are *primarily* valued in virtue of the insight and meaning discovered through their appreciation—smells and tastes are also denotative. Foods in ritualistic settings, for example, a harvest festival, are the clearest cases, but we also find meaning in everyday appreciation: "Routine uses of foods also may bestow upon them certain expressive properties. Chicken soup is a home remedy for illness in a number of cultures. There may be some medical reason for this. . . . Such palliative features are not likely to be part of the immediate experience of the soup, however, and more relevant for expressive properties such as 'soothing' and 'comforting' that are exemplified in chicken soup is the very fact that it is a home remedy and means that one is being taken care of."[26]

The value of Korsmeyer's argument is twofold, first because it sets out some good reasons for the cognitive value of smells and tastes, providing another reason to hold that smells and tastes are proper aesthetic objects; and second, it indicates one way that smells and tastes have meaning and importance in our lives. In the next section, I take a closer look at the significance of smells and tastes in everyday life.

EVERYDAY AESTHETICS

Thus far my strategy has been to elevate smells and tastes from their relegated place outside the aesthetic domain to proper objects of aesthetic appreciation. I started with traditional aesthetic theory to show that even smells and tastes can meet its strict criteria. If I have succeeded in this aim, then smells and tastes can be included within the aesthetic domain, even if they are rather different sorts of aesthetic objects than paintings, sculpture, and music. Smells and tastes will not always be the objects of careful discrimination and expert attention that many of my examples suggest. Smells and tastes pervade our ordinary lives, much more so than many works of art. So, any attempt to understand the place of smells and tastes in aesthetics needs to address the nature of their appreciation outside the more specialized contexts of connoisseurship.

Since I first tackled this topic in the late 1990s, philosophical aesthetics has broadened its scope more and more beyond its traditional concern for art, with growing areas of interest in everyday and environmental aesthetics.[27] Discussions in both areas are especially important for understanding how experiences that fall into the aesthetic domain extend beyond the narrower boundaries set by artistic aesthetics, traditional ideas of aesthetic experience, and the prejudices that accompany these views. Some philosophers writing in environmental and everyday aesthetics argue that a new starting point is needed when thinking through the domain of the aesthetic. Sibley recognized this, choosing to discuss a range of subject matter beyond art. More recently, through his theory of "aesthetics as engagement," Arnold Berleant has called for an environmental rather than art perspective.[28] This fits with my concerns here; and in particular, that the framework of everyday aesthetics is germane for the environment outlines just how we might understand the significance of smells and tastes in more quotidian contexts.

Sherri Irvin has recently defended the aesthetic status of some of our most everyday experiences: "I drink tea out of a large mug that is roughly egg-shaped, and I clasp it with both hands to warm my palms. When I am petting my cat, I crouch over his body so that I can smell his fur, which at different places smells like trapped sunshine or roasted nuts, a bit like almonds but not quite."[29] Turning to John Dewey's Art as Experience, one of the more generous treatments in recent times of everyday aesthetics, Irvin shows how these kinds of ordinary experiences meet Dewey's (rough) aesthetic criteria of conscious awareness, unity, closure, and complexity.[30] Irvin's argument hinges on the view that, although qualitatively different, these kinds of experiences nonetheless belong in the aesthetic domain. At the same time, she challenges Dewey's criteria, going further to show how, although such experiences may be "simple," "lacking in unity or closure," or "characterized by limited or fragmented awareness," aesthetic concepts are nonetheless applicable.[31]

Many everyday smells and tastes exhibit these qualities. Simplicity is often admired as an aesthetic quality in objects, and it is a style favored by many chefs in their approach to food (simple ingredients and flavors).[32] Walking through a forest can lack unity, being comprised of distinct, varying experiences: a fresh smell of pine in the background, catching sight of a chipmunk scampering away, the bright sound of a birdsong. A meal can be like this too, during which we attend to and savor different flavors and different combinations of flavors as they emerge while we eat. By no means do these different directions of attention need to come together for the experience to count as aesthetic. In terms of fragmented awareness, while eating a bun, I enjoy the richness of its soft, sweet doughiness, while also vaguely aware of a background spice—maybe cardamom. This kind of awareness may form a key aspect of the aesthetic character of eating the bun. It is worth pointing out that meaningful aesthetic experiences can involve fragmented experiences (and qualities), in the art world and beyond. Some artworks (video art, for instance) set out to be disruptive, to leave us without closure or some sort of consummatory experience.

In relation to complexity, Irvin emphasizes, rightly, that we need not turn to examples of expert criticism. Smelling her cat is a complex experience in itself. Consider my earlier example of smelling and eating raspberry yogurt. That experience exhibits complexity in so far as it involves attention to the creamy, slightly sour smell, combined with the sharpness of raspberry, and a creamy texture flecked with crunchy raspberry seeds. Unity and closure are possible too, as when two rather different ingredients in a meal work together just right, perhaps even creating some very new and distinctive flavor. My discussion of transience and stability earlier in this chapter lends further support for the complex qualities of smells and tastes.

As a pragmatist philosopher, Dewey was deeply interested in the connections between aesthetics and lived experience. What are these connections where smells and tastes are concerned? First and foremost, there is the great satisfaction acquired through fragrances and pleasurable smells as well as the delights of eating and drinking. The beautiful fragrance of jasmine or a delicious cheesecake are satisfactions that contribute to the good life. But there are less hedonic ways of understanding the value of these senses. First, the objects of sniffing and savoring can be unpleasant, repulsive, and disgusting.[33] So although we may not find positive aesthetic value as such, these experiences can be educative, even edifying, enabling us to grasp the diversity in our environment. Second, olfactory and gustatory experiences of everyday life help to situate us within environments and in relation to other people. These experiences might be said to contribute to both an environmental and a social aesthetic.[34] Where vision tends to distance us from our surroundings, smells and tastes involve the body integrated with environment—smelling through the nose and tasting through the mouth. As smell and taste environ us, they enable the discovery of meaning in the places and situations is which we find ourselves; through a particular kind of aesthetic orientation we both interpret and understand our place in the world.

Familiar and recognizable smells are key to habituating us in an environment, to making us feel at home. Consider Tom Robbins foregrounding of rich fragrances in an everyday environment: "Louisiana in September was like an obscene phone call from nature. The air—moist, sultry, secretive, and far from fresh—felt as if it were being exhaled into one's face. Sometimes it even *sounded* like heavy breathing. Honeysuckle, swamp flowers, magnolia, and the mystery smell of the river scented the atmosphere, amplifying the intrusion of organic sleaze."[35] The habituating effect holds true even when we quickly adapt and habituate ourselves to smells that we experience regularly. The smells associated with a particular house—often of food—can become so familiar that they become part of the background, so that we become only vaguely aware of them. The fact that we are not always aware of them covers up how crucial they can be to a sense of place. After being away for awhile, smells are more noticeable upon returning to a place, signaling a feeling of at-homeness (or in other contexts, a comforting feeling of familiarity).

The flip side of familiarity is unfamiliarity. Smells are important here too—they alert us to the strange, to what is dangerous, and make us feel alien to a place.[36] New and strange places have different, sometimes unrecognizable smells. Often there is pleasure in the unfamiliarity, in the freshness of something experienced for the first time. Less pleasurably, smell enables us to discover what we ought to avoid, such as food that's gone off or the stench of disease and death.[37] In his illuminating history of smell in French society, Alain Corbin cites the eighteenth-century fear of the cesspools of excrement that collected in urban centers. The source of the stench would have been something very familiar, yet in great quantities it became something strange, harmful, and fearful: "Thouret noted that exposure to air and sunlight rendered the faecal matter spread out in the Montfaucon basins innocuous, as was proved by the transmutations in the smells. If old excrement proved dangerous, it was because it had become 'alien to ourselves, our food, and our furnishings' by an interplay of 'decompositions' and 'recompositions.' It had lost the odor of the body. It had putrefied."[38]

We are typically attracted to things with pleasant odors and detracted from things with unpleasant odors. Sometimes the response is an immediate one—some smells just are repugnant, such as the smell of almost anything decomposing (autumn leaves being a nostalgic exception). The negative value we assign to the source of the smell follows the immediate response. But we also judge olfactory experiences as negative because of what we associate with them or know about their source. The smell of an animal decomposing is unpleasant and somewhat strange because it is associated with death and our fear of it as something to be avoided (a fear also played out in terms of a fear of the unknown). The meanings of smells and tastes are thus closely tied to the judgments we make about them and the environment in which we find them. In this way, smells and tastes play some role in determining our likes and dislikes or what we value in our environment.[39]

The familiarity and strangeness of smells and tastes contributes to our ability to use these senses to identify and recognize aspects of our environment. Along with our other senses, smell enables us to identify and individuate objects, particular places, and whole environments. I can tell the difference between two similar bath towels—one clean, the other dirty—not by how they look, but by the contrast in their smells. Turning again to a literary source, James Joyce creates rich images of urban places like Dublin through sensory descriptions in his various novels. Olfactory and gustatory qualities evoke an intimate feeling of the places visited in the daily lives of the two main characters in *Ulysses*, Stephen Dedalus and Leopold Bloom. Gustatory qualities are especially significant to Bloom's character and his routines. Bloom's visit to Davy Byrne's involves detailed, rambling descriptions of the pleasures and displeasures of his experience there, as shown by the lines cited at the beginning of this chapter. He has a special liking for "the inner organs of beasts and fowls"; and "most of all he liked grilled mutton kidneys which gave to his palate a fine tang of faintly scented urine."[40] Bloom also dwells on his wife's scents and wonders about his own—a way of identifying her and his body in relation to hers.[41]

Another striking way our noses facilitate recognition and identification is through olfactory memory. This dimension of memory is especially robust and lasting, and many physiological theories have been put forward to show that memory is better through the nose than through the eyes. It has been claimed, for example, that olfaction bypasses the conceptual part of the brain, the neocortex, whereas sights and sounds do not. The result is that odor-related memory is more immediate, called up more directly than memories connected to sight or sound.[42] Our ability to recognize a smell at some time in the present is dependent upon having had a past experience of the generic category of that smell.

In the present, our everyday recognition of various features of the places we live and work comes through smells. Consider the following smells. In the house: kitchen—warm baking bread, rich, red meat, gas oven, grease; bathroom—soap, perfumes, hamper, water. In institutions: library—dust, leather; hospital—sharp disinfectant, sanitized surfaces, illness, urine. In natural environments: sea—salt, fish, sun-scorched sand; mountains—damp, cold stone, dark earth, fresh leaves.

These examples show how olfactory memory operates to recognize and recall smells we associate with types of environments, but it also gives us the extraordinary capacity to call up very specific memories. A single whiff offers a door of recognition into a moment from the past. Recall the rich memories and emotions evoked of

Combray upon tasting a tea-soaked madeleine in Proust's *Remembrance of Things Past*. The emotional quality of olfactory memories can be quite strong—with childhood memories it is typically sentimental and nostalgic; with other memories it may simply leave one feeling despondent. Olfactory memory also recalls moments or stretches of *time*, acting as a historical record of smell experiences that provide a more fluid reference point for orientation to our environment. A particular smell is associated with a particular time in our lives or particular smells with times of the day or year. The morning is the smell of coffee; the winter is the smell of snow muffling other smells with its crisp, watery scent.

Much of my discussion has focused on the idea of individuals experiencing their environment. So far I have said nothing about human bodies, but the same environing roles of smell and taste apply in this most intimate of environments. Smells and perhaps tastes too help to establish our own identity and to recognize the identity of other people. For all sorts of reasons humans have body odors. They originate in our apocrine glands, which are found on various parts of the body, including the face and armpits. The fat in hair absorbs odors, and what we eat affects body odor (brunettes are said to smell differently than redheads, meat eaters different than vegetarians).[43] It is not surprising that we can recognize the smell of a particular person, especially someone we know well, and guess something about their habits based only on scent evidence. For people with no olfactory perception, or anosmia, the delights of food and the characteristic smell of a loved one are painfully missed.

The experience of smells and tastes in relation to other people—as well as to other things in our surroundings—may involve a relationship of reciprocity. Another sense, touch, offers the clearest case of this, since whatever you touch is somehow touching you back. Taste involves touch too, as we place food or other things in our mouths. When in close proximity to someone else, we smell their odor and they smell ours. Kant's views on this are disappointingly narrow, but consistent perhaps in their prudishness. Smells are the "most expendable" of the senses, and he argues that they repel us from things because most smells are unpleasant. He prefers taste because it promotes "sociability in eating and drinking."[44] Kant may be right about the centrality of taste as a social sense, but he ignores the environing quality of smells. The potential for promoting reciprocity indicates how these senses can establish a special sensory relation between ourselves and our environment.[45]

Let us not forget that individuals also experience themselves and have an identity in their environment. The olfactory geography of each person's body constitutes one dimension of bodily knowledge, and it is fundamental to charting the territory of our own bodies. Habituation to our own bodies means that we do not always notice these smells, but we do notice when something has changed. Unfamiliar smells may be due to something we have eaten, someone we have been with, or because of illness or disease. Strange or new smells are confusing to ourselves and others who know us.

Personal style is also to some extent an olfactory and gustatory matter. We are accustomed to how we fashion ourselves in visual ways: makeup on our faces, the adornments of jewelry, our choice of clothes, the bodily shape we present or aim for. We are also accustomed to the way we look at ourselves, as much as we are conscious of how others see us. Smell functions in these ways too. A personal style is created with a favorite perfume, and we cover up odors like sweat or garlic breath with scents we and others prefer to smell on our bodies. Our choices in food and drink become part of our identity in terms of our more particular, often consistent, likes and dislikes.

CONCLUSION

Smells and tastes rightly belong to the domain of aesthetics, and they are significant too for their place in orienting us in our environment and contributing to its meaning and value. If developing aesthetic sensitivity is considered, generally, a worthwhile activity, then becoming skilled in olfactory and gustatory perception should be part of this endeavor.

We might develop these senses in aesthetic appreciation in various ways. First, be aesthetically sensitive: make an effort, break conventions, sniff your food, savor the smell of a friend and describe what you smell to someone else. Practice identifying smells and combinations of them; while eating dinner out, try guessing the ingredients. Second, build a smell and taste vocabulary. This vocabulary is quite poor in most of us, but having it can open up a new sensory world by giving us the ability to express what we experience. J. D. Porteous suggests some useful ways to do this.[46] Explore and describe *smellscapes* and *tastescapes* instead of landscapes. Describe smell events and smell marks. Discuss ways in which you might play the role of a *nosewitness* instead of an eyewitness. Instead of hearsay, explore the idea of *nosesay*. Practice nose training and work out descriptions for what you discover. Generally, try to describe every smell or taste event you encounter, avoiding visual terms. Developing an aesthetic sensitivity for smells may have some real benefits: the possibility of more engaged aesthetic experience of our everyday environment; and the possibility of finding more meaning in it.

NOTES

Epigraph: James Joyce, *Ulysses*, ed. Hans Walter Gabler (Harmondsworth, UK: Penguin, 1986), 142.

1. Exceptions within philosophical aesthetics include Larry Shiner and Yulia Kriskovets, "The Aesthetics of Smelly Art," *Journal of Aesthetics and Art Criticism* 65, no, 3 (2007): 273–86; Frank Sibley, "Tastes, Smells, and Aesthetics," in *Approach to Aesthetics: Collected Papers on Philosophical Aesthetics*, ed. John Benson, Betty Redfern, and Jeremy Roxbee-Cox (Oxford: Oxford University Press, 2001),

207–55; D. McQueen, "Aquinas on the Aesthetic Relevance of Tastes and Smells," *British Journal of Aesthetics,* 33, no. 4 (1993): 346–56; N. Campbell, "Aquinas' Reasons for the Aesthetic Irrelevance of Tastes and Smells," *British Journal of Aesthetics,* 36, no. 2 (1996): 166–76. (See also note 3.) The aesthetic theories of J. O Urmson, Frank Sibley, and Harold Osborne are all more open to the idea that smells and tastes could be objects of aesthetic appreciation.

2. For discussion of this topic, see Marienne L. Quinet, "Food as an Art: The Problem of Function," *British Journal of Aesthetics* 21, no. 2 (Spring 1981): 159–71; Elizabeth Telfer, *Food for Thought: Philosophy and Food* (London: Routledge, 1996); Glenn Kuehn, "How Can Food Be Art?," in *The Aesthetics of Everyday Life,* ed. Andrew Light and Jonathan M. Smith (New York: Columbia University Press, 2005), 194–212; Carolyn Korsmeyer, "Food and the Taste of Meaning," in *Aesthetics in the Human Environment,* ed. Pauline von Bonsdorff and Arto Haapala (Helsinki: International Institute of Applied Aesthetics, 1999), 90–104; and Carolyn Korsmeyer, *Making Sense of Taste: Food and Philosophy* (Ithaca, NY: Cornell University Press, 1999).

3. Sibley, "Tastes, Smells, and Aesthetics."

4. Sibley, "Tastes, Smells, and Aesthetics," 213. Sibley refers to J. J. Gibson, *The Senses Considered as Perceptual Systems* (Boston: Houghton-Mifflin, 1966), chapter 8. Gibson's analysis of smells and tastes as a system is also the basis of Paul Rodaway's discussion of the senses in *Sensuous Geographies: Body, Sense and Place* (London: Routledge, 1994), 61–81.

5. See Korsmeyer, *Making Sense of Taste,* 83, and the author's reference to Valerie B. Duffy and Linda M. Bartoshuk, "Sensory Factors in Feeding," in *Why We Eat What We Eat,* ed. Elizabeth Capaldi (Washington, DC: American Psychological Association, 1996), 146.

6. It seems to be a biological fact that animals walking on all fours, close to the ground, have an especially keen sense of smell. See Diane Ackerman, *A Natural History of the Senses* (New York: Vintage, 1990), 30.

7. For a discussion of ocularcentrism, see David Abram, *The Spell of the Sensuous* (New York: Vintage, 1996).

8. See, for example, Ronald Hepburn's landmark paper, "Contemporary Aesthetics and the Neglect of Natural Beauty," reprinted in *Wonder and Other Essays* (Edinburgh: Edinburgh University Press, 1984), 9–35 and Allen Carlson's criticisms of the "scenery model" in *Aesthetics and Environment: The Appreciation of Nature, Art and Architecture* (New York: Routledge, 2000).

9. Plato, *Phaedo,* trans. G. M. A. Grube (Indianapolis, IN: Hackett, 1977), 64c–67d, 12ff.

10. John Stuart Mill, *Utilitarianism,* in *The Utilitarians* (Garden City, NJ: Dolphin Books, 1961), 410.

11. See Marcel Proust's *A Remembrance of Things Past* and James Joyce's *Ulysses, Dubliners,* and *Finnegans Wake.* J. D. Porteous gives several good examples in, "Smellscape," *Progress in Human Geography* 9, no. 3 (1985). See also Ackerman, *Natural History of the Senses,* 15–18.

12. Peter Süskind, *Perfume: The Story of a Murderer* (New York: Pocket Books, 1991)

13. For an illuminating discussion of olfactory art, see Shiner and Kriskovets, "Aesthetics of Smelly Art."

14. See Immanuel Kant, *Critique of Judgment,* trans. Werner Pluhar (Indianapolis, IN: Hackett, 1987). Monroe Beardsley also notes this line of argument, although it is not clear that he supports it. See Monroe Beardsley, *Aesthetics: Problems in the Philosophy of Criticism* (New York: Harcourt Brace, 1958), 98–99, 111.

15. This view has been held by Aquinas, Kant, Hegel, and some recent philosophers, such as Roger Scruton. See Aquinas, *Summa Theologiae* (several editions); Kant, *Critique of Judgment;* G. F. W. Hegel, *Aesthetics: Lectures on Fine Art,* vol. 1, trans. T. M. Knox (Oxford: Clarendon Press, 1975), 35; and Roger Scruton, *The Aesthetics of Architecture* (London: Methuen, 1979), 113–15, and *Art and Imagination* (London: Methuen, 1974), 156.

16. Kant, *Critique of Judgment,* §3, Ak. 205–7, 47–48.

17. Kant, *Critique of Judgment*, §14, Ak. 224–25, 70–71. Beardsley, *Aesthetics: Problems in the Philosophy of Criticism*, 98–99, and Scruton, *Aesthetics of Architecture*, 113, both make a similar claim. McQueen, in "Aquinas on the Aesthetic Relevance of Tastes and Smells," 351ff., also discusses Aquinas's objections in relation to complexity.

18. Judy Ridgway, *The Cheese Companion: The Connoisseur's Guide* (London: Apple Press, 1999), 93.

19. Ibid., 39.

20. Sibley, *"Tastes, Smells, and Aesthetics,"* supports this point, as does Telfer in *Food for Thought*, in relation to the composition of meals, although Telfer is less enthusiastic (see 48–49).

21. E. Morris, *Fragrance: The Story of Perfume from Cleopatra to Chanel* (New York: Scribner's, 1984), 234. Perfumers are best known for the ability to distinguish the mix of scents in a fragrance, but machines—gas chromatographs—can do it too.

22. *Smoke* (Summer 1998): 132. Cigar connoisseurs distinguish the complexity of the flavor and strength of a cigar, its aftertaste and its aroma, among other characteristics, and within each of these a mix of scents and tastes is common. In whisky tasting, the nose of a particular whisky, for example, might be a mix of fresh and floral aromas or, by contrast, "peaty with a burnt heather character and hints of ozone" (Talisker whisky, aged ten years). John Lamond and Robin Tucek, *The Malt Whisky File* (Edinburgh: Canongate, 1997), 210.

23. See Scruton, *Aesthetics of Architecture*; and Korsmeyer's helpful discussion of the presumed subjectivity of smells and tastes in *Making Sense of Taste*, 99ff.

24. See Yuriko Saito's discussion in "Everyday Aesthetic Qualities and Transience," in *Everyday Aesthetics* (Oxford: Oxford University Press, 2007), 149ff. She refers to the problem I discuss here as "stable identity" (24–25).

25. Telfer defends food as a minor art form because food is *nonrepresentational* in the way that art is. She argues, however, that food cannot be a *major* art form. See Telfer, *Food for Thought*, 58ff.

26. Korsmeyer, "Food and the Taste of Meaning," 98–99.

27. I should point out that eighteenth-century aesthetic theory had a wider conception of the aesthetic object than later periods and today. Aesthetic appreciation of nature was a common interest, and the range of objects identified as potentially sublime is myriad, including human character, animals, and even smells. Still, the other factors I have mentioned and the high/low distinction will have functioned to disqualify smells and tastes on many levels. Notable exceptions to art-centered aestheticians in the twentieth century are John Dewey, Frank Sibley, and J. O. Urmson.

28. See Arnold Berleant, *The Aesthetics of Environment* (Philadelphia: Temple University Press, 1992).

29. Sherri Irvin, "The Pervasiveness of the Aesthetic in Ordinary Experience," *British Journal of Aesthetics* 48, no. 1 (2008): 31.

30. John Dewey, *Art as Experience* (New York: Perigee, 1934).

31. Irvin, "Pervasiveness of the Aesthetic," 29.

32. Aki Kamozawa and H. Alexander Talbot, "Inspiration, Taste, and Aesthetics," in *Food and Philosophy*, ed. Fritz Allhoff and Dave Monroe (Malden, MA: Blackwell, 2007), 279.

33. See Carolyn Korsmeyer's excellent work on this, "Delightful, Delicious, Disgusting," in Allhoff and Monroe, *Food and Philosophy*, 145–61.

34. Arnold Berleant has worked toward a theory of social aesthetics in "Ideas for a Social Aesthetic," in *The Aesthetics of Everyday Life*, ed. Andrew Light and Jonathan M. Smith (New York: Columbia University Press, 2005), 23–38; and in his book *Sensibility and Sense* (Exeter: Imprint Academic, 2010).

35. Tom Robbins, *Jitterbug Perfume* (London: Bantam, 1991), 60.

36. For a discussion of how the strange and familiar operate in our urban sense of place, see Arto Haapala, "Strangeness and Familiarity in the Urban Environment," in *The City as Cultural Metaphor: Studies in Urban Aesthetics*, ed. Arto Haapala (Helsinki: Institute of Applied Aesthetics, 1998).

37. Kant remarks that this is the only redeeming quality of this sense. See Immanuel Kant, *Anthropology from a Pragmatic Point of View*, trans. Mary Gregor (The Hague: Martinus Nijhoff, 1974), Ak. 159, 37.

38. Alain Corbin, *The Foul and the Fragrant: Odor and the French Social Imagination* (Cambridge, MA: Harvard University Press, 1986), 28.

39. Smells and tastes also have significance in understanding different cultures and places. There is some evidence to show cultural differences in olfactory perception itself as well, which is connected to the variety of smells and tastes associated with a particular culture. For anthropological, sociological, and other perspectives, see Constance Classen, David Howes, and Anthony Synnott, *Aroma: The Cultural History of Smell* (London: Routledge, 1994); Jim Drobnick, ed., *The Smell Culture Reader* (Oxford: Berg, 2006); and Carolyn Korsmeyer, ed., *The Taste Culture Reader* (Oxford: Berg, 2005).

40. Joyce, *Ulysses*, 45.

41. Ibid., 306–7.

42. Morris, *Fragrance*, 37.

43. Ackerman, *Natural History of the Senses*, 22–23.

44. Kant, *Anthropology*, Ak. 159, 37.

45. J.D. Porteous, *Landscapes of the Mind: Worlds of Sense and Metaphor* (Toronto: University of Toronto Press, 1990).

46. See Rodaway, *Sensuous Geographies*, 37. I am grateful to Desna MacKenzie for drawing my attention to this relationship.

Ethical Gourmandism

Carolyn Korsmeyer

The ogre loved his children; he ate the children of others. Under the tyranny of the stomach, we are all of us, beasts and men alike, ogres. The dignity of labor, the joy of life, maternal affection, the terrors of death: all these do not count, in others; the main point is that the morsel be tender and savory.

JEAN-HENRI FABRE, *LIFE OF THE SPIDER*

To this epigraph from a naturalist, who arrived at his grim generalization from the study of spiders, I add a supplement that is lighter though no less macabre: A *New Yorker* cartoon by Charles Barsotti depicts a scene in a high-class restaurant. A respectably dressed lion, eyeglasses nestled into his mane and wine glass by his paw, sits at a table bedecked with a linen cloth and a small vase of flowers. Inspecting the menu, he concludes his order to the equally proper lion-waiter with the instruction: "And I'll have that lightly sedated, please."[1]

The contrast between gourmet sensibility and brutality, in this case, provokes laughter; Fabre's observation is closer to horror. In both cases there is a radical disharmony between the point of view of that which is devoured and the point of view of the eater, to whom the "tender and savory" morsel is the acme of taste pleasure and the only value on the table. On the assumption that the perspective of the tasty morsel is not just morally discountable, we may inquire more deeply about that taste pleasure. Are there two independent kinds of value at work here? Is this a collision of ethics and aesthetics, the rightness of action vying for primacy with the sensory pleasure of taste? Or is the very flavor of the morsel itself a complex property with both aesthetic and ethical valence inseparably present? Such questions echo a debate underway in the philosophy of art, where theorists argue about whether the moral properties of art are at the same time aesthetic virtues or flaws.

In this chapter I bring aspects of the latter debate to the question of gustatory taste, constructing an argument that, perhaps, will transfer back to the philosophy of art as well.

The relationship between aesthetic and ethical value raises old philosophical questions that are rooted most notably in Plato's wholesale condemnation of mimesis in the *Republic*. He worried that pleasures taken in imitation, whether enjoyment of misleading stories of the gods or the exciting arousal of emotions in response to tragedies, would nourish parts of the soul that vie with reason in pursuit of justice, thus damaging the ideal society. Contemporary debates today reflect the legacy of modern philosophy, which separated the concept of the aesthetic from other domains of value and even at times pursued the possibility that positively wicked works of art could still possess high aesthetic quality. The dominance of formalism in art theory for much of the twentieth century sidelined serious debate about moral issues and aesthetic worth, but there are few formalists writing these days, and the subject is a lively one at present.[2]

Advocates of the endeavor known as "ethical criticism" argue that an artwork's moral properties are also aesthetically salient, enhancing or compromising appreciative reception and artistic worth. (In this debate, "moral" and "ethical" are commonly used interchangeably, and I follow that usage here.) Opponents insist that aesthetic and ethical evaluations are independent phenomena. Those who maintain the separability of aesthetic and ethical properties in art may be dubbed "autonomists," for they endorse the idea that the value of art is independent from its instrumental, social, religious, or moral worth. As Richard Posner, a leading autonomist, asserts, "The moral content and consequences of a work of literature are irrelevant to its value as literature."[3] He goes on to list several indisputably great works of art whose moral content is questionable, including the *Iliad* and many of Shakespeare's plays.

There are a number of ways that advocacy of ethical criticism can be articulated, for there are multiple grounds for understanding the moral damage or benefit that art might impart. The ethical critic of art may consider whether exposure to violent movies can dispose audience members to antisocial behavior; whether reading finely wrought novels full of complex characters might help develop sympathetic capacities; whether exciting plots that rely on morally dubious actions manifest aesthetic defects; whether a beautiful work of art was made at the cost of human life or well-being. Those who maintain that such features can affect artistic or aesthetic value are labeled "ethicists" or "moralists." Within that large camp, there are degrees of endorsement of the aesthetic salience of moral properties, from "moderate" moralism, which holds that the moral worth of a work can sometimes also be an artistic boon or defect, to "complete" moralists (like Plato) who consider a moral defect always an artistic flaw. So named, these positions indicate camps within the philosophy of art that describe participants in the so-called analytic tradition.[4] But the subject of the ethics of criticism is equally prominent in recent Continental philosophy, where there is perhaps less doubt about the coimplication of the ethical and the aesthetic.[5]

Where might food and eating—in the practices of the lion, the spider, the human being—fit into this debate? Philosophy of all stripes is now more open-minded about matters concerning gustatory taste and eating than traditionally was the case, and here I carry some of the issues of ethical criticism to the subject of food. In particular, I investigate the nature of taste properties, those for which tender and savory morsels are appreciated. Provisionally, an autono-mist on the question of the aesthetic properties of taste would maintain that the deliciousness of a flavor stands on its own as a value to be assessed inde-pendently of other concerns. One who endorses what I call "ethical gourmand-ism" would argue that the aesthetic qualities of certain dishes are enhanced or compromised by the moral properties that they possess. Just what this might mean is pursued below.

I do not presume that meals are works of art, though I do think that flavors and tastes can occasion the kinds of experiences that we assess aesthetically.[6] In any case, the question of attaching moral valence to aesthetic properties does not depend on claiming food as an art form. Much of the debate over ethical criticism has focused on narrative arts, complex territory that introduces features of plot and character not found with eating. Therefore, I venture the comparison of ethical criticism and ethical gourmandism with caution, zeroing in on just one question: is the very taste of the food we eat imbued not only with flavor but also with moral valence? More specifically, are the *aesthetic properties* of foods—their flavor proper-ties and whether or not they are tasty, delicious, piquant, bland, yummy—related in important ways to what we might call the *moral properties* of foods, whether the tastant (what is tasted) is an edible or forbidden substance or whether it was produced in a morally dubious manner?[7]

Here, I argue affirmatively. To do so first requires making a case about the nature of taste sensation itself. I argue the following points, beginning with some fairly uncontentious claims and ending with a speculation: (1) Taste is a sense whose natural affinities are culturally developed. (2) Flavors—taste properties manifest in experience—are almost never simply pure sensations. They entail recognition of the object being tasted. In other words, tastes are experienced as *tastes of* something or other. (3) Cultivating and refining taste always requires knowing what one is eating. (4) Tastes possess aesthetic characteristics. Sometimes morally salient properties are also manifest in experience. (5) If one finds a food delicious, then one tacitly recognizes it as good to eat—that is, as nontransgres-sively edible, in a permissible food category. It is this last point that puts the capstone on ethical gourmandism.

CULTIVATING TASTE

That tastes for different kinds of food and drink can be cultivated, educated, learned, and refined is so obvious that it hardly needs argument. It forms the foundation of one of the most influential essays in aesthetics, Hume's "Of the Standard of Taste" (1757),[8] and it is extolled and exhorted by all manner of gourmands who promote the field of gastronomy.[9] But the subject is worth pondering, for it importantly complicates another obvious truth, and that is the inescapable need to eat—a need rooted in biological nature and shared with all other animals. Indeed, the physical necessity of eating is one of several factors that traditionally sidelined taste and food from philosophical attention in the Western tradition, as eating was often dismissed as a matter of the animal "body" rather than the uniquely human "mind."[10]

The tension between animal nature and human cultivation lies behind both the humor of the cartoon and the horror of the epigraph above. Beasts and men alike are driven by appetite, as Fabre observes, though whether that makes us "ogres" is debatable. Granting that appetite is a powerful physical drive by no means entails that the satisfaction of our appetites is accomplished simply by means of natural impulses. In fact, the cultivation of tastes dramatically distinguishes human beings from other animals. Of all the things that humans can eat, they choose to eat only a few; and of the things that they develop a liking for, only some are actually needed for nutrition. Others are chosen for reasons of convenience, culture, and pleasure, and some of those pleasures are both taxing and perplexing, requiring an enormous amount of cultivation that removes human taste and diet far away from natural impulses.

In their study of the development of human food preferences, psychologists P. Rozin and T. A. Vollmecke distinguish between "preference" and "liking" for foods. Preference implies choice among alternatives; liking refers to the hedonic response to flavors. The motivation to eat includes liking but is by no means indexed to it, they claim, for it is the "mental representation" of our foods that determines whether or not we consider them good to eat.[11] Liking, the pleasure valence of tastes, turns out to be a particularly interesting prompt for eating choices, for it represents an "internal motivation" to choose a particular food. External motivations are equally important, and they include recognition of good sources of nutrition, the need to participate in rituals, and the requirements of manners. (Eat your vegetables because they are good for you; have a piece of cake to be polite.) Absent the external motives, one might choose something else. In contrast, a positive liking for a taste is exercised readily. Thus, as Rozin and Vollmecke observe, internal motivation produces particularly *stable* patterns of eating behavior.[12]

What we like to eat, therefore, already possesses a whiff of ethics. Aristotle similarly links stable patterns of behavior with virtue when he notes that acts of a virtuous person spring from a firm and enduring character.[13] Among the several routes he recommends for developing virtue, learning to take pleasure in right action is among the most important, for it safeguards against temptations that occasion *akrasia*, or weakness of will. Where we regularly take pleasure informs practice as well as enjoyment.

The likings for foods that we develop are sometimes rooted in natural dispositions. The most obvious one is a tendency among mammals to like sweetness. How sweetness is delivered in human diets varies enormously, though the general propensity is common. Other taste likings, however, are not based in natural dispositions at all, and indeed some are actually strenuous developments out of natural *aversions*. These appear to be solely human proclivities, for Rozin and Vollmecke have not discovered anything comparable in the taste choices of nonhumans. They single out the affinity for hot chili peppers and for coffee as two widespread tastes for substances that at first are not particularly liked, being painfully hot and nastily bitter on initial exposure.[14] But many find the first swallow of coffee each morning blissfully good, and whole cultures savor the burn of chilis in their foods.

In short, human taste preferences and diets owe only a little to natural proclivities. We have to eat, but we don't have to eat the foods we do. Nor are we driven by a natural taste for the things we enjoy. This is an important preliminary step before assigning moral properties to foods (a locution to be explained shortly), for ethics cannot require behavior that is impossible. The point is that we cannot appeal to nature to account for what we eat or to exonerate the items in our diets.

TASTE AND ITS OBJECTS

We do not always know just what we are eating. Composite foods such as sausages, soups, and stews have so many ingredients that only the most attentive and practiced taster can sort them out. And in these days of mass-marketed food production, flavor and texture enhancers are likely to be hidden in supermarket products, detectable only by reading finely printed lists of chemical contents. The tangy orange flavor we enjoy, for example, may have been produced by chemical means that have nothing to do with oranges. These factors and the many more that contribute to the experiences of foods may suggest that taste *experiences* are quite separable from the *substances that cause* them. However, while on the level of microcontent we may be ignorant or deceived, it is still the case that we presume—erroneously or not—something about the things that we are eating. This section is designed to weld together tastes sensations and assumptions about the identity of what enters the mouth and to argue that the sensory properties of foods are inseparable from what we take the objects we eat to be.

While a presumption about the identity of food is not always the immediate object of awareness, when expectation is violated its presence is dramatically disclosed. Especially on those occasions when we ingest something unexpected, the interruption of taste pleasure demonstrates that a mistaken presumption was at work. If you pick up a glass of champagne in the belief that it is ginger ale, even the most expensive bottle of bubbly delivers an unpleasant shock. The tongue was expecting something tangy and gingery, and the sensation delivered is startling and bitter. It does not take long to readjust the mouth and the mind to champagne and appreciate the liquid appropriately. But only then does the taste come into focus such that it can be appreciated. It is not that the first taste manifested as bad champagne. Rather, the anticipated category of drink was so violated that the taste was simply inchoate and *wrong*.

This kind of example is not uncommon, for several foods and potable liquids look similar and might be mistaken for each other if one relies on the evidence of vision alone: whipped butter and lemon sherbet; wasabi and guacamole; suet and tofu; mayonnaise and blue cheese dressing; apple juice and chardonnay. Each of them (except suet) has a distinctive and potentially excellent flavor, but tasting one while mistaking it for the other does not deliver pleasurable taste. Assessing flavor, texture, and so forth can only occur with an understanding of the typical and ideal flavors that the substance is supposed to possess.[15]

Therefore, I think it evident that when we taste, whether we enjoy, criticize, reject, or tolerate a flavor, we virtually always presume something about the identity of what is being tasted. There is no other way for the sensation of taste to achieve order and coherence. Naturally, one can be wrong about the substance, but no sensory experience is foolproof against deception. What is more, not only identification but also assessment of flavor is highly dependent upon what the flavor is of. It makes no sense to praise or criticize a flavor all by itself; sourness is a positive quality of lemons but not of corn syrup. Taste experience is almost always a taste of a particularly identified substance, registering properties of some presumptive object or other.

It is evident from the above that this discussion trades on two "locations" for tastes, for I have been referring both to the *sensation* aroused in the mouth of the taster and to the *properties* of the objects tasted. Both uses are appropriate; taste is not just all in the mouth.[16] The fact that when we taste (subjective sensation) we discern something about the flavor of a substance (objective property—i.e., a property ascribed to the object) is one more piece of evidence that tastes are always tastes *of*.

THE DISCERNING TONGUE AND THE CULTIVATION
OF TASTE

Further proof of this point is provided by the deliberate cultivation of taste and the learned ability to discern subtleties in flavors, a capacity that requires knowledge of what is under assessment. Human communities develop preferences for foods and flavorings that characterize their cultures in what can become exceedingly complex manners. With sufficient elaboration over time, these qualify as "cuisines."[17] Within a cuisine, there can be certain flavors and foods that are particularly savored that outsiders positively loathe. Sometimes that loathing is a response to the identity of the tastant rather than the taste itself, such as a refusal to eat snails even when they are called escargots. But also there are flavors the very taste for which is so acquired and cultivated that one outside the acculturated group can't go near them. Such is the case with koumiss, a drink made from fermented mare's milk and consumed with relish in traditional Kazakhstan. Alan Outram reports that "to the modern Western palate it is utterly vile. It provokes all the body's natural reactions to rotten food."[18] But just as we can and do cultivate a taste for coffee and chili peppers, we could cultivate a taste for koumiss, given enough motivation. Because the milk has fermented to a point where it stinks of spoilage, to learn to enjoy it requires trust that one can drink without fear of poison. The initial step is to understand what it is and how it is supposed to taste—a point about cultivated taste that substantiates the necessity of identifying what one is tasting.

Examples of the necessity of cultivating a taste for a difficult substance may also be found closer to home. For a more familiar substance that is singularly repellent on first exposure, I nominate Scotch whisky. It is sharp, acrid, and burning; a large mouthful makes one cough; eyes water, nose runs. How does one learn to appreciate something like this? At a start, one discovers exactly what it is that one is supposed to taste, for without some knowledge and experience the sensations do not sort out distinctively enough to be appreciated. Here again we see the double face of taste: a sensation in the mouth, nose, and throat and the qualities nascent in the substance tasted. Both directions of taste are present in this expert description of a type of whisky: "The spirit has a fine, golden colour, got from long years in cask in a dark, stone-walled, slate-roofed, earth-floored warehouse above the river Spey. The nose is vinous, floral and smoky, like gardenias in a cigar box. It is not easily discerned, the flavours being closely integrated, but repays the effort expended in approaching it. A little diluted, it becomes green and grassy over a floral base. The floral note continues in the taste, but soon gives way to a savoury dryness, which continues long on the palate."[19]

A good deal of this description refers to the conditions that produced the drink, not just incidentally but as contributors to its flavor. Knowing how Scotch is made is an aid not only in understanding but also recognizing the qualities available to the appropriately educated palate. Moreover, a description such as this is a good entry to consideration of what counts as aesthetic properties of food and drink.

TASTE: AESTHETIC AND MORAL PROPERTIES

The term "aesthetic" admits a variety of uses and contexts, but for centuries it was not a term that was properly applied to food or drink at all. Traditionally, only the eyes and the ears were deemed "aesthetic" senses, the objects of which could be appreciated for beauty.[20] Such conceptual restrictions have relaxed considerably in the last generation of aesthetic theory, so I assume that there will be little objection to my referring to the aesthetic properties of food. But what are they?

Food has such a complex role in culture that it can take on many of the kinds of properties that we also attribute to artworks, including properties that are representational (Easter eggs, Passover matzo); expressive (comfort foods such as chicken soup, daring foods such as wasabi); and symbolic (sugar skulls and dead man's bread on the Day of the Dead in Mexico). The list of culturally embedded meanings for foods and their flavors is enormous and varies richly across the globe. A full catalog of the aesthetic characteristics of food must include all of these. For my purposes here, however, I focus solely on sensory taste properties, that is to say, to flavors, textures, and the experiences they occasion. Following current usage in aesthetics, we can single out both descriptive and verdictive properties for tastes.

For example: Chocolate ice cream possesses properties such as cold, smooth, chocolate (of course), and sweet over a hint of bitter. At least the last property is the sort of description that can count as "aesthetic," though a case could be made for all of them. For instance, one could complain that a dish of ice cream contains shards of ice crystals, nuts that are too soft, and artificial sweetener. The kinds of descriptive properties that enter into an assessment of the ice cream's taste are the sorts that also qualify as aesthetic. That the dish contains three ounces of ice cream does not qualify; that the ice cream is chocolate or raspberry, sweet or slightly sour, creamy or sugary, or flavored with artificial vanilla—these are descriptive properties that are also aesthetic inasmuch as they are appealed to when accounting for quality and satisfaction in the product. Descriptive properties support verdictive properties, which in the case of foods is usually something like "delicious." (The artistic equivalent verdict is "beautiful.") Or one could just say "Yum!" Negative assessments are possible as well, of course, from "disappointing in flavor and texture" to "Yuck."

More complex properties enter into the assessment of a substance such as wine, and here the recourse to metaphoric description to identify flavor makes it clear that the descriptive properties singled out align with aesthetic discourse in the more familiar domain of art: warm tones, hints of blackberry and pepper, woodsy, and so forth are descriptive aesthetic properties that support a verdict such as "fine cabernet."[21] Critical discourse about wines and foods confirms that our hedonic responses to what we ingest are premised upon assumptions about what is in our mouths. We may start with "Yum!" but to figure out just what makes the wine so delectable we sort through the taste properties detected in the experience, tracing the verdict (delicious!) to the balance of ingredients, depth of flavors, and whatever else is appropriate to the substance being tasted.[22] This last qualification is crucial: what we find delicious must be a flavor property that is appropriate for the kind of substance in question. Again, whenever we taste, we presume that we know something about the identity of what is in our mouths.

Any aspect of flavor or texture, including the haptic qualities of heat, such as the tang of pepper, can be a property that not only describes what one is eating but also describes it in a way that is critical or appreciative, that indicates *savoring*. Savoring is a central instance of aesthetic experience of food and drink.[23] One can savor the qualities of foods in ways quite parallel to savoring the round, warm tones of a violin. To return to the description of the Scotch whisky quoted above, we see that nearly every property described is potentially of aesthetic relevance. Even the slate roof of the warehouse might impart a subtle (very subtle) quality. Hence literal description (of the roof) becomes an aesthetic description (of the quality discernable in the drink). Needless to say, such nuances are easily missed, but that is not to say that ascription is unjustified.

Ascribing moral properties to foods requires a more indirect approach, for moral properties such as "wicked," brave," "honest," and so forth are typically and literally applied only to persons or to their actions. A piece of meat on a plate does not act, and while a meal may poison, it is the cook who is the poisoner, not the food. The Scotch whisky so praised may intoxicate and cause obnoxious behavior, but the whisky itself is neither drunk nor morally responsible for drunkenness. So how can we establish the grounds for ethical gourmandism? How can the properties of taste be fit into a category suited for moral assessment?

Some of the same problems face ethical criticism, for a movie or a book is neither a person nor an action. They are, however, the results of actions, and this is one way to transfer the moral qualities of the human endeavor that brought art into being to the artworks themselves.[24] In the case of taste, it is the identity of the tastant and its preparation that link taste properties with moral valence. Because taste qualities are always qualities *of* their objects, one tacitly grants the appropriateness of eating those objects in the act of savoring. One cannot cultivate a taste for foie gras without cultivating a taste for fatty liver of a force-fed goose. In this way taste is, as it were, transparent. It is certainly possible to enjoy foie gras without knowing much about how it is produced. But the connoisseur cannot be both knowledgeable and innocent.

This observation parallels a strain of ethical criticism that has been dubbed "means moralism." As Alessandro Giovanelli claims, "A work that is produced by ethically blameworthy means is a worse work of art for that reason." He goes on to note that "consuming something that has been produced immorally arguably makes one participate in, in some sense approve of, the process of production."[25] In the case of foods, that consumption is literal: one incorporates into one's own body the dubiously produced object. Giovanelli targets the aesthetic relevance of the means of production of an artwork by specifying that there be a "trace" of the means of production that is perceivable in the work. A particularly direct example of such a trace is provided by the phenomenon of brush strokes in paintings—a literal trace in this case. The properties of the brush strokes are not only their immediately discernible traits, such as thickness of paint, but also recognition of how they were deposited on a canvas: by a brush wielded in the conventional way, by the artist's hair, or by a fish that was dipped in paint and left to thrash about as it expired.

Means moralism seems especially apt for the assessment of foods and their enjoyments because cultivating tastes frequently requires noticing flavors that are the result of the way they were produced. The description of Scotch above is full of references to the means that brought the whisky into being, traces of which remain in the flavor. When I was a child and drank milk from local farms, the milk in the spring was often redolent of the sprouting onion grasses that the cows grazed on. In that case, the assessment of the means was aesthetically negative, though morally neutral. The point is that an aspect of the means of milk production had a direct causal effect on the flavor. A trace of the means remains in the product. When those means are morally condemnatory or praiseworthy, we have moral properties infused in the taste properties of food. Traces of means in flavors are by no means the only indication of moral aspects of eating. Tuna caught in nets that also kill dolphins are harvested in ways that use unfortunate means, but this is not evident in the flavor of the tuna.[26] It is the flavor trace that binds together the aesthetic and moral elements of taste, and here the case for ethical gourmandism is most strongly rooted.

The means of food production are complex and prompt reflection on many areas where ethical quality matters: uses of pesticides or genetically engineered plants, factory conditions, additives, use of underpaid or forced labor. Many deplorable factors in the production of what we eat may not be directly manifest in what we taste, but some are. The moral valence of taste is probably most apparent in the eating of things that might not want to be eaten—that is, other animals.

CROCODILE TEARS

These serpents slay men, and they eat them weeping.
—SIR JOHN MANDEVILLE, CA. 1400[27]

The above discussion has proceeded in the conditional: *if* certain kinds of meal preparation are morally dubious, and *if* the object and its preparation impart a trace on flavor, *then* this quality is simultaneously aesthetic and moral. I have not established that certain foods should not be eaten; it would take a different set of arguments to prove that. Rather, in this section I advance the claim that because of the coimplication of aesthetic and moral quality in taste, if one truly enjoys a dish, one must accede to the appropriateness of what is eaten. There can be no such thing as saying "I really ought to be a vegetarian, but I just love lamb." If you love the taste of lamb, you do not consider it wrong to eat a sheep.

Strong advocates for animal rights dispute the idea that there can be degrees of moral valence to meat eating. If it is wrong to eat another sentient being, they assert, than assuring that it is killed kindly does not lift the moral weight. Tom Regan dismisses the goal of kindness in the raising and slaughter of animals as an illegitimate cloak that covers the absolute wrong of killing for food.[28] He correctly observes that kindness of intent is no assurance against wrongness of action. Nonetheless, the issues are importantly separable for ethical gourmandism, for the morality of eating animals is a debatable question in ethics, and cruelty is not. Therefore we can take cruelty of means of production as a fairly clear example of how aesthetic taste properties merge with moral taste properties, advancing the idea that if a trace of cruelty is present in flavor, this is an instance of a moral defect being at the same time an aesthetic defect.

In this argument I depart from some other philosophers who have examined the phenomena of taste qualities and pleasures. Kent Bach, for example, separates the pleasurable savor of wine from cognition of the properties of wine, positing that taste experience is already complete before one comes to know the ingredients and means of producing flavor.[29] My own inclination is to believe that such separation is not only difficult but impossible. As I have argued above, both aesthetic and moral properties of food are combined in taste experience, which is, at least in the cultivated taster, always the flavor *of* a substance, not just a bare sensation. Therefore, *if* one holds that the means of producing a food are wrong, then the food's taste will register that wrong. If one still enjoys the taste, then this is evidence that one is not committed to the moral evaluation. Therefore, positive aesthetic assessment is pro tanto a positive moral assessment when it comes to tastes.

Here are some examples to test this surmise. They are taken from the writings of a great gourmand, Alexandre Dumas *père*, author of adventure novels and of

Le Grand Dictionnaire de Cuisine, published posthumously in 1873. They are not ghastly examples of unusual cruelty, and therefore they are ripe for comparison with the ordinary eating of today. One may or may not discover moral valence in the tastes of the traces of the means of production and preparation of these dishes that Dumas recommends, but I believe one will grant that the traces themselves are present.

> We will explain the method which produces in poultry the best possible taste and at the same time the best quality of fat. . . . Feed them for a few days with ground barley, bran and milk. Put them in a cage in a dark place, but one which is not damp. Finally, always leave within easy reach of them some barley which has been kneaded with milk.
>
> The meat of the deer, venison, is better when the animal is killed in action.
>
> In Toulouse they have a special way of fattening ortolans which is better than anywhere else; when they want to eat them, they asphyxiate them by immersing their heads in a very strong vinegar, a violent death which has a beneficial effect on the flesh.[30]

The last entry in particular spells out the trace of the means on the flavor of the meat. The ortolan, a kind of warbler, is a tiny bird formerly eaten as a delicacy. Both its preparation and its consumption require studied attention, and no one who indulged in it would have failed to attend to the savor of its flesh and the elements that went into its production. Therefore, the "violent death" of the ortolan would be among those properties present on the tongue. The eater who attends with relish to the aesthetic taste properties cannot help but be aware of the moral valence of the taste as well. If it is delicious, then it is also deemed good to eat.

This conclusion may appear unreasonably strict. Sometimes discovery of what one is eating turns it to ashes in the mouth, as when a vegetarian discovers that her hot dog is made from pork rather than soy. But there are many things that we *furtively* enjoy, not entirely approving of our own actions yet savoring them nonetheless. Am I therefore ignoring the possibility of guilty pleasures? Indeed of pleasures that are all the sweeter because they are sinful? After all, we often say, "I know I shouldn't have any, but I just love X" (where X can be anything from chocolate to gin, foie gras, or milk-fed veal). Isn't this evidence that my claim about inseparability of aesthetic pleasure and moral valence is wrong? I don't think so, but it does lead to complexities in what counts as a moral valence for taste qualities, and to even greater complexities about the consistency of the values we practice.

Many times with indulgence in a so-called guilty pleasure, the guilt is directed to oneself. Perhaps one is on a restricted diet or wants to lose weight. Such proscriptions can be serious (avoidance of a heart attack) or relatively trivial (wanting to fit more comfortably into new jeans). But they are also directed toward oneself, and when we ourselves are both the actors and the targets of action we allow ourselves a bit of leeway in assessing the rightness or wrongness of choice. But with 'eating a creature killed with cruelty and relishing the tastes that reflect that death, the guilty pleasure is directed otherward. In cases such as these, I believe, enjoyment either indicates acceptance that the means of production is acceptable, or it indicates that the diner is simply ignoring something about the taste he or she is enjoying.

By such reasoning, the latter kind of guilty pleasure is also guilty of willful moral ignorance. If you reply, "Oh come on. It's only a bird," then that lifts the guilt by denying the moral weight, essentially confirming that the gustatory pleasure is appropriate and the object tasted is an acceptable thing to consume. What I think is problematic is the attempt both to claim an unqualified taste pleasure and to acknowledge that the taste includes morally unsavory qualities. Savoring the unsavory would be a kind of contradiction in which the inseparable aesthetic and moral properties of a flavor struggle to separate.

And here the practical application of my speculation begins to run aground, for I don't think there is any reason to think that we are consistently minded creatures. Kendall Walton suggests that when art confronts us with morally repugnant situations, our imaginations come up against our own moral beliefs, which intervene in the imaginative world the artwork has conjured, bringing aesthetic engagement to a halt.[31] Even more optimistically, Kant considered harboring a contradiction to be a kind of mental pain that the rational being immediately rejects.[32]

It would help my case if I could claim that the same thing happens with ethical gourmandism: that when we taste the delicate flavor of the ortolan, its vinegary drowning evident in our mouths, its savor diminishes. However, in practice I doubt this happens so readily. If one says that eating lamb is wrong and continues to enjoy it, that assertion betrays a kind of inconsistency that separates the aesthetic and moral valence in a way that cannot sustain scrutiny. On the other hand, it is quite easy to avoid scrutiny of one's taste likings and easy therefore to live with inconsistency. In practice, then, ethical gourmandism confronts a particularly resilient brand of *akrasia*.

CODA: BYPASSING THE MORAL COSTS OF FLAVOR

Much of my argument concerning taste properties assumes both a causal account of taste properties and the awareness of those causes when one eats. When you taste X flavor, you typically know that you are eating X. However, as I noted at the outset, it is possible to detach the production of a flavor from the typical cause, for an artificially induced taste can be an orange flavor without being the flavor of an orange. The chemistry of flavor production is proceeding apace, and it is not out of the question that there will come a time when the morally fastidious can have foie gras made from lentils or gluten. Would this be a taste liking that could be cultivated free from moral compromise? That is, can we with clear conscience look forward to a world where we can have all those delicious flavors free from the moral taint that presently turns them (or perhaps should turn them) to ashes in the mouth?

I am not sure.

It sounds unproblematic at first. If you presently eschew foie gras because of the cruel way it is produced, why not enjoy goose liver without the goose? If a happy calf can be genetically engineered to drop dead onto a platter at the age of seven weeks, why not relish a veal cutlet? But considering a darker example reveals a problem. Suppose human flesh tastes delectable. Is it okay to cultivate a taste for faux human being? Isn't there something enduringly terrible about having a taste for human flesh, even if that taste is to be satisfied by means of a substitute?

I leave the subject with this question dangling, for it raises the possibility of a diet of foods that merely simulate the original sources of flavor. Serious considerations about such inventions may lie in the future. If so, they would direct discussion of imitation foods and flavors back toward the old territory of artistic mimesis that Plato so eloquently decried, uniting ethical criticism and ethical gourmandism even more firmly in the same venerable debate.

NOTES

Epigraph: Jean-Henri Fabre, *The Life of the Spider*, trans. Alexander Teixeira de Mattos (New York: Dodd, Mead, 1913), ch. 8, www.e-fabre.com/en/virtual_library/life_of_the_spider/chap08 .htm.

1. Charles Barsotti cartoon, *The New Yorker*, June 5, 2000, www.cartoonbank.com.

2. Recent books on this subject include Berys Gaut, *Art, Emotion and Ethics* (Oxford: Oxford University Press, 2007); Jerrold Levinson, ed., *Aesthetics and Ethics: Essays at the Intersection* (Cambridge: Cambridge University Press, 1998); Garry Hagberg, ed., *Art and Ethical Criticism* (Malden, MA: Blackwell, 2008); and Martha Nussbaum, *Love's Knowledge* (New York: Oxford University Press, 1990).

3. Richard Posner, "Against Ethical Criticism," *Philosophy and Literature* 21, no. 1 (1997): 1.

4. For a review of the varieties of positions taken in the debates over ethical criticism, see Noël Carroll, "Art and Ethical Criticism: An Overview of Recent Directions of Research," *Ethics* 110, no. 2 (2000): 350–87.

5. For a small sampling of work that draws on Continental sources, see Tobin Siebers, *The Ethics of Criticism* (Ithaca, NY: Cornell University Press, 1988); and Robert Eaglestone, *Ethical Criticism* (Edinburgh: Edinburgh University Press, 1997).

6. I make this case in *Making Sense of Taste: Food and Philosophy* (Ithaca, NY: Cornell University Press, 1999).

7. The equivalent question in ethical criticism is, are the moral properties of art also aesthetically relevant properties? For an argument in the affirmative, see Mary Devereaux, "Beauty and Evil: The Case of Leni Riefenstahl's *Triumph of the Will*," in Levinson, *Aesthetics and Ethics*, 227–56.

8. David Hume, "Of the Standard of Taste," in *The Philosophical Works of David Hume*, vol. 3. (Boston: Little, Brown and Company, 2004).

9. In the nineteenth century, especially in France and England, gastronomy was promoted alongside the developing philosophies of taste and art. For the history of this movement, see Denise Gigante, *Taste: A Literary History* (New Haven, CT: Yale University Press, 2005); and Denise Gigante, ed., *Gusto: Essential Writings in Nineteenth-Century Gastronomy* (New York: Taylor and Francis, 2005).

10. For a contrasting discussion of the union of aesthetic and gustatory refinement in Chinese culture, see Joanna Waley-Cohen, "The Quest for Perfect Balance," in *Food: The History of Taste*, ed. Paul Freedman (Berkeley: University of California Press, 2007), 98–133.

11. P. Rozin and T. A. Vollmecke, "Food Likes and Dislikes," *Annual Review of Nutrition* 6 (1986): 434.

12. Ibid., 441.

13. Aristotle, *Nicomachean Ethics* bk. 2.

14. Rozin and Vollmecke, "Food Likes and Dislikes," 438, 445. For speculation about the origin of early human diets, see Alan K. Outram, "Hunter-Gatherers and the First Farmers: The Evolution of Taste in Prehistory," in Freedman, *Food: The History of Taste*, 35–61.

15. Compare recognition of standard and counterstandard properties of art in Kendall Walton, "Categories of Art," *Philosophical Review* 89 (1970): 339–67.

16. For an analysis of the nature of taste properties and their claims for objectivity (being of the object), see Barry C. Smith, "The Objectivity of Tastes and Tasting," in *Questions of Taste: The Philosophy of Wine*, ed. Barry C. Smith (Oxford: Signal Books, 2007), 41–77.

17. Jack Goody, *Cooking, Cuisine and Class* (Cambridge: Cambridge University Press, 1982).

18. Outram, "Hunter-Gatherers and the First Farmers," 42.

19. Phillip Hills, *Appreciating Whisky: A Connoisseur's Guide to Nosing, Tasting, and Appreciating Scotch* (Glasgow: HarperCollins, 2000), 171. The whisky described is a Glenfiddich eighteen-year-old single malt.

20. See *Making Sense of Taste*, ch. 2.

21. For discussions of wine and its properties, see essays in Smith, *Questions of Taste*; and Fritz Allhoff, ed., *Wine and Philosophy: A Symposium on Thinking and Drinking* (Malden: Blackwell, 2008).

22. This roughly follows Nick Zangwill's analysis of the direction of the relation between aesthetic verdicts and descriptions in *The Metaphysics of Beauty* (Ithaca, NY: Cornell University Press, 2001).

23. See Elizabeth Telfer on "aesthetic eating" in *Food for Thought: Philosophy and Food* (London: Routledge, 1996), 57.

24. Mary Devereaux, "Moral Judgments and Works of Art: The Case of Narrative Literature," *Journal of Aesthetics and Art Criticism* 62 (2004): 3–11.

25. Alessandro Giovanelli, "By the Means of Art" (paper presented at the Eastern Division of the American Society for Aesthetics, Philadelphia, April 3–4, 2009). I thank the author for making his manuscript available to me.

26. Ibid.

27. *Oxford English Dictionary*, compact ed., vol. 1 (Oxford: Oxford University Press, 1971), 606.

28. Tom Regan, "The Case for Animal Rights," in *Exploring Ethics*, ed. Steven M. Cahn (New York: Oxford University Press, 2009), 315.

29. Kent Bach, "Knowledge, Wine, and Taste: What Good is Knowledge?" in Smith, *Questions of Taste*, 37.

30. Alexandre Dumas, from *Dumas on Food: Selections from Le Grand Dictionnaire de Cuisine,* trans. Alan and Jane Davidson (London: The Folio Society, 1978), 97, 111, 200.

31. Kendall Walton, *Mimesis as Make-Believe: On the Foundations of the Representational Arts* (Cambridge, MA: Harvard University Press, 1990). See also Ted Cohen, "On Consistency in One's Personal Aesthetics," in Levinson, *Aesthetics and Ethics*, 106–25.

32. Immanuel Kant, *Grounding for the Metaphysics of Morals*, trans. James W. Ellington (Indianapolis, IN: Hackett Publishing, 1981). The operation of the categorical imperative rides on the inability to countenance inconsistency.

6

Two Evils in Food Country

Hunger and Lack of Representation

Michiel Korthals

THE PRODUCTION OF FOOD: ONE OR TWO BATTLES?

Hunger is for nearly all human beings an evil. The fact that a lot of food in the world is not fairly or equally distributed, either because of lack of resources or because of lack of access and management, is widely seen as shameful. The ethical issues around hunger are easy to identify: food is simply not equally and fairly divided, which means that principles of equality and fairness are distorted and that some people are fat and have at least normal bellies and others are extremely thin, undernourished, or even starving. Although there are many different interpretations of the principles of justice and fairness, identifying these phenomena of misdistribution is a rather easy job, because these principles appeal to common sense and refer to phenomena that everyone can perceive, such as hunger and the thin belly.

However, in many cases, even when hunger is not the primary problem, people additionally speak of "food deserts" or feel humiliated by the food products they are offered because they do not correspond with their choices. This feeling of humiliation can even be expressed by the hungry. In this chapter, I make a plea for considering these cases, which express a different evil than hunger but are as important. These cases in the food and agricultural sector are very much entwined with hunger but also have some features of their own: the lack of pluralism and the lack of representation of food styles and choices in the dominant food culture.

The Battle against Hunger Due to Lack of Resources and Fair Distribution

Colleen Tigges is director of EAT First!, an organization that fights misinformation surrounding environmental issues, especially as they relate to agriculture. She recently coauthored *A Field Manual for the Green War* and writes in the *AgBioNews* newsletter, "Ideology means nothing to people who have no energy to power homes and businesses, no indoor plumbing, and who don't have enough to eat. These people will choose any opportunity to stop their children from starving—do they have any other choice?" (Tigges 2004).

The history of agriculture can be seen as an ongoing battle against nature to end famine and hunger. The evil here, the enemy so to speak, is the constant threat of hunger and undernourishment; and the good here is food, whatever it may be. Good food is any food. This battle, as all battles, has its proponents and its opponents. Proponents are in favor of more and higher yields; opponents are critics of high-yielding agriculture and intensification. For proponents, ending famine and hunger is the main ethical problem, and opponents of high-yield methods are reproached for delaying this effort. In the view of proponents, agriculture is mainly an issue of farmers who are willing to intensify or not; and over the twentieth century to today, farmers have been increasingly assisted by professional agricultural scientists, which indeed has resulted in the doubling and tripling of yields (LaFollette 2005).

The Battle against Lack of Pluralism and Misrepresentation of Food Styles

In contrast to the misdistribution of food, lack of pluralism in food styles is more difficult to identify, although its outcome can be as disastrous and shameful as the first evil of hunger. That outcome is always something like misrepresentation, which in the food sector means that not all food styles are represented in the market, in production, in governments, or in research. Bluntly said, it means that some groups have no voice in the food sector and some have more (disproportionate) voice. This presupposes that the right of food choice, of either collectives or individuals, is not respected. When, for example, the cheapest and most accessible type of food is fast food, and people in their own homes are encouraged to eat processed food with little preparation required; when in the production of food the only target is more yields, regardless of the quality of the food, of the environment, of the landscape, of the animals involved; that indeed only one food style is dominant and suppresses all others—all of this indicates misrepresentation of food styles.

Lack of pluralism in food styles is undeniable when seen in light of the controversial concept of the *quality of food*. The multi-interpretable concept of "quality" is defined by different cultures in various ways. Quality of food for a Muslim is different than for a Hindu or a Jewish person, to name only the most well-known and broadest lifestyle groups. Although quality of food is controversial, some general aspects can be discerned, which makes it possible to compare different food styles. These aspects are, for example, the measure of respect for the animals involved, the landscape, and the environment. Food styles differ with respect to these aspects. However, what aspects an individual chooses to live by and why is up to that individual.

In this chapter, I start with the ethical meaning of representation, focusing on food, to illustrate that misrepresentation of food styles is indeed a serious evil. Then I discuss the dominance of one food style in the Western world, followed by descriptions of some other food styles, and I explain what an ethical and acceptable representation of these food styles would require and what the difficulties are of coexistence with the dominant food style. Finally, I compare the two evils—hunger and misrepresentation—and make clear why the evil of misrepresentation can only explicitly be distinguished in recent times, when there has developed such a huge gap between citizen-consumers and producers.

THE FAIR REPRESENTATION OF FOOD STYLES

Several cases have inspired me.

In Mali, Maurice Mamanlawal Salé, from the private charity Eden, is angry. Normally, in times of lesser yields of the national staple crop sorghum, people eat wild plants and certain insects. However, because of the lesser value that nowadays is attached to these plants and insects, and the higher respect that Western foods garner, plus the ease of getting food from international charities, people do not collect these foodstuffs anymore (*NRC Handelsblad,* March 4, 2006). The standards that determine which things are perceived to be edible and which are not depend not only on information and knowledge—metaphors play a role as well in differentiating the edible from the not edible.

Gene R. DeFoliart (1999) describes how attitudes affect food choices, in his article "Insects as Food." DeFoliart writes of what the earlier researcher, Carl Axel Silow, found in Zambia in the 1970s:

> Silow describes how European influence has undermined the traditional attitudes toward caterpillars: In connection with the independence movement a reaction spread, especially in the towns, maintaining that caterpillars are excellent African food. The course of development, according to which modern, enlightened people should not eat the larvae, appears, however, to be stronger. Already at the primary schools many children learn from their teachers that caterpillars are bad food. Even if they generally keep the food habits of their parents, they have become a little

hesitant about them. The pupils of the secondary schools, who spend their terms at boarding-schools with mainly non-African teachers, often refuse to eat caterpillars.

According to Silow (1976): "It is known that some missionaries have condemned winged termite eating as a heathen custom."

The United Nations and its aid organizations produce crises of food through their incompetent actions. "White people like me were flying in to save little children," says a Dutch aid worker, "as if the local inhabitants of Niger aren't able to do this themselves." He tells about a competent local physician who instructed mothers in traditional cooking and food education, using local products, to improve their diets. But this doctor was compelled to stop his efforts because UNICEF required that even lightly undernourished children had to be fed with the Unimix food from abroad, although this normally is required only for severely undernourished children (*NRC Handelsblad,* December 18, 2005).

Prices of tropical commodities decrease on the world market. People in the West, it seems, do not prefer fruits such as bananas, mangos, and other directly edible tropical products. Or, better said, supermarkets and food industries offer consumers in the West increasingly processed food, in which tropical commodities are only ingredients and sugar and fats are main ingredients. This in turn determines what farmers in the global South can farm and earn. Robbins (2003) calls the result of this change in the food industry's buying strategy "stolen fruit: the tropical commodities disaster."

Changing preferences in the North determine food sovereignty in the South. The shifting preference from petroleum-based fuel to biofuel increases the demand for soybeans. Soy is now a money machine, and a kind of soy gold rush is happening in the South. In Mato Grosso do Sul, in Brazil, grass on the pampas is increasingly being replaced by soy. In ten years, the area under soybean cultivation has increased from 18 to 38 million hectares (eleven times the size of the Netherlands), according to the Commisao Pastoral da Terra and the Brazilian Research Office. The consequences are widespread deterioration of living conditions in rural areas (Dros 2004).

The introduction of new foodstuffs always takes the path of assimilating the unknown to the known. This according to Montanari (2006, 109), who supplies ample evidence in his historical works on famines and food affluence. Thus in Mediterranean Europe since Roman times, bread was central, and hence the European preference for bread (Montanari 2006, 134). Thus at first potatoes were made into bread forms, and the same happened with corn that was first shaped into polenta (polenta is the form in which corn is cooked). New foods succeed because of people "treating—or, believing [they] can treat—new products by traditional procedures and methods of food preparation" (Montanari 2006, 109). In periods of hunger, when there is lack of grain, other ingredients like acorns have been harvested. "The famished poor then tried to bake the acorns into bread," writes Montanari (2006, 107). Every new food item is in this way assimilated by existing food styles, which implies that new foodstuffs are always adapted to local contexts, which in turn means that they will have some intercontextual commonality with the traditional food style but will never be identical to it.

The Ethical Meaning of Representation

These six examples reveal the importance of established food styles. Neglecting or even disrespecting established food styles causes hunger, not due to lack of resources but due to lack of sovereignty over food. The social forces that determine what crops should be produced and eaten do not represent the farming and food preferences of local inhabitants; rather, social forces suppress these preferences, which are then not represented. The situation is a showcase of *lack of representation,* or *misrepresentation.*

Hannah Pitkin, in her 1967 book *The Concept of Representation,* says that representation "involves treating something as present which is 'nevertheless not present literally or in fact'" (9). The "something" in her book consists of the various opinions of citizen-consumers about political issues, such as power distribution, responsibilities, and other public issues. Mostly, in democracies at least, citizens do have a voice. But because of various reasons and constraints, citizens are not present in the decision-making process. Instead, they decide to let others speak for them, to act and decide on their behalf. So, citizens have a voice and the right to delegate this voice to their representatives—and also the right to hold their representatives accountable.

Fair representation of food styles is not directly connected with these political issues but with making present in the food chain and networks the voices of different food styles. Fair representation in this sense covers production and availability of food products and everything connected with these processes: labeling, marketing, public debates, research, regulations of markets (concerning industry, farming, communication and information, etc.). With the absence of representation, food styles do not have a voice in the food chain (be it in supermarkets, food production, food research, or food regulation). Because food is an important aspect of social and cultural identities, individuals and groups deeply appreciate their food choices (and implicitly or explicitly the production processes), and they are often unwilling to change their eating habits. Food products, more than other products, are directly linked with cultural self-esteem and respect.

Fair representation of food styles means that products of the different styles must in fact be produced and available. The products must also be affordable, that is, prices of foodstuffs in the different styles must be more or less comparable. Moreover, choice of whatever foodstuffs must be without constraint; people should be able to choose, for example, the vegetarian food style without being ostracized or in a more innocent way punished for their lifestyle. Finally, reliable information about the products of a food style must be available, for example, that no pork proteins have been used in halal food, no genetically modified ingredients in organic food.

UN Ethical Justification of the Fair Representation of Food Styles

The right of food choice received a canonical stamp in 1999 with the Right to Adequate Food (Article 11), a convention of the UN Economic and Social Council of the Human Rights Commission. According to the convention (UN Economic and Social Council 1999), the right to adequate food covers several issues:

1. The States Parties to the present Covenant recognize the right of everyone to an adequate standard of living for himself and his family, including adequate food, clothing and housing, and to the continuous improvement of living conditions. The States Parties will take appropriate steps to ensure the realization of this right, recognizing to this effect the essential importance of international co-operation based on free consent.

2. The States Parties to the present Covenant, recognizing the fundamental right of everyone to be free from hunger, shall take, individually and through international co-operation, the measures, including specific programmes, which are needed:

   (a) To improve methods of production, conservation and distribution of food by making full use of technical and scientific knowledge, by disseminating knowledge of the principles of nutrition and by developing or reforming agrarian systems in such a way as to achieve the most efficient development and utilization of natural resources;

   (b) Taking into account the problems of both food-importing and food-exporting countries, to ensure an equitable distribution of world food supplies in relation to need.

   . . . .

8. The Committee considers that the core content of the right to adequate food implies: The availability of food in a quantity and quality sufficient to satisfy the dietary needs of individuals, free from adverse substances, and acceptable within a given culture. The accessibility of such food in ways that are sustainable and that do not interfere with the enjoyment of other human rights;

   . . . .

11. Cultural or consumer acceptability implies the need also to take into account, as far as possible, perceived non nutrient-based values attached to

food and food consumption and informed consumer concerns regarding the nature of accessible food supplies.

The Fair Representation of Food Styles
as an Ethical Principle

Traditionally, especially in medical ethics, informed choice is conceptualized as a form of individual autonomy. However, informed choice exerted in the food sector is different, because of the large- and small-scale social effects and social contexts of this type of choice. First, food choice addresses itself to a market and production sector that, on a daily basis, provides products that should be bought. Second, food choice takes into account the network the chooser is in, be it made up of relatives, friends, or others he or she is eating with. Therefore, food choice can never be modeled on individual informed choice. A food choice is something like choosing according to one's lifestyle and corresponding food style, and it is collectively exercised, with collective presuppositions and implications.

In contrast to the battle against hunger, the battle with respect to fair representation of food styles does not appeal to principles of just distribution but to principles of respect and voice. According to the principles of just distribution, equal and fair distribution of goods (food) is ethically justified because food is an important instrument for survival, or, better, because it allows you to live the life you want to live. According to the principles of respect and voice, fair representation of food styles is ethically justified because food is an intrinsic part of living a good life that people, mostly collectively, choose to live. *Respect for food choices* implies respecting them even when they seem, from another point of view, unhealthy or irrational. (As a matter of fact, constraints should regulate which ideal of the good life is ethically permissible and which is not, but that is not my point here.) *Voice* means that the respected food choices are indeed realized in food production, preparation, and consumption. Collective food choices should be heard in the production chain and in the market, reflected by the establishment of farming and food styles that correspond to the chosen styles.

Fair representation of food styles can be justified both in the deontological theory of Immanuel Kant and in the utilitarian theory of John Stuart Mill. Kant (1991) writes that

> laziness and cowardice are the reasons why such a large part of humanity, even long after nature has liberated it from foreign control *(naturaliter maiorennes)*, is still happy to remain infantile during its entire life, making it so easy for others to act as its keeper. It is so easy to be infantile. If I have a book that is wisdom for me, a therapist or preacher who serves as my conscience, a doctor who prescribes my diet,

then I do not need to worry about these myself. I do not need to think, as long as I
am willing to pay.

Because food choices involve a person's autonomy, consumers should decide
about their own food (diet); as a consequence, markets should follow. Kant presupposes that an adult is *educated,* has *capabilities,* and gets (reliable) *information* about
the diets available. Kant also presupposes that production processes and markets
deliver the goods and services an autonomous person prefers. Ideally, fair representation would mean that all food styles are treated equally in farming and production
and find their expression in corresponding farming and production styles.

From a utilitarian perspective, fair representation of food styles can also be
justified, although in a different way, as is clear from John Stuart Mill's statement:
"The only freedom which deserves the name, is that of pursuing our own good in
our own way, so long as we do not attempt to deprive others of theirs, or impede
their efforts to obtain it. Each is the proper guardian of his own health, whether
bodily, or mental or spiritual" (Mill 1978, 15).

Because each person is the guardian of his or her own health, food choices
should be freely made, not restricted by market monopolies and other forms of
demand restrictions. Mill formulates a classical restriction: "His own good, either
physical or moral is not a sufficient warrant. The only purpose for which power
can rightfully be exercised over any member of a civilized community, against his
will, is to prevent harm to others" (Mill 1978, 12). Again, from this perspective,
the autonomous person should be enabled to strive for his or her own good and
food through education, regulation, reliable information, and responsive markets.

Fair representation is a contested concept, and the history of agriculture is a
continuous battle fought between parties already represented in agriculture and
others that have faced exclusion. Fair representation is an ideal, and more often
than not misrepresentation is the outcome of these battles. The bones of contention
in these battles reflect the three aspects of representation. First, food products of the
various food styles must be available and the production process must be so structured that these products are indeed produced. Second, the foodstuffs must also
be affordable, that is, consumer prices must be more or less comparable without
too many differences between basic foodstuffs. Finally, foodstuffs must be able to
be enjoyed without constraint, without being culturally repressed. People should
be able to choose, for example, a vegetarian food style without being ostracized
or in another way punished because of their lifestyle; stronger even, they must be
respected because of their food choices.

What Is a Food Style?

To clarify the meaning of fair representation and to justify the concept of fair
representation of food styles, it is necessary to pay some attention to what a

food style is. Generally speaking, a food style can be understood as a food regime that is part of a lifestyle. It includes a certain type of information about food; the type of shopping, preparing, and cooking it involves; eating out or at home, together or alone; and the form of fulfillment it takes. It bears a similarity to Bourdieu's (1977) concept of habitus, though in his theory the ethical aspects of representation and misrepresentation (and their implications, such as feelings of disgust and humiliation) are not explicitly taken in to account.

A group of social researchers, hard at work trying to render the concept of food-related lifestyle a valid instrument, have distinguished as least twenty-three elements of a food style, divided into five categories: ways of shopping, cooking methods, quality aspects, consumption associations, and purchasing motives (Grunert 1997). Although this list is already rather complex, it still is not complex enough because it does not take into account the more ethical and cognitive values often at stake in a food style. For example, vegetarianism is not covered, nor is halal and kosher food.

A food style is also a way of disciplining yourself and others: it can promote an ideal of health (in the sense of living according to certain standards for an ideal body) or can be hedonistically enjoyable. A food style is often gendered, because in many cultures women do the cooking, but it is also influenced by age and stage in the life course and by the type of social engagement involved (e.g., cohabitation or not). A food style, as it is a component of lifestyle, has relationships with culture and cultural practices.

Generally, in most European states, we have five or six different food styles that have a more or less equal number of adherents (Rozin 1996). Roughly speaking, these styles concentrate on either traditional (regional or national) food, health food, natural (organic) food, international (cosmopolitan) food, or fast food (Korthals 2004). Many consumers do not adhere only to one style but are rather eclectic. Some people, following different food styles, can indeed consume the same kind of foodstuffs, but their motivations can be totally different. Health, for example, can be a motive for following a vegetarian, natural food style; whereas for others, animal sensibility can be a reason to eat only vegetables.

All kinds of causal determinants are responsible for a certain lifestyle and food style, but these empirical relationships are, from an ethical point of view, not always relevant. In general, we can distinguish different ways of relating to food, such as being less or more involved with food, as in the example of cultures that eat to live or cultures that live to eat. Moreover, cultures have different attitudes toward food advice, traditional and new ways of cooking and eating, eating out or not, and toward gendered forms of eating or not (Warde 1997; Miele and Murdoch 2002a).

Five Objections to the Fair Representation
of Food Styles

A first objection concerns the fact that food is very important for the health of human beings, a concern nowadays usually assessed by medical and other experts. Is human health not in jeopardy if everyone is more or less autonomous in his or her food choices? Should it not be recommendable that food experts prescribe healthy food styles and exclude unhealthy ones? The answer to this objection, on principle, is of course that people should be allowed to make their own food choices, even if experts consider these choices unhealthy, as long as the choices do not harm others. However, from a more practical point of view, one could assume that experts' recommendations adhere to only a minimum standard, for example, not eating too much animal fat or not eating enough vegetables, thus leaving ample room for diverging food choices of the average eater.

A second objection concerns the possible social effects of the fair representation of food styles and addresses the possible pillorization and subsequent fragmentation of society into secluded or excluded communities. I doubt, however, that such severe effects would result from the fair representation of food styles. Most societies have continued to live with many different food styles; this diversity became a problem when states (in particular since World War II, as a consequence of widespread famines in Europe) assumed increasing responsibility for food production and tried to support only one style, but that is waning.

A third objection is that fair representation of food styles might result in a total individualization of food choice, if indeed everyone chooses his or her own food type. Again, I think this is an exaggeration, because (in Europe at least) most people still enjoy common meals and prepare their meals in cooperation with others. Exactly because of the social function of food, it is so important for societies that common meals and preparation activities be supported, because these have such a fundamental positive effect on social respect and, indeed, on humanitarian feelings (as Kant would say in *Anthropology from a Pragmatic Point of View*).

A fourth objection could be that some people might like to experiment with all kinds of less desirable or acceptable food styles, such as cannibalism, or to behave irresponsibly and adopt food styles linked to risks for disease (e.g., obesity). The principal answer here is that people are indeed allowed to adopt unhealthy food styles, as long as they do not harm others. However, an extreme liberal standpoint is not desirable here, because many people do not foresee what the consequences of their actions can be. Therefore, governments should recommend minimum health levels, making it easier for people to live healthily and more difficult to live unhealthily. Nevertheless, this does not distort the right to autonomous food choices, because prescribing or recommending a minimum standard is different than prescribing the whole diet of an individual.

Last but not least, a fifth objection says there are all kinds of practical barriers to the fair representation of food styles, such as lack of representatives and structures of legitimacy and accountability, and the fact that food production is a fully commercial, market-oriented sector. It could be that fair representation would contribute to making a market sector a kind of governmental branch, but not necessarily. The deliberative perspective of this issue of representation emphasizes the role of civil society as a broad palette of different types of citizens groups that act together to structure their communicative power (in the sense of Hannah Arendt). Indeed, fair representation could mean that consumer groups have a larger say in commercial food companies but without overriding market strategies and mechanisms. On the contrary, from a deliberative point of view, markets and private enterprises have a their own value, which should not be neglected.

From a pragmatic liberal point of view, these objections should be taken seriously, but they are not compelling reasons to adhere to the existing situation with its one dominant food style (fast food).

FEATURES OF THE FAIR REPRESENTATION
OF FOOD STYLES

The fair representation of food styles is made up of components similar to those of political representation (see Pitkin 1967). In general, fair representation of food styles requires pluralism and comprises at least four components: the features of the represented (i.e., the type of persons represented); the aspects or subject matter represented; the features of the representatives; and, finally, the justification of representation, or its legitimacy.

The first issue concerns the type of persons represented. Because the subject here concerns food choices, in which collective choices or personal food choices in aggregate make up a food style, it is a group of persons or a food style that should be represented. This group should have considerable size.

The second issue is the subject matter that should be represented, which in the case of food styles means the foodstuffs represented. First, food choices can only be voiced and represented by humans; second and most important, food products show up in the market according to preferred food production processes. Consumer groups made up of neighbors, or other consumer organizations, could exert influence in this arena.

The third issue is the question of what and who the representatives are. On one level, the representatives could be a neutral body of decision makers or, in accordance with the deliberative democracy ideal, could be representatives of the various food styles themselves.

The fourth issue, concerning the legitimacy of representation, is more or less the same as in political representation. Someone who chooses fast food cannot really represent slow food, and so on. Moreover, accountability and responsibility are main components of legitimacy. This means that, in the end, representatives can be held responsible and, if found unsatisfactory, can be removed from their positions of authority and replaced. Such requirements can make the food chain and its networks much more transparent.

TYPES OF MISREPRESENTATION OF FOOD STYLES

Political misrepresentation means that people do not get the representatives they thought they were getting, whether because of fraud or because their representatives do not have the corresponding political power. Food misrepresentation manifests in similar ways. By appealing to universal features, a food style can gain dominance as the healthy one, the profitable one, and so on; and then other food styles cannot exert their power. The consequence is underrepresentation of a food style, inadequate representation, or even no representation at all.

Misrepresentation in the first instance has nothing to do with food security. Food security is a policy aim, seen from the perspective of the fair distribution of food; but it is too vague an aim to be of use in the context of misrepresentation. Indeed, there can be food security and even abundance of food without fair representation, as in the case of genetically modified (GM) food that people refuse to eat.

What happens very often is that a food style is used as an instrument of power to dominate people, that is, as a kind of geopolitics with food. GM crops nowadays are often used that way. During the cold war, food was often used by the superpowers to contain unrest or to pacify resistant nations (Perkins 1997). But food styles also operate within a country's political landscape, often as a kind of prize mechanism to buy a political clientele, as in the case of types of food aid. In Peru, a vast amount of money is used for buying and selling milk, to satisfy political clienteles of the dominant elites (Aguiar et al. 2006).

In the Western world, fast food has an enormous advantage, both in marketing and advertising and also in research and even cooking. This misrepresentation means that everything is biased toward fast food, even though consumers never asked for fast food, for magnums, for eight mealtimes a day. In the production sector of fast food, all attention is on yields, yields, yields, on calories, protein, and other ingredients. In research as well, this food style is dominant, focused on more yields, still tasteless but healthy food. When something like taste *is* incorporated, it is blind tasting, which cannot be called human tasting, because that is always contextual (dependent on the history and circumstances).

In consumption, the fast food style belongs to a cooking style that can be called "scissor cooking." Prepackaged ingredients and foodstuffs, which you open with a scissor, require only short preparation time. Fast food's only competitor in the market and production realms, ironically, is health food (with "health" defined quite narrowly). The main metaphor that characterizes the fast food style in consumption and production is food as fuel. And the resulting dominance of the fast food style thwarts fair representation of other food voices and choices.

Example of extreme misrepresentation of food: *Darwin's Nightmare.* Hubert Sauper's 2004 documentary film, *Darwin's Nightmare,* treats the hellish edges of the Western food system. It shows the monoculture production of Victoria perch in Tanzania's Victoria Lake. Local residents produce clean and hygienic fish for export but themselves have to live on the offal, head and bones, which are mostly in a terrible state as cast off by the fish industry.

The system produces numerous injustices, such as the neglect of children, the abuse of women, and the interplay of fish transport and illegal arms transport. The Sukumas, the region's original inhabitants, traditionally lived from cattle and some crops, but because of the total destruction of their habitat they are compelled to eat fish remains. The way these remains are stored and processed mirrors the total disrespect that the Sukumas encounter. The movie makes it clear that misrepresentation in the case of food styles seldom comes alone but rather can be accompanied by other forms of misrepresentation and injustice.

Example of simple misrepresentation of food: the case of GM food. The efforts to introduce GM crops in western Europe are a good example of a large offensive to change food styles against the will of the people involved. The case is analyzed in some excellent studies (Charles 2001) and has everything to do with the food choices that European consumers want to exert, along with associated desires for labeling and transparent information. Producers did not want to label food for the European market and thereby infringed this right of food choice. Trade interests and even political pressure was brought to bear. However, in the end, the right to food choice prevailed in Europe, the result being that GM crops are separately harvested, transported, and processed.

Example of slow food versus fast food. Vegetarian, organic, and animal welfare–friendly food are all examples of food styles. There are many ways to classify food production and consumption styles, and depending on these classifications they overlap or exclude each other. Also, the motivations for adopting whatever food style can be different. At least in Europe, it seems that pluralism of food styles is increasing, with ensuing diversification of food styles and corresponding farming and production styles.

A food style that has been gaining attention is "slow food." Slow food was born in Italy as a protest against fast food and the standardization and lack of quality of food: the fast, quick way to cook everything and the neglect of quality, enjoyment, health, the environment, and the landscape. Slow food emphasizes local production and local tradition, which it tries to preserve as much as possible, although it does not disregard the connection between craftsmanship and science. Slow food views food not as fuel, as fast food does, but as art—like a book or a theater play. In contrast to fast food, slow food is not in favor of boosting calories or proteins but of increasing taste. In Italy, slow food is not an elite movement; it produces products that can be offered on a larger scale but without betraying slow food principles.

Slow food production is defended by showing, for example, that modern hygienic standards are taken into account or that complying with fast food standards is not always necessary. More proactively, science could contribute much to slow food by investigating the numerous agronomic, biological, and marketing issues that slow food products bring to light. Because of misrepresentation, however, nutrition and agricultural sciences until now have not contributed to the development of slow food (Winter 2004).

PROBLEMS OF THE INTERACTION BETWEEN FAIRLY REPRESENTED FOOD STYLES

Even when food styles are fairly represented, they can conflict with or even contradict each other. Coexistence is not always possible. Food styles can conflict in terms of established ethical norms and values or in terms of more technical norms, such as sanitary and veterinary standards. Both the deontological and utilitarian perspectives in ethics pay some attention to these conflicts, which can be conceptualized in terms of rights and obligations.

An interesting ethical controversy between several food styles concerns the way animals should be treated. Although animal welfare is high on the agenda of slow food, for example, as are food crafts and traditions, slow food also protects products that do not respect animal welfare (e.g., foie gras) or animal biodiversity (e.g., the processing of rare woodcocks and thrushes, as in the recipe for *sformato di uccelletti*).

Fast food also has its share of conflicts, as in its conflicts with normal standards of healthy food; the fast food connection with obesity is rather well established. Compared to the huge impact on human health of fast food, the rare occasions that slow food consumers are contaminated by raw milk products (and are exposed to *Listeria*) or contract prion diseases from eating cervella are not ethically significant.

Solutions to these conflicts between food styles should not be too quickly generalized. However, in some cases, food science could play a role. For example, research could supply replacements for the ugly aspects of foie gras production, or perhaps thrushes could be cloned, as already happens with the San Marzano tomato.

DIFFERENCES BETWEEN THE TWO EVILS: HUNGER
AND MISREPRESENTATION

For the various stakeholders, the differences between the two evils of hunger and misrepresentation are considerable. Consumers suffer differently from lack of food or misrepresentation than producers do, and governments have different jobs to do in each case.

Differences from a consumer perspective. For consumers, the two cases are differently structured. In the case of hunger, consumers do not get (enough) food because they lack purchasing power or because food simply is not available, whether through lack of production or distribution. Misdistribution means that consumers have no choice between not having and having food, whereas with misrepresentation they have no choice between different types of food and so cannot make their own choices. Continuing with the second case, misrepresentation, the supply of food can be sufficient but consumers can reject it because of preferences, or can grudgingly accept it only to later discover negative implications (such as obesity or food-related diseases). In fact, in most cases, acts of misrepresentation concern consumers; in the end, consumers will have to accept foodstuffs even if these do not meet their food choices.

Differences from a producer perspective. For producers, the first evil of hunger, or misdistribution, means that they are not able to produce in sufficient amount the food needed, whether constrained by military or political force or by sheer force of nature. In the second case, however, with misrepresentation, they are able to produce, but not the type of foodstuffs they think are acceptable according to their perception of the market or demand, again whether because of military, political, or economic force. Control over land and resources is an important factor in both cases, but it manifests differently. In the case of misdistribution, farmers do not have access to seeds and other resources. In the case of misrepresentation, farmers do not get the resources they prefer; they are under pressure to accept, for example, the seed and other resources on offer. Kloppenburg's (1990) history of hybrid maize is an example of this second situation. Kloppenburg makes it clear that the financial pressures on farmers to accept industrial-produced hybrid maize seeds in the early twentieth century were considerable, even though farmers lost the possibility of reusing their own seed. He also shows that, at the same time, there were alternatives to the hybrid seeds that were not chosen, because of the pressure from industrial and governmental actors. Henry A. Wallace, US secretary of agriculture in the 1930s, at that time also founded Pioneer Hibred, the company that produced the seeds. So, in this case, misdistribution was not at stake but rather something akin to the lack of representation of (and sufficient resources for) alternatives to hybrid maize.

Differences from a regulatory point of view. Governments have a severe problem when their population is starving, whether because of production or distribution problems. In the case of misrepresentation, on the other hand, people are not able to act according to their own rights. In the Western world, because of the gap between consumers and producers, producers do not know what the preferences of consumers are; and, vice versa, consumers do not know what producers are doing. This situation results in temporary food scares. As shown by the Eurobarometer, the European Commission's public opinion analysis arm, distrust of authorities common; and organizations farthest removed from the food chain, such as environmental organizations, are trusted the most. In the case of misrepresentation, authorities encounter waves of severe mistrust.

Some governments, for political reasons, use the two types of evils: hunger is often manipulated, as is misrepresentation, in attacking and suppressing rival political parties. Hunger can also be used in exterior policies, by boycotting or destroying harvests of foreign nations. The latter is particularly effective in humiliating cultural groups such as minorities.

Implications for the history of agriculture. Seen from the perspective of battles for representation, the history of agricultural intensification is not only a battlefield for higher yields but also for farming and production styles, which compete for dominance or, if possible, peaceful coexistence. The history of agricultural intensification is a complex network of roads taken or only halfway taken, of crucial decisions on mixing different farming and food styles.

This interplay between diverging types of agriculture has been intertwined with the battle against nature for higher yields. Protests against displacement of labor can be seen as phenomena that fit into the perspective of the battle for representation, and they are well-known events in the history of agriculture. They occurred not only with the advent of machines or pesticide- and herbicide-resistant variants but also when sheep or specific crops were introduced.

Seen from the possibility of misrepresentation, power not only plays a role in enabling farmers to have access or not to preferred seeds, resources, and technologies, but also in preventing consumers from having access to preferred foodstuffs. There are several possibilities here, including that consumers are supplied with foodstuffs but not their preferred ones, and they refuse to consume. This does not happen often, because under most circumstances people want to survive and are willing to feed their children whatever is supplied. What happens more often is that consumers (and farmers) grudgingly accept the food supplied but feel denigrated and disrespected or instrumentalized. Consumers and farmers are trapped, because they have to consume and produce; presented with resources and without choice, in the end consumers will have to accept whatever is offered.

TABLE 1 Characteristics of the Two Evils: Hunger and the Misrepresentation of Food Styles

	Misdistribution of Food (Hunger)	Misrepresentation of Food Styles
Social evil	Hunger, malnutrition (destitution)	Repression of food styles
Ethical evil	Injustice (no equal distribution)	Disrespect (against sovereignty, voice)
Ethical emotions	Feeling of lack	Feeling of humiliation
Social abuse	Food as power instrument: blackmailing with hunger	Food, agriculture as instrument of repression: disrespecting
Moral ideologies of abuse	The hungry do not deserve food, their own fault	Disrespected food style is unhealthy, risky, harmful
Power object	Farmers	Consumers
Government: inside	Food as instrument against inner opposition	Politics against unwilling minorities
Government: outside	Geopolitics against different social systems	Geopolitics against different food cultures

Table 1 lists the various features of both the battle against hunger and against misrepresentation, distinguishing how the respective evils are socially structured, ideological shaped, and politically fought over (in particular by governments).

REFERENCES

Aguiar, C., J. Resenfeld, B. Stevens, S. Thanasombat, and H. Masud. 2007. *An Analysis of Malnutrition Programming and Policies in Peru.* Ann Arbor: International Economic Development Program, Gerald R. Ford School of Public Policy and School of Public Health, University of Michigan.

Aiken, W., and H. LaFollette, eds. 1996. *World Hunger and Morality.* New York: Prentice Hall.

Arnold, D. 1998. *Famine: Social Crises and Historical Change.* Oxford: Blackwell.

Bourdieu, P. 1977. *Outline of a Theory of Practice.* Cambridge: Cambridge University Press.

Charles, D. 2001. *Lords of the Harvest: Biotech, Big Money, and the Future of Food.* New York: Basic Books.

De Beaufort, I. 2004. "Justice, Genetics and Lifestyles." In *A Companion to Genethics,* ed. J. Burley and J. Harris, 325–33. Malden, MA: Blackwell.

DeFoliart, G. R. 1999. "Insects as Food: Why the Western Attitude Is Important." *Annual Review of Entomology* 44:21–50.

Dros, J. M. 2004. *Managing the Soy Boom: Two Scenarios of Soy Production Expansion in South America.* Amsterdam: AIDEnvironment.

George, S. 1984. *Ill Fares the Land: Essays on Food, Hunger, and Power.* Washington, DC: Institute for Policy Studies.

Grigg, D. 1993. *The World Food Problem.* Oxford: Blackwell.

Grunert, K. 1997. "Food Related Lifestyle: Results from Three Continents." *Asian Pacific Advances in Consumer Research* 2:64–65.

Islam, N., ed. 1995. *Population and Food in the Early Twenty-first Century: Meeting Future Food Demand of an Increasing Population.* Washington, DC: World Bank.

Kant, I. 1991. "An Answer to the Question: What is Enlightenment?" In *Kant: Political Writings,* trans. H. B. Nisbet. Cambridge: Cambridge University Press.

———. 2006. *Anthropology from a Pragmatic Point of View.* Ed. Robert B. Louden. Cambridge: Cambridge University Press.

Kloppenburg, J., Jr. 1990. *First The Seed: The Political Economy of Plant Biotechnology, 1492–2000.* Cambridge: Cambridge University Press.

Korthals, M. 2004. *Before Dinner.* Dordrecht, Netherlands: Springer.

Kriflik, L. S., and H. Yeatman. 2005. "Food Scares and Sustainability: A Consumer Perspective." *Health, Risk and Society* 7 (11): 11–24.

LaFollette, H. 2005. "World Hunger." In *A Companion to Applied Ethics,* ed. R. G. Frey, 238–53. Oxford: Blackwell.

Lyson, T. 2002. "Advanced Agricultural Biotechnologies and Sustainable Agriculture." *Trends in Biotechnology* 20 (5): 193–98.

Miele, M., and J. Murdoch. 2002a. "Fast Food/Slow Food: Standardising and Differentiating Cultures of Food." In *Globalization, Localization and Sustainable Livelihoods,* ed. R. Almas, 23–41. Aldershot, UK: Ashgate.

———. 2002b. "The Practical Aesthetics of Traditional Cuisines: Slow Food in Tuscany." *Sociologia Ruralis* 42 (42): 312–28.

Mill, J. S. 1978. *On Liberty.* Indianapolis, IN: Hackett Publishing. First published 1863.

Montanari, M. 2006, *Food Is Culture.* New York: Columbia University Press.

Murcott, A. 2000. "Understanding Life-Style and Food Use: Contributions from the Social Sciences." *British Medical Bulletin* 56 (1) (May 1): 121–32.

Pelletier, D., C. McCullum, V. Kraak, and K. Asher. 2003. "Participation, Power and Beliefs Shape Local Food and Nutrition Policy." *The Journal of Nutrition* 133 (1): 301S–304S.

Perkins, J. H. 1997. *Geopolitics and the Green Revolution: Wheat, Genes, and the Cold War.* New York: Oxford University Press.

Phillips, F. 1992. *The World Food Problem: Tackling the Causes of Undernutrition in the Third World.* Boulder, CO: Lynee Rienner.

Pitkin, H. 1967. *The Concept of Representation.* Berkeley: University of California Press.

Robbins, P. 2003. *Stolen Fruit: The Tropical Commodities Disaster.* London: Zed.

Rogers, B. 2003. *Beef and Liberty, Roast Beef, John Bull and the English Nation.* London: Chatto and Windus.

Rozin, P. 1996. "Sociocultural Influences on Human Food Selection." In *Why We Eat what We Eat: The Psychology of Eating,* ed. E. D. Capaldi, 233–63. Washington, DC: American Psychological Association.

Rozin, P., C. Fischler, S. Imada, A. Sarubin, and A. Wrzesniewski. 1999. "Attitudes to Food and the Role of Food in Life in the U.S.A., Japan, Flemish Belgium and France: Possible Implications for the Diet–Health Debate." *Appetite* 33:163–80.

Schroder, M., and M. McEachem. 2004. "Consumer Value Conflicts Surrounding Ethical Food Purchase Decisions: A Focus on Animal Welfare." *International Journal of Consumer Studies* 28 (2): 168–78.

Silow, C. 1976. *Edible and Other Insects of Mid-Western Zambia: Studies in Ethno-Entomology.* Uppsala: Institutionen för allmän och jämförande etnografi vid Uppsala universitet.

Tigges, C. 2004. "EAT First!—Choice? What Choice." *AgBioNews,* August 3. www .agbioworld.org/newsletter_wm/index.php?caseid=archive&newsid=2205.

UN Economic and Social Council. 1999. The Right to Adequate Food (Art. 11). E/C.12/1999/5. Geneva: UN Office of the United Nations High Commissioner for Human Rights. http:// daccess-ods.un.org/TMP/1177052.63197422.html.

Warde, A. 1997. *Consumption, Food and Taste, Culinary Antinomies and Commodity Culture.* London: Sage.

Winter, M. 2004. "Geographies of Food: Agro Food Geographies—Farming, Food and Politics." *Progress in Human Geography* 28 (5): 664–70.

Ethics and Genetically Modified Foods

Gary Comstock

Much of the food consumed in the United States is genetically modified. Genetically modified (GM) food derives from microorganisms, plants, or animals manipulated at the molecular level to have traits that farmers or consumers desire. These foods often have been produced using techniques in which "foreign" genes are inserted into the microorganisms, plants, or animals. Foreign genes are genes taken from sources other than the organism's natural parents. In other words, genetically modified plants contain genes they would not have contained if researchers had only used traditional plant-breeding methods.

Some consumer advocates object to GM foods, and sometimes they object on ethical grounds. When someone opposes GM foods on ethical grounds, the person typically has some reason or other for the opposition. We can scrutinize the person's reasons and, when we do so, we are doing applied ethics. Applied ethics involves identifying people's arguments for various conclusions and then analyzing those arguments to determine whether the arguments support the conclusions. A critical goal here is to decide whether an argument is sound. A sound argument is one in which all of the premises are true and no mistakes have been made in reasoning.

Ethically justifiable conclusions inevitably rest on two kinds of claims: (a) empirical claims, or factual assertions about how the world *is,* claims ideally based on the best available scientific observations, principles, and theories; and (b) normative claims, or value-laden assertions about how the world *ought to be,* claims ideally based on the best available moral judgments, principles, and theories.

Is it ethically justifiable to pursue GM crops and foods? There is an objective answer to this question, and we will try here to figure out what it is. But we must begin with a proper, heavy dose of epistemic humility, acknowledging that few ethicists at the moment seem to think that they know the final answer.

Should the law allow GM foods to be grown and marketed? The answer to this, and every, public policy question rests ultimately with us—citizens who will in the voting booth and shopping market decide the answer. To make up our minds, we will use feelings, intuition, conscience, and reason. However, as we citizens are, by and large, not scientists, we must, to one degree or other, rest our factual understanding of the matter on the opinions of scientific experts. Therefore, ethical responsibility in the decision devolves heavily upon scientists engaged in the new GM technology.

ETHICAL RESPONSIBILITIES OF SCIENTISTS

Science is a communal process devoted to the discovery of knowledge and to open and honest communication of knowledge. Its success, therefore, rests on two different kinds of values.

Epistemological values are values by which scientists determine which knowledge claims are better than others. The values include clarity, objectivity, capacity to explain a range of observations, and ability to generate accurate predictions. Claims that are internally inconsistent are jettisoned in favor of claims that are consistent and that fit with established theories. (At times, anomalous claims turn out to be justifiable, and an established theory is overthrown, but these occasions are rare in the history of science.) Epistemological values in science also include fecundity, the ability to generate useful new hypotheses, simplicity, the ability to explain observations with the fewest number of additional assumptions or qualifications, and elegance.

Personal values, including honesty and responsibility, are a second class of values, values that allow scientists to trust their peers' knowledge claims. If scientists are dishonest, untruthful, fraudulent, or excessively self-interested, the free flow of accurate information so essential to science will be thwarted. If a scientist plagiarizes the work of others or uses fabricated data, the scientist's work will become shrouded in suspicion, and otherwise reliable data will not be trusted. If scientists exploit those who work under them, or discriminate on the basis of gender, race, class, or age, then the mechanisms of trust and collegiality undergirding science will be eroded.

The very institution of scientific discovery is supported, indeed permeated, with values. Scientists have a variety of goals and functions in society, so it should be no surprise that they face different challenges.

University scientists must be scrupulous in giving credit for their research to all who deserve credit; careful not to divulge proprietary information; and painstaking in maintaining objectivity, especially when funded by industry. Industry scientists must also maintain the highest standards of scientific objectivity, a particular challenge since their work may not be subject to peer-review procedures as strict as those faced by university scientists. Industry scientists must also be willing to defend results that are not favorable to their employers' interests. Scientists employed by nongovernmental organizations face challenges as well. Their objectivity must be maintained in the face of an organization's explicit advocacy agenda and in spite of the fact that their research might provide results that might seriously undermine the organization's fund-raising attempts. All scientists face the challenges of communicating complex issues to a public that receives them through media channels often not equipped to communicate the qualifications and uncertainties attaching to much scientific information.

At its core, science is an expression of some of our most cherished values. The public largely trusts scientists, and scientists must in turn act as good stewards of this trust.

A METHOD FOR ADDRESSING ETHICAL ISSUES

Ethical objections to GM foods typically center on the possibility of harm to persons or other living things. Harm may or may not be justified by outweighing benefits. Whether harms are justified is a question that ethicists try to answer by working methodically through a series of questions:[1]

1. What is the harm envisaged? To provide an adequate answer to this question, we must pay attention to how significant the harm or potential harm may be (will it be severe or trivial?); who the "stakeholders" are (that is, who are the persons, animals, even ecosystems, who may be harmed?); the extent to which various stakeholders might be harmed; and the distribution of harms. The last question directs attention to a critical issue, the issue of justice and fairness: are those who are at risk of being harmed by the action in question different from those who may benefit from the action in question?

2. What information do we have? Sound ethical judgments go hand in hand with thorough understanding of the scientific facts. In a given case, we may need to ask two questions: Is the scientific information about harm being presented reliable, or is it fact, hearsay, or opinion? And, what information do we not know that we should know before making the decision?

3. What are the options? In assessing the various courses of action, emphasize creative problem solving, seeking to find win-win alternatives in which everyone's interests are protected. Here we must identify what objectives each stakeholder wants to obtain; how many methods are available by which to achieve those objectives; and what advantages and disadvantages attach to each alternative.

4. What ethical principles should guide us? There are at least three secular ethical traditions:
   · Rights theory holds that we ought always to act so that we treat human beings as autonomous individuals and not as mere means to an end.
   · Utilitarian theory holds that we ought always to act so that we maximize good consequences and minimize harmful consequences.
   · Virtue theory holds that we ought always to act so that we act the way a just, fair, good person would act.

   Ethical theorists are divided about which of these three theories is best. We manage this uncertainty through the following procedure. Pick one of the three principles. Using it as a basis, determine its implications for the decision at hand. Then, adopt a second principle. Determine what it implies for the decision at hand. Repeat the procedure with the third principle. Should all three principles converge on the same conclusion, then we have good reasons for thinking our conclusion morally justifiable.

5. How do we reach moral closure? Does the decision we have reached allow all stakeholders either to participate in the decision or to have their views represented? If a compromise solution is deemed necessary in order to manage otherwise intractable differences, has the compromise been reached in way that has allowed all interested parties to have their interests articulated, understood, and considered? If so, then the decision may be justifiable on ethical grounds.

There is a difference between *consensus* and *compromise*. *Consensus* means that the vast majority of people agree about the right answer to a question. If the group cannot reach a consensus but must, nevertheless, take some decision or other, then a *compromise* position may be necessary. But neither consensus nor compromise should be confused with the right answer to an ethical question. It is possible that a society might reach a consensus position that is unjust. For example, some societies have held that women should not be allowed to own property. That may be a consensus position, or even a compromise position, but it should not be confused with the truth of the matter. Moral closure is a sad fact of life; we sometimes must decide to undertake some course of action even though we know that it may not be, ethically, the right decision, all things considered.

ETHICAL ISSUES INVOLVED IN THE USE OF GENETIC TECHNOLOGY IN AGRICULTURE

Discussions of the ethical dimensions of agricultural biotechnology are sometimes confused by a conflation of two quite different sorts of objections to GM technology: intrinsic and extrinsic. It is critical that we not only distinguish these two classes but keep them distinct throughout the ensuing discussion of ethics.

Extrinsic objections focus on the potential harms consequent upon the adoption of genetically modified organisms (GMOs). Extrinsic objections hold that GM technology should not be pursued because of its anticipated results. Briefly stated, the extrinsic objections go as follows: GMOs may have disastrous effects on animals, ecosystems, and humans. Possible harms to humans include perpetuation of social inequities in modern agriculture, decreased food security for women and children on subsistence farms in developing countries, a growing gap between well-capitalized economies in the Northern Hemisphere and less capitalized peasant economies in the South, risks to the food security of future generations, and the promotion of reductionistic and exploitative science. Potential harms to ecosystems include possible environmental catastrophe, inevitable narrowing of germplasm diversity, and irreversible loss or degradation of air, soils, and waters. Potential harms to animals include unjustified pain to individuals used in research and production.

These are valid concerns, and nation-states must have in place testing mechanisms and regulatory agencies to assess the likelihood, scope, and distribution of potential harms through a rigorous and well-funded risk-assessment procedure. It is for this reason that I have said, above, that GM technology must be developed responsibly and with appropriate caution. However, these extrinsic objections cannot by themselves justify a moratorium, much less a permanent ban, on GM technology, because they admit the possibility that the harms may be minimal and outweighed by the benefits. How can one decide whether the potential harms outweigh the potential benefits unless one conducts the research, field tests, and data analysis necessary to make a scientifically informed assessment?

In sum, extrinsic objections to GMOs raise important questions about GMOs, and each country using GMOs ought to have in place the organizations and research structures necessary to ensure their safe use. There is, however, an entirely different sort of objection to GM technology, a sort of objection that, if it is sound, would indeed justify a permanent ban.

Intrinsic objections allege that the process of making GMOs is objectionable *in itself*. This belief is defended in several ways, but almost all of the formulations are related to one central claim, the unnaturalness objection: *It is unnatural to genetically engineer plants, animals, and foods* (UE).

If UE is true, then we ought not to engage in bioengineering, however unfortunate may be the consequences of halting the technology. Were a nation to accept UE as the conclusion of a sound argument, then much agricultural research would have to be terminated and potentially significant benefits from the technology sacrificed. A great deal is at stake.

In *Vexing Nature? On the Ethical Case against Agricultural Biotechnology,* I discuss fourteen ways in which UE has been defended.[2] For present purposes, those fourteen objections to GMOs can be summarized as follows: (1) To engage in agricultural biotech is to *play God*. (2) To engage in agricultural biotech is to *invent world-changing technology*. (3) To engage in agricultural biotech is *illegitimately to cross species boundaries*. (4) To engage in agricultural biotech is to *commodify life*. Let us consider each claim in turn.

(1) To Engage in Agricultural Biotech Is to Play God

In a Western theological framework, humans are creatures, subjects of the Lord of the Universe, and it would be impious for them to arrogate to themselves roles and powers appropriate only for the Creator. Shifting genes around between individuals and species is taking on a task not appropriate for us, subordinate beings. Therefore, to engage in bioengineering is to play God.

There are several problems with this argument. First, there are different interpretations of God. Absent the guidance of any specific religious tradition, it is logically possible that God could be a being who wants to turn over to us all divine prerogatives; or who explicitly wants to turn over to us at least the prerogative of engineering plants; or who doesn't care what we do. If God is any of these beings, then the argument fails because playing God in this instance is not a bad thing.

The argument seems to assume, however, that God is not like any of the gods just described. Assume that the orthodox Jewish and Christian view of God is correct, that God is the only personal, perfect, necessarily existing, all-loving, all-knowing, and all-powerful being. In this traditional Western theistic view, finite humans should not aspire to infinite knowledge and power. To the extent that bioengineering is an attempt to control nature itself, the argument would go, bioengineering would be an acceptable attempt to usurp God's dominion.

The problem with this argument is that not all traditional Jews and Christians think that this God would rule out genetic engineering. I am a practicing evangelical Christian and the chair of my local church's council. In my tradition, God is thought to endorse creativity and scientific and technological development, including genetic improvement. Other traditions have similar views. In the mystical writings of the Jewish Kabbalah, God is understood as one who expects humans to be cocreators, technicians working with God to improve the world. At least one Jewish philosopher, Baruch Brody, has suggested that biotechnology may be a vehicle ordained by God for the perfection of nature.[3]

I personally hesitate to think that humans can "perfect" nature. However, I have become convinced that genetic modification might help humans to rectify some of the damage we have already done to nature. And I believe God may endorse such an aim. For humans are made in the divine image. God desires that we exercise the spark of divinity within us. Inquisitiveness in science is part of our nature. Creative impulses are not found only in the literary, musical, and plastic arts. They are part of molecular biology, cellular theory, ecology, and evolutionary genetics too. It is unclear why the desire to investigate and manipulate the chemical bases of life should not be considered as much a manifestation of our godlike nature as the writing of poetry and the composition of sonatas. As a way of providing theological content for UE, then, argument (1) is unsatisfactory because it is ambiguous and contentious.

(2) To Engage in Agricultural Biotech Is to Invent World-changing Technology

Let us consider (2) in conjunction with similar objection (2a).

(2a) To Engage in Agricultural Biotech Is to Arrogate Historically Unprecedented Power to Ourselves

The argument here is not the strong one, that biotech gives us divine power, but the more modest one, that it gives us a power we have not had previously. But it would be counterintuitive to judge an action wrong simply because it has never been performed. In this view, it would have been wrong to prescribe a new herbal remedy for menstrual cramps or to administer a new anesthetic. But that seems absurd. More argumentation is needed to call historically unprecedented actions morally wrong. What is needed is to know to what extent our new powers will transform society, whether we have witnessed prior transformations of this sort, and whether those transitions are morally acceptable.

We do not know how extensive the agricultural biotech revolution will be, but let us assume that it will be as dramatic as its greatest proponents assert. Have we ever witnessed comparable transitions? The change from hunting and gathering to agriculture was an astonishing transformation. With agriculture came not only an increase in the number of humans on the globe but the first appearance of complex cultural activities: writing, philosophy, government, music, the arts, and architecture. What sort of power did people arrogate to themselves when they moved from hunting and gathering to agriculture? The power of civilization itself.[4]

Agricultural biotech is often oversold by its proponents. But suppose that they are right, that agricultural biotech brings us historically unprecedented powers. Is this a reason to oppose it? Not if we accept agriculture and its accompanying advances, for when we accepted agriculture, we arrogated to ourselves historically unprecedented powers.

In sum, the objections stated in (2) and (2a) are not convincing.

(3) To Engage in Agricultural Biotech Is Illegitimately to Cross Species Boundaries

The problems with this argument are both theological and scientific. I will leave it to others to argue the scientific case that nature gives ample evidence of generally fluid boundaries between species. The argument assumes that species boundaries are distinct, rigid, and unchanging while, in fact, species now appear to be messy, plastic, and mutable. To proscribe the crossing of species borders on the grounds that it is unnatural seems scientifically indefensible. It is also difficult to see how (3) could be defended on theological grounds. None of the scriptural writings of the Western religions proscribe genetic engineering, of course, because genetic engineering was undreamed of at the time the holy books were written. Now, one might argue that such a proscription may be derived from Jewish or Christian traditions of scriptural interpretation. Talmudic laws against mixing "kinds," for example, might be taken to ground a general prohibition against inserting genes from "unclean" species into clean species. Here's one way the argument might go: For an observant Jew to do what scripture proscribes is morally wrong; Jewish oral and written law proscribe the mixing of kinds (for example, eating milk and meat from the same plate; yoking donkeys and oxen together); bioengineering is the mixing of kinds; therefore, for a Jew to engage in bioengineering is morally wrong.

But this argument fails to show that bioengineering is intrinsically objectionable in all of its forms for everyone. The argument might prohibit *Jews* from engaging in certain kinds of biotechnical activity but not all; it would not prohibit, for example, the transferring of genes *within* a species, nor, apparently, the transferring of genes from one clean species to another clean species. Incidentally, it is worth noting that the Orthodox community has accepted transgenesis in its food supply. Seventy percent of cheese produced in the United States is made using a GM product, chymosin. This cheese has been accepted as kosher by Orthodox rabbis.[5]

In conclusion, it is difficult to find a persuasive defense of (3) either on scientific or religious ground.

(4) To Engage in Agricultural Biotech Is to Commodify Life

The argument here is that genetic engineering treats life in a reductionistic manner, reducing living organisms to little more than machines. Life is sacred and not to be treated as a good of commercial value only, to be bought and sold to the highest bidder.

Could we apply this principle uniformly? Would not objecting to the products of GM technology on these grounds also require that we object to the products of ordinary agriculture on the same grounds? Is not the very act of bartering or exchanging crops and animals for cash vivid testimony to the fact that every culture on earth has engaged in the commodification of life for centuries? If one accepts commercial trafficking in non-GM wheat and pigs, then why should we object to commercial trafficking in GM wheat and GM pigs? Why should it be wrong for us to treat DNA the way we have previously treated animals, plants, and viruses?[6]

While (4) may be true, it is not a sufficient reason to object to GM technology, because our values and economic institutions have long accepted the commodification of life. Now, one might object that various religious traditions have never accepted commodification and that genetic engineering presents us with an opportunity to resist, to reverse course. Leon Kass, for example, has argued that we have gone too far down the road of dehumanizing ourselves and treating nature as a machine, writing that we should pay attention to our emotional reactions against practices such as human cloning.[7] Even if we cannot defend these feelings in rational terms, our revulsion at the very idea of cloning humans should carry great weight. Mary Midgley has argued that moving genes across species boundaries is not only "yucky" but, perhaps, a monstrous idea, a form of playing God.[8]

Kass and Midgley have eloquently defended the relevance of our emotional reactions to genetic engineering but, as both admit, we cannot simply allow our emotions to carry the day. As Midgley writes, "Attention to . . . sympathetic feelings [can stir] up reasoning that [alters] people's whole world view."[9] But as much hinges on the reasoning as on the emotions.

Are the intrinsic objections sound? Are they clear, consistent, and logical? Do they rely on principles we are willing to apply uniformly to other parts of our lives? Might they lead to counterintuitive results?

Counterintuitive results are results we strongly hesitate to accept because they run counter to widely shared, considered moral institutions. If a moral rule or principle leads to counterintuitive results, then we have a strong reason to reject it. For example, consider the following moral principle, which we might call the doctrine of naïve consequentialism: *Always improve the welfare of the most people* (NC).

Were we to adopt NC, then we would not only be permitted but required to sacrifice one healthy person if by doing so we could save many others. If six people need organ transplants (two need kidneys, one needs a liver, one needs a heart, and two need lungs), then NC instructs us to sacrifice the life of the healthy person so as to transplant that person's six organs to the other six. But this result, that we are obliged to sacrifice innocent people to save strangers, is wildly counterintuitive. This result gives us a strong reason to reject NC.

I have argued that the four formulations of the unnaturalness objection considered above are unsound insofar as they lead to counterintuitive results. I do not take this position lightly. Twelve years ago, I wrote "The Case against bGH," an article, I have been told, that "was one of the first papers by a philosopher to object to agricultural biotech on explicitly ethical grounds." I then wrote a series of other articles objecting to GM herbicide-resistant crops, transgenic animals, and, indeed, all of agricultural biotechnology.[10] I am acquainted with worries about GM foods. But, for reasons that include the weakness of the intrinsic objections, I have come to change my mind. The sympathetic feelings on which my anti-GMO worldview was based did not survive the stirring up of reasoning.

WHY ARE WE CAREFUL WITH GM FOODS?

I do not pretend to know anything like the full answer to this question, but I would like to be permitted the luxury of a brief speculation about it. The reason may have to do with the natural, completely understandable, and wholly rational tendency to take precautions with what goes into our mouths. When we are in good health and happy with the foods available to us, we have little to gain from experimenting with a new food and no reason to take a chance on a potentially unsafe food. We may think of this disposition as the precautionary response.

When faced with two contrasting opinions about issues related to food safety, consumers place great emphasis on negative information. The precautionary response is particularly strong when a consumer sees little to gain from a new food technology. When a given food is plentiful, it is rational to place extra weight on negative information about any particular piece of that food. It is rational to do so, as Dermot Hayes points out, even when the source of the negative information is known to be biased.[11]

There are several reasons for us to take a precautionary approach to new foods. First, under conditions in which nutritious, tasty food is plentiful, we have nothing to gain from trying a new food if, from our perspective, it is in other respects identical to our current foods. Suppose on a rack in front of me there are eighteen dozen maple-frosted Krispy Kreme doughnuts, all baked to a golden brown, all weighing three ounces. If I am invited to take one of them, I have no reason to favor one over the other.

Suppose, however, that a naked man runs into the room with wild hair flying behind him yelling that the sky is falling. He approaches the rack and points at the third doughnut from the left on the fourth shelf from the bottom. He exclaims, "This doughnut will cause cancer! Avoid it at all costs, or die!" There is no reason to believe this man's claim and yet, since there are so many doughnuts freely available, why should we take any chances? It is rational to select other doughnuts, since all are alike. Now, perhaps one of us is a mountain climber who loves taking risks. He might be tempted to say, "Heck, I'll try that doughnut." In order to focus on the right question here, the risk takers should ask themselves whether they would select the tainted doughnuts to take home to feed to their two-year-old daughter. Why impose any risk on your loved ones when there is no reason to do so?

The Krispy Kreme example is meant to suggest that food tainting is both a powerful and an extraordinarily easy social act. It is powerful because it virtually determines consumer behavior. It is easy because the tainted does not have to offer any evidence of the food's danger at all. Under conditions of food plenty, rational consumers do and should take precautions, avoiding tainted food no matter how untrustworthy the tainted.

Our tendency to take precautions with our food suggests that a single person with a negative view about GM foods will be much more influential than many people with a positive view. The following experiment lends credibility to this hypothesis. In a willingness-to-pay experiment, Hayes and colleagues paid eighty-seven primary food shoppers forty dollars each. Each participant was assigned to a group ranging in size from a half-dozen to a dozen members. Each group was then seated at a table at lunchtime and given one pork sandwich. In the middle of each table was one additional food item, an irradiated pork sandwich. Each group of participants was given one of three different treatments: (a) the *pro-irradiation* treatment, (b) the *anti-irradiation* treatment, or (c) the *balanced* treatment.

Each treatment began with all of the participants at a table receiving the same, so-called natural description of an irradiated pork sandwich. The description read, in part, like this: The U.S. FDA has recently approved the use of ionizing to control *Trichinella* in pork products. This process results in a ten-thousand-fold reduction in *Trichinella* organisms in meat. The process does not include measurable radioactivity in food.

After the participants read this description, they would proceed to conduct a silent bid in order to purchase the right to exchange their nonirradiated sandwich for the irradiated sandwich. Whoever bid the highest price would be able to buy the sandwich for the price bid by the second-highest bidder. In order to provide participants with information about the opinions of the others at their table so that they could factor this information into their future bids, the lowest and highest bids of each round were announced before the next round of bidding began. At the end of the experiment, one of the ten bidding rounds would be selected at random, and the person bidding the highest amount in that round would have to pay the second-highest price bid during that round for the sandwich.

After five rounds of bidding, the second-highest bids in all three groups settled rather quickly at an equilibrium point, roughly twenty cents. That is, someone at every table was willing to pay twenty cents for the irradiated pork sandwich, but no one in any group would pay more than twenty cents. The bidding was repeated five times in order to give participants the opportunity to respond to information they were getting from others at the table and to ensure the robustness of the price.

After five rounds of bidding, each group was given additional information. Group (a), the so-called pro group, was provided with a description of the sandwich that read, in part, "Each year, 9,000 people die in the United States from food-borne illness. Some die from Trichinella in pork. Millions of others suffer short-term illness. Irradiated pork is a safe and reliable way to eliminate this pathogen. The process has been used successfully in twenty countries since 1950."

The pro-group participants were informed that the author of this positive description was a pro-irradiation food-industry group. After the description was read, five more rounds of bidding began. The price of the irradiated sandwich quickly shot upward, reaching eighty cents by the end of round ten. A ceiling price was not reached, however, as the bids in every round, including the last, were significantly higher than the preceding round. The price, that is, was still going up when the experiment was stopped.

After its first five rounds of bidding, group (b) was provided with a different description. It read, in part: In food irradiation, pork is exposed to radioactive materials. It receives 300,000 rads of radiation—the equivalent of 30 million chest X-rays. This process results in radiolytic products in food. Some radiolytic products are carcinogens, and linked to birth defects. The process was developed in the 1950s by the Atomic Energy Commission.

This source of this description was identified to the bidders as Food and Water, an anti-irradiation activist group in England. After group (b) read this description, it began five more rounds of bidding. The bid went down, quickly reaching zero. After the first five rounds produced a value of twenty cents in group (b) for the pork sandwich described in a "neutral" way, *no one* in this group would pay a penny for the irradiated sandwich described in a "negative" way. This result was obtained even though the description was clearly identified as coming from an activist, nonscientific group.

After five rounds of bidding on the neutral description, the third group, group (c) received *both* the positive and the negative descriptions. One might expect that this group's response would be highly variable, with some participants scared off by the negative description and others discounting it for its unscientific source. Some participants might be expected to bid nothing while others would continue to bid highly.

However, the price of the sandwich in the third, so-called balanced group, also fell quickly. Indeed, the price reached zero as quickly as it did in group (b), the negative group. That is, even though the third group had both the neutral and the positive description in front of them, no one exposed to the negative description would pay two cents for the irradiated sandwich.

Hayes's study illuminates the precautionary response and carries implications for the GM debate. Given neutral or positive descriptions of GM foods, consumers initially will *pay more* for them. Given negative descriptions of GM foods, consumers initially will *not* pay more for them. Finally, and this is the surprising result, given *both* positive and negative descriptions of GM foods, consumers initially will not pay more for them. Both sides in the GM food debate should be scrupulous in providing reasons for all of their claims, but especially for their negative claims.

In a worldwide context, the precautionary response of those facing food abundance in developed countries may lead us to be insensitive to the conditions of those in less fortunate situations. Indeed, we may find ourselves in the following ethical dilemma.

For purposes of argument, make the following three assumptions. (I do not believe that any of the assumptions is implausible.) First, assume that GM foods are safe. Second, assume that some GM "orphan" foods—such as rice enhanced with iron or vitamin A, or virus-resistant cassavas, or aluminum-tolerant sweet potatoes—may be of great potential benefit to millions of poor children. Third, assume that widespread anti-GM information and sentiment, no matter how unreliable on scientific grounds, could shut down the GM infrastructure in the developed world.

Under these assumptions, consider the possibility that by tainting GM foods in the countries best suited to conduct GM research safely, anti-GM activists could bring to a halt the range of money-making GM foods marketed by multinational corporations. This result might be a good or a bad thing. However, an unintended side effect of this consequence would be that the new GM orphan crops mentioned above might not be forthcoming, assuming that the development and commercialization of these orphan crops is dependent upon the answering of fundamental questions in plant science and molecular biology that will only be answered if the research agendas of private industry are allowed to go forward along with the research agendas of public research institutions.

Our precautionary response to new food may put us in an uncomfortable position. On the one hand, we want to tell "both sides" of the GM story, letting people know both about the benefits and the risks of the technology. On the other hand, some of the people touting the benefits of the technology make outlandish claims that it will feed the world while some of the people decrying the technology make unsupported claims that it will ruin the world. In that situation, however, those with unsupported negative stories to tell carry greater weight than those with unsupported positive stories. Our precautionary response, then, may well lead in the short term, at least, to the rejection of GM technology. Yet, the rejection of GM technology could indirectly harm those children most in need, those who need what I have called the orphan crops.

Are we being forced to choose between two fundamental values, the value of free speech versus the value of children's lives?

On the one hand, open conversation and transparent decision-making processes are critical to the foundations of a liberal democratic society. We must reach out to include everyone in the debate and allow people to state their opinions about GM foods, whatever their opinion happens to be, whatever their level of acquaintance with the science and technology happens to be. Free speech is a value not to be compromised lightly.

On the other hand, stating some opinions about GM food can clearly have a tainting effect, a powerful and extraordinarily easy consequence of free speech. Tainting the technology might result in the loss of this potentially useful tool. Should we, then, draw some boundaries around the conversation, insisting that each contributor bring some measure of scientific data to the table, especially when negative claims are being made? Or are we collectively prepared to leave the conversation wide open? That is, in the name of protecting free speech, are we prepared to risk losing an opportunity to help some of the world's most vulnerable?

THE PRECAUTIONARY PRINCIPLE

As a thirteen-year-old, I won my dream job, wrangling horses at Honey Rock Camp in northern Wisconsin. The image I cultivated for myself was the weathered cowboy astride Chief or Big Red, dispensing nuggets to awestruck young rider wannabes. But I was, as they say in Texas, all hat.

"Be careful?" was the best advice I could muster.

Only after years of experience in a western saddle would I have the skills to size up various riders and advise them properly on a case-by-case basis. You should slouch more against the cantle and get the balls of your feet onto the stirrups. You need to thrust your heels in front of your knees and down toward the animal's front hooves. You! Roll your hips in rhythm with the animal, and stay away from the horn. You, stay alert for sudden changes of direction.

Only after years of experience with hundreds of different riders would I realize that my earlier generic advice, well-intentioned though it was, had been of absolutely no use to anyone. As an older cowboy once remarked, I might as well have been saying, "Go crazy!" Both pieces of advice were equally useless in making good decisions about how to behave on a horse.

Now, as mad cow disease grips the European imagination, concerned observers transfer fears to genetically modified foods, advising: "Take precaution!" Is this a valuable observation that can guide specific public-policy decisions? Or is it well-intentioned but ultimately unhelpful advice?

As formulated in the 1992 Rio Declaration on Environment and Development, the precautionary principle states that "lack of full scientific certainty shall not be used as a reason for postponing cost-effective measures to prevent environmental degradation."[12] The precautionary approach has led many countries to declare a moratorium on GM crops on the supposition that developing GM crops might lead to environmental degradation. The countries are correct that this is an implication of the principle. But is it the only implication?

Suppose global warming intensifies and comes, as some now darkly predict, to interfere dramatically with food production and distribution. Massive dislocations in international trade and corresponding political power will follow global food shortages, affecting all regions and nations. In desperate attempts to feed themselves, billions will begin to pillage game animals, clear-cut forests to plant crops, cultivate previously nonproductive lands, apply fertilizers and pesticides at higher-than-recommended rates, and kill and eat endangered and previously nonendangered species.Perhaps not a likely scenario, but not entirely implausible either. GM crops could help to prevent it, by providing hardier versions of traditional plant lines capable of growing in drought conditions, or in saline soils, or under unusual climactic stresses in previously temperate zones, or in zones in which we have no prior agronomic experience. On the supposition that we might need the tools of genetic engineering to avert future episodes of crushing human attacks on what Aldo Leopold called "the land," the precautionary principle requires that we develop GM crops. Yes, we lack full scientific certainty that developing GM crops will prevent environmental degradation. True, we do not know what the final financial price of GM research and development will be. But if GM technology were to help save the land, few would not deem that price cost-effective. So, according to the precautionary principle, lack of full scientific certainty that GM crops will prevent environmental degradation shall not be used as a reason for postponing this potentially cost-effective measure.

The precautionary principle commits us to each of the following propositions: (1) We must not develop GM crops. (2) We must develop GM crops. As (1) and (2) are plainly contradictory, however, defenders of the principle should explain why implications are not incoherent.

Much more helpful than the precautionary principle would be detailed case-by-case recommendations based on a wide review of nonindustry-sponsored field tests conducted by objective scientists expert in the construction and interpretation of ecological and medical data. Without such a basis for judging this use acceptable and that use unacceptable, we may as well advise people in the GM area to go crazy. It would be just as helpful as "Take precaution!"

RELIGION AND ETHICS

Religious traditions provide an answer to the question, How, overall, should I live my life? Secular ethical traditions provide an answer to the question, What is the right thing to do? When in a pluralistic society a particular religion's answers come into genuine conflict with the answers arrived at through secular ethical deliberation, we must ask how deep the conflict is. If the conflict is so deep that honoring the religion's views would entail dishonoring another religion's views, then we have a difficult decision to make. In such cases, the conclusions of secular ethical deliberation must override the answers of the religion in question.

The reason is that granting privileged status to one religion will inevitably discriminate against another religion. Individuals must be allowed to follow their consciences in matters theological. But if one religion is allowed to enforce its values on others in a way that restricts the others' ability to pursue their values, then individual religious freedom has not been protected.

Moral theorists refer to this feature of nonreligious ethical deliberation as the *overridingness* of ethics. If a parent refuses a lifesaving medical procedure for a minor child on religious grounds, the state is justified in overriding the parent's religious beliefs in order to protect what secular ethics regards as a value higher than religious freedom: the life of a child.

The overridingness of ethics applies to our discussion only if a religious group claims the right to halt GM technology on purely religious grounds. The problem here is the confessional problem, of one group attempting to enforce its beliefs on others. I mean no disrespect to religion; as I have noted, I am a religious person, and I value religious traditions other than my own. Religious traditions have been the repositories and incubators of virtuous behavior. Yet each of our traditions must in a global society learn to coexist peacefully with competing religions and with nonreligious traditions and institutions.

If someone objects to GM technology on purely religious grounds, we must ask on what authority she speaks for her tradition; whether there are other, conflicting, views within her tradition; and whether acting on her views will entail disrespecting the views of people from other religions. It is, of course, the right of each tradition to decide its attitude about genetic engineering. But in the absence of other good reasons, we must not allow someone to ban GM technology for narrowly sectarian reasons alone. To allow such an action would be to disrespect the views of people who believe, on equally sincere religious grounds, that GM technology is not necessarily inconsistent with God's desires for us.

MINORITY VIEWS

When in a pluralistic society the views of a particular minority come into genuine conflict with the views of the majority, we must ask a number of questions: How deep is the conflict? How has the minority been treated in the past? If the minority has been exploited, have reparations been made? If the conflict is so deep that honoring the minority's views would entail overriding the majority's views, then we have a difficult decision to make. In such cases, the conclusions of the state must be just, taking into account the question of past exploitation and subsequent reparations, or lack thereof. This is a question of justice.

The question of justice would arise in the discussion of GM technology if the majority favored GM technology, while the minority claimed the right to halt GM technology. If the minority cited religious arguments to halt GMOs, yet the majority believed that halting GMOs would result in loss of human life, then the state faces a decision very similar to the one discussed in the prior section. In this case, secular policy decisions may be justified in overriding the minority's religious arguments insofar as society deems the value of human life higher than the value of religious freedom.

However, should the minority cite past oppression as the reason that their values ought to predominate over the majority's, then a different question must be addressed. Here, the relevant issues have to do with the nature of past exploitation; its scope and depth; and the sufficiency of efforts to rectify the injustice and compensate victims. If the problem is long-standing and has not been addressed, then imposing the will of the majority would seem a sign of an unjust society insensitive to its past misdeeds. If, on the other hand, the problem has been carefully addressed by both sides and, for example, just treaties arrived at through fair procedures have been put in place, are rectifying past wrongs, and are preventing new forms of exploitation, then the minority's arguments would seem to be far weaker. This conclusion would be especially compelling if it could be shown that the lives of other disadvantaged peoples might be put at risk by honoring a particular minority's wish to ban GMOs.

CONCLUSION

Earlier I described a method for reaching ethically sound judgments. It was on the basis of that method that I personally came to change my mind about the moral acceptability of GM crops. My opinion changed as I took full account of three considerations: (a) the rights of people in various countries to choose to adopt GM technology (a consideration falling under the human rights principle); (b) the balance of likely benefits over harms to consumers and the environment from GM technology (a utilitarian consideration); and (c) the wisdom of encouraging discovery, innovation, and careful regulation of GM technology (a consideration related to virtue theory).

Is it ethically justifiable to pursue genetically modified crops and foods? I have come to believe that three of our most influential ethical traditions converge on a common answer. Assuming we proceed responsibly and with appropriate caution, the answer is yes.

NOTES

1. In describing this method, I have drawn on an ethics assessment tool devised by Courtney Campbell, in the Philosophy Department of Oregon State University, and presented at the Oregon State University Bioethics Institute in Corvallis in the summer of 1998.

2. Gary Comstock, *Vexing Nature? On the Ethical Case against Agricultural Biotechnology* (Boston: Kluwer Academic Publishers, 2000).

3. Brody Baruch, private communication, 1994.

4. William McNeill, "Gains and Losses: A Historical Perspective on Farming" (1989 Iowa Humanities Lecture, National Endowment for the Humanities and Iowa Humanities Board, Oakdale Campus, Iowa City, 1989).

5. Jonathan Gressel, observation at the Annual Meeting of the Weed Science Society of America, Chicago, February 10, 1998. See also, Alan Ryan et al., *Genetically Modified Crops: The Ethical and Social Issues* (London: The Royal Society, 1999), sec. 1.38.

6. Dorothy Nelkin and M. Susan Lindee, *The DNA Mystique: The Gene as Cultural Icon* (New York: Freeman, 1995).

7. Leon R. Kass, *Toward a More Nature Science: Biology and Human Affairs* (New York: Free Press, 1998), and "Beyond Biology: Will Advances in Genetic Technology Threaten to Dehumanize Us All?" *New York Times*, August 23, 1998, www.nytimes.com/books/98/08/23/reviews/980823.23kassct .html.

8. Mary Midgley, "Biotechnology and Monstrosity: Why Should We Pay Attention to the 'Yuk Factor,'" *Hastings Center Report* 30, no. 5 (2000): 7–15.

9. Ibid., 10.

10. Gary Comstock, "The Case against bGH," *Agriculture Human Values* 5 (1998): 26–52. The other essays are reprinted in Comstock, *Vexing Nature?* chs. 1–4.

11. Dermont Hayes, John A. Fox, and Jason F. Shogren, "Consumer Preferences for Food Irradiation: How Favorable and Unfavorable Descriptions Affect Preferences for Irradiated Pork in Experimental Auctions," *Journal of Risk and Uncertainty* 24, no. 1 (2002): 75–95.

12. UN Environment Programme, "Rio Declaration on Environment and Development," www .unep.org/Documents.Multilingual/Default.asp?documentid=78&articleid=1163.

The Ethics of Food Safety
in the Twenty-First Century

Who Keeps the Public Good?

Jeffrey Burkhardt

In theory, a fully informed consumer might decide which food-related risks to take and which to avoid. But in the real world, average citizens cannot collect detailed information about the wide array of food safety issues and make their own decisions. For the most part, these decisions are delegated to responsible authorities in government agencies and the food industries. (FAO 2002)

A safe and secure food system is a public good: this means that an individual benefiting from a safe and secure food system does not reduce availability of the benefit for others and that no one can be effectively excluded from receiving these benefits (Samuelson 1954). Although individuals and private entities have a role to play in ensuring a safe and secure food system, governments are the primary agents to secure, or "keep," this public good (Caswell 1998). Identifying food safety as a public good also means that governments have ethical obligations to their citizens to protect, or "keep," that public good. Utilitarian and rights-based ethical theories converge on this issue: food safety is both a social goal to be optimized and a right that individuals have that the government must help protect (Thompson 2001).

In modern, industrialized, and urbanized societies, the complexities of the food system have long made fulfilling this obligation difficult and costly (Starbird 2005). Several factors have made carrying out this responsibility more serious and difficult in the present era. Government agencies responsible for food safety now face an evolving set of conditions that affect their abilities to fulfill their responsibilities. Among these new conditions are (1) the increasingly concentrated corporate control over the food chain from farm to market; (2) a rapidly growing global market in even basic food staples; and (3) hostile international political movements, which raise the threat of terrorist activities that could severely affect the food system. Each of these considerations is enough to warrant enhanced governmental oversight, regulation, inspection, and so on.

As noted in the FAO report cited in the chapter epigraph (FAO 2002), there are good, science-based strategies for strengthening government (and private) oversight. However, taken together, these new concerns may imply a more radical approach to keeping the public good associated with a safe and secure food system. Some have argued that more reliance on locally produced foods would not only better ensure food safety but have other benefits as well, such as social and environmental sustainability.

This chapter (a) defines "food safety" and what assuring it ethically implies in practical terms; (b) examines the means that governments and corporate actors (and individuals to a lesser extent) employ to address their ethical responsibilities vis-à-vis the food system; (c) looks individually at each of these new concerns for the various agencies responsible for our food and assesses the adequacy of current policies and practices to ensure food safety; and (d) critically assesses the argument that our food system should be restructured in order to ensure better oversight and control over issues of safety and security. Regarding this last point, I maintain that, while restructuring the food system to allow better local control over matters of safety and security may be a better (more ethical, efficient, and effective) alternative to the present situation, it is both unlikely to occur and may not in fact be the alternative preferred by the majority of consumers.

THE ETHICS OF FOOD SAFETY

The ethical mandate for governmental regulatory and oversight functions derives from two features of our urbanized society and our modern, industrial agricultural production system: (1) there are many ways in which foods can cause harm; and (2) the food system as a whole is complex. Regarding the first point, it is estimated that approximately seventy-six million cases of food-caused illnesses occur each year in the United States, resulting in 323,000 hospitalizations and 5,200 deaths (Kux, Sobel, and Fain 2007). Recently, milk contaminated with melamine (as a means of increasing protein/nitrogen content) in infant formula produced in China resulted in 4 deaths and sickness in 53,000 children. This was followed by deaths and illnesses of thousands of pets in the United States that ate pet food linked with the same toxin (CNN 2008; Fan 2008). These and other disturbing events prompted the creation of a US national food safety working group and the call for tighter food inspection following US president Obama's announcement banning "downer" cows from the food system (Associated Press 2009).

There are many actors in the food system and many stages between the farm and the dinner table. At each stage, problems can arise that may ultimately cause harm. From the perspective of rights theory, people have a right not to be harmed (or placed in harm's way). Utilitarian ethics demands that the greatest social good be pursued; this would imply that people should not be placed at risk without any overriding benefit. Either way, the possibility of harm, risk, or hazard—however one characterizes a potential threat to life or health—establishes a moral responsibility on the part of *someone* to try to prevent or reduce that threat. It is commonly thought that that someone should be governments.

Ensuring food safety is not simple. Food safety policy in the United States consists of three components: risk assessment, management, and communication. A first step in any food safety determination is to perform a science-based analysis that identifies any potential harm and how likely it is to occur. This involves hazard identification, dose response, and exposure analysis. In other words, if a foodstuff or food additive (or process) is potentially harmful, it is critical to know how it would cause adverse effects and what the likelihood is that people would be exposed to those effects. Scientific risk assessment is never unequivocally certain or complete, so the second component of food safety policy is risk management. This is a process of weighing policy alternatives to accept, minimize, or reduce assessed risks and to select and implement options. In essence, this involves judgments about whether any risks associated with a given food are within limits defined by a predetermined set of standards. For example, one such standard is "No detectable adverse effects": there may be potentially hazardous substances in the food but in a low enough dose or concentration (e.g., parts per million) that no one would be put at risk consuming them. It is important to note that a judgment that a foodstuff or some ingredient is "safe" does not mean there are "no risks"; indeed, what makes food safety an ethically challenging issue is that sometimes risks must be allowed because of a broader public benefit (Fischoff et al. 1993). As it is usually stated, safety means simply "acceptable risk."

A final stage in food safety policy is communication. This involves exchange of information and options about risks among risk assessors, risk managers, and other interested parties, including the public. It is at this stage that judgments are made about whether warning labels, information labels, or other sorts of information campaigns are necessary to show the potential consumer that the food meets government standards. Clearly, much time and resources are needed to determine whether a particular food is safe. To ensure that the food system as a whole is safe and secure requires an even greater amount of time and resources. President Obama's food safety working group is a good example of additional resources (beyond current regulatory/inspection agencies) being committed to address this issue.

Most of the problems with food safety globally are associated with bacterial/ viral contamination or spoilage, and much of the government's management and communication effort has gone into reducing these hazards or risks in the United States. When (where) people either grow their own food or rely on local sources from known growers or distributors, the primary responsibilities for ensuring food safety rest with those who grow and who prepare food for consumption. Simple practices like washing produce and adequately cooking meats (and keeping a clean cooking and dining area) are sufficient to discharge the ethical responsibilities producers and preparers had (and have) to protect the rights or ensure the welfare of those they feed. But producers and preparers have to know their responsibilities and take the practical steps necessary to secure safe food.

In modern societies with industrialized agricultural systems, risks from microbial contamination and spoilage still exist, but other potential hazards pose concern and complicate the ethics of food safety. Among these "modern" hazards are agricultural chemicals (such as pesticides, herbicides, fungicides), industrial chemicals (such as mercury and other heavy metals entering the food chain via air and water pollution), and foreign material (such as animal excrement, toxic plant material, and other undesirable biological material) (Henson and Caswell 1999).

Add to these that the industrialized agricultural system is not transparent to the ordinary consumer. That is, most people in an urban society do not know much if anything about how food is produced, where it is produced, who produces it, nor how it gets from the farm gate to produce aisle, meat cooler, or frozen and canned sections of the supermarket. There may be some ethical responsibilities on the part of preparers to wash fresh produce and adequately cook raw meat, but with so much food processed, prepackaged, ready to eat, and so on, the ethical responsibility of the individual food preparer is limited. Some people want to place the burden of ensuring food safety on farmers, citing, for example, the 2006 *E. coli* contamination of fresh spinach that sickened two hundred people and killed five (Runsten 2008). Environmental critics of agriculture have long focused on agricultural and industrial contamination as the primary risk factors affecting food safety (Berry 1977). However, farmers are just one set of players in the *system*. And farmers' techniques have evolved. For example, excessive chemical applications to crops have been reduced as new technologies have emerged and best management practices have been adopted (BLM 2009).

THE FOOD SAFETY SYSTEM

It is tempting to impute the ethical responsibility for ensuring food safety to every actor in the food system, from farmers to consumers. For example, Henson and Spencer (2001) argue that private (i.e., corporate) entities that process, transport, and distribute food have the primary responsibilities with respect to securing public food safety, and excessive regulation can actually hinder good management practices. It is true that when a private actor such as a processing facility, distributor, wholesaler, or supermarket has been shown to have put consumers at risk (sometimes even unknowingly), there is clear warrant for moral reprimand (if not legal remedy). I will return to the issue of private, corporate actors below. The issue here is, however, not to blame or punish actors for unethical or illegal activities that have already caused harm (from sickness to death), but to ensure *ex ante* that the food system is safe and secure. That is, the primary ethical responsibility is to prevent harm. Everyone may have a part in this collective responsibility, but it is up to governments, acting on behalf of people's rights or the general welfare, to safeguard consumers and citizens as far as possible.

In the United States, there are practical problems surrounding the government's attempt to act on its ethical responsibilities to consumers in this regard. These arise in part from the fact that different agencies are responsible for different links in the food system chain, with different risk factors tied to different links. The Animal and Plant Health Inspection Service (APHIS) and the Food Safety and Inspection Service (FSIS) of the US Department of Agriculture (USDA) are responsible for ensuring that healthy animals and nontoxic plants are used in agricultural production. The Environmental Protection Agency (EPA) is responsible for controlling potential chemical contaminants in production systems. The Food and Drug Administration (FDA) is the arbiter of whether or not processed foods, food additives, and new food products are safe for public consumption. The FDA also determines whether certain foods need to be labeled as having certain ingredients, beyond their nutritional composition. Overall, the FDA currently regulates about 80 percent of the food supply, ensuring the safety of domestic and imported food products except for meat and poultry. The FSIS is responsible for the remaining 20 percent, inspecting cattle, sheep, swine, and goats before and after slaughter. The two agencies share responsibility for egg safety.

Legislation has been proposed (Food Safety Enhancement Act of 2009) that would, among other things, give the FDA oversight of on-farm production activities, charge facilities an annual $500 registration fee, require additional record keeping, and expand FDA authority to quarantine geographic areas for food safety problems. The point is to provide a more centralized (and presumably more efficient) control point for food safety assurance.

Currently, the (ethical) responsibilities of each of these agencies are built into their mission statements (see this chapter's appendix). Directors, managers, and employees of these agencies take their responsibilities seriously (Sebelius 2009; Vilsack 2009). However, their resources are limited. As I detail below, it has become increasingly difficult for the regulators and inspectors to do their jobs. The government's ability to act on its ethical responsibilities has become perhaps too difficult if not impossible in some cases.

The FDA and USDA have faced an especially difficult situation since the introduction in the 1980s of genetically modified (GM) plants (and more recently animals). In the view of at least some people, foods that contain such material as seeds or oils or even proteins derived from GM plants and animals are ethically unacceptable. The USDA supported and encouraged farmers to adopt GM crops as a way of reducing use of pesticides and herbicides, and the EPA supported this policy. However, the FDA faced considerable pressure from consumer advocates and citizen groups to prevent GM material from entering the food system, or at least to label foods that contain GM material. After deciding that most genetically modified organisms (GMOs) are safe for human consumption—a controversial decision in its own right—the FDA decided that labels are unnecessary.

The no-labeling decision of the FDA appeared to contradict a basic ethical consideration: People have a moral right to choose what they put in their bodies, especially what they eat. If some people object to GMOs or biotechnology generally on religious or cultural grounds, or perceive risks in GMOs, then governments must respect their right not to consume such items. Even if those who object to GMOs are scientifically incorrect in their assessment of risk, they are nevertheless entitled to have their rights protected. This is an ongoing ethical dilemma that the FDA will face as long as GM foods are allowed on the market and are not labeled (Thompson 2007).

NEW CHALLENGES

Industrialization and Concentration

The industrialization of agriculture during the twentieth century was marked by numerous changes in both the methods and structure of agriculture. The "industrialization of agriculture" is a catchphrase for a broad set of changes that have occurred in agriculture in the United States and other developed countries over the last one hundred years. Its main features are as follows:

- The transition from animal-powered farming techniques to machine power, with its attendant need for electrical or petrochemical fuel.
- The transition from the use of inputs (seed, fertilizers, and pest control measures) produced on the farm and reused yearly to the purchase of inputs from nonfarm sources, such as seed companies.
- The transition from small- to medium-sized farms, worked by a farm family and a few hired hands, to large-scale farms where

all workers are hired and the farm manager may not even be the
farm owner.
- The transition from localized and seasonal farm markets to regional,
national, and international markets and "seasonal" produce available
year-round.
- The transition from numerous independent farm producers supplying
markets and processing firms to a relatively small number of large farm
producers supplying commodities under contract to processing firms.

The industrialization of agriculture is not simply the transition from a primarily
manual labor–based enterprise to a more technologically based production system.
The biological, economic, and sociological dimensions of agricultural have changed
in important ways as well.

Two socioeconomic changes stand out: (1) the first related to the structure of
the agricultural sector; and (2) the second concerning the size and number of food
processors. Currently the United States has what is called a "bipolar" agricultural
structure. Of the nearly two million farms in the United States, fewer than 25
percent produce more than 80 percent of foodstuffs Americans consume. Ownership patterns have changed as well. While most small- and midsize farms are
single-family proprietorships or family-owned corporations, many of the largest
and greatest revenue-producing farms are owned by corporations whose primary
enterprise is not agricultural. For example, many farms are owned by petrochemical companies, restaurant chains, and a consortium of urban-based investors.

One could argue that the structural changes are simply the logical result of
the technological transformation of agriculture. As long as consumers continue
to spend a relatively small portion of their income on agricultural products and
remain happy with the outcome of agriculture's industrialization, there is little
cause for concern, economic, ethical, or otherwise. The cause for concern with
increased size and concentration of production in farms is that, despite USDA
and EPA regulations and a general adherence to the standards for Good Agricultural Practices (GAP) stipulated by the Food and Agricultural Organization of the
United Nations (FAO), mistakes and oversights happen. Even though most farmers
are committed to the goals of GAP—improving the safety and quality of food and
other agricultural products—consider the number outbreaks of food contamination from produce grown by large farm operations in the United States.

While anecdotal, these outbreaks suggest that the size and market control of
modern industrial farm operations may make them more prone to mishandling
their produce. This is not to say all do; indeed, one might find these numbers amaz-
ingly low compared to the total amount of produce grown and shipped. Still, as the
FAO (2009) points out, "GAP implementation and especially record keeping and
certification will increase production costs," and these costs increase exponentially

with the size of farms. It is not surprising that there are risks associated with the production of so much food by so few large-scale operations, as farm operations attempt to minimize costs—including costs of implementing GAP.

Food safety is also affected by the large size of and small number of food product processors ("manufacturers"). As Hendrickson and Heffernan (2006) point out, in 2005,

- four beef-packing firms controlled 85 percent of the market;
- four millers controlled 63 percent of milled grain market;
- five firms control 57 percent of supermarket sales; and
- four firms control 57 percent of poultry processing.

As critics of "agribusiness" frequently argue, this kind of corporate control inevitably affects the riskiness of foods. The Food Safety and Inspection Service inspected over five thousand meat-processing plants in 2006 and found that only 50 percent tested raw meat before further processing; only 21 percent tested raw poultry before processing (FSIS 2007b). As recent scares over contaminated ground beef indicate (FSIS 2007a), there are serious flaws in the animal products processing/distribution system that can be attributed in part to the power the agribusiness firms have over the food chain—and their frequent lack of attention to their responsibility to test to assure the safety of the foods they process and sell. Little wonder that consumers have reported concern about processed, packaged foodstuffs marketed by large agribusiness firms (Food Processing.com 2007).

The USDA and FDA anticipated these concerns by introducing, in 1996, the HACCP System—Hazard Analysis and Critical Control Points—which is intended to be a public-private collaborative effort to reduce food risks. Essentially, HACCP identifies points in the production-processing chain (mainly in food animal production) where hazards are likely to occur and then permits companies to certify that hazards at those "control points" have been minimized (FDA 2009a). Companies are supposed to have a trained inspector and HACCP plan for every product produced. However, as of 2006, only 50 percent of the 5,300 meat-processing plants surveyed by FSIS had a quality-control agent or department (FSIS 2007b). Ideally intended to reduce the need for USDA inspections, promoters of HACCP have pointed to successes in preventing more occurrences of contaminated meats. Yet outbreaks have continued to occur, and consumers remain concerned that neither the manufacturers nor government agencies are fulfilling their obligations.

Globalization

A second trend that is affecting food safety concerns and raising ethical questions is the globalization of the food system, in particular, food imports into the United States. Closely connected with the concentration of production and processing/distribution, the United States currently imports over 40 percent of its fruit, 15 percent of its vegetables, and 80 percent of its fish and seafood (Hoffman and Hooker 2009). While the majority of fruit and vegetables are imported from NAFTA trading partners Canada and Mexico, the remainder of those items and most seafood are brought into the United States through its ports. The 361 US commercial ports receive 95 percent of imports by weight and 75 percent by value, with the nine million shipping containers that arrive yearly accounting for 66 percent of total maritime trade value (Frittelli 2005). Although food accounts for only 4.2 percent of total US imports (WRI 2009), it has been estimated that the average American diet includes 18 percent of imported food per year (Brooks, Buzby, and Regmi 2009; Jerardo 2005).

The ethical issues in this situation arise from two factors: (1) many other nations from whom we import do not have the same environmental or health regulations and practices as the United States; and (2) the US regulatory system is not equipped to inspect or guarantee the safety of all the food imported into the country. As a result, consumers are being put at risk once again, with no visible recourse.

Despite the environmental and human health provisions of the North American Free Trade Agreement (NAFTA), the Central American Free Trade Agreement (CAFTA), and the "sanitary and phytosanitary" rules governing trade established by the World Trade Organization (WTO), many nations do not have acceptable (to the United States) environmental and health regulations and practices. Four-fifths of total US food imports are from high-income countries such as Canada and the European Union, which do have high standards and practices. However, there has been a loss of market share for these countries since 2007, which has been accompanied by a growth in US import market share from developing countries, particularly middle-income countries such as Mexico, Chile, and China. In many cases, middle- and lower-income countries do not have as extensive or effective food safety standards, practices, and regulations in place as those in the United States or other more developed countries. As Buzby and Regmi (2009) have pointed out, most food safety violations come from these middle- and lower-income countries, and the Food and Drug Administration has a policy of refusing imports from countries with a history of food safety or environmental violations. The FDA issues "Import Alerts" to its field agents and inspectors when a nation or manufacturer or particular shipper has been found in violation of food safety regulations, and the agency can then apply a "Detain without Physical Examination" order for those imports until proof is offered about the safety of the imported goods (FDA 2009b).

However, in 2007, the FDA conducted inspections on only 1.3 percent of the food that it regulates (vegetables, fruit, seafood, grains, dairy, and animal feed) at ports and southern and northern borders—down from an already disconcertingly low 8 percent prior to NAFTA and WTO agreements. Only 11 percent of beef, pork, and chicken imported in 2007 was inspected at the US-Canadian and US-Mexican borders by the US Department of Agriculture (Public Citizen 2009).

Although products enter the United States through 361 ports, in 2007 the FDA had inspectors on-site at only 90 of these ports. In 2009 the agency likely covered half that number. To increase inspections of FDA-regulated imports to 10 percent (still a strikingly low figure) would require an additional 1,600 full-time inspectors. To double that figure to 20 percent import inspection would require 3,200 full-time inspectors and $540 million, according to FDA estimates recently reported to the Subcommittee on Oversight and Investigations (of the House Energy and Commerce Committee) (DeWaal 2007). Even with the call for stepped-up inspections by the Obama administration, such additional funding is unlikely. Hence, Americans remain at risk for food safety contamination from imported foods. The government is unable to keep the public good associated with food safety from these sources.

Agri-Food Bioterrorism

Since the September 11, 2001, terrorist attacks on the United States, the notion of food safety has taken on a new meaning, closely associated with what used to be called food security. Because of how vulnerable consumers are to intentional food contamination with anything from toxins to carcinogens, and despite calls for stepped-up efforts to protect agriculture, monitor food processing more closely, and more aggressively inspect food distribution centers, the US food system remains vulnerable.

There have only been 365 cases of malicious food poisonings documented worldwide since 1950 (72 percent of which were caused by an individual attempting to kill or injure another single person) (Dalziel 2009). Nevertheless, since early 2002, the Food and Drug Administration, the US Department of Agriculture, the US Department of Homeland Security, and nearly every state government have instituted some sort of plan or policy regarding agri-food bioterrorism (National Center for Food Protection and Defense 2009). Although the United States has not had a direct terrorist attack since 2001, government agencies maintain that the threat of agri-food bioterrorism remains very real.

Risks from agri-food bioterrorism are of course closely connected with the concentration of agricultural production/processing/distribution and with global trade in food, but there are two other independent reasons why this is a unique threat: (1) the "wide-open spaces" nature of American farms and ranches; and (2) the national nature of our food distribution network, that is, the lengthy distances that most of our food travels from farm gate to consumer, sometimes called "food miles."

The United States is a land of farms. Farms and ranches cover roughly 40 percent of the land in the Lower 48 states, with the predominance of croplands situated in the middle third of the country. With so much land in farming and ranching, and with the freedom of movement that citizens and visitors (legal or illegal) enjoy across the country, a deliberate act of terrorism against agricultural production is not only possible but feasible. As Wheelis (2000) argues, many potential sites for release of an animal contaminant, such as auction houses, have very low security. Access to large numbers of animals with destinations all over the country or a region is simple and easy. Seeds, fertilizers, and pesticides provide routes for infection of crop plants, although of somewhat higher (but still not robust) security. And of course pastures and fields themselves have essentially no security at all.

The Food Safety and Inspection Service has encouraged farmers and ranchers to implement what it calls functional food defense plans (FFDPs) (FSIS 2007b). These are on-site strategies whereby farmers look for vulnerable points at the establishment, determine what the risk factor is for each point, develop defense measures at each point identified as high risk, and create a written plan to implement defense measures. Defense measures are actions taken to build barriers or shields around vulnerable areas to prevent intentional product adulteration. The defense measures that an establishment develops can be physical barriers such as locks, fences, and cameras, or the measures can be changes in procedures such as limited access, escorting visitors, or supervising contract employees. Despite the national security and food safety rationale for FFDPs, the FSIS 2006 survey of producers showed that growers' adoption of such plans as of August 2006 was only 27 percent. The FSIS goal of a food defense plan adoption rate of 90 percent by 2010 was not reached. However, survey results showed that, in 2010, 74 percent of respondents had a defense plan in place. FSIS now has set a 90 percent adoption rate as its 2015 goal. How likely it is that this will be reached is not clear; given many farmers' continued negative perceptions of government "intervention," a 90 percent adoption rate may be slow to arrive or may never be achieved.

Clearly associated with the geographical size of the United States and the placement of its "breadbasket" far from most major urban centers on both coasts, is the fact that food travels great distances, even within the country, to major markets. A 2003 study showed that for sixteen typical fresh produce items, the "weighted average source distance" (in this case to Iowa, in the middle of the breadbasket) was 1,494 miles, and the sum of food miles for the same sixteen items was 25,301 miles—greater than the circumference of the earth (Pirog and Benjamin 2003). Much of this produce is shipped via railroad: as anyone who has observed railcars filled with corn or oats can attest, access at grain elevators, switching yards, and even due to the slow movement of long trains is virtually unlimited. For foods shipped via truck, the porous system of truck stops, highways, back roads, and the like also make access easy. Anyone intending to introduce a microbial or chemical contaminant would have a clear opportunity.

While the US Department of Agriculture has 723 plant quarantine and inspection stations located across the country, mostly at ports, border crossings, and frequently on interstate highways, the agency does not check for chemical or biological contamination, instead focusing on examination of the physical properties of the products inspected: is a product legal, intact, spoiled, mispackaged in some way? Again, it would be relatively easy for a bioterrorist to introduce a biotoxin into a shipment, which may not even be detected when the product reaches its final destination at a processing plant, distribution warehouse, or commercial outlet. It is actually surprising that even homegrown terrorists have not used the food system as a means to generate harm or fear. Despite the efforts of government agencies, the agri-food system remains a viable target for such activities.

A Fatally Flawed System of Oversight?

Given the above, it might be argued that the new challenges facing US food safety inspection/regulatory agencies and their responses to date show how antiquated, poorly conceived, and inefficient these agencies are, and how therefore they necessarily fail to keep the public good associated with food safety. The rejoinder is that governments—not just in the United States—have always had to monitor private industry involved in food production, processing, and distribution. Governments have always had to control imports and exports of any merchandise, food included. And the nature of agriculture, especially in a large land mass such as the United States (or Brazil, Canada, France, Russia, China, India, etc.) has always posed a problem in terms of vulnerability to natural or human-made disasters, and in terms of the need to transport foods over long distances to more heavily populated urban centers.

The current situation illustrates how important it is that sufficient personnel and resources be devoted to this effort—to satisfy the government's ethical responsibility to keep our food supply safe and secure. The problem is not that the government is not trying to fulfill its responsibilities. There are just too many actors, factors, and product and information "flows" for governments to perform perfectly, given current constraints. Defenders of the USDA, FSIS, and FDA can legitimately point out that the occasional "food scares," whether the result of domestic mistakes or tainted imports, are just that: occasional. The fact that there have been no documented agri-food bioterrorist attacks (even since September 11, 2001) suggests either that no attempts have been made or—more likely—that any planned attacks were prevented by good intelligence and hasty action. In sum, the government agencies responsible for securing our food seem to have acted responsibly both in terms of their official missions and their ethical responsibilities.

Nevertheless, a number of calls have come forth for a restructuring of our food system. A variety of reasons have been offered for this, from the presumed inherent environmental and health risks associated with industrial agriculture and a global and national market distribution system, to the "more sustainable" and controllable nature of a system of small, local producers and distribution centers.

LOCAL FOOD: A NEW FOOD SAFETY PARADIGM?

There is an underlying theme in the missions and visions of various social networks and activist movements concerned with local or community-supported agriculture, and now the "slow food" movement, that locally grown and marketed foods are safer than conventionally grown and processed foods, that is, the foods provided to us long-distance by industrial agriculture and the large food manufacturing and importing firms. Two lines of thought can be gleaned from this theme: (1) locally grown and marketed meats and produce are usually marketed as "whole foods" and hence are not subjected to the industrial processes that even unintentionally go awry: botulism in canned vegetable, *E. coli* in ground meats, *Salmonella* in chickens, and so on. That is, locally grown and marketed foods are less susceptible to the unintentional contamination that comes with some imported foods or any intentional adulteration that might be induced by a bioterrorist (see LocalHarvest.org 2009; Locavores.com 2009). And (2) locally grown and distributed food systems represent a structure that is more sustainable. By "sustainability," advocates mean that a local food system is more environmentally friendly and hence healthier for humans and animals, is more economically viable over the long term, and is more socially just. Sustainability advocates further argue that a local food system is fundamentally more safe and secure than our current system, since monitoring, rules enforcement, and quality assurance operate in a generally informal, community-based fashion (see SustainableTable.org 2009).

It is true that most locally produced and marketed foods are sold as whole foods. Smaller supermarkets in some cities rely on local growers to supply meat, eggs, and produce, which they frequently can sell at prices below major supermarket chain prices. Moreover, they can (legitimately) advertise their food as "fresh from the farm" and (truly) "vine-ripened" tomatoes. The same is true at local farmers' markets. (In fact, some farmers' markets have rules against selling any processed or "value-added" items such as fruit jams or sun-dried vegetables, for example, sun-dried tomatoes.) Local supermarkets and farmers' markets frequently have their own "sanitation" rules—products purchased locally must be washed and dried by the producer and delivered within a specified period after harvest (usually a day or two). Individual states' laws govern the sale of unpasteurized (raw) milk and homemade sausages (Kennedy 2004).

While local and farmers' markets have existed probably since the beginning of agriculture, the impetus for the growth of these entities in recent years (and the heightened calls for public policy to encourage and support them) stemmed in part from some consumers' expressed desire for organic foods, which for a long time were only available from smaller-scale local operations in some areas. The idea of pesticide-free produce and biologic-free meat products conjures up images of "wholesome" and "healthy" food in many people's minds, and farmers and local communities converged to establish markets for these commodities. There are of course trade-offs: organic production is (or at least has been until now) a more labor-intensive form of production, and hence produce and meats are more expensive. Nevertheless, community-supported local organic production spurred the greater movement toward local production and distribution in general. Even in large cities there are now markets (either supermarket types or farmers' markets) that are either exclusively or predominantly organic. In either case, the vast majority of the products in these markets are locally grown.

Despite the common conception that locally grown whole and especially organic foods are more safe than those produced on large-scale industrialized farms, numerous studies have shown that (a) safety depends on the actual agricultural methods used by local growers; and (b) organic foods may contain no inorganic pesticide residues or animal biologics but still may not be as safe as an imported counterpart. Indeed, in the case of the farmer, there must be some guarantee (certified organic, certified HACCP, certified GAP) that what is delivered to market actually is free of known food risk factors. There is no a priori reason to believe that just because the weighted average source distance from farm to market is, say, 56 miles, the food is any safer than the identical commodities shipped 1,800 miles across country. Moreover, some studies suggest that most organic plants contain high levels of nitrogen and carcinogens produced by plants themselves fighting off diseases and pests (see, e.g., Trewavas 2001; Lovejoy 1994). Whole foods—regardless of the source—may *seem* healthier and more nutritious than processed and packaged foods, but that is in part because the consumer prepares a "wholesome" real meal at home. However, it has been shown that the vitamin content of fresh and frozen vegetables is the same (Favell 1998).

Locally grown and purchased whole foods (whether organic or not) might address some of the emerging issues in food safety, but in the end the geographical size of the United States, the relatively long distances from our most productive agricultural areas, the diverse climates, and ultimately, the ever-present threat to food systems—global, national, and local—from potential agri-food terrorists are enough reasons to believe that this option is not the answer to food safety concerns. Moreover, consumers want fresh produce out of their local season, and the demand for imported chocolates, wines, and cheeses continues to grow. The appeal of locally produced foods and local markets may be motivated in part by a concern for food safety. However, the stronger appeal may be that local or community food systems are more sustainable than the current structure of global industrial agriculture. A thorough discussion of the theory and practice of "sustainability" is far beyond the scope of this chapter, but some remarks concerning sustainability, safety, and the public good are in order. The theory of sustainability is the idea that we should "meet present needs without compromising the ability of future generations to meet their needs" (WCED 1987). In practice, this means that our society—and all our practices, including food production—should be structured so that we are economically viable over the long term and conservation- and restoration-oriented in our use of natural resources, and that our institutions are just and equitable. These are the so-called three legs of the sustainability stool, or the triple bottom line, of a socially responsible accounting.

Making local agriculture sustainable means avoiding the "unsustainable" practices of industrial agriculture, especially the use of petroleum-based agricultural chemicals, and eschewing the lengthy food miles that global industrial agriculture entails. It means that local communities engage in better stewardship over their natural resource base—which includes farms and ranches. And it means that small-scale farmers should be rewarded for their efforts in producing food for local consumption and taking care of their farms and families. There is no direct connection to food safety as it is generally thought of, but the idea is that a sustainable community/society/world will necessarily be healthier in both a human and environmental sense. Hence, a safe and secure food supply is a fortuitous by-product of sustainable practices. In fact, in a future utopian sustainable community on a global level, environmental problems will have been solved, alternative energy sources for food production and all industry will have been found, the poverty and ignorance that breeds much terrorist ideology and practices will have been eliminated, and the world's population will have stabilized at levels that would allow greater food self-sufficiency at the local level. A safe and secure food system would be taken for granted.

CONCLUDING REFLECTIONS

Most ethical considerations of food safety have for the past several years focused on: (a) ethical concerns about the theory and practice of using scientific risk assessment in determining the safety of new products or ingredients; (b) concerns about the process by which the Food and Drug Administration approves new foods and especially new food additives; and (c) concerns about whether food labels—when required by the FDA—give consumers all the information they might want in order to make informed choices about the foods they purchase. Each of these concerns made their way into larger public debate in the case of GM foods or ingredients of foodstuffs.

Regarding the ethical concerns about using scientific risk assessment to determine food safety, it has been argued that scientific risk assessment (and management) is an imprecise tool. Test results are only as good as the tests; and while the tests have rapidly improved over the years (e.g., ascertaining parts per billion as opposed to parts per million), there remains a degree of uncertainty associated with any judgment that risks associated with a food are acceptable. Critics of GM foods claimed early on that the novelty of these foods and food ingredients, and the fact that there was no long-standing scientific or regulatory history associated with them, demanded a stronger testing requirement and generally a go-slow approach. It was suggested, for example, that a "precautionary principle" should be followed in assessing GM foods: these new foods should be evaluated using a "guilty till proven innocent" criterion. In other words, GM foods should not be allowed on the market until it can be shown, through years of rigorous testing, that there are absolutely no harmful effects associated with them.

The FDA responded by invoking what is called the doctrine of "substantial equivalence," which means focusing on the specific product being proposed for approval, rather than the means by which the product came to be, and determining whether the new product is the same as the previously approved one for regulatory purposes. That a new soybean happens to have been genetically engineered means nothing if it is physically, biologically, and chemically the same as a conventionally bred soybean. GM foods that meet the doctrine of criterion equivalence need no additional testing. This debate still goes on, now supplemented with the concern that the whole FDA regulatory apparatus is flawed (see Thompson 2007; Burkhardt 2008).

Indeed, regarding food labels, the issue is that, until recently, the FDA did not require companies submitting new food products for approval to provide the data from their internal (or contracted-out) food safety evaluations. Instead, the FDA required only a report on the results of those tests. When the product (e.g., a GM food) had already been determined to be substantially equivalent and the new product and its ingredients fell within "generally recognized as safe" guidelines, no further analysis was needed (Shanklin and Sánchez 2005). Critics suggested that this revealed collusion between the food industry and the FDA and risked endangering the public; the industry can falsify data and results in order to get a product approved. The FDA responded that companies have good public relations and criminal liability reasons not to falsify reports submitted to the FDA. Although the agency did begin requesting data from companies in 2001, and now requires companies seeking FDA approval to submit a summary of data, the FDA is unlikely to examine most of the data.

The food labeling issue that has raised most of the ethical concern and public debate has surrounded GM foods, which, as noted above, was resolved in favor of the industry's claims (and the FDA's judgment) that no labels are necessary for GM foods already deemed safe (see Burkhardt 2008). Nevertheless, the principle that consumers have the right to know what is in their food, even if the government has determined that the food is safe, remains important. As one critic recently wrote, "Our food choices are not simply a matter of satisfying our biological needs. Indeed, our consumption more broadly reflects a whole mess of values that are not simply economic" (Stemwedel 2009). As Thompson (2007) has argued in a variety of forums, freedom of choice or autonomy is an utmost ethical consideration in the food ethics arena, and governments cannot legislate what is or is not important to individuals. Some companies have begun to voluntarily label their non-GM foods as "GM free" or "Contains no genetically modified ingredients" as a way of capturing a market niche for individuals opposed to GM foods for reasons of a "whole mess of values." Given that the European Union does require labeling for GM foods, this is one issue that will not be resolved anytime soon.

The importance of the concerns about the scientific adequacy and impartiality of FDA regulation, and the ethical correctness of decisions about there being no food safety–related reasons for labeling GM foods, are indisputable. However, my focus in this chapter is not on individual consumers' preferences or individuals versus the government when it comes to food safety decisions. Individuals do matter, and consumers and farmers and food corporations do have interests and rights regarding food safety. However, my concern is with the food system as a whole and the responsibilities of actors who are part of this system. I have argued that governments are the best agents to ensure the safety of the food system and the food this system provides us. The means governments have employed to address their ethical responsibilities vis-à-vis the food system may have flaws and may occasionally appear overly paternalistic or even corrupt. But government-led efforts to induce private actors into safer practices such as GAP and HACCP suggest that regulation and monitoring are improving, as are public communications encouraging consumers to engage in safe handling practices. In the end, when we look at trends such as concentration of agricultural production and manufacturing, the globalization of the food trade, and also at the threat of agri-food bioterrorism, good government action is the best alternative to address the safety (and security) issues these situations call for. It is governments' ethical responsibility to keep the public good, whether with regard to food safety, environmental health, national security, or social justice. As citizens, we should hold our government agencies accountable for this responsibility, demand efficiency and effectiveness, and support the allocation of resources to allow them to better fulfill their responsibilities to secure the public good.

APPENDIX 1

US Government Agencies Responsible for Food Safety:
Mission Statements

Food and Drug Administration. The Food and Drug Administration of the US Department of Health and Human Services is responsible for protecting the public health by assuring the safety, efficacy, and security of human and veterinary drugs, biological products, medical devices, our nation's food supply, cosmetics, and products that emit radiation. The Food and Drug Administration is also responsible for advancing the public health by helping to speed innovations that make medicines and foods more effective, safer, and more affordable; and helping the public get the accurate, science-based information they need to use medicines and foods to improve their health.

Environmental Protection Agency. The mission of the Environmental Protection Agency is to protect human health and the environment. Since 1970 the Environmental Protection Agency has been working for a cleaner, healthier environment for the American people.

US Department of Agriculture, Animal and Plant Health Inspection Service. The Animal and Plant Health Inspection Service is responsible for protecting and promoting US agricultural health, administering the Animal Welfare Act, and carrying out wildlife-damage management activities.

US Department of Agriculture, Food Safety and Inspection Service. The Food Safety and Inspection Service is the public health agency in the US Department of Agriculture responsible for ensuring that the nation's commercial supply of meat, poultry, and egg products is safe, wholesome, and correctly labeled and packaged.

Sources: US government agency websites.

REFERENCES

Associated Press. 2009. "Obama Bans 'Downer' Cows from Food Supply: President Says Current Food Safety System is a 'Hazard to Public Health.'" March 14. www.msnbc.msn .com/id/29691788.

Berry, W. 1977. *The Unsettling of America.* San Francisco: Sierra Club Books.

BLM (Bureau of Land Management). 2009. "What Are Best Management Practices?" US Department of the Interior, BLM. www.blm.gov/wo/st/en/prog/energy/oil_and_gas/ best_management_practices.html.

Brooks N., J. C. Buzby, and A. Regmi. 2009. "Globalization and Evolving Preferences Drive U.S. Food Import Growth." *Journal of Food Distribution Research* 40 (1): 39–46.

Burkhardt, J. 2008. "The Ethics of Agri-Food Biotechnology: How Can an Agricultural Technology be so Important?" In *What Can Nanotechnology Learn from Biotechnology*, ed. L. David and P. Thompson, 55–78. New York: Academic Press.

Buzby, J.C., and A. Regmi. 2009. "FDA Refusals of Food Imports by Exporting Country Group." *Choices* 24 (2): 11–15.

Buzby, J.C., L. Unnevehr, and D. Roberts. 2008. *Food Safety and Imported Food: An Analysis of FDA Food-Related Import Refusal Reports.* EIB 39. Washington, DC: US Department of Agriculture, Economic Research Service.

Caswell, J. A. 1998. "Valuing the Benefits and Costs of Improved Food Safety and Nutrition." *Australian Journal of Agricultural and Resource Economics* 42 (4): 409–24.

CDC (Centers for Disease Control and Prevention). 2009. "FoodNet Facts and Figures." www.cdc.gov/foodnet/factsandfigures/2009/trends.html.

CNN. 2008. "EU Bans Baby Food with Chinese Milk." September 25. http://edition.cnn.com/2008/WORLD/asiapcf/09/25/china.milk/index.html.

Dalziel, C. R. 2009. *Food Defense Incidents 1950–2008: A Chronology and Analysis of Incidents Involving the Malicious Contamination of the Food Supply Chain.* Singapore: Centre of Excellence for National Security (CENS), S. Rajaratnam School of International Studies, Nanyang Technological University. www.rsis.edu.sg/CENS/publications/reports/RSIS_Food%20Defence_170209.pdf.

DeWaal, C. S. 2007. "Import Inspection Failures and What Must Be Done." *Testimony Before the United States House of Representatives Energy and Commerce Committee's Subcommittee on Oversight and Investigations,* 110th Cong. (July 17).

Fan, M. 2008. "Top Chinese Food Inspector Resigns amid Milk Scandal." *Washington Post,* September 23. www.washingtonpost.com/wpdyn/content/article/2008/09/22/AR2008092200257.html.

FAO (Food and Agricultural Organization of the United Nations). 2002. "Expert Consultation on Food Safety: Science and Ethics." www.fao.org/DOCREP/006/j0776e/j0776e06.htm.

———. 2009. Good Agricultural Practices. www.fao.org/prods/GAP.

Favell, D. J. 1998. "A Comparison of the Vitamin C Content of Fresh and Frozen Vegetables." *Food Chemistry* 62 (1) (May): 59–64.

FDA (Food and Drug Administration). 2009a. "Hazard Analysis and Critical Control Points (HACCP)." www.fda.gov/Food/FoodSafety/HazardAnalysisCriticalControlPointsHACCP/default.htm.

———. 2009b. "Import Alert Retrieval System (FIARS)." www.fda.gov/ora/fiars/ora_import_alerts.html.

Fischoff, B., S. Lichtenstein, P. Slovic, S. L. Derby, and R. Keeney. 1993. *Acceptable Risk.* Cambridge: Cambridge University Press.

Food Processing.com. 2007. "Survey Reveals Eroding Consumer Confidence in Packaged Goods Brands." July 10. www.foodprocessing.com/industrynews/2007/093.html.

Frittelli, J. 2007. *Port and Maritime Security: Background and Issues for Congress.* CRS Report for Congress, Report RL31733. Washington, DC: Congressional Research Service, the Library of Congress.

FSIS (Food Safety Inspection Service). 2007a. "California Firm Recalls Ground Beef for Possible *E. coli* O157:H7 Contamination." Press release, June 3. www.fsis.usda.gov/ News_&_Events/Recall_025_2007_Release/index.asp.

———. 2007b. "Third Food Defense Plan Survey." www.fsis.usda.gov/OPPDE/rdad/ FSISNotices/48-08.pdf.

———. 2010. "Food Defense Plan Survey Results." www.fsis.usda.gov/food_defense_%26_ emergency_response/Food_Defense_Plan_Survey_Results/index.asp.

Hendrickson, M., and W. Heffernan, 2005. *Concentration of Agricultural Markets.* Columbia, MO: Department of Rural Sociology, University of Missouri.

Henson, S., and J. Caswell. 1999. "Food Safety Regulation: An Overview of Contemporary Issues." *Food Policy* 24 (6): 589–603.

Henson, S., and N. H. Hooker. 2001. "Public Sector Management of Food Safety: Public Regulation and the Role of Private Controls." *International Food and Agribusiness Management Review* 4:7–17.

———. 2009. *"Theme Overview:* Emerging Issues in Food Safety.*"* Choices 24 (2): 4–5.

Jerardo, A. 2005. "Americans Have Growing Appetites for Imported Foods." *Amber Waves,* April. www.ers.usda.gov/AmberWaves/April05/findings/GrowingAppetite.htm.

Kennedy, P. 2004. "Summary of Raw Milk Statutes and Administrative Codes." www .realmilk.com/milk-laws-2.html.

Kux, L., J. Sobel, and K. M. Fain. 2007. "Control of Foodborne Diseases." In *Law in Public Health Practice,* ed. R. A. Goodman, 361–84. Oxford: Oxford University Press.

LocalHarvest.org. 2009. www.localharvest.org.

Locavores.com 2009. www.locavores.com.

Lovejoy, S. B. 1994. "Are Organic Foods Safer?" www.inetport.com/~texasbot/lovejy .htm.

National Center for Food Protection and Defense. 2009. "Resources." www.ncfpd.umn .edu/resources.cfm.

Pirog, R., and A. Benjamin. 2003. *Checking the Food Odometer: Comparing Food Miles for Local versus Conventional Produce Sales to Iowa Institutions.* Ames: Leopold Center for Sustainable Agriculture, Iowa State University.

Public Citizen. 2009. "Imported Food and Product Safety." www.citizen.org/trade/food.

Runsten, D. 2008. "Defending Family Farmers: Industrial Food Safety Fallout." www .wildfarmalliance.org/Press%20Room/Runsten_FS.pdf.

Samuelson, P. 1954. "The Pure Theory of Public Expenditure." *Review of Economics and Statistics* 36 (4): 387–89.

Sebelius, K. 2009. "Secretary Sebelius Statement of Food Safety Working Group." US Department of Health and Human Services, press release, May 13.www.hhs.gov/news/ press/2009pres/05/20090513a.html.

Shanklin, A. P., and E. R. Sánchez. 2005. "Regulatory Report: FDA's Food Contact Substance Notification Program." *Food Safety Magazine,* October–November. www.fda.gov/Food/ FoodIngredientsPackaging/FoodContactSubstancesFCS/ucm064161.htm.

Sherry, K. 2009. "Farmers Critical of Food Safety Bill." *Los Angeles Times,* July 17. www .latimes.com/news/nationworld/nation/la-na-food-safety17-2009jul17,0,5036101.story.

Starbird, S. A. 2005. "Moral Hazard, Inspection, and Food Safety." *American Journal of Agricultural Economics* 87 (1): 15–27.

Stemwedel, J. 2009. "Look for the GMO label." *Cognitive Daily,* January 9. http://scienceblogs.com/cognitivedaily/environment.

SustainableTable.org. 2009. www.sustainabletable.org/issues/eatlocal.

Thompson, P. B. 2001. "Risk, Consent and Public Debate: Some Preliminary Considerations for the Ethics of Food Safety." *International Journal of Food Science and Technology* 36 (8) (December): 833–43.

———. 2007. *Food Biotechnology in Ethical Perspective.* 2nd ed. Dordrecht, Netherlands: Springer.

Trewavas, A. J. 2001. "Urban Myths of Organic Farming." *Nature* 410:409–10.

Vilsack, Tom, 2009. "Agriculture Secretary Vilsack's Statements at Food Safety Working Group." US Department of Agriculture, press release, May 13. www.usda.gov/wps/portal/!ut/p/_s.7_0_A/7_0_1OB?contentidonly=true&contentid=2009/05/0164.xml.

WCED (World Council on Economic Development). 1987. "What Is Sustainable Development?" UNESCO. http://portal.unesco.org/en/ev.php-URL_ID=1071&URL_DO=DO_TOPIC&URL_SECTION=201.html.

Wheelis, M. 2000. "Agricultural Biowarfare and Bioterrorism: An Analytical Framework and Recommendations for the Fifth BTWC Review Conference." www.fas.org/bwc/agr/agwhole.htm.

WHO (World Health Organization). 2009. "Food Safety and Foodborne Illness Fact Sheet." www.who.int/mediacentre/factsheets/fs237/en.

WRI (World Resources Institute). 2009. EarthTrends, the Environmental Information Portal. http://earthtrends.wri.org/searchable_db/index.php?theme=8&variable_ID=236&action=select_countries.

The Myth of Happy Meat

Richard P. Haynes

Happy Meats is proud to be listed in the River Cottage Meat Book and be a Rick Stein Food Hero. We are a specialist producer of superb free range, rare breed meat, where welfare is put first. Traditional old British and Irish breed of pig, lamb and cattle are reared outside on chemical free food. The result is quality tasty meat which you can trust.

Our rare breed animals have a great life. Our Gloucester old spot pigs are born and raised outside and fed on simple, natural additive free food. We avoid the use of routine antibiotics and do not use artificial fertilizers and sprays on our land. Our Soay and Jacobs lamb, Dexter and Belted Galloway cattle roam freely and graze on the lush grass and traditional pasture herbs in the lovely Teme Valley. (HappyMeats 2011)

While the idea of transferring the happiness of a live animal to its dead body—the meat—may seem absurd, the real message here is that animals raised under certain conditions are happy (well-off, have a high quality of life, have good welfare) and that their premature death does not affect this happiness. This thesis is common to what is often referred to as the "animal welfare movement" as opposed to the "animal rights" or "animal liberation" movement.[1] Animal welfarists, while advocating the reform of current practices in the use of nonhuman animals in research and for food, argue that suitably reformed practices would make these practices morally acceptable because they would be consistent with promoting the welfare of the animals used. Even though most animals used in research are eventually euthanized, and animals used for meat are slaughtered at a premature age,[2] welfarists tend to claim that death is not a harm, or that it is a fair exchange for the services provided for the animal during its lifetime.[3] Other justifications of animal use in science include the claim that scientists have an interest in animal welfare because happy animals make the best models for good science and that professional caretakers, such as attending veterinarians, are the best judge of the welfare of the animals under their care. Animal rightists or liberationists, on the other hand, oppose these uses, though it is not clear the extent to which Peter Singer, for example, would oppose adequately reformed practices.[4]

The disagreement between welfarists and liberationists clearly hinges on how we conceptualize welfare or happiness and then apply this conceptualization to nonhuman animals.[5] Although discussions about how to properly conceptualize (or define) animal welfare has played only a background role among scientist users of animals in research, the topic has came to play a major role among farm animal welfare scientists, mostly in Europe and Canada.[6] Most of the conceptualizations offered,[7] I argue, are mistaken; with correct conceptualizations, the difference between welfarists and liberationists would, for all practical purposes, disappear. That is the major thesis of this chapter.

In what follows, I first present what I consider to be the most plausible theory of human welfare. Then I show how this theory can be applied to nonhuman animals. Finally, I lay out what I consider to be the ethical implications of this application concerning how we should treat nonhuman animals.

A THEORY OF HUMAN WELFARE

Appleby and Sandøe (2002), in arguing that there are no conclusive reasons to support a particular theory of animal welfare, first lay out the three types of theories of human welfare (quality of life) and claim that there are no clear reasons to support any one of them over the rest. They first divide theories of human welfare into objective and subjective theories; then they subdivide subjective theories into hedonistic and preference satisfaction theories. Objective theories provide a list of goods, the possession of which warrant us to say that the possessor has a high quality of life, whether or not the possessor concurs in this judgment. Hedonistic theories claim that the possession of certain subjective states, such as feelings of pleasure, make the possessor well-off. Preference satisfaction theories maintain that someone is well-off to the extent that his or her preferences are satisfied (whether the person knows that or not).

These authors do not mention another subjective theory, the one that I consider to be the most plausible. This is the theory developed by Sumner (1996).[8] After finding fault with objective theories and with the two versions of subjective theories described by Appleby and Sandøe, Sumner offers his own theory and then defends it. Sumner's theory is that someone is well-off to the extent that he or she is justifiedly satisfied with life. Justified satisfaction is important because someone may be satisfied with life owing to oppressive socialization to expect little. Sumner uses the term "autonomy" to convey this requirement. Even though it is reasonable to develop a list of things that standardly have prudential value for humans (or for other species), such as good health, good functioning capacities, and so on, everyone is entitled to decide what criteria to use in evaluating their own life, as long as these criteria are arrived at autonomously. But Sumner's view suggests that individuals have the capacity to appraise their life and their goals, while it is not clear that nonhuman animals have this ability unless they are aware of possibilities that may not be part of their experience. So how can this theory be applied to nonhuman animals?[9]

SUMNER'S THEORY APPLIED TO NONHUMAN ANIMALS

Nonhuman animals may not be in a position to appraise their lives unless they are aware of possible lives they could lead were not these possibilities withheld from them. While they might appear to be satisfied with their current lives (they do not seem bored or in pain), this satisfaction cannot be arrived at autonomously. We could say that they have been raised under oppressive conditions and have learned to adapt to them. Therefore, in order to apply Sumner's theory to nonhuman animals, we must step in and perform the role of appraiser. To do this, we would have to be aware of the sorts of activities and amenities a particular animal and its species are capable of enjoying or finding rewarding. How to do this is a problem. Even animals in the wild, especially in harsh conditions, may lead a far from ideal life. But if we narrow the context to animals raised by humans, or animals whose environment humans control, which is relevant to the question of whether animals raised for food or for use in research (or for any other form of work, in fact) have an acceptable life, then the question of an adequately rich environment seems to become more manageable.

Here, a knowledge of what enables an animal to flourish, to use a word that Martha Nussbaum and others use, is helpful. According to Nussbaum, the (good) capabilities that nonhuman animals share with humans, and that animals are entitled to enjoy include life, bodily health, bodily integrity, senses, imagination, and thought, emotions, practical reason, affiliation, living with other species, play, and control over one's environment (Nussbaum 2004).[10] While Nussbaum seems to hold an objectivist theory of welfare, the list she provides can still be used as a list of things that standardly have prudential value for animals of different species. Her account of animals flourishing is certainly preferable to the efforts of food animal welfare scientists to find out what sorts of environments food animals prefer.[11]

The "preference tests" that food animal welfare scientists suggest employing are generally set against the background of a given environment, the one usually used in raising an animal for food, and seem only to seek out what single changes might improve the animal's welfare (e.g., single or wide stalls, perches or wire floors).[12] Perhaps an important exception to this narrower use of preference tests is the "pig park" suggested by Stolba and Wood-Gush (1984). It seems typical of the efforts of food animal welfare scientists, as well as others seeking to reform but not eliminate the raising of animals for food, to assume that raising animals for food under suitably reformed conditions makes the practice morally acceptable. But this assumption is based on the claim that a premature death is not a harm and does not affect the quality of life of the animals; or, that it is a reasonable price for an animal to pay for the room, board, and health care provided for it. Since this assumption raises the question about what our moral responsibilities are toward the animals we raise for food, let us now turn to that question.

WHAT DO WE OWE ANIMALS WE RAISE?

If we raise an animal or otherwise control its environment, then we stand in a custodial-ward relationship to it analogous to the parent-child relationship. By controlling the animal's environment, we limit the ability of that animal to choose its own life, making us responsible for providing the best life possible for it. This is not only true for animals removed from the wild but for animals that are not capable of fending for themselves were they to become feral. Most domesticated animals fit into this category. Just as a prospective parent must consider whether he or she has the means and ability to adequately provide for a prospective child, animal custodians have the same responsibilities. They should not undertake to limit an animal's ability to choose the sort of life that is best for it unless they are willing and able to provide that life for it. I am not sure what moral principle supports this claim other than the principle that we should not undertake responsibilities that we are not able and willing to fulfill. What implications does this principle have for what relationships with animals are morally acceptable and what uses are morally permissible?

As I have argued elsewhere (Haynes 2008, ch. 17), animals as workers present several problems, whether the custodian bred and raised the animal or acquired it from others. Included in the worker category are a large range of activities, such as working dogs (watchdogs, seeing-eye dogs, police dogs), draft animals, animals used in research, animals used for their products (eggs, wool, milk, manure), animals used for pest control and for maintaining pastures or controlling the growth of unwanted vegetation, and animals used in entertainment and in displays, such as zoos and aquariums. Since the custodian generally controls the off-work environment of the working animal, this environment must be such as to foster the animal's flourishing when it is not working. The off-work environment must provide the working animal with the social environment that it needs to flourish. In cases where the social environment is a human one, then the person(s) using the animal must provide a loving atmosphere that encourages human-animal bonding. If an animal is acquired, then presumably it has been taken from a different environment, and this change of environment poses special problems. A separate problem is whether the working animal (assuming that the work is not just the exercising of some capability that permits a flourishing activity) receives a fair exchange of value for its work.

Possible exceptions to the very demanding responsibilities undertaken by an animal custodian are cases of rescuing animals in distress or of protecting ourselves or others from a dangerous animal. Here our obligations depend on what other resources are available elsewhere and what we can afford.

The general point here is that responsible animal custodians must eliminate any exploitative uses of their animal wards and must make every reasonable effort to promote their welfare. Of course, this implies that the use of animals in terminal studies in science is prohibited, as is the premature "euthanization" of animals when they are retired, and it certainly prohibits a premature termination of an animal's life in order to use it for food.[13] In short, a *true welfarist* who accepts my account of animal welfare would be a sterner liberationist than Singer, for example, who does not consider death for most animals a harm. Singer would fall into the camp of those welfarists who think that suitably reformed practices would permit the raising and killing of animals for food. But if we agree with Sapontzis (1987, ch. 9), for example, that life is instrumentally good because it enables us to experience good things, then taking it deprives its victim of this ability.

CONCLUSION

As I said above, the disagreement between welfarists and liberationists clearly hinges on how we conceptualize welfare or happiness and then apply this conceptualization to nonhuman animals. Most of the conceptualizations offered, I argue here, are mistaken; with correct conceptualizations, the difference between welfarists and liberationists would, for all practical purposes, disappear. Happy meat is simply a myth.

NOTES

1. For a detailed account of the history of these two movements in the United States, see Jasper and Nelkin (1992).

2. Pigs used for meat rarely live beyond nine months, and the life span of lamb and veal is obvious.

3. See, for example, Appleby (1999) and Rollin (1995). For a critique of these arguments, see Haynes (2008, ch. 16).

4. Singer (1979) does not think that death for most nonhuman animals is a harm, and Regan (2004, e.g., 285) seems to allow for the death of an animal when a choice has to be made between a human and a nonhuman death. Varner (1994) argues that liberationists and welfarists are not that far apart, and that a convergence is possible. My thesis is that if welfare is properly conceptualized, the two should be identical.

5. Although Henry Salt (1980) used the term "animal welfare" on at least one occasion, its current use seems to have derived from the use given it by Major C. W. Hume, who founded the University of London Animal Welfare Society in 1926, which subsequently became Universities Federation of Animal Welfare (UFAW). For an account of Hume and the UFAW, see Haynes (2008, ch. 2) as well as the UFAW website (www.ufaw.org.uk/History). The use of the term was imported into the United States by Robert Gesell, whose daughter, Christine Stevens, founded the Animal Welfare Institute (AWI). Prior to this, scientist welfarists in the United States considered themselves part of the animal care movement. For an account of the Animal Care Panel and its subsequent influences, and for the role of the AWI in challenging this movement and in influencing US animal welfare legislation, see Haynes (2008, chs. 3 and 4).

6. See, for example, the works of Rollin (1995); Mensch (1993, 1998); Duncan (1981, 1996, 2004); Fraser (1993); Fraser and Duncan (1998); Fraser and Matthews (1997); Appleby (1999); Appleby and Sandøe (2002); Sandøe (1996, 1999); Sandøe, Christiansen, and Appleby (2003); and Nordenfelt (2006). For an account and critique of farm animal welfare scientists' efforts to define animal welfare, see Haynes (2008, chs. 8–14).

7. In this literature, there seems to be some confusion between defining animal welfare and offering a list of goods that have prudential value to a particular species of animal.

8. Appleby and Sandøe (2002) mention Sumner but refer only to an earlier article.

9. For a more detailed account of Sumner's view and the problems with applying it to nonhumans, see Haynes (2008, xiv–xviii).

10. For my brief account of Nussbaum's theory, see Haynes (2008, ch. 13) and Haynes (2007).

11. The notion of food animal welfare science seems to have arisen from the mandates of the Brambell Commission report in 1965, which was stimulated by the public's reaction to Ruth Harrison's book *Animals Machines* (1964). The report called for studies to find out what would eliminate the more objectionable conditions that food animals are subjected to. For a brief account of the reactions to this report, see Mench (1998) and my account of her summary in Haynes (2008, ch. 7).

12. For an account of, partial support for, but a critique of the dangers of using preference tests, see Duncan and Fraser (1997), Fraser and Matthews (1997), and Haynes (2008, chs. 10 and 11).

13. Comstock (2000) argues that it would be acceptable to euthanize an animal whose life is no longer tolerable and then to use it for food; and Sapontzis (1987, ch. 11) argues that it would be acceptable to use roadkill for food.

REFERENCES

Appleby, M. C. 1999. *What Should We Do about Animal Welfare?* Oxford: Blackwell Science.

Appleby, M. C., and P. Sandøe. 2002. "Philosophical Debate on the Nature of Well-Being: Implications for Animal Welfare." *Animal Welfare* 11 (2002): 283–94.

Brambell, F. R. 1965. *The Report of the Technical Committee to Enquire into the Welfare of Animals Kept under Intensive Livestock Husbandry Systems.* Command Paper no. 2836. London: Her Majesty's Stationery Office.

Comstock, G. L. 2000. "An Alternative Ethic for Animals." In *Livestock, Ethics, and Quality of Life,* ed. J. Hodges and K. Han, 99–118. Wallingford, UK: CABI.

Duncan, I. J. H. 1981. "Animal Rights—Animal Welfare: A Scientific Assessment." *Poultry Science* 60:489–99.

———. 1996. "Animal Welfare Defined in Terms of Feelings." *Acta Agricolae Scandanavica, Section A, Animal Science,* suppl. 27: 29–35.

————. 2004. "A Concept of Welfare Based on Feelings." In *The Well-Being of Farm Animals: Challenges and Solutions*, ed. J. Benson and B.E. Rollin, 85–101. Oxford: Blackwell.

Duncan, I.J.H., and D. Fraser. 1997. "Understanding Animal Welfare." In *Animal Welfare*, ed. M.C. Appleby and B.O. Hughes, 19–31. Wallingford, UK: CABI.

Fraser, D. 1993. "Assessing Animal Well-Being: Common Sense, Uncommon Science." In *Food Animal Well-Being 1993—Conference Proceedings and Deliberations, April 13–15, 1993*, 37–74. Indianapolis, IN: Purdue University, Office of Agricultural Programs.

Fraser, D., and I.J.H. Duncan. 1998. "'Pleasures', 'Pains' and Animal Welfare: Toward a Natural History of Affect." *Animal Welfare* 7:383–96.

Fraser, D., and L.R. Matthews. 1997. "Preference and Motivational Testing." In *Animal Welfare*, ed. M.C. Appleby and B.O. Hughes, 159–71. Wallingford, UK: CABI

Happy Meats. 2011. "Welcome to Happy Meats." www.happymeats.co.uk.

Harrison, R. 1964. *Animal Machines*. London: Vincent Stuart.

Haynes, R. 2007. "Animal Rights and Animal Equality: A Review of Three Recent Books; *Animal Rights: Current Debate and New Directions*, edited by Cass R. Sunstein and Martha C. Nussbaum (Oxford University Press, 2004), *Animal Equality: Language and Liberation*, by Joan Dunayer (Ryce Publishing, 2001), *Speciesism*, by Joan Dunayer (Ryce Publishing, 2004)." *Journal of Agricultural and Environmental Ethics* 20 (6): 533–42.

————. 2008. *Animal Welfare: Competing Conceptions and Their Ethical Implications*. Dordrecht, Netherlands: Springer.

Jasper, J.M., and D. Nelkin. 1992. *The Animal Rights Crusade: The Growth of a Moral Protest*. New York: Free Press.

Mench, J.A. 1993. "Assessing Welfare: An Overview." *Journal of Agricultural and Environmental Ethics* 6 (suppl. 2): 43–53.

————. 1998. "Thirty Years after Brambell: Whither Animal Welfare Science?" *Journal of Applied Animal Welfare Science* 1 (2): 91–102.

Nordenfelt, L. 2006. *Animal and Human Health and Welfare: A Comparative Philosophical Analysis*. Oxford: CABI.

Nussbaum, M.C. 2004. "Beyond 'Compassion and Humanity': Justice for Nonhuman Animals." In *Animal Rights: Current Debates and New Directions*, ed. C.R. Sunstein and M.C. Nussbaum, 299–320. New York: Oxford University Press.

Regan, Tom. 2004. *The Case for Animal Rights*, Updated edition. Berkeley: University of California Press.

Rollin, Bernard E. 1995. *Farm Animal Welfare. Social, Bioethical, and Research Issues*. Ames, IA; Iowa State University Press.

Sandøe P. 1996. "Animal and Human Welfare—Are They the Same Kind of Thing?" *Acta Agriculturae Scandinavica, Section A, Animal Science*, suppl. 27: 11–15.

————. 1999. "Quality of Life: Three Competing Views." *Ethical Theory and Moral Practice* 2:11–23.

Sandøe, P., S.B. Christiansen, and M.C. Appleby. 2003. "Farm Animal Welfare: The Interaction of Ethical Questions and Animal Welfare Science." *Animal Welfare* 12: 469–78.

Salt, H. 1980. *Animals Rights*. London: Centaur Press. First published 1894 by Macmillan.

Sapontzis, S. F. 1987. *Morals, Reason, and Animals*. Philadelphia: Temple University Press.

Singer, P. 1979. *Practical Ethics*. Cambridge: Cambrige University Press.

Stolba, A., and D. G. M. Wood-Gush. 1984. "The Identification of Behavioural Key Features and Their Incorporation into a Housing Design for Pigs." *Annals of Veterinary Research* 15:287–98.

Sumner, L. W. 1996. *Welfare, Happiness, and Ethics*. Oxford: Clarendon Press.

Varner, G. E. 1994. "The Prospects for Consensus and Convergence in the Animals Rights Debate." *Hastings Center Report* 24 (1): 24–28.

Animal Welfare, Happy Meat, and Veganism as the Moral Baseline

Gary L. Francione

The dominant position on the matter of animal ethics, at least in the United States and most Western countries, is that although animals have some moral value, they have less moral value than do humans, and, therefore, it is acceptable to use animals for our purposes as long as we treat them "humanely" and do not inflict "unnecessary" suffering on them. This position is known as the "animal welfare" approach to animal ethics. The animal welfare approach is also the position most often promoted by large animal advocacy organizations, including by many that call themselves "animal rights" organizations. These organizations often claim that they promote welfare reform not as an end itself but as a means to the eventual abolition of animal use or, at least, the significant reduction of animal use. I have referred to these advocates as "new welfarists."[1] In any event, traditional welfarists and new welfarists all share in common the notion that nonhumans have less moral value than do humans, and that the primary concern of animal ethics is to ensure that animals have a reasonably pleasant life and a relatively painless death.

Our most numerically significant animal use is for food: we kill approximately fifty-six billion animals a year (worldwide) for food, and this staggering number does not include fish and other aquatic animals. There is an emerging and broad social consensus that the vast majority of animals exploited for food are raised in horrendous circumstances, exposed to considerable pain and suffering during their brief lives, and slaughtered in a way that can be described only as barbaric. The new welfarists maintain that the response to this social concern is to promote what they claim is more progressive welfare reform and to encourage people to be "conscientious omnivores" of the resulting "happy meat" and animal products.

I am critical of the new welfarist approach.

First, I reject the notion that is accepted by virtually all welfarists that animals have less moral value than humans. Second, I maintain that because animals are property, welfare reform will not provide significant protection for animal interests. Third, I argue that the happy meat/animal products movement is actually counterproductive in that it makes us feel comfortable about continuing to exploit animals. Fourth, I propose that the only position consistent with the recognition that all sentient nonhumans have a right not to be treated exclusively as a means to the ends of humans is veganism.

THE MORAL SIGNIFICANCE OF NONHUMAN ANIMALS

Animal welfare emerged in Britain in the nineteenth century, primarily in the writings of utilitarian theorists such as Jeremy Bentham and John Stuart Mill.[2] A central tenet of this position is that although animals can suffer and, based on that characteristic alone, are entitled to some moral consideration, they are morally inferior to humans because they have different sorts of minds. Animals are not self-aware and do not have an interest in continued existence; they do not care *that* we use them because they are not self-aware; they care only about *how* we use them because they suffer. Therefore, although animals have some moral significance, they count less than humans because their minds are not similar to those of humans.

This notion about the supposed moral inferiority of nonhumans based on cognitive differences is also represented in contemporary animal welfare theory, the leading figure of which is Peter Singer. Singer, also a utilitarian like Bentham and Mill, maintains that animals have an interest in not suffering but have lives that are less valuable than those of humans:

> While self-awareness, the capacity to think ahead and have hopes and aspirations for the future, the capacity for meaningful relations with others and so on are not relevant to the question of inflicting pain . . . these capacities are relevant to the question of taking life. It is not arbitrary to hold that the life of a self-aware being, capable of abstract thought, of planning for the future, of complex acts of communication, and so on, is more valuable than the life of a being without these capacities.[3]

According to Singer:

> An animal may struggle against a threat to its life, even if it cannot grasp that it has "a life" in the sense that requires an understanding of what it is to exist over a period of time. But in the absence of some form of mental continuity it is not

easy to explain why the loss to the animal killed is not, from an impartial point of view, made good by the creation of a new animal who will lead an equally pleasant life.[4]

That is, Singer argues that because animals do not know what it is they lose when we kill them, they do not have any interest in continuing to live and, therefore, death is not a harm to them. They do not care that we use and kill them for our purposes. They care only about not suffering as a result of our using and killing them. He argues that as long as they have a reasonably pleasant life and a relatively painless death, our use of animals may be ethically defensible:

> If it is the infliction of suffering that we are concerned about, rather than killing, then I can also imagine a world in which people mostly eat plant foods, but occasionally treat themselves to the luxury of free range eggs, or possibly even meat from animals who live good lives under conditions natural for their species, and are then humanely killed on the farm.[5]

Singer maintains that similar human and nonhuman interests in not suffering ought to be treated in a similar fashion, as required by the principle of impartiality, or, as Singer refers to it, the principle of equal consideration. He claims that because humans have "superior mental powers,"[6] they will in some cases suffer more than animals and in some cases suffer less, but he acknowledges that making interspecies comparisons is difficult at best and perhaps even impossible.

The rights/abolitionist position that I have developed concedes that, for purposes of argument, and given that humans are, at least as far as we know, the only animals who use symbolic communication and whose conceptual structures are inextricably linked to language, it is most probably the case that there are significant differences between the minds of humans and the minds of nonhumans.[7] But my response to this is, so what? Any differences that may exist between human and animal minds do not mean that animals have no interest in continuing existence or that their suffering has a lesser weight than does that of humans. We cannot justify using nonhumans as human resources irrespective of whether we treat animals "humanely" in the process.

It is not necessary to come to any conclusion about the precise nature of animal minds to be able to assess the welfarist view that death itself does not harm nonhuman animals because, unlike humans, they live in what Singer describes as "a kind of eternal present."[8] The only cognitive characteristic required is that nonhumans be *sentient;* that is, that they be perceptually aware.[9] Sentience is necessary to have interests at all. If a being is not sentient, then the being may be alive, but there is nothing that the being prefers, wants, or desires. There may, of course, be uncertainty as to whether sentience exists in a particular case, or with respect to classes of beings, such as insects or mollusks. But the animals we routinely exploit—the cows, chickens, pigs, ducks, lambs, fish, rats, and so on—are all, without question, sentient.

To say that a sentient being—any sentient being—is not harmed by death is decidedly odd. After all, sentience is not a characteristic that has evolved to serve as an end in itself. Rather, it is a trait that allows the beings who have it to identify situations that are harmful and that threaten survival. *Sentience is a means to the end of continued existence.* Sentient beings, by virtue of their being sentient, have an interest in remaining alive; that is, they prefer, want, or desire to remain alive. Therefore, to say that a sentient being is not harmed by death denies that the being has the very interest that sentience serves to perpetuate. It would be analogous to saying that a being with eyes does not have an interest in continuing to see or is not harmed by being made blind. The Jains of India expressed it well long ago: "All beings are fond of life, like pleasure, hate pain, shun destruction, like life, long to live. To all life is dear."[10]

Singer recognizes that "an animal may struggle against a threat to its life," but he concludes that this does not mean that the animal has the mental continuity required for a sense of self. This position begs the question, however, in that it assumes that the only way that an animal can be self-aware is to have the sort of autobiographical sense of self-awareness that we associate with normal adult humans. That is certainly one way of being self-aware, but it is not the only way. As biologist Donald Griffin, one of the most important cognitive ethologists of the twentieth century, notes, if animals are conscious of anything, "the animal's own body and its own actions must fall within the scope of its perceptual consciousness."[11] We nevertheless deny animals self-awareness because we maintain that they cannot "think such thoughts as 'It is *I* who am running, or climbing this tree, or chasing that moth.'" Griffin maintains that "when an animal consciously perceives the running, climbing, or moth-chasing of another animal, it must also be aware of who is doing these things. And if the animal is perceptually conscious of its own body, it is difficult to rule out similar recognition that it, itself, is doing the running, climbing, or chasing." He concludes that "if animals are capable of perceptual awareness, denying them some level of self-awareness would seem to be an arbitrary and unjustified restriction." It would seem that any sentient being must be self-aware in that to be sentient means to be the sort of being who recognizes that it is that being, and not some other, who is experiencing pain or distress. When a sentient being is in pain, that being necessarily recognizes that it is she who is in pain; there is some*one* who is conscious of being in pain and has a preference, desire, or want not to have that experience.

We can see the arbitrary nature of the welfarist assumption if we consider humans who have a condition known as transient global amnesia, which occurs as a result of a stroke, seizure, or brain damage. Those with transient global amnesia often have no memory of the past and no ability to project themselves into the future. These humans have "a sense of self about one moment—now—and about one place—here."[12] Their sense of self-awareness may be different from that of a normal adult, but it would not be accurate to say that they are not self-aware or that they are indifferent to death. We may not want to appoint such a person as a teacher or allow her to perform surgery on others, but most of us would be horrified at the suggestion that it is acceptable to use such people as forced organ donors or as nonconsenting subjects in biomedical experiments even if we did so "humanely." Even if animals live in a sort of eternal present, that does not mean that they are not self-aware or that they have no interest in continued existence or that death is not a harm for them. A similar analysis holds for what Singer identifies as "any other capacity that could reasonably be said to give value to life."[13] Some humans will not have the capacity at all, some will have it less than other humans, and some will have it less than other nonhumans. This deficiency or difference may be relevant for some purposes but it does not allow us to conclude that, as an empirical matter, a human lacking the capacities that Singer identifies as giving value to life does not have an interest in continuing to live or that death is not a harm for her.

Also arbitrary is the welfarist notion that humans have "superior mental powers" so that in assessing animal pain, or in trying to determine whether human pleasure or the avoidance of human pain justifies imposing pain and suffering on animals, we keep in mind Mill's notion that "it is better to be a human being dissatisfied than a pig satisfied."[14] What, apart from self-interested proclamation, makes human characteristics "superior" or allows us to conclude that we experience more intense pleasure when we are happy than a pig does when she is happily rooting in the mud or playing with other pigs? Just as in the case about the harm of death, such an analysis works only if we assume what we are setting out to prove.

If we restrict our analysis to human beings, the problem with the welfarist approach becomes clear. Assume we have two humans: a philosophy professor and a factory worker who has no higher education and has no interest in having any discussions that would be regarded by the philosopher as intellectually stimulating. If we were to say that it is better to be a philosophy professor dissatisfied than a factory worker satisfied, such an assertion would, quite rightly, be viewed as arbitrary and elitist.

To the extent that humans and nonhumans have different sorts of minds, those differences may be relevant for some purposes, just as differences between and among humans may be relevant for some purposes. Mary's greater ability at math may justify our giving her a scholarship over Joe, who lacks ability at math. The rescued dogs that live with my partner and me very much like to sit with us when we watch movies, but we do not consider their likes and dislikes in movies when we go to the video store because, at least as far as we can tell, they do not have any. So there are relevant differences between the minds of humans and the minds of nonhumans. Any differences, however, are not logically relevant to, for instance, whether we use dogs in painful experiments or kill them for other purposes, just as Joe's inability at math is not relevant to whether we should take his kidney to save Mary or use him in an experiment to get data that may benefit Mary. We cannot claim that humans are superior based on humans having more interests, or more intense interests, than nonhumans, without begging the question and engaging in reasoning that, if applied in the human context, would quite rightly be seen as blatantly arbitrary and elitist.

The rights position, as I have developed it, rejects the notion that some non-humans, such as the nonhuman great apes, are more deserving of moral status or legal protection than are other animals because they are more like humans. The fact that an animal is more like us may be relevant to determining what other sorts of interests the animal has, but with respect to the animal's interest in her life and the harm to her of death, or her interest in not being made to experience pain and suffering, her being similar to humans is simply not relevant.

There is general agreement that humans have an interest in not being treated exclusively as the resource of another and that this interest ought to be protected by a basic, prelegal right that prohibits chattel slavery. We certainly do not treat everyone equally in that, for instance, we often pay more money to people who are considered to be more conventionally intelligent or to be better baseball players. But for purposes of treating humans exclusively as the resources of others—as far as human slavery is concerned, at least as a matter of moral theory and cus-tomary international law—we regard all humans, irrespective of their individual characteristics, as having equal inherent value. If animals matter morally, then we must apply the principle of equal consideration and ask whether there is a good reason to accord the right not to be treated as property to nonhumans as well. Is there a justification for using animals in ways we would consider it inappropriate to use humans?

The answer is clear. There is no rational justification for our continuing to deny this one right to sentient nonhumans, however "humanely" we treat them. As long as animals are property, they can never be members of the moral community. The interests of animal property will always count for less than the interests of animal owners. We can fall back on religious superstition and claim that animal use is justified because animals do not have souls, are not created in God's image, or are otherwise inferior spiritually. Alternatively, we can claim that our use of animals is acceptable because we are human and they are not, which is nothing more than speciesism and is no different from saying that it is acceptable for whites to dis-criminate against blacks based simply on differences in skin color or for men to exploit women based simply on differences of gender.

The animal rights position does not mean releasing domesticated nonhumans to run wild in the street. If we took animals seriously and recognized our obligation not to treat them as things, we would stop producing and facilitating the production of domestic animals altogether. We would care for the ones whom we have here now, but we would stop breeding more for human consumption and we would leave nondomesticated animals alone. We would stop eating, wearing, or using animal products and would regard veganism as a clear and unequivocal moral baseline. We would then avoid the overwhelming number of false conflicts that so trouble those who advance the animal welfare position.[15] These conflicts appear to exist only because we assume that the cow is there to be used as a resource, and there is an ostensible conflict between the property owner and the property sought to be exploited. Once we see that we cannot morally justify using animals—however "humanely"—then these conflicts disappear.

ANIMALS AS PROPERTY AND THE ECONOMICS OF WELFARE REGULATION

Animals are property.[16] They are economic commodities; they have a market value. Animal property is, of course, different from the other things that we own, in that animals, unlike cars, computers, machinery, or other commodities, are sentient and have interests. All sentient beings have interests in not suffering pain or other deprivations and in satisfying those interests that are peculiar to their species. But it costs money to protect animal interests. In general, we spend money to protect animal interests only when it is justified as an economic matter—only when we derive an economic benefit from doing so. For example, the Humane Slaughter Act in the United States, enacted originally in 1958, requires that larger animals slaughtered for food be stunned and not be conscious when they are shackled, hoisted, and taken to the killing floor.[17] This law protects the interests that animals have at the moment of slaughter but does so only because it is economically beneficial for producers and consumers.[18] Large animals who are conscious and hanging upside down and thrashing as they are slaughtered will cause injuries to slaughterhouse workers and will incur expensive carcass damage. Therefore, stunning large animals makes good economic sense. Of course, these animals have many other interests throughout their lives, including an interest in avoiding pain and suffering at times other than at the moment of slaughter, which are not protected because it is not economically effective to do so. Moreover, the Humane Slaughter Act has not been interpreted to apply to smaller animals, including poultry, which account for about 95 percent of the animals slaughtered for food in the United States. The reason for this exclusion is that given the number of birds slaughtered, and their relatively smaller size and lesser value, it has not been considered as economically efficient to protect the interests of chickens as it is to protect the interests of cows. Welfarists are campaigning for more "humane" poultry slaughter on the basis that recent studies in agricultural economics indicate that the proposed reforms will be economically beneficial to the producers of animal products.[19]

There are laws that require that we treat animals "humanely" and that we not inflict "unnecessary" suffering on them.[20] These laws, however, do not prohibit uses that are unnecessary; they only supposedly prohibit treatment that is not necessary to achieve a given use.[21] For example, as I mentioned at the outset, we kill and eat approximately fifty-six billion land animals every year. No one maintains that it is necessary to eat animals to lead an optimally healthy lifestyle, and an increasing number of mainstream health care professionals tell us that animal foods are detrimental to human health. Animal agriculture is a disaster for the environment because it involves a very inefficient use of natural resources and creates water pollution, soil erosion, and greenhouse gasses. The only justification we have for the pain, suffering, and death that we impose on these billions of animals is that we enjoy eating animal foods, or that it is convenient to do so, or that it is just plain habit. Our use of animals in entertainment and for sport hunting also cannot be considered necessary. The only use of animals that cannot be dismissed as transparently trivial involves biomedical research that will supposedly result in cures for serious human illnesses (most of which are related to our consumption of animal products); and even in this context, which involves a miniscule number of animals relative to our other uses, there are serious questions about the need to use animals.[22]

Because animal welfare laws do not question use and purport only to regulate treatment, they generally either explicitly exempt what are considered "normal" or "customary" practices of institutionalized animal use, or courts interpret pain and suffering imposed pursuant to those practices as "necessary" and "humane."[23] That is, the law defers to industry to set the standard of "humane" care. This deference is based on the assumption that those who produce animal products—from the breeders to the farmers to the slaughterhouse operators—will not impose more harm on animals than is required to produce the particular product, just as the rational owner of a car would not take a hammer to her car and dent it for no reason. The result is that the level of protection for animal interests is linked to what is required to exploit animals in an economically efficient way. And that allows for a standard of treatment that, if applied to humans, would constitute torture. Animal welfare provides little protection for animal interests.

It is, of course, possible as a theoretical matter to achieve protection for animal interests that goes beyond what is necessary to exploit them as economic commodities; it is, however, highly unlikely as a practical matter. Any regulation that is not cost-justified will generate powerful opposition from producers and consumers alike. Contemporary welfarist campaigns promoted by animal advocates demonstrate that animal welfare reform remains firmly rooted in the notion of animals as economic commodities; despite the claims of new welfarists, supposedly more progressive welfare reform does not differ significantly from traditional welfare reform.[24] These campaigns do nothing to move away from the property paradigm and to accord value to animal interests that goes beyond their value as human resources.

For example, the Humane Society of the United States (HSUS), in conjunction with Farm Sanctuary and other groups, is leading efforts in the United States to have conventional gestation crates for pigs banned in favor of larger individual crates or group housing systems employing an electronic sow feeder (ESF) to reduce aggression at feeding time. The HSUS argues that studies indicate that "sow productivity is higher in group housing than in individual crates, as a result of reduced rates of injury and disease, earlier first estrus, faster return to estrus after delivery, lower incidence of stillbirths, and shorter farrowing times. Group systems employing ESF are particularly cost-effective."[25] In addition, "conversion from gestation crates to group housing with ESF marginally reduces production costs and increases productivity."[26] The HSUS cites one study showing that "the total cost per piglet sold is 0.6-percent lower in group ESF systems, while the income to the piglet farmer is 8-percent higher, because of increased productivity,"[27] and another showing that "compared to gestation crates, group housing with ESF decreased labor time 3 percent and marginally increased income per sow per year."[28]

The HSUS claims that "savings at the sow farm can be passed onto the fattening farm, where the cost per unit weight decreases 0.3 percent."[29] This will result in at least some decrease in the retail price of pork and a small increase in demand. The HSUS concludes, "It is likely that producers who adopt group housing with ESF could increase demand for their products or earn a market premium."[30] HSUS claims that despite the greater efficiency of alternative production systems, pork producers in the United States are only slowly adopting those economically more desirable systems because of "inertia and producers' lack of familiarity with ESF."[31]

This is one example. It is, however, difficult to think of any welfare reform that does not fit this model of analysis.

ANIMAL WELFARE: MAKING HUMANS FEEL BETTER ABOUT ANIMAL EXPLOITATION

Many animal advocates recognize the limitations of welfare reform but argue that welfare regulation will, at some point in the future, lead to the abolition of animal exploitation or, at least, to a significant reduction in animal use. The new welfarists are vague as to exactly how welfare reform will lead in an incremental way toward abolition or to significantly reduced animal use. One argument they make frequently is that welfare reform will sensitize people to the problem of animal suffering and that this greater sensitivity will lead people gradually along a path to abolition. The problem with the new welfarist position is that there is absolutely *no* empirical evidence to support it. We have had animal welfare, both as a prevailing moral theory and as part of the law, for more than two hundred years now, and we are using more nonhuman animals in more horrific ways than at any time in human history.

What new welfarists conveniently ignore in claiming that welfare reform will lead incrementally toward reduced animal use, or even to abolition in the long term, is that animal welfare not only does not reduce demand or sensitize society in a way that moves it incrementally in a positive direction, but welfare reforms actually make people feel more comfortable about continuing to exploit animals by reassuring them—falsely—that standards have been improved in meaningful ways. This false reassurance reinforces the notion, which is deeply embedded in our speciesist culture, that it is morally acceptable to use animals as long as they are treated "humanely." The welfarist approach actually supports and strengthens the property paradigm and does not move away from it.

Making society feel more comfortable about animal exploitation is more often than not an explicit goal of animal welfare campaigns and organizations. For example, many of the large animal advocacy groups in the United States and Britain promote labeling schemes under which the flesh or products of nonhumans are given a stamp of approval. For example, Humane Farm Animal Care (HFAC), with its partners HSUS, American Society for the Prevention of Cruelty to Animals, World Society for the Protection of Animals, and others, promotes the Certified Humane Raised and Handled label,[32] which HFAC describes as "a consumer certification and labeling program" to give consumers assurance that a labeled "egg, dairy, meat or poultry product has been produced with the welfare of the farm animal in mind."[33] HFAC emphasizes that "in 'food animals, stress can affect meat quality . . . and general [animal] health,'"[34] and that the label "creates a win-win-win situation for retailers and restaurants, producers, and consumers. For farmers, the win means they can achieve differentiation, increase market share and increase profitability for choosing more sustainable practices."[35] Retailers win as well because "natural and organic foods have been among the fastest growing grocery categories in recent years. Now grocers, retailers, restaurants, food service operators and producers can benefit from opportunities for sales and profits with Certified Humane Raised & Handled."[36] The Humane Society International, an arm of HSUS, has launched a Humane Choice label in Australia that "will guarantee the consumer that the animal has been treated with respect and care, from birth through to death."[37]

Whole Foods, a chain of supermarkets in the United States, Canada, and Great Britain, is developing an Animal Compassionate Standards label and the Royal Society for the Prevention of Cruelty to Animals (RSPCA) in Britain has the Freedom Food label, which is "the farm assurance and food labelling scheme established by the RSPCA, one of the world's leading animal welfare organisations.

The scheme is a charity in its own right, set up in 1994 to improve the welfare of farm animals and offer consumers a higher welfare choice."[38]

Putting aside the matter that these labeling schemes are explicitly intended by animal advocates to make the public feel more comfortable about animal exploitation, there are serious questions as to whether these schemes translate into any significant welfare benefit for nonhuman animals. For example, a number of producers who have the RSPCA Freedom Food label have been exposed as engaging in heinous animal abuse.[39] One scholar who has looked at the Whole Foods Animal Compassionate Standards has raised serious questions about whether these standards will amount to anything more than deceptive corporate branding.[40]

In addition to labeling schemes, animal welfare groups give awards to animal exploiters. For example, People for the Ethical Treatment of Animals (PETA) gave a Best Animal-Friendly Retailer Award to Whole Foods, claiming that the corporation "has consistently done more for animal welfare than any retailer in the industry, requiring that its producers adhere to strict standards,"[41] and a Visionary Award to slaughterhouse designer and meat-industry consultant Temple Grandin, whose "improvements to animal-handling systems found in slaughterhouses have decreased the amount of fear and pain that animals experience in their final hours, and she is widely considered the world's leading expert on the welfare of cattle and pigs."[42] PETA, HSUS, Farm Sanctuary, Peter Singer, and others issued a statement to "express their appreciation and support for the pioneering initiative being taken by Whole Foods Market in setting Farm Animal Compassionate Standards."[43] A leading vegetarian magazine in the United States, VegNews, featured Whole Foods CEO John Mackey on its cover and declared him Corporate Exec of the Year in 2005.[44] Compassion in World Farming gives Good Egg Awards to those who use, sell, or promote cage-free eggs. Recipients include McDonald's, Sainsbury's, Carrefour, Hellmann's Mayonnaise, and Whole Foods.[45] Animal welfarists also praise animal exploiters who adopt welfare reforms that improve production efficiency.

All of this is intended to make people feel better about the exploitation of nonhuman animals, and that is precisely the effect it is having. There is increasingly abundant media coverage about how people are feeling better about eating meat because they have become "compassionate carnivores."[46] One Reuters report noted that "some vegetarians, and those who have reduced their meat consumption because of their conscience or politics, are beginning to eat sustainable meat, choosing products that are not the result of industrial farming practices."[47] Celebrity chefs on both sides of the Atlantic are leaders in promoting happy meat and animal products.[48] A popular author, Catherine Friend, who raises animals for slaughter, writes about her "respect" for animals and, in an almost unfathomable expression of moral schizophrenia, shares a "Letter to My Lambs" that she wrote to her lambs being sent to slaughter: "I wish you a safe journey, and I honor your role in my life."[49] A "safe journey" to the slaughterhouse? Friend argues that by not "remaining 'at the table,'"[50] those who do not consume animal products do nothing to shift animal production away from intensive farming and toward "humane," sustainable practices, such as those Friend claims to use. In other words, those who do not consume happy animal flesh and products are actually harming animals. Similarly, in promoting the KFC faux chicken sandwich, PETA was asked about the fact that the patty was cooked in the same oil as was the non-faux chicken. PETA responded that advocates should not complain lest "we run the risk of making vegetarianism/veganism appear to be difficult, unpleasant, or outright annoying, which will likely turn off others from even considering adopting a vegetarian diet—and that does harm animals."[51]

That this is not recognized as outright absurdity is attributable in large part to the fact that Peter Singer, often referred to as the "father of the animal rights movement," describes being a "conscientious omnivore" as a "'defensible ethical position,'"[52] and he claims that those concerned about animal ethics can still indulge in "the luxury" of eating "humanely" raised and slaughtered meat and animal products.[53] And we should not be surprised that PETA is telling people they should eat a nonvegan sandwich fried in the same oil as chicken lest they harm animals by making veganism "appear to be difficult, unpleasant, or outright annoying." After all, Singer explicitly argues that we may have a moral obligation not to be vegan in situations in which others will be annoyed or disconcerted about insistence on veganism.[54]

In sum, the new welfarists have enthusiastically embraced the position that the moral issue is not that we are using animals but only how we use them, and our use of nonhumans is morally justifiable as long as our treatment is acceptable. Rather than representing incremental steps toward abolition or reduced animal use, the new welfarist approach perpetuates and perhaps even increases animal exploitation, first by encouraging an unsuspecting public to believe that our treatment of animals has improved and that they can now consume animals without a guilty conscience and second by reinforcing the traditional welfarist notion that animal use is morally acceptable as long as the level of treatment is acceptable. Institutionalized exploiters recognize this. For example, Randy Strauss of Strauss Veal and Lamb International, claims to want "to revolutionize the veal industry" by replacing the traditional veal crate with group stalls over the next several years.[55] Strauss, citing the European experience, where consumers increased their consumption of veal when Europe converted from the crate to the group stalls, recognizes that "there are a growing number of people who, if they feel good about what they're eating, will eat veal." Strauss wants to "capture that market" so that he can "increase the 0.6-pound per capita consumption market resulting in a healthier veal industry." A consistent theme that runs through the literature of

industrial suppliers of animal products is the recognition that the public perception of increased animal welfare can only help the particular industry by boosting
demand. Given that most welfare reforms actually increase production efficiency,
welfare reform is very smart business.

The new welfarist approach has made business partners out of the animal
advocacy movement and institutional exploiters. The animal advocacy groups
get to declare victory—and to fund-raise—when legislation or voluntary industry
agreement results in a change in practice that was inefficient and that would have
been changed anyway, or a change that adds a de minimis amount to production
costs but that has no real effect on the bottom line either because demand for the
product is inelastic given the price increase or because "compassionate consumers"
will actually increase demand for the product. Industry gets to reassure the public
that they really do care about animals and that consumers can, in the words of
Randy Strauss, "fully enjoy veal with the satisfaction of knowing that veal calves are
raised in a humane manner." Corporations such as McDonald's, Kentucky Fried
Chicken, and Whole Foods can point to the endorsement of large animal advocacy
organizations and prominent animal advocates. They can even get direct marketing
help from animal advocates if they adopt one of an increasing number of labeling
schemes sponsored and approved by animal organizations and animal advocates,
telling the public that "we support certified humane programs, we support other
farmers, we work with farmers, we think farming is a noble profession."[56]

THE THEORETICAL AND PRACTICAL SOLUTION: VEGANISM

New welfarists often argue that the animal rights/abolitionist approach is utopian
or idealistic and does not provide any practical normative guidance. According
to these critics, abolitionists want nothing short of the immediate abolition of
exploitation and they reject any sort of incremental or practical change as a means
to achieving that abolition.[57] The new welfarists are certainly correct to say that
abolitionists want to end all animal exploitation and would like to see it all end
tomorrow, or even later today. But no one thinks that is possible, and the welfarists
are wrong to say that abolitionists reject incremental change. The abolitionists
reject regulatory change that seeks to make exploitation more "humane" or that
reinforces the property status of animals and, instead, seek change that incrementally eradicates the property status of nonhumans and recognizes that nonhumans
have inherent value. The abolitionist position provides definite normative guidance
for incremental change both on an individual level and on the level of social and
legal change.

On the individual level, rights theory prescribes incremental change in the
form of ethical veganism.[58] Although veganism may represent a matter of diet or

lifestyle for some, ethical veganism is a profound moral and political commitment to abolition on the individual level and extends not only to matters of food but to the wearing or use of animal products. Ethical veganism is the personal rejection of the commodity status of nonhuman animals, the notion that animals have only external value, and the notion that animals have less moral value than do humans. Indeed, ethical veganism is the *only* position consistent with the recognition that, for purposes of being treated as a thing, the lives of humans and nonhumans are morally equivalent. Ethical veganism must be the unequivocal moral baseline of any social and political movement that recognizes that nonhuman animals have inherent or intrinsic moral value and are not resources for human use.

The more people who become vegan for ethical reasons, the stronger will be the cultural notion that animals have a moral right not to be treated as commodities. If we are ever going to effect any significant change in our treatment of animals and to one day end that use, it is imperative that there be a social and political movement that actively seeks abolition and regards veganism as its moral baseline. As long as a majority of people think that eating animals and animal products is a morally acceptable behavior, nothing will change. There may be a larger selection of happy meat and other fare for affluent "conscientious omnivores" or "compassionate consumers," but this will not abolish animal exploitation or do anything other than make society more comfortable with exploitation and thereby entrench it more deeply. The welfarist says, in essence, "If we are going to eat meat (or some other animal product), this is the morally better meat (or other product) to eat." This position sidesteps the "if" clause. The rights position maintains clearly that there is no normal circumstance where the behavior in the "if" clause is morally acceptable. The rights position promotes veganism because only after people see that the "if" is problematic will they even recognize our use of nonhuman animals as the fundamental moral issue and appreciate the problem with animal welfare, which focuses only on treatment. We will never even be able to see the moral problem with animal use as long as we are continuing to use animals. We will never find our moral compass as long as animals are on our plates, on our backs or feet, or in the lotions that we apply to our faces. We will never adequately address our moral schizophrenia as long as animals are nothing more than resources or economic commodities whose interests, including their interest in continuing to exist, can be ignored if we get some benefit from doing so.

Animal advocates who claim to favor animal rights and to want to abolish animal exploitation but continue to eat or use animal products are no different from those who claimed to be in favor human rights but who continued to own slaves. We marvel that people who campaigned so passionately for the "rights of man" could exclude slaves and women. Those campaigners were locked in their eighteenth-century "if" clause, in that they assumed it was acceptable to deny personhood to women and slaves and the only question was how they were treated. Just as slavery represented the institutionalized commodification of humans, meat, dairy, eggs, animal clothing, and animal products represent the institutional commodification of nonhumans. Moreover, there is no coherent distinction between meat and dairy or eggs. Animals exploited in the dairy or egg industries live longer, are treated worse, and end up in the same slaughterhouse as their meat counterparts. There is as much, if not more, suffering and death in dairy or egg products as in flesh products, but there is certainly no morally relevant distinction between or among them. To say that one does not eat beef but drinks milk is as silly as to say that one eats flesh from large cows but not from small cows. Moreover, there is also no morally relevant distinction between a cow and a fish or other sentient sea animal for purposes of treating either as a human resource. We may more easily recognize the pain or suffering of a cow because, like us, she is a mammal. But that is not a reason to ignore the suffering or death of the billions of sentient fish and other sea animals we kill annually.

The most important form of incremental change on a social level is creative, nonviolent education about veganism and the need to abolish, not merely to regulate, the institutionalized exploitation of animals. The animal advocacy movement in the United States has seriously failed to educate the public about the need to abolish animal exploitation. Although there are many reasons for this failure, a primary one is that animal advocacy groups find it easier to promote welfarist campaigns aimed at reducing "unnecessary" suffering that have little practical effect and are often endorsed by the industry involved. Such campaigns are easy for advocates to package and sell and they do not offend anyone. It is easier to tell people—including donors, many of whom are omnivores—that they can be morally conscientious omnivores than it is to take the position that veganism is a moral baseline. That, however, is precisely the problem. No one disagrees with the principle that it is wrong to inflict "unnecessary" suffering and that we ought to treat animals "humanely." But, as two hundred years of animal welfare have made plain, these are merely platitudes in light of the property status of animals. We have not come to grips with the "if" of whether we are justified in using animals.

Veganism and creative, positive, nonviolent vegan education provide practical and incremental strategies both in terms of reducing animal suffering now and in terms of building a movement in the future that will be able to obtain more meaningful legislation in the form of prohibitions of animal use rather than mere "humane" welfare regulation. If, in the late 1980s—when the animal advocacy community in the United States decided very deliberately to pursue a welfarist agenda rather than an abolitionist one—a substantial portion of movement resources had been invested in vegan education and advocacy, there would likely be many hundreds of thousands more vegans than there are today. That is a very conservative estimate, given the tens of millions of dollars that have been expended by animal advocacy groups to promote welfarist legislation and initiatives. The increased number of vegans would reduce suffering more by decreasing demand for animal products than all of the supposed welfarist successes put together. Increasing the number of vegans would also help to build a political and economic base required for the social change that is a necessary predicate for legal change. Given that there is limited time and there are limited financial resources available, expansion of traditional animal welfare is not a rational and efficient choice if we seek abolition in the long term. Indeed, in light of the insignificant level of protection provided by welfare regulation, the often extremely long "phase-in" times, and the always present list of exceptions, traditional animal welfare is also not an effective way of reducing animal suffering in the short term.

Moreover, it is important for animal advocates to be engaged in efforts to educate society at all levels and through all media about animal exploitation and the moral basis for its abolition. At the present time, the prevailing moral norm, reflected in the law, is that it is morally acceptable to use nonhumans for human purposes as long as animals are treated "humanely." As a result, the social debate focuses on what constitutes "humane" treatment, and many advocates spend their time trying to convince members of the public that larger cages are better than smaller cages, or that gassing chickens is better than stunning them. The debate should be shifted in the direction of animal use and the indisputable fact that humans have no coherent moral justification for continuing to use nonhumans, however "humanely" they are treated. This requires that advocates educate themselves about the ethical arguments against animal use and that they engage in creative ways to make those arguments accessible to the general public. Given that most people accept that nonhumans are members of the moral community in some sense—that is, they already at least think that they reject the notion that animals are merely things—it is challenging, but not impossible, to get people to see that membership in the moral community *means* that we stop using animals altogether.

Educational efforts can take myriad forms and are limited only by imagination. It is not necessary to have a great deal of money or be part of a large organization to be an effective educator. Indeed, the sort of pervasive social change that is necessary requires a strong grassroots movement where neighbors educate neighbors. The paradigm shift will not occur as the result of a highly salaried corporate welfarist coming to town, giving a lecture, and flying out. As I have discussed elsewhere, the corporate movement has very deliberately eviscerated grassroots activism in the United States and is well on the way to doing so in Europe as well.[59] Activism has become writing a check to an organization that, most of the time, already has a great deal of money. But the pendulum is swinging back, largely as the result of the Internet, which has lowered the opportunity costs of communication and has facilitated networking among similarly minded activists, who can bypass the large organizations and their efforts to control the discourse about issues. These activists, often from different countries, can work together to create materials and provide mutual support, and they can take the fruits of their efforts into their local communities. Advocates do not have to have graduate degrees or be professional educators to be able to engage in effective abolitionist education. They need only have the willingness to learn some basic ideas and to think about how to bring those ideas to life in a creative way that will resonate with the public, much of which already cares about animals and is surprisingly receptive to arguments about animal rights and the abolition of animal use.

NOTES

Special thanks to Anna E. Charlton for comments and to Brienne DeJong and Randy Sandberg for research assistance. This essay is dedicated to Robert, a little stray who was found under a car and who came to live with us. And to Gwyneth, our late lamented rescue dog.

To ensure that cited online material remains available to the reader, where possible that material has been captured and is available on my website, www.abolitionistapproach.com. In the following notes, citations to online material include original URLs if those addresses were accurate at the time of this book's publication, and the link to my website follows in parentheses.

1. See Gary L. Francione, *Rain Without Thunder: The Ideology of the Animal Rights Movement* (Philadelphia: Temple University Press, 1996).

2. For a further discussion of the issues discussed in this section, see Gary L. Francione, *Animals as Persons: Essays on the Abolition of Animal Exploitation* (New York: Columbia University Press, 2008), and *Introduction to Animal Rights: Your Child or the Dog?* (Philadelphia: Temple University Press, 2000).

3. Peter Singer, *Animal Liberation*, 2nd ed. (New York: New York Review of Books, 1990), 20.

4. Ibid., 228–29.

5. Rosamund Raha, "Animal Liberation: An Interview with Professor Peter Singer," *The Vegan* (Autumn 2006): 19.

6. Singer, *Animal Liberation*, 16.

7. For excellent discussion of the nature of animal cognition and the confusion it has caused in moral theory about animals, see Gary Steiner, *Animals and the Moral Community: Mental Life, Moral Status, and Kinship* (New York: Columbia University Press, 2008), 1–55, and *Anthropocentrism and Its Discontents: The Moral Status of Animals in the History of Western Philosophy* (Pittsburgh: University of Pittsburgh Press, 2005), 18–37.

8. Raha, "Animal Liberation: An Interview with Professor Peter Singer," 19.

9. For a further discussion of the role of sentience in rights/abolitionist theory, see Francione, *Animals as Persons*, 129–47, 165–66.

10. "Âkârâṅga Sûtra," in *The Sacred Books of the East: Vol. 22: Jaina Sutras, Part 1*, trans. Hermann Jacobi, ed. F. Max Müller (Delhi: Motilal Banarsidass Publishers, 1989), 19. I recognize that Jainism maintains that plants have one sense—the sense of touch. However, it appears that the sense in which the Jains use "sentience" in this context is different from the way that term is understood when it is applied to mobile, multisensed beings. Jains are forbidden from killing the latter but are allowed to kill and eat plants. Therefore, to the extent that Jains regard plants as sentient, they still draw a distinction between plants and other sentient beings.

11. Donald R. Griffin, *Animal Minds: Beyond Cognition to Consciousness* (Chicago: University of Chicago Press, 2001), 274. Subsequent quotes this paragraph are also from this source.

12. Antonio R. Damasio, *The Feeling of What Happens: Body and Emotion in the Making of Consciousness* (New York: Harcourt, 1999), 16.

13. Singer, *Animal Liberation*, 18.

14. John Stuart Mill, "Utilitarianism" in *Utilitarianism and Other Essays: J. S. Mill and Jeremy Bentham*, ed. Alan Ryan (Harmondsworth, UK: Penguin, 1987), 281.

15. For a discussion of conflicts between humans and animals, see Francione, *Introduction to Animal Rights*, 151–62.

16. The property status of animals has been a consistent theme in my work and was the exclusive focus of Gary L. Francione, *Animals, Property, and the Law* (Philadelphia: Temple University Press, 1995).

17. Humane Methods of Slaughter Act of 1958, Pub. L. No. 85–765, 72 Stat. 862 (codified at 7 U.S.C. §§ 1901–1907 [2000]).

18. The "findings and declarations of policy" of the Humane Slaughter Act make clear the importance of economic considerations in assessing matters of animal welfare: "The Congress finds that the use of humane methods in the slaughter of livestock prevents needless suffering; results in safer and better working conditions for persons engaged in the slaughtering industry; brings about improvement of products and economies in slaughtering operations; and produces other benefits for producers, processors, and consumers which tend to expedite an orderly flow of livestock and livestock products in interstate and foreign commerce" 7 U.S.C. § 1901 (2000).

19. For a discussion of the campaign for controlled-atmosphere killing or stunning, see Gary L. Francione and Robert Garner, *The Animal Rights Debate: Abolition or Regulation?* (New York: Columbia University Press, 2010), 30–36.

20. For a discussion of the necessity of animal use, see Francione, *Introduction to Animal Rights*, 1–49. Courts have explicitly recognized that prohibitions against "unnecessary" suffering or "needless" killing must be interpreted by reference to institutional uses that are clearly unnecessary; and courts have also recognized that practices regarded as "cruel," as we normally use that term in ordinary discourse, are permitted within the meaning of anticruelty laws. See Francione, *Introduction to Animal Rights*, 58–63; and Francione, *Animals, Property, and the Law*, 146.

21. Robert Garner argues that the welfarist approach is "not trying to show that the use of animals is morally wrong regardless of the benefits to humans. Rather, the movement is trying to show that most, if not all, of the cruel and harmful techniques currently employed on animals are unnecessary in the sense that they do not produce human benefits or that such benefits can be achieved in other ways." Robert Garner, "Animal Welfare: A Political Defense," *Journal of Animal Law and Ethics* 1 (2006): 161, 167. Garner claims that I accept this analysis and that it is "somewhat ironic" that I do so given my criticism of his defense of welfarism. Robert Garner, *Animals, Politics and Morality*, 2nd ed. (Manchester, UK: Manchester University Press 2004), 41n2. Garner fails to understand that my discussion of necessity concerns animal use per se and not the treatment of animals, which, as he correctly notes, is the focus of the welfarist approach.

22. Even if animal use in vivisection is "necessary," in that it cannot be dismissed as trivial and justified only by human amusement, pleasure, or convenience, animal use in this context cannot be justified morally. See Francione, *Animals as Persons*, 170–85.

23. New Jersey Society for the Prevention of Cruelty to Animals vs. New Jersey Department of Agriculture, 196 N.J. 366 (2008), is one of the few cases that has questioned the interpretation of "humane" as conforming to "routine husbandry practices." The Court held as arbitrary and capricious administrative regulations that exempted from the anticruelty statute "routine husbandry practices" defined as those "commonly taught" at veterinary schools, agricultural colleges, and so on, where

the New Jersey Department of Agriculture did not even review what these institutions teach or consider whether what was commonly taught reflected welfare concerns. The Court made clear that if the agency had engaged in a proper review, its decision to exempt these practices would be largely immune from legal attack.

24. For a further discussion of reforms after 1995 and how these reforms have failed to provide a significant welfare benefit for animals and are generally linked to the efficient exploitation of animal property, see Francione, *Animals as Persons,* 72–96. See also Francione and Garner, *Animal Rights Debate,* 175–270.

25. Humane Society of the United States, *An HSUS Report: The Economics of Adopting Alternative Production Systems to Gestation Crates,* 1,, www.hsus.org/web-files/PDF/farm/econ_gestation.pdf (www.abolitionistapproach.com/philosophy-of-food/endnotes/28.pdf).

26. Ibid.

27. Ibid., 2.

28. Ibid.

29. Ibid.

30. Ibid.

31. Ibid., 1.

32. Humane Farm Animal Care, "Certified Humane Raised and Handled," www.certifiedhumane .org (www.abolitionistapproach.com/philosophy-of-food/endnotes/35.pdf).

33. Humane Farm Animal Care, "What Is Certified Humane Raised and Handled?," www .abolitionistapproach.com/ philosophy-of-food/endnotes/36.pdf.

34. Ibid., quoting an unspecified article in *Agricultural Research.*

35. Humane Farm Animal Care, "Why Produce Certified Humane Raised and Handled?," www .abolitionistapproach.com/philosophy-of-food/endnotes/38.pdf.

36. Humane Farm Animal Care, "Why Carry Certified Humane Raised and Handled?," www .abolitionistapproach.com/philosophy-of-food/endnotes/39.pdf.

37. Humane Society International, "Humane Choice," www.humanechoice.com.au (www .abolitionistapproach.com/philosophy-of-food/endnotes/40.pdf).

38. Royal Society for the Prevention of Cruelty to Animals, "Freedom Food—Welcome," www .rspca.org.uk/servlet/Satellite?pagename=RSPCA/RSPCARedirect&pg=FreedomFoodHomepage& marker=1&articleId=1125387930357 (www.abolitionistapproach.com/philosophy-of-food/endnotes/ 41.pdf).

39. These exposés, which have been presented by BBC, ITV, Channel 4, and other media, were investigated by Hillside Animal Sanctuary in Norwich. The group's website provides links to some of the media presentations. See www.hillside.org.uk (www.abolitionistapproach.com/philosophy-of-food/endnotes/42a.pdf). In at least one situation, the RSPCA claimed that it had conducted an inspection of an egg producer that had the Freedom Food stamp of approval but had failed the producer for various violations. Nevertheless, the RSPCA allowed the producer to keep its Freedom Food accreditation and we continue to see its products with the logo. Chris Semple, "Freedom Farm Cruelty' Exposed," *The Sun,* June 23, 2008, www.thesun.co.uk/sol/homepage/news/article1328275.ece (www.abolitionistapproach.com/philosophy-of-food/endnotes/42b.pdf).

40. Darian M. Ibrahim, "A Return to Descartes: Property, Profit, and the Corporate Ownership of Animals," *Law and Contemporary Problems* 70 (2007): 89, 109–11.

41. "Best Animal-Friendly Retailer," 2004 PETA Proggy Award, www.peta.org/feat/proggy/2004/ winners.html#retailer (www.abolitionistapproach.com/philosophy-of-food/endnotes/44.pdf).

42. "Visionary," 2004 PETA Proggy Award, www.peta.org/feat/proggy/2004/winners.html #visionary (www.abolitionistapproach.com/philosophy-of-food/endnotes/45.pdf).

43. For a copy of the statement, see www.abolitionistapproach.com/philosophy-of-food/ endnotes/46.pdf.

44. Mackey was on the cover of *VegNews*, April 2004, and the issue contained a lengthy interview with him. *VegNews*, November–December 2005, 36, announced the Corporate Exec of the Year award.

45. Compassion in World Farming, "Good Egg Awards," www.compassioninfoodbusiness.com/awards/good-egg-awards/ (www.abolitionistapproach.com/philosophy-of-food/endnotes/49.pdf).

46. See, for example, Connie Mabin, "Animal-Friendly Labels Appeal to Buyers," *Boston Globe*, February 5, 2007, www.boston.com/news/world/europe/articles/2007/02/05/animal_friendly_labels_appeal_to_buyers (www.abolitionistapproach.com/philosophy-of-food/endnotes/50a.pdf); and Megan Lane, "Some Sausages Are More Equal Than Others," *BBC News Magazine*, February 1, 2007, http://news.bbc.co.uk/2/hi/uk_news/magazine/6295747.stm (www.abolitionistapproach.com/philosophy-of-food/endnotes/50b.pdf).

47. Terri Coles, "Humane Farming Eases Pangs for Some Vegetarians," Reuters, August 14, 2007, www.reuters.com/article/healthNews/idUSSCH47468520070814?sp=true (www.abolitionistapproach.com/philosophy-of-food/endnotes/51a.pdf). See also Christine Lennon, "Why Vegetarians Are Eating Meat," *Food and Wine*, August 2007, www.foodandwine.com/articles/why-vegetarians-are-eating-meat (http://www.abolitionistapproach.com/philosophy-of-food/endnotes/51b.pdf).

48. For example, in the United States, "celebrity chef Wolfgang Puck is cooking up kinder, gentler menus. As part of a new initiative to fight animal cruelty, Puck said Thursday he will no longer serve foie gras, the fatty liver produced by overfeeding ducks and geese." Moreover, his restaurants, casual eateries, and catering facilities "will use only eggs from hens that have lived cage-free; veal from roaming calves; and lobsters that have been removed from their ocean traps quickly to avoid crowded holding tanks." "Chef Wolfgang Puck Bans Foie Gras," *Washington Post*, March 23, 2007, www.washingtonpost.com/wp-dyn/content/article/2007/03/22/AR2007032200954_pf.html (www.abolitionistapproach.com/philosophy-of-food/endnotes/52a.pdf). In the United Kingdom, television chef Hugh Fearnley-Whittingstall led an unsuccessful effort to force Tesco, a supermarket chain, to carry poultry bearing the RSPCA Freedom Food label. See "TV Chef Loses Tesco Chicken Vote," *BBC News*, June 27, 2008, http://news.bbc.co.uk/2/hi/business/7476829.stm (www.abolitionistapproach.com/philosophy-of-food/endnotes/52b.pdf).

49. Catherine Friend, *The Compassionate Carnivore: Or, How to Keep Animals Happy, Save Old MacDonald's Farm, Reduce Your Hoofprint, and Still Eat Meat* (Cambridge, MA: Da Capo, 2008), 158, 160.

50. Ibid., 247. In a review of Friend's book, one writer remarks that, according to Friend, "to be a compassionate carnivore, you don't have to cut out factory-farmed meat, you don't have to eat organic (her own small farm is humane, but non-organic) you don't have to shun conventional farming. All you have to do is respect animals and be prepared to make a little effort to search for what Friend calls 'happy meat.'" Tim Lott, "How to Love Animals and Eat Them," *The Telegraph*, June 1, 2008, www.telegraph.co.uk/arts/main.jhtml?xml=/arts/2008/06/01/bofri101.xml (www.abolitionistapproach.com/philosophy-of-food/endnotes/54.pdf).

51. "Calling All Canadians: Eat Some Vegan Chicken at KFC," *PETA2 Daily Blog*, July 21, 2008, http://blog.peta2.com/2008/07/calling_all_canadians_eat_some.html (www.abolitionistapproach.com/philosophy-of-food/endnotes/55.pdf).

52. Patrick Barkham, "Alfalfa Male Takes On the Corporation," *The Guardian*, September 8, 2006, quoting Peter Singer, www.guardian.co.uk/environment/2006/sep/08/food.ethicalliving (www.abolitionistapproach.com/philosophy-of-food/endnotes/56.pdf). See also Peter Singer and Jim Mason, *The Way We Eat: Why Our Food Choices Matter* (Emmaus, PA: Rodale, 2006), 81–183 ("The Conscientious Omnivores"), www.nerve.com/Opinions/Singer/heavyPetting/main.asp.

53. See Raha, "Animal Liberation: An Interview with Professor Peter Singer."

54. See "Singer Says," *Satya* (October 2006), www.abolitionistapproach.com/philosophy-of-food/endnotes/58.pdf.

55. Quoted in Bryan Salvage, "Revolutionizing the Veal Industry," *Meat Processing*, December 2006, 15. All Strauss quotes are from this source.

56. See "AgriTalk Interview with Wayne Pacelle," *Bovine Veterinarian*, June 30, 2009, www.cattlenetwork.com/bovine-vet/regulatory-government/agritalk-interview-with-wayne-pacelle-113984724.html, www.abolitionistapproach.com/philosophy-of-food/endnotes/62.pdf).

57. See Garner, *Animals, Politics, and Morality*, 221.

58. See Francione, *Animals as Persons*, 107–51. See also www.abolitionistapproach.com for essays and materials concerning the centrality of veganism to the animal rights/abolitionist approach.

59. See Francione, *Rain Without Thunder*.

Animal Ethics and Food Production in the Twenty-First Century

David Fraser

The use of animals to create human food has been a controversial issue since classical times. In ancient Greece the followers of Pythagoras (born about 580 B.C.) saw strong bonds of kinship between humans and animals, and on this basis they rejected the then-common practice of killing animals for food or religious sacrifice.[1] The philosopher Porphyry (232–309), in a culture where animals were widely used for food production, wrote a book-length treatise arguing that the purity and self-discipline of a vegetarian diet are important for an intellectual life, and that animals deserve moral consideration because they have the capacity "to feel distress, to be afraid, to be hurt, and therefore to be injured."[2] St. Augustine (354–430), the early Christian writer, argued against contemporary proponents of vegetarianism on the grounds that there is "no association or common bond" that links animals to humans.[3] More recently, concern for animals underwent a significant revival in the English-speaking world during the 1700s, and the century ended with a rash of books and essays criticizing the prevalent use of animals in food production.[4]

Today, ethical debate about the use of animals in food production continues, but its scope has been enlarged by many new developments. These include the rapid expansion of global animal production and its growing ecological effects; the diverse effects of animal-based foods on human health; the increasing use of quasi-industrial production methods and the complex effects they have on the welfare of animals; and a rapidly growing human population whose nutritional needs will require major reconsideration of the use of global agricultural resources. These new developments create many complex, real-life problems that urgently require ethical analysis.

Fortunately, during the last decades moral philosophers have taken significant interest in animal issues, including the use of animals in food production, to the point that we can identify an emerging field of animal ethics philosophy. But does animal ethics philosophy, as it has evolved to date, lay a suitable foundation for ethicists to engage in the issues raised by the contemporary use of animals in food production? Or do we need new approaches—even a new generation of animal ethics philosophers operating in different ways—to deal with issues of food animal ethics?

I will start by sketching the magnitude and some of the complexity of the issues, then identify what I see as some common shortcomings in the animal ethics philosophy of the recent past, and finally indicate some of the features that will be required of animal ethics philosophy if it is to be applied effectively to food production in the twenty-first century.

THE MAGNITUDE AND COMPLEXITY OF ANIMAL USE IN FOOD PRODUCTION

The use of animals to produce food is a vast activity that increases every year to a new record level. In the industrialized nations, production of meat increased steadily from the 1960s to the close of the century. The increase was seen mainly in animal species that are fed on grain, and it occurred partly in response to the surplus production of grain that resulted from the Green Revolution. Thus, poultry production (which is largely grain-based) increased fivefold from 1961 to 2001 in the industrialized countries, and pig production nearly doubled. The increase was less pronounced for production of bovine species, which are fed on both forage and grain; and production of sheep and goats, which are generally fed on forage, remained largely unchanged.

These developments were overshadowed, however, by changes in the less industrialized countries, where increases in animal production were so rapid that they have been termed the Livestock Revolution.[5] In these countries, production of bovine meat, mutton, and goat trebled from 1961 to 2001, and production of poultry and pig meat increased more than tenfold. As a result, the less industrialized nations, which accounted for only a quarter of world meat production in the mid-twentieth century, were producing the majority of the world's meat by 2001. In summary, then, by the beginning of the current century, animal production had tripled over the previous forty years, and an increasingly large majority of global production was occurring outside the long-industrialized nations where animal production was formerly concentrated.

But the use of animals in food production is complex as well as vast. Animals are raised in a wide variety of production systems, including nomadic herding, subsistence "village" production, small- and medium-scale commercial farms, and large, vertically integrated food businesses. The majority of food-producing animals are raised for meat, but many (such as cattle in much of India) produce milk and manure but may not be eaten. An estimated 400 million animals are used for labor, in many cases to till the land or carry agricultural products.[6] The animals themselves have very different quality of life: some live fairly natural and healthy lives, for example on rich pasture; some eke out an existence on garbage dumps or arid scrubland; some live their entire lives in buildings with automated feeding systems and mechanical ventilation.

To avoid any temptation to overgeneralize about such a diverse global activity, let us consider four instructive contradictions.

First, the production of animal products both increases and decreases human access to food. Some 600 million of the world's poorest people, including many landless people, depend significantly on animals for their livelihood, both as a source of food and for income to buy grain.[7] Not surprisingly, therefore, many international development agencies actively promote small-scale animal production as a way of helping people lift themselves out of poverty and malnutrition.[8] For example, Heifer International, a development-oriented nongovernmental organization, has adopted as its mission "to work with communities to end hunger and poverty and to care for the earth" by "providing appropriate livestock, training and related services to small-scale farmers and communities worldwide."[9] On the other hand, the large increase in demand for animal products has driven up the cost of cereals;[10] while this may advantage low-income cereal producers, it could reduce access to food among the very poor. Moreover, much of the increased demand for meat occurs in cities and is likely to lead to more intensive production in periurban areas, possibly to the detriment of poorer farmers in remote areas. The situation has led to calls for policy to guide the current increase in animal production so as to allow the poor to benefit.[11]

Second, animal products are both valuable and harmful to human health. In poorer countries, foods of animal origin are believed to play an important role in improving human nutrition, especially by providing adequate intakes of micronutrients such as vitamin A, riboflavin, vitamin B12, iron, zinc, and calcium.[12] For example, a review of the Nutrition Collaborative Research Support Program noted that intake of animal-source foods had significant benefits for growth, activity, and cognitive function in children in low-income countries.[13] On the other hand, the high consumption of animal products seen in wealthy countries is believed to have harmful effects on health. For example, an extensive study of an American population found that high meat consumption was associated with greater risk of obesity and many correlated health problems, including hypertension, diabetes, ischemic heart disease, and certain forms of cancer.[14] The 2007 report of the World Cancer Research Fund and the American Institute for Cancer Research concluded that consumption of red and processed meat increases the risk of colorectal cancer. Based on its findings, the report recommended that individuals limit red meat intake to 500 grams per week (about 70 grams per day) as well as limiting alcohol intake and avoiding sugary drinks, fast food, and weight gain during adulthood.[15] Taking both overconsumption and underconsumption into account, McMichael and colleagues proposed, as an international target, a meat intake of 90 grams per person per day. This would require large reductions of intake in the richer countries and significant increases in low-income countries.[16]

Third, animal production can be both an integral part of sustainable food production systems and a major source of environmental pollution. In the traditional mixed farming systems of western Europe and elsewhere, animals were grazed on "outfields"—more remote land often of marginal quality—and their manure maintained the quality of the soil in "infield" areas closer to human habitations where crops were cultivated.[17] As human population increased, more of the outfields were cultivated and the amount of land left for grazing became insufficient for the production of manure. One response was to use external inputs, especially fertilizers manufactured using reserves of petroleum and phosphates, to avoid depleting the soil, but the overuse of such products has led to excessive nutrient loading. The appropriate use of animals could help shift back to more ecologically sound forms of agriculture,[18] and in less prosperous countries, where such external fertilizer is not available or affordable, manure remains an important part of sustainable crop production.[19] On the other hand, global animal production is a major cause of pollution. According to one important study, livestock production is a major cause of the greenhouse gases that are driving climate change, and it accounts for more than 8 percent of global human water use as well as being an important cause of water pollution and soil erosion.[20] Some of the harmful effects, such as the use of pesticides and water for feed crop production, might be reduced by shifting toward more extensive grazing systems rather than grain-feeding systems, but other aspects—such as production of ammonia from manure and methane from rumen fermentation—would occur regardless of the production system used.

As a final example, raising animals for food production can create both benefits and harms for the health and welfare of the animals themselves. In principle, we might expect that animals that live under human care should have healthier lives than those that do not. This is true in certain respects but not in others. Many infectious diseases are reasonably well controlled in farm animals. Rinderpest—a horrible and usually fatal disease of ruminants—killed an estimated 200 million cattle in Europe during the 1700s,[21] but today the disease has very nearly been eradicated from the world. On a regional level, many countries have become free from many serious animal diseases. Canada, for example, is considered free from

African swine fever, bluetongue, classical swine fever (hog cholera), contagious bovine pleuropneumonia, foot-and-mouth disease, velogenic Newcastle disease, and others.[22] And on a local level, keeping animals confined in buildings—whatever its other effects—has often allowed medium- to large-scale animal producers to create disease barriers so that even locally common diseases and parasites are excluded from their herds or flocks. On the other hand, the so-called production diseases—conditions caused by breeding and feeding animals for very high productivity—have become more common. There is strong evidence, for example, that breeding for very high production in dairy cattle has increased the incidence of ketosis (a metabolic disorder), mastitis (inflammation of the mammary glands), leg problems, and reproductive failure.[23] The net result is that dairy cattle today live shorter lives than several decades ago,[24] largely because of production-related diseases.

A similar mixture of harms and benefits is seen when we consider changes in animal housing. In the early 1900s, when semioutdoor systems were in widespread use, the mortality rate of newborn pigs was typically 25 percent or more because many piglets died from chilling, starvation and injury.[25] As pigs were brought into more controlled, indoor conditions where they could be protected from drafts, dampness, and clumsy movements of the sow, this value typically fell to 10–15 percent.[26] Such a large reduction in starvation, chilling, and injury must count as a significant animal welfare gain.[27] On the other hand, the same indoor environments seem poorly suited for the adult breeding animals who are commonly exposed to long-term restriction of movement and, in some cases, heat stress and feeding methods that cause extreme excitement.[28] Likely as a result of such factors, mortality rate among adult sows has increased substantially, at least in the United States, where problems such as heart failure, urinary tract infections, and torsion of abdominal organs may lead to 10 percent or even 20 percent of breeding sows dying per year—a phenomenon that clearly indicates "compromised welfare."[29]

To summarize, food animal production can help improve access to food and it can reduce access to food; animal production can contribute to the sustainability of agriculture and it can pollute the environment; eating animal products can promote health and it can cause illness; and modern production methods can have both positive and negative effects on the health and welfare of the animals themselves. The situation calls for careful analysis.

The issues are partly technical and are being addressed (although not nearly enough) by scientists. In particular, scientists can provide the elements that are traditionally called "factual." Thus scientists may study the influence of diet on micronutrient deficiency and heart disease, the recycling of manure, the generation of greenhouse gases, and the animal welfare problems of confined or free-range production systems.

But the issues are also fundamentally ethical. We need to decide how to balance competing benefits and harms while also taking account of other considerations such as social justice, freedom of choice, preservation of traditions, and the inherent value of animals themselves. Does animal ethics philosophy, as it is currently undertaken, provide a good basis for providing the type of guidance that is needed?

SOME FEATURES OF RECENT ANIMAL ETHICS PHILOSOPHY

I believe that several features commonly seen in animal ethics philosophy stand in the way of ethicists playing the role that I feel is needed.

Simplistic Analysis

Some animal ethics philosophy appears to me to engage in simplistic analysis of the kind of complex issues described above. To take a single example, several philosophers have used arguments about world hunger to advocate an end to the use of animals for food. Specifically, they have argued that people should stop eating animal products because the land used to produce animals would feed more people if used to produce plant products instead. In *Deep Vegetarianism,* for instance, philosopher Michael Allen Fox (quoting John Robbins's *Diet for a New America*) proposed that "a given acreage can feed twenty times as many people eating a pure vegetarian (or vegan) diet-style as it could people eating the standard American diet-style."[30] And in a chapter called "Becoming Vegetarian," philosopher Peter Singer, noting that many poor people suffer from inadequate protein intake, calculated that "one acre of fertile land" could produce "between three hundred and five hundred pounds of protein" if the land is used to produce high-protein plant products, but only "between forty and fifty-five pounds of protein" if the acre is used to grow crops to feed animals that are then killed and eaten.[31]

There is certainly merit in such arguments in cases where large amounts of arable land—that is, land that is suitable for tillage and production of crops—are used to support animal production. According to data collected by the Food and Agriculture Organization of the United Nations (FAO), there are about 1.4 billion hectares of arable land in the world,[32] and a significant fraction of this land—possibly a third—is used to grow feed crops for animals.[33] However, the world also contains a much larger area (about 3.4 billion hectares) of permanent pasture and meadow.[34] Much of this land cannot be tilled for crops (as least not sustainably), typically because of poor soil quality, excessive slope, or inadequate rainfall. If land of this type were used for production of field crops, it could become degraded or eroded and go out of production entirely. However, it can be used for the permanent production of grasses and other forage plants and can therefore support ruminant animals as long as overgrazing is prevented. On the surface, therefore, it would seem that the argument of world hunger would lead us not to stop producing animals but, rather, to use arable land principally to grow crops for human consumption and to continue using the much larger area of permanent pasture and meadow principally to produce animals. However, even that suggestion is oversimplified for a number of reasons. For instance, some level of animal production on arable land may serve valuable roles in crop rotation to maintain soil quality, as well as providing fertilization, weed control, and disposal of crop residues such as straw, oilseed meal, and low-quality grain.[35]

Especially as world food supplies become more tenuous, there is an urgent need to critically analyze and improve our use of agricultural resources. We need to decide how to proceed in a context of conflicting ethical imperatives to (for example) provide adequate food for people now, sustain food production capacity for the future, respect individual choices, and so on. For ethicists to provide guidance on such issues, rather than creating seemingly logical but oversimplified arguments, they will need to conduct (or participate in) careful analysis that combines ethical reflection with a robust understanding of food production.

Lack of Understanding of Animals Themselves

During the Renaissance, philosophy included the natural sciences together with such branches of modern philosophy as ethics and metaphysics. Today, with the specialization of knowledge, philosophers cannot be expected to be scientists as well. In many cases, however, philosophers writing about animal ethics have based their arguments on factual claims about the mental powers and emotional states of animals, but with little apparent awareness of the relevant empirical evidence. For example, three philosophers responded to early arguments about the moral standing of animals by claiming certain fundamental differences between humans and other species.

Philosopher Peter Carruthers made the claim that "all mammals, at least, have beliefs, desires and sensations," but he nonetheless claimed that "human beings are unique amongst members of the animal kingdom in possessing conscious mental states." Carruthers proposed that because animals do not have conscious mental states, their beliefs, desires, and sensations are not consciously experienced, and even "their pains must all be non-conscious ones." He concluded, "Since their pains are non-conscious, they make no real claims upon our sympathy."[36]

In *Against Liberation: Putting Animals in Perspective*, philosopher Michael Leahy allowed only a certain degree of consciousness in other species. He claimed that an animal "will be aware of its prey in that it consciously perceives, pursues, and devours it," but, given that the animal lacks language, "there will be no possibility of *self*-consciousness entering the equation." In the same vein, Leahy acknowledged that animals can "manifest relatively short-term distress at, say, the loss of a mate," but "without language it cannot *consider* its plight." Thus, he concluded, "lacking language, animal behavior does not have *meaning* for them as it can for us." In some respects, philosopher R. G. Frey went further. He claimed that because animals do not have language, they lack not only self-consciousness but beliefs as well. Lacking beliefs and self-consciousness, they cannot have consciously held desires. And lacking such desires, Frey concluded "that animals have neither interests nor moral rights."[38]

At the time when the philosophers were making these claims about animals, scientists were studying states of emotion and cognition in a wide range of animal species. To take one illustrative example, in a scientific book titled *Reaching into Thought: The Minds of the Great Apes,* the authors of one chapter reviewed the available scientific literature to understand whether great apes (chimpanzees, gorillas, and orangutans) show evidence of having a sense of self. They proposed that five elements comprise a sense of self: (1) objective self-awareness, or the ability to distinguish oneself from the rest of the world; (2) subjective self-awareness, consisting of identification or emotional involvement with those stimuli that correspond to oneself; (3) possession of personal memories; (4) the ability to form representations of oneself; and (5) the ability to hold theories about oneself, such as what parts of oneself are central and how different facets of oneself are interrelated. Based on the scientific literature available, the authors concluded that the great apes show evidence of possessing the first four attributes but no evidence (at that time) of the fifth.[39] This type of evidence provides insights that would seem fundamental to any analysis of the mental capacities of animals and their moral implications.[40]

To be fair, Carruthers, Leahy, and Frey were working in part from assumptions about the role of language in (human) consciousness, and they may have felt that empirical research on the cognitive and emotional capacity of animals was not relevant because nonverbal species could not have consciousness of the type that they saw as morally relevant. And admittedly, research on the emotions and cognitive abilities of animals is a growing science and was less readily available when Carruthers, Leahy, and especially Frey wrote their works. But I look forward to seeing a new generation of animal ethics philosophers whose analysis will be based on a robust understanding of the empirical research on the mental abilities and emotional states of animals. Such an approach might also contribute to traditional philosophical issues of language and consciousness.

The Use of Dubious Sources of Information

The treatment of animals can be such an emotional subject that trustworthy analysis—even trustworthy sources of information—are difficult to find. Witness, for example, the following two descriptions of confinement animal production, one by an advocate of vegetarianism and one by a promoter of the swine industry. The first, from *67 Ways to Save the Animals* by popular writer Anna Sequoia, describes modern animal production as a world where

> animals have become the immobilized machine parts of great automated assembly lines in darkened factories—tools whose sole purpose is to convert various feedstuffs, including some quite toxic substances, into flesh for human eating. Absolutely no consideration is given to the comfort of these animals, except to keep them alive in large enough numbers to make the animal factories profitable.[41]

In contrast, a brochure promoting the US swine industry claims that many hogs

> are kept indoors in buildings where the pork producer can control the temperature, humidity and other environmental factors. These buildings are well lit and clean, so that the producer can monitor and promote the health of the hogs. Sows may live in individual stalls because it helps give them their own space and also allows the producer to feed and observe each sow individually to meet her needs.[42]

Obviously both of these accounts were written more to persuade than to inform. I think of these as advocacy writing, in the sense that the authors are writing less to analyze a situation than to advocate for a position to which they are committed. Thus, Sequoia, as an advocate of vegetarianism, uses negative words and disturbing images to create a sense of revulsion at animal production. The swine industry writer, being committed to promoting the industry's interests, uses positive words and creates an image of a conscientious producer carefully monitoring the health of the animals and keeping animals indoors for their own benefit. In these and many other examples, people are exposed to rhetorical advocacy but do not know what to believe or what guidance to follow.

Academic moral philosophers could be the trustworthy sources of information and analysis that are needed to guide the public through the rhetorical claims and counterclaims of the advocacy writers.[43] Philosophers are, for the most part, educated in ethics, mandated to conduct and publish research, free from the short deadlines of commercial journalism, and free from the industry-funded research contracts that put many scientists into conflicts of interest when they are asked to comment on industry practices.

However, instead of investigating the issues, many philosophers have used the shortcut of taking their facts secondhand from advocacy sources. For example, in *Animal Liberation*, philosopher Peter Singer drew some of his empirical material about meat production from such books as *Diet for a New America* and *A Vegetarian Sourcebook*.[44] In describing the environmental impact of meat production, philosopher M. A. Fox referred readers to *Diet for a New America*, noting that the "findings are substantiated by many other authors" and citing fellow philosopher J. L. Hill as an example.[45] However, Hill had also relied heavily on advocacy literature for his information on how animal agriculture affects human health and the environment, citing three such sources, namely *Diet for a New America, Beyond Beef,* and *The New Vegetarians,* in over ninety of the book's footnotes.[46]

In my view, this reliance on advocacy sources constitutes a serious problem of scholarship. If moral philosophers base their analysis on biased accounts, they may draw faulty conclusions. They may also lend an aura of authenticity to biased or incorrect accounts by repeating them in academic books and scholarly articles. As a result they may seriously mislead their readers.

To trace one example, a brief 1978 article in the magazine *Farm Journal* reported losses that had been incurred the previous year by the US swine industry from various types of disease and injury.[47] Two years later, social critic Jim Mason and philosopher Peter Singer, in citing this work, stated,

> According to the Livestock Conservation Institute, an industry group that specializes in losses associated with animal production, pig producers lose more than $187 million each year from dysentery, cholera, abscesses, trichinosis, and other swine diseases.[48]

The original article did list trichinosis and dysentery, although obviously referring to swine dysentery, not the human disease. Neither cholera (a bacterial disease of people) nor hog cholera (a viral disease of pigs) was mentioned in the 1978 article, presumably because cholera is rarely seen in the industrialized countries and hog cholera had been eradicated in the United States in 1976. However, Mason and Singer may have been recalling the costly hog cholera eradication program that was still a recent memory.

Eight years later, advocacy writer John Robbins, although citing the original *Farm Journal* article as his source, gave what appeared to be simply a rewording of the Mason and Singer text, including their addition of "cholera":

> The Livestock Conservation Institute reports that pig producers lose more than $187 million each year from dysentery, cholera, abscesses, trichinosis, and other swine diseases.[49]

There then followed a repeated reworking of these statements in many advocacy publications and websites where various embellishments were added and any distinction between the human diseases (dysentery, cholera) and the swine diseases (swine dysentery, hog cholera) was lost. The sources claimed, for example, that many pigs "die of dysentery, cholera, trichinosis and other diseases";[50] that "dirt, dust and toxic gases" in swine barns encourage diseases such as "cholera, dysentery and trichinosis";[51] and that "chronic diseases such as dysentery, cholera, trichinosis and other ailments" are "fostered by factory farming."[52]

Then in a 2004 book, philosopher Tom Regan, in a paragraph beginning with a reference to swine production in the United States, stated, "Dysentery, cholera, trichinosis, and other diseases are common."[53] The statement was unreferenced, but elsewhere Regan cited the Mason and Singer text plus other works by philosophers and advocacy writers. More recently, in a scholarly article published in 2008, philosopher Nancy M. Williams repeated, "Dysentery, cholera, trichinosis and other diseases are common," again without a specific citation, but elsewhere on the same page she acknowledged works by Regan and Singer.[54]

Regan and Williams did not specify which country they were writing about, but in both works the sentence occurred in a paragraph that made reference to the United States, and readers would almost certainly assume from the context that the claims applied to that country. What, then, was the status of these diseases in the United States at that time? As noted above, hog cholera had last been seen in the United States in 1976.[55] Trichinosis had been in decline for many decades. National surveys found only 5 cases out of 3,048 animals tested in 1990 (0.16 percent) and 1 case out of 7,987 animals tested in 1995 (0.013 percent); the six farms with positive animals had known risk factors, especially poor rodent control.[56] Swine dysentery remained more common in the United States. A survey found 11 percent of US farms affected in 1989–1991, but the 2006 edition of *Diseases of Swine* reported that the disease was thought to be "much less common" by that time, partly because of the shift toward larger, indoor units with more successful disease prevention.[57] In fact, contrary to the implications of the philosophers and the advocacy writers, the confinement of pigs in indoor facilities has almost certainly been a major factor in reducing the incidence of both swine dysentery and trichinosis; specifically, it has limited the spread of swine dysentery from farm to farm and has prevented pigs from coming into contact with wild animal vectors of trichinosis.

Without question, the health of swine raises important ethical issues. Freedom from hog cholera and numerous other animal diseases is maintained in many countries by killing any animals in or near infected herds. Sometimes millions of animals are killed in such disease-eradication programs and sometimes by methods that would not meet the standard of humane slaughter required at slaughter plants. Moreover, some of these diseases could be controlled by vaccination instead of eradication, but countries using vaccination may lose their disease-free status for purposes of international trade. This creates a complex moral problem: how should we act when faced with legitimate animal health benefits that can be achieved in different ways, each of which has different implications for animal welfare and international trade? The control of swine dysentery raises a different issue. The low incidence of the disease is clearly a health benefit for the animals, but currently this benefit is achieved partly by keeping the animals permanently indoors where the pathogen can be excluded. In such cases, how should we balance freedom from disease *versus* freedom to live under less confined circumstances, and can we find solutions that better accommodate both issues? These and many other aspects of animal health pose genuine ethical problems; a high incidence of trichinosis, cholera, and dysentery in US swine production does not.

To be fair, the standard of scholarship shown by the philosophers cited above was not below that of many of their colleagues. Indeed, in relying on the advocacy and philosophical literature for information on animal health and production, they were simply conforming to a relatively common practice in animal ethics philosophy. Yet because of this practice, some animal ethicists have misled their readers on factual matters, while also damaging their own credibility and integrity in the eyes of those who are involved in the subject.

Fairness to People

In defending animals, have animal ethicists been fair to people?

The number of people who raise animals has dropped drastically during the past fifty years in most of the industrialized countries. In Denmark, as an example of a major animal-producing country, the number of pig farms declined from 120,000 to only 13,000 from 1970 to 2000, and the number of cattle producers declined from 103,000 to only 23,000.[58] Nonetheless, a great many people continue to be primary producers of animals. In Canada, for example, the 2006 Census of Agriculture identified a total of 148,000 farm operators raising animals, where "farm operator" is defined as "those persons responsible for the management decisions" on a farm, ranch, or other agricultural operation. The number included some 86,000 beef producers, over 25,000 dairy farmers, and 9,000 swine producers.

Remarkably little research has been done on how this large and diverse group of people view animals and proper animal care, but based on many years of involvement with this community, let me suggest the following as hypotheses for further study. My impression is that cow-calf ranchers—the tens of thousands of ranchers in Canada who breed beef cows and sell their progeny after they have grazed on pasture for roughly a year—tend to have a strong attachment to animals, to the land, and to the traditions of cattle ranching; many of them take pride in being what they see as good stewards of both animals and the environment. Pig farmers, working almost entirely indoors, tend to be focused strongly on disease prevention, putting any new animals into quarantine, disinfecting rooms between groups of animals, and requiring workers to change to clean clothing before entering. For them, good animal welfare is, above all, a question of good health, and the rapid growth that their animals achieve is taken as an indication that the animals are thriving. Dairy farmers, who must follow strict routines to maintain the hygiene of the product they ship each day, are the most likely to see themselves as professionals, willing to adopt standards (including animal welfare standards) and apply them to their operations. They are also the most likely to openly discuss the comfort of their animals, and they see animal comfort as reflected in high milk yield. For the most part, all groups feel that providing for the needs of animals is integral to their personal and financial success; and most attach relatively little significance to short-term pain such as is caused by hot-iron branding or castration of young animals. Nonetheless, my experience is that all groups include a very wide range of values and attitudes: a few producers have struck me as callous, a very few even as brutal, but the majority I would describe as independent, conscientious people who like dealing with animals and are willing to work hard and make personal sacrifices to provide a level of animal care that they consider fitting.

The portrait painted by some animal ethics philosophers is very different. To take a few examples, in writing about farm animals Tom Regan claimed that "pain and deprivation are heaped upon them in amounts beyond human calculation."[59] Mark Rowlands claimed that "intensively farmed" animals "live a life of utter misery, wretchedness and desolation, characterized by physical and psychological deprivation and torment."[60] And J.L. Hill claimed that farm animals "typically live in desperately cramped and dangerously unclean living conditions, are not properly fed or exercised, are shot up with hormones and other chemicals that render animals seriously ill through much of their lives" and are "seriously abused and exploited."[61]

Because these statement are generally written in the passive voice, they tend only to imply (rather than state explicitly) that the "torment" and "abuse" are caused by the farmers and ranchers; but for the farmers and ranchers themselves, the sense of being wronged and misrepresented by such statements is nonetheless very strong. In other cases the accusations are more explicit. For example, philosopher Mark Bernstein, in seeking to explain to readers why no one stops the illegal abuse of animals that he claimed was common at slaughter plants, blamed the veterinarians who are hired to enforce the law. The veterinarians, Bernstein wrote, "are typically not helpful. They are often otherwise retired and (like people in general) by and large want to be troubled as little as possible and to avoid any physical or unpleasant work." Thus, he claimed, the veterinarian will "let the plant run as it illegally does. A vet who makes no waves enjoys increased chances of becoming a consultant. Consultants collect a USDA pension while working a relatively cushy job."[62] Here again, my own experience is very different. I know many veterinarians who are diligent and self-sacrificing in their attempts to protect animals; frankly, I can also think of one or two who merited Bernstein's unflattering description.

Without question, there are serious problems in the treatment of animals in food production.[63] Some relate to reprehensible conduct, such as neglect and brutal handling. Here the standards are often uncontroversial—such conduct is illegal in many jurisdictions—but enforcement is difficult. Other problems require standards to be set; for example, should pain relief be provided for short-lived but painful procedures like castration? However, I believe the most important issues are systemic ones and that they richly merit ethical deliberation.

One example involves economic constraints. In the United States during the late 1970s, the average profit received by pig producers was roughly $21 per pig sold, but by the 1990s this had fallen to less than $4.[64] Given the additional effect of inflation, farms needed to expand roughly tenfold over those two decades to generate the same effective income: if 100 breeding sows generated a decent family income in the 1970s, 1,000 sows were needed in the 1990s. The drastic decline in profits was likely due in part to the concentration of the slaughter industry, whereby thousands of producers found themselves selling to relatively few large buyers, and the pressure to reduce prices was intense. The decline in profits was undoubtedly a major reason why the number of farms fell over these decades

In addition, the decline in profit arguably had important effects on the animals. Specifically, with very low profit per animal, even producers with the best of values will be extremely constrained in the amount of staff time, bedding, space, veterinary care, and other amenities that they can devote to each animal.[65] Is this acceptable? In a market economy, we tend to allow market competition to influence or determine production methods for manufactured goods; as a result, the most cost-efficient methods tend to prevail and the less cost-efficient disappear. But when the products are (or involve) sentient beings, and when production methods greatly affect their quality of life, can we, ethically, allow market economics to determine how production occurs? And what options (consumer awareness, product labeling, supply management, legislation) might help to protect animals, perhaps while empowering producers to raise animals in ways that they themselves consider most appropriate? Ethicists could play an important role in these issues, for example by helping producers to articulate the constraints that they face in providing animal care and how these constraints might be overcome; but this will require a generation of ethicists who can engage successfully with people who are involved in food production.

Focus on Personal Choice Decisions to the Exclusion of Social Policy Decisions

Some years ago I found myself increasingly disturbed by the effect of cars on North American society. Cars had become the number-one killer of children and young people; they were a major factor in the deteriorating state of the planet; and they play an important role in the current epidemic of obesity and related health problems. For these and other reasons I decided to stop owning a car. However, regardless of the logic of my reasoning and the beneficial effects of this decision on my life, I have to recognize that the global use of cars is increasing, not decreasing, especially as prosperity grows in emerging economies. Hence, there is a pressing need for guidance not only at the level of personal-choice decisions such as whether or not to use cars, but also at the level of social policy—for instance on legal measures to reduce the amount of death and injury caused by cars, on infrastructure to support alternative forms of transportation, and on health programs to try to restore a healthier level of physical activity.

Some of the animal ethics philosophy of recent decades seemed to approach the issues in a manner that led to personal-choice decisions but not to social policy reform. Singer's *Animal Liberation* contained strong criticism of food animal production, followed by an admonition that readers "cease to eat animals."[66] Regan, in *The Case for Animal Rights*, concluded that his theory required "the total dissolution of commercial animal agriculture as we know it."[67] Such arguments can certainly be applied to the personal-choice decisions that people make as individuals—to buy dairy products or soy products, to wear a leather belt or a plastic belt.

However, animal production and its rapid growth also raise many issues at the level of social policy. Policy makers do not have the latitude to rule that global animal production should cease, but they do need guidance on many issues that can influence how it is carried out. For example, we are now seeing the emergence of laws, corporate policies, and international agreements designed to protect the welfare of animals.[68] These create a need for guidance on the various policy options. Here, by way of illustration, are three specific cases.

First, in the past twenty years, many jurisdictions have created legislation intended to protect the welfare of food-producing animals. However, if one jurisdiction bans a particular cost-saving production practice (cages for hens, crates for calves) but cannot close its borders to competing products from other jurisdictions, then domestic suppliers who are required to observe the ban may simply be replaced by foreign suppliers who are not. In some cases, animals may even be transported from the jurisdiction where the ban is in effect to be raised in less regulated jurisdictions, with the result that the animals suffer from long-distance transport as well as the banned rearing conditions.[69] In cases such as these, how should policy balance the public's desire for reform, the interests of domestic suppliers, and the actual welfare of the animals?

As a second illustration, consider that many retail and restaurant companies have adopted policies to source animal products from suppliers that meet certain animal welfare standards. The companies could conduct their own audits of suppliers, but in such cases the company may want to restrict purchases to a few large suppliers in order to minimize the amount of auditing required. Alternatively, companies could require suppliers to arrange and pay for their own audits through a third party, but this is generally more burdensome for smaller farms than for large ones. Should retail and restaurant companies organize their animal welfare assurance programs so as to avoid disadvantaging smaller producers, and how might this be done?

Finally, in Namibia, meat is an important export product, and a labeling program (Farm-Assured Namibian Meat) ensures high standards of animal health and welfare, while also providing access to export markets for thousands of Namibian cattle producers.[70] The program seems likely to contribute to the welfare of both people and animals in rural Namibia. In contrast, some other countries export grain-fed chicken while some of their own local people have difficulty buying grain. How can trading agreements and labeling programs enable importing nations to purchase animal products in ways that benefit, rather than harm, local people in the exporting nation?

In pointing out these questions, my purpose is not to criticize animal ethicists for approaching the subject at the personal-choice level. Undoubtedly there is a need for guidance on personal-choice decisions. However, in a world of vast and ever-increasing animal production, there is also a need for guidance that policy makers, veterinary officials, agricultural leaders, and others can apply within the latitude of decision making that they can exercise.

ANIMAL ETHICS FOR THE TWENTY-FIRST CENTURY

In all likelihood, the predominant reality of the twenty-first century will be the increase in the world's human population, combined (if the trend continues) with an increase in economic prosperity that may allow billions of people to engage in a level of materialism that has previously been confined to wealthy people and wealthy nations. Before turning specifically to food production, let us consider more broadly the range of impacts that the burgeoning human population will have on the nonhuman inhabitants of the planet.

One set of effects will arise from major increases in human-built structures such as roads, tall buildings, and communication towers. These are already taking a huge but largely ignored toll on animals. A review article on the effects of roads on wildlife concluded that roughly a million vertebrates are killed per day on roads in the United States, and that roads and vehicles have now replaced hunting as the leading direct human cause of death of wild terrestrial vertebrates.[71] Towers and tall buildings are another overlooked problem. A single tower can kill thousands of birds per year, and the increasing global use of cellular telephones and other technology will likely lead to the construction of many thousands of new towers every year.[72]

Other effects will involve increased international travel, trade, and other activities that contribute to the transmission of animal diseases. The devastating 2001 outbreak of foot and mouth disease in the United Kingdom likely began with the illegal importation of contaminated meat from a country where the disease was present.[73] The 1998 outbreak of Nipah virus in Malaysia, which resulted in many pigs and several hundred humans becoming infected, is believed to have been caused when deforestation and large-scale forest burning forced infected bats out of their natural habitat and into orchards where their feces came into contact with domestic pigs.[74]

And perhaps the greatest effects will occur more indirectly, through the impact of human activities on climate change, destruction and fragmentation of habitat, pollution of oceans, and introduction of exotic species. As a single example, climate change is predicted to alter the living conditions of wild animals so drastically as to put many species on a course to extinction.[75]

By any measure, however, food production will rank as one of our most significant impacts on the animals of the world. Numerically, food production already involves far more animals than all other direct forms of animal use (companionship, entertainment, research) combined.[76] Moreover, economic prosperity appears almost inevitably to lead to greater demand for animal products.[77] Hence, any lowering of consumption in the wealthy nations, for health or other reasons, will be more than offset by growing demand in emerging economies. We must prepare for this growth through education, policy, international development strategies, trade agreements, and other means, so that the people of the world can achieve their legitimate aspirations while also safeguarding, as best we can, the welfare of the animals that will be used in the process.[78]

However, the effects of food production on animals is by no means confined to the production of animal products. Producing food for nine billion or more people—by whatever method—will put enormous pressure on the landscapes of the world and their nonhuman inhabitants. Consider, for instance, how animals are affected by routine agricultural procedures. The density of mammals in agricultural land varies widely depending on rainfall and other factors, but for farmlands of the temperate zone and steppe, rodent densities have been reported at 143–490 animals per hectare.[79] The few available studies suggest that agricultural operations have devastating effects on these animals. In one study, 17 of 22 radio-tagged Polynesian rats (Rattus exulans) living in sugarcane fields were killed by the harvesting equipment, either through traumatic injury or suffocation when they were trapped in their burrows under compacted soil.[80] In another case, 17 of 33 radio-tagged wood mice (Apodemus sylvaticus) disappeared within a week of grain harvesting, likely because of predation when the covering vegetation was removed.[81] A study of common voles (Microtus arvalis) found that virtually all the animals disappeared immediately after plowing, and this was presumed to be "mainly due to decreased survival."[82] When practices such as these are applied to the 1.4 billion hectares of arable land in the world, the number of mammals injured and killed is likely to exceed the number affected by any other human activity.

For the most part, philosophers have tended to ignore issues such as these or to downplay their moral significance for various reasons, for instance because the killing is accidental rather than deliberate.[83] Yet killing animals by traumatic injury or suffocation, destroying their shelters and offspring, removing their cover so that they cannot escape from predators—these must surely count as ethically problematic, whether one formulates the concerns in terms of speciesism, pain and suffering, reverence for life, violation of rights, or the virtue of care and compassion. Thus, as we broaden the focus of animal ethics to include the overall impacts of a vast and intrusive human population, food production systems will be a major focus of concern, and they will need to be considered in their entirety.[84] How might this be attempted?

I believe that the issues require an approach based on what Stephen Toulmin has called "practical philosophy."[85] I see a practical approach (applied to food animals) as addressing the real-life moral problems of people engaged in food production, veterinary medicine, and agricultural policy, rather than being focused on theoretical concepts such as the grounds for moral considerability of other species. Thus a practical approach would be attentive to facts and context; it would communicate with nonphilosophers engaged in practical occupations; and it would be effective in achieving good outcomes in practice. Such an approach has much in common with the philosophic pragmatism of John Dewey, William James, and others.[86] However, my goal in this chapter is not to explore the historical roots of the approach I am suggesting, nor to derive such an approach from the thinking of pragmatic philosophers. Rather my goal is to use real-life complexities and facts concerning animals in food production to argue that a practical approach is needed.

Any attempt to achieve good outcomes—to achieve "benefits" and reduce "harms"—rests on certain normative assumptions, but it need not be limited to the conception of benefits and harms from any one ethical theory. For example, a practical approach would not necessarily limit harm to violations of individual rights, nor focus only on hedonic states such as pleasure and pain. As a practical approach, we might begin by taking everyday conceptions of benefit and harm as a starting point for action. For example, if it is uncontroversial that causing sentient beings to die from starvation is a harm, that inflicting suffering is a harm, that driving vertebrate species to extinction is a harm, and that destroying the life-sustaining ecological processes of the planet is a harm, then we have ample scope for taking action now, even while we debate those cases where genuine disagreement remains.

With a focus on real-life problems, a practical approach will require a solid understanding of the problems themselves, as may be obtained by a combination of scholarship, experience, and engagement. For example, in making recommendations about how food should be produced, practical ethicists will have a good working knowledge of food production methods; in drawing conclusions about the emotions and mental capacities of animals, practical ethicists will be aware of the scientific research that has been done on these subjects. This is likely to mean working partly in cooperation with specialists in other disciplines. Thus a practical approach to animal ethics is likely to include multidisciplinary projects involving veterinarians, animal welfare scientists, agriculturalists, economists, and development specialists, and tackling the complex trade-offs that arise among competing concerns. In so doing, animal ethicists would move closer to the approaches used by bioethicists who engage closely with issues and decision making in medical practice.

Moreover, given that so many aspects of food production are influenced by social policy, a practical ethic needs to provide guidance not only at the level of personal-choice decisions but also at the level of policy decisions. It needs to relate to the issues faced by legislators, veterinary officials, international agencies, farmer organizations, corporations, and other bodies. In formulating this ethic, animal ethicists will need to be mindful of other important values and concerns that must be considered at the policy level. For example, proposals intended to benefit animals may prove ineffective if they conflict strongly with worker safety, environmental protection, human health, and other considerations.

Finally, given the vast number of people who own, care for, or otherwise directly affect food-producing animals, a practical approach to food animal ethics will require that ethicists interact with the people who are directly involved. Ethicists may, for example, need to understand the motivations of animal producers and the constraints that limit their freedom of action, and work with them to articulate a vision of the future that will engage animal producers and others in a process of ethical reflection and reform.

CONCLUDING REMARKS

During the 1700s and 1800s, much of the moral concern about animals was channeled into attempts to eliminate acts of cruelty. Cruelty was seen as a vice, and the movement for the prevention of cruelty to animals was seen as part of a broader program of social reform and "moral progress."[87] During the 1900s, the emphasis broadened to include forms of harm caused not by individual acts of cruelty but by institutionalized forms of animal use, especially in biomedical research and large-scale food production.

I believe that the twenty-first century will require a further broadening of the focus of animal ethics to include the full spectrum of the effects of a burgeoning human population on the other inhabitants of the planet, and indeed on its life-sustaining ecological processes. By any measure, the use of animals in food production will be a major issue requiring a combination of technical knowledge, ethical analysis, practical innovation, and policy development. A new generation of ethicists could play a crucial role in the process by focusing on the complexities of real-life problems and acting as credible guides to competing moral interests.

NOTES

I am grateful to colleagues Michael McDonald, Jeff Spooner, Raymond Anthony, and Robert Friendship for valuable comments and advice. This work was supported by the Industrial Research Chair program of the Natural Sciences and Engineering Research Council, by the Social Sciences and Humanities Research Council of Canada, and by the many donors to the UBC Animal Welfare Program listed on our website at www.landfood.ubc.ca/animalwelfare.

1. R. Sorabji, *Animal Minds and Human Morals: The Origins of the Western Debate* (Ithaca, NY: Cornell University Press, 1993).

2. Porphyry, *On Abstinence from Killing Animals*, trans. G. Clark (London: Duckworth, 2000), 91.

3. Saint Augustine, *The City of God*, trans. G. G. Walsh, D. M. Zema, G. Monahan, and D. J. Honan, ed. V. J. Bourke (New York: Image Books, 1958). The quotation is from bk. 1, ch. 20, p. 56.

4. Examples of the works are Humphry Primatt, *The Duty of Mercy and the Sin of Cruelty to Brute Animals* (1776); George Nicolson, *On the Conduct of Man to Inferior Animals* (1797); Joseph Ritson, *An Essay on Abstinence from Animal Food as a Moral Duty* (1802); and Thomas Young, *An Essay on Humanity to Animals* (1798). These are described in R. Preece, "Introduction to An Essay on Humanity to Animals" (1798), by Thomas Young, ed. R. Preece (Lewiston, NY: Edwin Mellen, 2001), 1–37.

5. A. G. Brown, ed., *The Livestock Revolution: A Pathway from Poverty?* (Parkville: Australian Academy of Technological Sciences and Engineering, 2003).

6. N. S. Ramaswamy, "Draught Animals and Welfare," *Revue Scientifique et Technique de l'Office International des Epizooties* 13 (1994): 195–216.

7. C. Seré, "Not by Bread Alone: The Next Food Revolution," in Brown, *Livestock Revolution*, 6–12.

8. F. Dolberg, "Review of Household Poultry Production as a Tool in Poverty Reduction with Focus on Bangladesh and India," *Pro-Poor Livestock Policy Initiative Working Paper No. 6* (Rome: Food and Agriculture Organization of the United Nations, 2003).

9. Heifer International, "Heifer International: Ending Hunger, Caring for the Earth," 2009, www .heifer.org (accessed April 2009).

10. Z. Zhou, "Feed versus food: The Future Challenge and Balance for Farming," in Brown, *Livestock Revolution*, 40–53.

11. P. Pinstrup-Andersen, P. Pandya-Lorch, and M. W. Rosegrant, *World Food Prospects: Critical Issues for the Early Twenty-First Century* (Washington, DC: Food Policy Report, International Food Policy Research Institute, 1999).

12. Food and Agriculture Organization of the United Nations (FAO), *The State of Food and Agriculture 2009: Livestock at the Turning Point* (Rome: FAO, 2009).

13. L. H. Allen, "Interventions for Micronutrient Deficiency Control in Developing Countries: Past, Present and Future," suppl. *Journal of Nutrition* 133 (2003): 3875S–78S.

14. G. E. Fraser, "Associations between Diet and Cancer, Ischemic Heart Disease, and All-Cause Mortality in Non-Hispanic White California Seventh-Day Adventists," suppl. *American Journal of Clinical Nutrition* 70 (1999): 532S–38S.

15. L. Miles, "The New WCRF/AICR Report—Food, Nutrition, Physical Activity and the Prevention of Cancer: A Global Perspective," *Nutrition Bulletin* 33 (2008): 26–32.

16. A. J. McMichael, J. W. Powles, C. D. Butler, and R. Uauy, "Food, Livestock Production, Energy, Climate Change, and Health," *The Lancet* 370 (2007), doi:10.1016/S0140-6736(07)61256-2.

17. J. B. Schiere, and H. van Keulen, "Harry Stobbs Memorial Lecture, 1997. Rethinking High Input Systems of Livestock Production: A Case Study of Nitrogen Emissions in Dutch Dairy Farming," *Tropical Grasslands* 33 (1999): 1–10.

18. J. B. Schiere, M. N. M. Ibrahim, and H. van Keulen, "The Role of Livestock for Sustainability in Mixed Farming: Criteria and Scenario Studies under Varying Resource Allocation," *Agriculture, Ecosystems and Environment* 90 (2002): 139–53.

19. M. C. Rufino, P. Tittonell, M. T. van Wijk, A. Castellanos-Navarrete, R. J. Delve, N. de Ridder, and K. E. Giller, "Manure as a Key Resource within Smallholder Farming Systems: Analysing Farm-Scale Nutrient Cycling Efficiencies with the NUANCES Framework," *Livestock Science* 112 (2007): 273–87.

20. H. Steinfeld, P. Gerber, T. Wassenaar, V. Castel, M. Rosales, and C. de Haan, *Livestock's Long Shadow: Environmental Issues and Options* (Rome: Food and Agriculture Organization of the United Nations, 2006).

21. J. Blancou, *History of the Surveillance and Control of Transmissible Animal Diseases* (Paris: OIE, 2003).

22. Canadian Food Inspection Agency, "Animal Diseases," www.inspection.gc.ca/english/anima/disemala/disemalae.shtml (accessed May 2009).

23. W. M. Rauw, E. Kanis, E. N. Noordhuizen-Stassen, and F. J. Grommers, "Undesirable Side Effects of Selection for High Production Efficiency in Farm Animals: A Review," *Livestock Production Science* 56 (1998): 15–33.

24. W. Knaus, "Dairy Cows Trapped between Performance Demands and Adaptability," *Journal of the Science of Food and Agriculture* 89 (2009): 1107–14.

25. H. R. Davidson, *The Production and Marketing of Pigs* (London: Longmans, Green and Company, 1949); D. C. Lay Jr., R. L. Matteri, J. A, Carroll, T. J. Fangman, and T. J. Safranski, "Preweaning Survival in Swine," *Journal of Animal Science* 80 (2002): E74–E86.

26. P. R. English, "Improving Piglet Survival by Getting Things Right for the Smallest Pigs at Birth," *Practical Pig Review* (July): 16–20; Lay et al., "Preweaning Survival in Swine."

27. D. Fraser, "Behavioural Perspectives on Piglet Survival," suppl. *Journal of Reproduction and Fertility* 40 (1990): 355–70.

28. M. Morin, R. Sauvageau, J.-B. Phaneuf, E. Teuscher, M. Beauregard, and A. Lagace, "Torsion of Abdominal Organs in Sows: A Report of 36 Cases," *Canadian Veterinary Journal* 25 (1984): 440–42.

29. S. D'Allaire and R. Drolet, "Longevity in Breeding Animals," in *Diseases of Swine*, 9th ed., ed. B. E. Straw, J. J. Zimmerman, S. D'Allaire, and D. J. Taylor (Oxford: Blackwell, 2006), 1011–25, quotation on p. 1016.

30. M. A. Fox, *Deep Vegetarianism* (Philadelphia: Temple University Press, 1999), quotation on p. 99, referring to J. Robbins, *Diet for a New America* (Walpole, NH: Stillpoint, 1987), 352.

31. P. Singer, *Animal Liberation*, rev. ed. (New York: Avon, 1990),165.

32. Food and Agriculture Organization of the United Nations (FAO), "ResourceSTAT: Land," http://faostat.fao.org/site/377/default.aspx#ancor (accessed April 2009).

33. FAO, *State of Food and Agriculture 2009.*

34. FAO, "ResourceSTAT: Land."

35. Schiere and van Keulen, "Harry Stobbs Memorial Lecture, 1997."

36. P. Carruthers, *The Animals Issue: Moral Theory in Practice* (Cambridge: Cambridge University Press, 1992), quotations on pp. 184 and 186.

37. M. P. T. Leahy, *Against Liberation: Putting Animals in Perspective* (London: Routledge, 1991), quotations on pp. 156, 133, and 139.

38. R. G. Frey, *Interests and Rights: The Case against Animals* (Oxford: Clarendon, 1980), 167.

39. D. Hart and M. P. Karmel, "Self-Awareness and Self-Knowledge in Humans, Apes, and Monkeys," *Reaching into Thought: The Minds of the Great Apes*, ed. A. E. Russon, K. A. Bard, and S. T. Parker (Cambridge: Cambridge University Press, 1997), 325–47.

40. D. Fraser and R. Preece, "Animal Ethics and the Scientific Study of Animals: Bridging the 'Is' and the 'Ought,'" *Essays in Philosophy* 5, no. 2 (2004). http://sorrel.humboldt.edu/~essays/fraser.html.

41. A. Sequoia, 67 Ways to Save the Animals (New York: Harper Collins, 1990), 45.

42. National Pork Producers Council (NPPC), How Hogs Are Raised Today (Des Moines, IA: NPPC, 1997).

43. In referring to academic moral philosophers, I am thinking primarily of individuals holding university appointments and teaching or publishing in the area of moral philosophy. Of the authors cited in this chapter, the group would include Mark Bernstein, Peter Carruthers, David DeGrazia, Michael Allen Fox, G. L. Francione, R. G. Frey, J. L. Hill, Ramona Christina Ilea, A. Lamey, Michael Leahy, Tom Regan, Bernard Rollin, Mark Rowlands, Peter Sandøe, Peter Singer, Paul Thompson, Gary Varner, and Nancy M. Williams.

44. Singer, Animal Liberation; Robbins, Diet for a New America; K. Akers, A Vegetarian Sourcebook (New York: Putnam, 1983).

45. Fox, Deep Vegetarianism, 85.

46. J. L. Hill, The Case for Vegetarianism: Philosophy for a Small Planet (Lanham, MD: Rowman and Littlefield, 1996); Robbins, Diet for a New America; J. Rifkin, Beyond Beef: The Rise and Fall of the Cattle Culture (New York: Dutton, 1992); P. Amato and S. A. Partridge, The New Vegetarians: Promoting Health and Protecting Life (New York: Plenum, 1989).

47. "Pig Health Losses Total $187 Million," Farm Journal, September 1978, p. Hog-2.

48. J. Mason and P. Singer, Animal Factories (New York: Crown, 1980), 76.

49. Robbins, Diet for a New America, 94.

50. "The State of: The Environment, Food Chain and Animal Protection," www.ecovegevents.com/eve/theStateOf.htm (accessed May 2009).

51. In Defence of Animals (IDA), "Factory Farming Facts," www.idausa.org/facts/factoryfarmfacts.html (accessed May 2009).

52. Jim Motavalli, "So Why Are You Still Eating Meat?" E Magazine, January 3, 2002, www.veggieuniverse.com (accessed May 2009).

53. T. Regan, Empty Cages: Facing the Challenge of Animal Rights (Lanham, MD: Rowman & Littlefield, 2004), 94.

54. N. M. Williams, "Affected Ignorance and Animal Suffering: Why Our Failure to Debate Factory Farming Puts Us at Moral Risk," Journal of Agricultural and Environmental Ethics 21 (2008): 371–84, quotation on p. 375.

55. S. Edwards, A. Fukusho, P.-C. Lefevre, A. Lipowski, Z. Pejsak, P. Roehe, and J. Westergaard, "Classical Swine Fever: The Global Situation," Journal of Veterinary Microbiology 73 (2000): 103–19.

56. H. R. Gamble and E. Bush, "Seroprevalence of Trichinella Infection in Domestic Swine Based on the National Animal Health Monitoring System's 1990 and 1995 Swine Surveys," Veterinary Parasitology 80 (1999): 303–10.

57. D. J. Hampson, C. Fellström, and J. R. Thomson, "Swine Dysentery," in Straw et al., Diseases of Swine, 785–805, quotation on p. 788.

58. D. Fraser, Animal Welfare and the Intensification of Animal Production: An Alternative Interpretation, FAO Readings in Ethics Number 2 (Rome: Food and Agriculture Organization of the United Nations, 2005).

59. Regan, Empty Cages, 94.

60. M. Rowlands, Animals Like Us (London: Verso, 2002), 111.

61. Hill, Case for Vegetarianism, 40.

62. M. H. Bernstein, Without a Tear: Our Tragic Relationship with Animals (Chicago: University of Illinois Press, 2004), 98.

63. D. Fraser, J. Mench, and S. Millman, "Farm Animals and Their Welfare in 2000," in State of the Animals 2001, ed. D. J. Salem and A. N. Rowan (Washington, DC: Humane Society Press, 2001), 87–99.

64. Fraser, "Animal Welfare and the Intensification of Animal Production," reproducing data kindly provided by Dr. John Lawrence.

65. Fraser, "Animal Welfare and the Intensification of Animal Production."

66. Singer, *Animal Liberation*, 159.

67. T. Regan, *The Case for Animal Rights* (Berkeley: University of California Press, 1983), 351.

68. D. Fraser, "Animal Welfare Assurance Programs in Food Production: A Framework for Assessing the Options," *Animal Welfare* 15 (2006): 93–104.

69. D. Fraser, *Understanding Animal Welfare: The Science in its Cultural Context* (Oxford: Wiley-Blackwell, 2008), 219.

70. D. Bowles, R. Paskin, M. Gutierrez, and A. Kasterine, "Animal Welfare and Developing Countries: Opportunities for Trade in High Welfare Products from Developing Countries," *Revue Scientifique et Technique de l'Office International des Epizooties* 24 (2005): 783–90.

71. R. T. T. Forman and L. E. Alexander, "Roads and Their Major Ecological Effects," *Annual Review of Ecology and Systematics* 29 (1998): 207–31.

72. C. A. Kemper, "A Study of Bird Mortality at a West Central Wisconsin TV Tower from 1957–1995," *The Passenger Pigeon* 58 (1996): 219–35; P. K. Anderson, "Wireless Telecommunications and Night Flying Birds: We May be Sacrificing Millions of Migrants for Convenience, Entertainment and Profit," *Biodiversity* 4, no. 1 (2003): 10–17.

73. J. M. Scudamore, *Origin of the UK Foot and Mouth Disease Epidemic in 2001* (London: Department for Environment, Food and Rural Affairs, 2002).

74. K. B. Chua, "Nipah Virus Outbreak in Malaysia," *Journal of Clinical Virology* 26 (2003): 265–75.

75. C. D. Thomas et al. "Extinction Risk from Climate Change." *Nature* 427 (2004): 145–48.

76. Figures from 2007 show slaughtered meat-producing animals at roughly 50 billion chickens, 1.4 billion pigs, 0.6 billion sheep, 0.4 billion goats, and 0.3 billion cattle. Companion animals would be the next most numerous group, estimated by the World Society for the Protection of Animals at 0.5 billion dogs and a similar number of cats. Food and Agriculture Organization of the United Nations (FAO), "Livestock Primary and Processed," 2007, http://faostat.fao.org/site/569/default.aspx (accessed March 2008); World Society for the Protection of Animals (WSPA), "Stray Animal Control," 2009, www.wspa-usa.org/pages/1995_stray_animal_control.cfm (accessed March 2009).

77. J. A. L. Cranfield, T. W. Hertel, J. S. Eales, and P. V. Preckel, "Changes in the Structure of Global Food Demand," *American Journal of Agricultural Economics* 80 (1998): 1042–50.

78. D. Fraser, R. M. Kharb, C. M. E. McCrindle, J. Mench, M. J. R. Paranhos da Costa, K. Promchan, W. Song, A. Sundrum, P. Thornber, and P. Whittington, *Capacity Building to Implement Good Animal Welfare Practices: Report of the FAO Expert Meeting* (Rome: Food and Agriculture Organization of the United Nations, 2009).

79. W. Jędrzejewski and B. Jędrzejewska. "Rodent Cycles in Relation to Biomass and Productivity of Ground Vegetation and Predation in the Palearctic," *Acta Theriologica* 41 (1996): 1–34.

80. R. D. Nass, G. A. Hood, and G. D. Lindsey, "Fate of Polynesian Rats in Hawaiian Sugarcane Fields during Harvest," *Journal of Wildlife Management* 35 (1971): 353–56.

81. T. E. Tew and D. W. Macdonald, "The Effects of Harvest on Arable Wood Mice Apodemus sylvaticus," *Biological Conservation* 65 (1993): 279–83.

82. J. Jacob, "Short-Term Effects of Farming Practices on Populations of Common Voles," *Agriculture, Ecosystems and Environment* 95 (2003): 321–25, quotation on p. 324.

83. A. Lamey, "Food Fight! Davis versus Regan on the Ethics of Eating Beef," *Journal of Social Philosophy* 38 (2007): 331–48.

84. D. Fraser, "Animal Ethics and Animal Welfare Science: Bridging the Two Cultures," *Applied Animal Behaviour Science* 65 (1999): 171–89; S. L. Davis, "The Least Harm Principle May Require That Humans Consume a diet Containing Large Herbivores, Not a Vegan Diet," *Journal of Agricultural and Environmental Ethics* 16 (2003): 387–94.

85. S. Toulmin, *Cosmopolis: The Hidden Agenda of Modernity* (New York: Free Press, 1990). The term appears on pp. 34–35 and 186–92.

86. The application of philosophic pragmatism to animal issues has been extensively explored in E. McKenna and A. Light, *Animal Pragmatism: Rethinking Human-Nonhuman Relationships* (Bloomington: Indiana University Press, 2004), especially in chapters by Paul B. Thompson ("Getting Pragmatic about Farm Animal Welfare") and Ben A. Minteer ("Beyond Considerability: A Deweyan View of the Animal Rights-Environmental Ethics Debate").

87. Fraser, *Understanding Animal Welfare*, 22.

Nature Politics and the Philosophy of Agriculture

Paul B. Thompson

The word "environmentalism" is often used to describe a loosely organized social movement that emerged in the closing decades of the nineteenth century, leading to the formation of national parks and wildlife preserves. The most active early period in the United States coincided with the terms of President Theodore Roosevelt. The movement enjoyed a resurgence during the 1970s with the passage of key environmental legislation such as the Clean Water Act and the creation of the Environmental Protection Agency. It has reemerged in recent times in connection with opposition to globalization and response to climate change. The idea of sustainability has considerably broadened the concerns of the environmental movement at the same time that it has helped bring environmentalism itself into the mainstream. Popular books such as Michael Pollan's *Omnivore's Dilemma* have brought questions of diet and farming practice under the umbrella of sustainability and have successfully made agriculture into a focus of the environmental movement.[1] But do these popular treatments have a philosophy?

THINKING ABOUT AGRICULTURE

Agriculture is an almost ideal subject matter for examining the interface between traditional political theory, on the one hand, and the newly emergent ideas of environmental philosophy, on the other. By the early decades of the twentieth century, industrialization and the rise of the factory system had already given rise to competing philosophical visions of political life. Some of these visions stressed the efficiency of market processes for allocating the productive resources of society and advocated a vigorous defense of private property as both a key to this efficiency and a brake on state tyrannies that threaten individual freedom. Other visions emphasized the continually worsening condition of the poor and working classes and advocated principles for inclusion of their interests and voices in political decision making. These latter views would eventually recognize that race, gender, and sexual orientation had also been used as forms of exclusion that deprive marginalized people of their political rights. But prior to World War II, the focus was on working people and urban areas. Works of social theory by writers such as Karl Kautsky[2] and novels such as John Steinbeck's *Grapes of Wrath* extended the terms of these political debates to the countryside. Capitalist exploitation could apply to rural as well as urban labor, and on-farm industrialization was likely to involve wasteful and destructive exploitation of nature, as exemplified by the American Dust Bowl of the 1930s. A left-leaning critique of exploitative farming practices was thus in place well before anyone had thought up the idea of "agribusiness," and this critique had an explicitly environmentalist dimension.

Within the broader social sciences, this linking of political theory and environmental themes has continued apace. James O'Connor has analyzed exploitation of nature in terms of "the second contradiction of capitalism," for example, while sociologists such as Fred Buttel, Riley Dunlap, and William Friedland have built a large proportion of environmental sociology on the foundations of Kautsky's 1898 critique of capitalist encroachment on traditional farming.[3] Aldo Leopold, generally hailed as a founding figure for present-day environmental philosophy, was quite cognizant of agriculture and aware of the ironies of industrialization. "There are two spiritual dangers in not owning a farm. One is the danger of supposing that breakfast comes from the grocery, and the other that heat comes from a furnace," he wrote in a widely quoted passage from *A Sand County Almanac,* and a few pages later he notes acerbically that the agricultural experiment station seemed to think that its job was "to make Illinois safe for soybeans."[4] But though Leopold is in many respects the prototypical environmental philosopher, his willingness to take agriculture seriously is *not* typical.

In fact, most environmental philosophy has been shaped by the early history of international movements to establish national parks and to preserve wildlife populations. The focus was on that comparatively small portion of the land mass that was to be set aside and protected *from* agriculture, and environmental thought was preoccupied with developing good reasons to do just that. The debate between John Muir and Gifford Pinchot over the future of American wilderness set the stage for an environmental ethics that has largely ignored land and water used for farm production.[5] Muir was a Scot who immigrated to the United States as a young man. He wrote a number of influential books on the American West and eventually founded the Sierra Club. Disciples of Muir believe in the preservation of woodlands and other wild areas. They argue for the intrinsic value of ecosystems and have developed ethical approaches that are "ecocentric" in that they view that natural world as having moral value and significance wholly apart from any use that humans may have for it. They decry those who decide nature's fate by calculating the economic value of wild species or habitat, and they support political initiatives to remove natural areas from the threat of development by timber and mining companies or by public water projects.

Pinchot founded the School of Forestry at Yale and was a leader of the US Forest Service as well as governor of Pennsylvania. Disciples of Pinchot argue for conservation and wise use of nature, but they see no problem in describing forests and protected areas as resources that must be set aside for future use. They think of environmental ethics in terms of duties to future generations of human beings. They are thus "anthropocentric" in taking the moral value that we associate with the natural world to reside ultimately in the way that human beings do in fact place value on it. It is, for example, the subjective feeling of well-being that a human being places upon simply knowing that certain ecosystems exist that provides the ultimate basis for setting aside parks and wilderness areas. This kind of well-being may become the target of an economic analysis: so-called existence value. In real life, Pinchot and Muir were frequently political allies. Thus, anthropocentric conservationists may support many of the same political goals as their ecocentric preservationist philosophical opponents, but the anthropocentrist sees nothing inherently wrong with weighing nature's loss against humanity's gain.

Muir and Pinchot represent two ways of understanding environmental values, and their respective philosophies also arose in debates over the future of African wildlife and European woodlands. This type of debate continues to be crucial for the fate of endangered species, such as the giant panda, and over the third of the world's land mass that is now forested. This tension usefully illuminates issues in the way that urban encroachment, energy consumption, and thermal pollution threaten large land areas where human use has until recently had marginal and indirect effect on wildlife and ecosystem processes. It is also quite appropriate for *some* questions involving agriculture. The encroachment on Amazonian rain forest by cattle ranching provides an excellent example of a situation in which farming creates practical environmental problems that fit this traditional model of environmental philosophy reasonably well. However, the fact that some of the ranchers doing the encroachment are themselves poor and marginalized peoples shows that there are political issues not fully conveyed by Muir/Pinchot dichotomy. Yet by organizing environmental philosophy around the dichotomy represented by the perspectives of Muir and Pinchot, environmental ethicists have tended to place agriculture squarely on one side (usually Pinchot's) or the other. And this makes the political questions somewhat difficult to address.

That is, agriculture is seen as a *part of* the industrial economy just as surely as factories or urban sprawl. Given this orientation, the goal of an ecocentric Muir-style environmental philosophy is to protect nature *from* agriculture. The planting of a field is seen as just another impact *on* the environment and as a failure typical of Pinchot-style utilitarianism. For their part, even the followers of Pinchot have typically adopted a "weak anthropocentrism" that advocates protection of wild areas "because we love them" or, alternatively, for the appreciation and edification of future generations. Even here, the emphasis on wildness leaves an agricultural field out of the picture. (It is, perhaps, worth mentioning that this tendency is far more evident in North America than in long-settled areas such as Asia and Europe, where farms are much more likely to be seen as part *of* the environment.) This approach lines up well enough with standard political theory when it is large companies and the interests of capital that are doing the farming (e.g., exploiting), but there are tensions created when protecting the property rights of small farmers seems to be at issue. Are they just exploiters too?

The other extreme is in evidence when people (not just philosophers) presume that traditional small farms or organic methods are just as "natural" as a genuine wilderness. This kind of thinking leads to the conclusion that these farming methods are just fine already from an environmental perspective. The possibility that desperately poor farmers or organic growers might collectively engage in exploitative destruction of nature never comes up. Notice that, in this view, farming is seen as a *part of* the natural environment that needs to be protected *from* industrialization. In either case it becomes altogether too easy to overlook hard questions about the productivity of a given farming system and its ability to meet the needs of both farmers (often themselves quite poor) as well as those in extreme poverty who depend on the productivity of the system in order to meet their needs for food.

FROM ENVIRONMENTALISM TO THE PHILOSOPHY OF AGRICULTURE: THE CASE OF ANCIENT GREECE

In fact, many of agriculture's environmental impacts should not be thought of as consequences, outcomes, or endpoints that are the *result* of human action. They are better understood as components in dynamic feedback systems that regulate both ecosystem processes and a wide range of human interests. In this connection, it is useful to recall the difference between moral philosophies that emphasize case-by-case decision making and the pattern of moral thinking characteristic of classical Greek philosophy. For the Greeks, human activity is thought to reflect and be shaped by the social and natural milieu. It is impossible to be a good person in a bad society, and the place and manner in which one derives a living plays a large role in making a society good. Victor Davis Hanson, a contemporary scholar of the ancient Greeks, believes that philosophers such as Socrates, Plato, and Aristotle must be read in light of agrarian ideals that were the foundations of life throughout Greek city-states. His book *The Other Greeks* argues that the Greek worldview incorporates both nature and society into an enveloping environment that aids or inhibits action in a selective way.[6] Human goodness involves the realization of potential that is latent in human character, but the character and potential for this realization is not wholly under any individual person's control. One will develop virtues and vices as a result of the way that one's environment rewards or penalizes patterns of conduct in a systematic way. There is, to repeat, no good person without a good environment. And for the Greeks a good environment was not a pristine environment but a farm environment.

This type of thought places individuals within concentric webs: family, community, and nature. These webs work as interacting hierarchies to establish feedback loops, ensuring that individuals internalize the consequences of their actions into habits of personal character. It is not that one stands back from the impact of one's conduct and wonders how to *value* the outcome, as a contemporary economist might. Rather, one sees the whole organic situation as creating more specific value commitments, understood as virtues that integrate and preserve the whole. Families provide an environment for the growth and development of children, but communities, in turn, provide an environment that can either help or hinder the proper functioning of family life. Communities themselves take on unique characteristics of the regional environment in which they exist. In an integrated and healthy moral environment, tensions between family loyalty, citizenship, and stewardship are actually a creative and positive force. They counterbalance one another and prevent the exclusive or obsessive development of any one character tendency over others. A balance or harmony of the virtues signals right action. Decline occurs when otherwise virtuous conduct tends toward excess, veering in the direction of vice.

In Hanson's view, the polis or city-state typical of ancient Greece had a social organization that depended on a type of agriculture that had theretofore not been seen. Relatively small family units formed households, generally supported by family labor and that of a small number of slaves. These household units were mainly self-supporting, but they did produce enough extra food and fiber for the support of craftsmen and artisans, whose skills vastly improved the quality of life (and also made the agriculture itself more productive). Previous agricultures had been organized around large-scale public works for irrigation and distribution of harvests. They demanded massive numbers of slaves as well as a highly stratified elite (the priesthood) to manage the system. The unique mountainous geography of Greece was not only ill suited to such large-scale, top-down irrigated agriculture; the nature of Greek soils and rainfall permitted the cultivation of a broader variety of crops, including olive trees and grape vines. But these tree and vine crops in turn required lifetime investments of labor and maintenance. The farming people (including household slaves, by the way) thus gained an interest in maintaining long-term control over their lands that slave laborers in Egypt or China never experienced.

This was, in Hanson's view, the root of mutual self-interest binding a number of households into a community. Each household had more autonomy than anyone (save the emperor or pharaoh himself) in a top-down agriculture, but each also was highly dependent on the community as a whole. Hanson emphasizes the way that this interdependence played out in the emergence of a unique military innovation, the phalanx, and subsequently in the emergence of citizenship, relative equality, and limited democracy throughout the Peloponnesian Peninsula. The Greek polis; the Greek ideals of citizenship, equality, and freedom; and the Greek conception of morality all rest, in Hanson's view, on the unique organization of Greek agriculture.

Because ancient Greece is also widely thought to be the birthplace for contemporary philosophy and democracy, it is worth taking some care to examine Hanson's views from a critical perspective. Hanson feels that the political events that spawned the golden age of Athenian philosophy were precipitated by changes in marine technology—by a shift in the way that Athens was situated in respect to its biological environment. In the first phase, Athens enjoyed a dramatic economic and military expansion owing to its sea power, but these changes then fed back into the character of the Athenian people themselves. New economic interests emerged. Unlike the interests of those who derived their livelihood and security from the lands surrounding Athens, these new interests derived wealth from trade. They demanded protection of sea-based trading routes and incessant expansion of the Athenian sphere of influence through military conquest. In response, Athenian moral philosophers attempted to articulate ideals that would express the importance of loyalty to the polis.

In short, Hanson argues that key elements in the thought of ancient Greece can only be appreciated when we understand they were arguments that rest upon agrarian ideals. Here I take Hanson's history at face value, treating it as an elaborate thought experiment for examining the philosophical dimensions of farming and food systems. In another context, the adequacy of Hanson's analysis as a history of the ancient world might be tested more carefully.

AGRICULTURE AS A MODEL FOR
ENVIRONMENTAL PHILOSOPHY

If Hanson is right, agrarian ideals are actually implicit in our most venerable sources of ethical thinking. Although philosophies of agriculture are seldom formulated explicitly today, competing philosophies of agriculture continue to be implicit in many if not most of the twentieth-century scientific and policy changes that created the modern world. Like an environmental philosophy, a philosophy of agriculture is a somewhat coherent set of beliefs or principles that express the purpose or guiding vision of farming or animal husbandry—the principal (though not exclusive) vocations that we associate with food and fiber production. It goes without saying that the purpose of food and fiber production is producing fiber and food, of course, but the Greeks understood these productive activities to be interwoven with more comprehensive human purposes and social ideals. Furthermore, any productive activity takes place within the context of a social consensus on appropriate rules, constraints, and institutions. Thus for Socrates, Plato, and Aristotle it was conceivable to propose that human slavery was consistent with one's philosophy of agriculture, but it is not conceivable today.

Of course, few people ever think about what the philosophy of agriculture might include. I first began to think about it when I was asked to teach a course on agricultural ethics in 1982. Not long into my second attempt at the course, a professor of agricultural economics accosted me one day for what he presumed was my naïve and nostalgic advocacy of family farm. In fact, at that time I had not conceived of agricultural ethics having anything to do with family farms, and I had developed a course covering world hunger, animal welfare, and the environmental issues associated with agricultural chemicals. "Methinks thou dost protest too much," I said to myself. It took me several years to understand why my colleague assumed I was an advocate for family farms and even longer to link this question to the main themes of environmental philosophy, but I will try to explain the connections here in just a few pages.

The percentage of farmers among the overall population in industrializing countries has been getting smaller for a long, long time. At the same time the average size of farms has been getting larger, whether we measure size in acres or hectares, numbers of animals, or the value of the food and fiber commodities produced. These farms have also become much more specialized. Most large farms now produce just one or two things, while farms of yore would have produced a dozen or more crops or animals, both for home consumption and for sale. There are some exceptions to these trends. *Very* small farms have actually prospered throughout North America during recent times, though these operations seldom derive all of their income from growing crops and raising animals. Nevertheless, the trend to fewer and larger farms has been a hallmark of industrialization. In addition to his writings on the Greeks, Hanson has written books on this trend in modern agriculture, suggesting that just as the shift away from family farms led to decline in ancient Athens, so might it for us today.[7] The reason my former colleague cautioned me against a naïve endorsement of small farms is that, in his view, industrialization has forever changed the way we should understand agriculture. He was endorsing what I call an *industrial philosophy of agriculture*. According to this view, whatever might have been the case in the past, we should now see agriculture as just another sector in the industrial economy. This means that society is best served when farmers, ranchers, and other animal producers make their products available at the lowest possible cost. They should not, of course, impose costs on others in order to do so. There are still important ethical issues that must be addressed in an industrial philosophy of agriculture, environmental impacts or fairness to workers and animals themselves among them. But we now live in an industrialized world and perhaps we should simply face up to that fact.

I will call the opposing point of view an *agrarian philosophy of agriculture*. Others prefer terms such as "alternative" or "multifunctional" agriculture, and still others associate the word "sustainability" itself with the agrarian way of thinking. This view sees agriculture as performing a social function above and beyond its capacity to produce food and fiber goods such as meat, milk, leather, or wool. The exact nature of these broader social functions may vary from one situation to another. One starting point is the fact that some people—a minority, perhaps—have very strong feelings both *for* small-scale and traditional or diversified family-style farming and *against* the larger and more specialized farms that are typical of the industrial era. The strength of these feelings and the intensity with which they are expressed is alone a reason to see the opposition between industrial and agrarian views of agriculture as a debate with ethical and philosophical dimensions. It is this debate that becomes the heart of agricultural ethics.

INDUSTRIAL AGRICULTURE: THE CASE FOR SPECIALIZATION

Perhaps the trend toward fewer, larger, and more specialized farms is a good thing. This is the view of Jeffrey Sachs, an economist known for his work on problems of poverty reduction, debt cancellation, and disease control for the developing world. Sachs describes the talents of the traditional diversified farmer as "truly marvelous. [They] typically know how to build their own houses, grow and cook food, tend to animals, and make clothing." But there is more: "They are also deeply inefficient. Adam Smith pointed out that specialization, where each of us learns just one of those skills, leads to a general improvement in everybody's well-being."[8] Farmers who concentrate on raising just one or two types of crop or who raise just one species of livestock can become especially adept at the skills needed for that kind of work. They can exploit whatever advantages their soils or weather conditions might afford for a particular production activity to their fullest. This kind of specialization allows them to produce at the lowest possible cost.

The *ethical* argument for such specialization is that when goods are produced at the least possible cost they can be sold at the lowest price. This means that people who eat (i.e., all of us) spend less on food, freeing up more of their income for other things; low-cost food is especially important for those who have the least income. In fact, there are two ethical arguments at work here: First, selling *anything* for less is good on utilitarian grounds, because when people have more discretion to spend elsewhere they can allocate their spending to those things they see as making the greatest contribution to their personal well-being. Technologies that improve efficiency serve the greatest good for the greatest number. Second, selling *food* for less is good on egalitarian grounds, since the reduction in cost is of relatively greater importance to the poor than to the rich. Technologies that reduce the cost of necessities (like food) are ethically better than technologies that reduce the cost of luxury goods (like entertainment) because they are especially beneficial to people with lower income.

There is a cost to this productivity, and it winds up being borne by those farmers who are slow to utilize the most productive technology available. The price of farm commodities will reflect the average costs of all producers. If farmers cannot recover their costs, they do not remain farmers for long. Early adopters of more productive technology have lower average costs but sell at the higher rate. They make landfall profits. But as the new technology becomes the norm, average production costs fall, and prices fall too. Those who have the new technology can still recover costs even at the new lower price. They stay in business. Those still using the old technology have costs well above the average. They cannot recover their costs in the new economic environment and eventually they will go out of business. Who buys their farms? Clearly, it is the early adopters (who had several years of high profits) who now have the wherewithal to snap up these bankrupt farms. Increases in technology thus cause a treadmill effect. Individual farmers must now run harder (produce more) to stay in place (recover their costs). For the farm sector as a whole, every turn of the treadmill means fewer and larger farms.

If the technology treadmill results in fewer, larger, and more specialized farms, it also results in a general lowering of prices for food consumers. If we are inclined to view the ethics of agricultural technology as a problem of trade-offs, any harm or loss we associate with the changing structure of farming must be weighed against the benefits noted above: although the farmers who disappear from farming when the treadmill turns are "losers," the winners are not only very numerous (all of us) but the comparatively disadvantaged among us win comparatively more. So, especially in circumstances where those displaced from farming can find employment in other fields, the technological treadmill looks like a bargain to development-oriented economists like Jeffrey Sachs.

The economic details can complicate the moral calculation of trade-offs. For example, benefits captured by biotechnology companies or the food industry may not be passed on to consumers. Details such as these matter a great deal for any final analysis of the sustainability or moral acceptability of industrial agriculture, and they are discussed at greater length in my book *The Agrarian Vision*. But before considering a few more examples of the complications that arise in comparing trade-offs, it is important to stress a more general point about the underlying ethical logic of the case for specialization.

Notice that this argument does not treat agriculture differently from any other sector of the economy. Specialization in *any* sector can lower costs. Efficiencies in manufacturing can lower the cost of automobiles or video games. More efficient energy production that results in lower consumer prices will be welcomed by all—and may be almost as valuable to the poor as efficiencies that reduce the cost of food. Lower-cost health care methods would, like cheaper food or energy, find moral support on both utilitarian and egalitarian grounds. What is more, government policy that slowed the introduction of more efficient technology in manufacturing, energy, or health care would be viewed as offering unfair advantages to established producers. When corporations such as oil companies or the insurance industry interfere in the political process solely to protect their profits, it is regarded as a form of political corruption. If this is how we react to protecting the economic interests of those who produce health services, energy, or manufactured goods, why should we see protecting the interests of those who produce food any differently?

The argument for specialization applies across all sectors of an industrial economy. If we think that a norm of specialization and encouragement of the most productive technical means should not be applied in farming or livestock production, we are claiming that farmers are a special case. Some reasons for thinking they might be will be discussed below, but it is important to recognize that Sachs's adaptation of Adam Smith creates a burden of proof for those who think that agriculture is different. In contrast, the industrial philosophy of agriculture— the view that agriculture is *not* different from every other sector of the industrial economy—sees more productive technology as a good thing on both utilitarian and egalitarian grounds.

As already noted, there is no true efficiency when there is no true reduction in cost. Lower prices can sometimes be achieved by deferring maintenance or investment costs. This means that these costs will have to be paid sometime in the future, and the lower price does not reflect a true increase in efficiency. Lower prices can also be achieved by forcing costs upon third parties. A company that lowers costs by lowering wages can sell for less, but it is simply the workers, rather than the company, who are bearing these costs. In these cases, lower prices might benefit consumers, but they do not reflect the true costs of production. Considering such trade-offs is critical to the ethical legitimacy of an industrial philosophy of agriculture, and that is where the discussion must turn next.

INDUSTRIAL AGRICULTURE: THE TRUE COST
OF FOOD

Some critics of industrial agriculture argue that the relatively low prices consumers pay for food and fiber goods in industrial societies conceal a host of hidden costs. Jeffery Sachs praises Green Revolution technologies in agriculture for increasing the yields of farmers in India.[9] But Vandana Shiva argues that such calculations neglect the way that older farming methods returned nutrients and maintained soil structure.[10] Soil-depleting practices defer costs into the future, especially if rising energy costs also increase the cost of artificial fertilizers. Bill McKibben picks up on the energy theme, noting that the alleged efficiencies in the industrial food system conceal that enormous quantities of fossil fuel energy are used not only for synthetic fertilizers, pesticides, and farm machinery but also in transporting food commodities from distant markets.[11] Our society's reliance on inexpensive fossil fuels has institutionalized a system that is imposing costs on future generations through practices that deplete resources and stimulate climate change.

These points are also noted by Michael Pollan in his enormously popular book *The Omnivore's Dilemma*. Pollan adds the more straightforward point that animal production in the United States and Canada is made to seem cheaper than it is by taxpayer-supported farm subsidies paid to grain farmers. These price-support payments have lowered the costs of animal feeds far below what would have been established simply by the economic forces of supply and demand. Other costs take the form of direct harm to public health. Yale professor John Wargo has argued that weak laws regulating agricultural pesticides in the United States have unaccounted costs in the form of long-term health problems and the attendant medical expenditures allocated to addressing them.[12] To the extent that the efficiencies extolled by Sachs depend on tax subsidies or entail costs in the form of harm to health, there are costs imposed upon present-day generations that have not been reflected in the prices paid by food consumers. They are, in the parlance of economics, "externalities."

There are also more philosophically controversial costs associated with industrial animal production. Modern feedlots and dairy operations utilize feeding practices that speed weight gain or increase milk production, but at the expense of gastric distress and increased rates of diseases such as mastitis. Modern egg production places hens in crowded conditions where they cannot express instincts to flap their wings, bathe in dust, or build a nest. Pregnant sows are kept in narrow crates throughout the gestation period, unable to even turn around. Broiler chickens have been bred to have such exaggerated breasts that they suffer from skeletal deformities. Gene Baur, the founder of Farm Sanctuary, argues that these are costs imposed upon the animals themselves and are not accounted for in the prices that consumers pay for animal products.[13] Animal biotechnologies have the potential to both mitigate and exacerbate some of these impacts on animals.

Now, the precise way that we want to understand costs that are not reflected in the market price of a good is open to a number of different ethical interpretations. The language of cost may suggest a form of benefit-cost weighing that is familiar to utilitarian ethical thinking. Here, benefits from lower food costs might be thought to offset costs, and the crucial ethical questions revolve around how we estimate the value of costs and benefits and then aggregate them in an attempt to determine whether or not the value of costs outweighs the value of benefits. A utilitarian might ask whether the benefits to consumers (especially poor consumers) exceed costs in taxes or medical expenditures as well as costs for future generations or animals.

But one might also argue that certain types of harm should not be viewed as being offset by compensating benefits. In the libertarian tradition of ethics, harms to health or liberty are regarded as overriding benefit-cost calculations. When affected parties lack effective legal means to prevent such harms, this is regarded as morally unacceptable. The libertarian approach to ethics is grounded in principles that regard social (or governmental) compulsion of individual action as requiring severe tests of legitimacy. In standard treatments, one should be willing to limit one's freedom to *harm* others in exchange for the assurance that government will protect oneself from harmful acts *by* others. We are justly compelled to respect each other's liberty and property, in this view, but acts of beneficence are morally legitimate only on the condition that they are undertaken voluntarily. All the costs described above (arguably) qualify as violations of libertarian moral rights, though there are difficult conceptual issues to work out with respect to animals or future generations.

Given the multiple ways in which we might approach these views, there is thus more philosophical work to do in specifying the exact way that we want to approach the unaccounted-for costs noted by Shiva, McKibben, Pollan, Wargo, and Baur. But it is not my purpose to pursue lessons in basic moral theory, so these important issues will be set aside here. A different philosophical point *is* worth noticing. While this litany of harm serves as an important qualification for the case for specialization, the moral force of these claims is wholly consistent with the industrial philosophy of agriculture. Recall that this philosophy states that we should treat farming just like every other sector of the economy. Certainly we are just as worried about adverse impacts on health or unjustified tax subsidies in industries such as energy or manufacturing. (Indeed, these are frequently the subject of moral critiques of these industries.) Similarly, there is nothing particularly unique about agriculture when it comes to costs imposed on future generations. Costs to future generations in the form of climate change would appear to be due primarily to transportation and household energy consumption, for example.

In a similar vein, activities such as the use of animals in medical experiments have been the focus of protest by advocates for animal rights. The claim that we should account for all the costs of an activity, including those to nonhumans, is consistent with the main thrust of industrial thinking, even if the argument for animal rights remains controversial. So all these critiques that have been leveled at industrial-style farming are well within the purview of a philosophy that states that agriculture should be viewed as an ordinary sector of the industrial economy. Disagreement between someone like Sachs, who advocates more industrial farming, and critics who seem to want less of it will derive from one of two sources. First, it might be disagreement about the outcomes that specialization has actually produced. Second, it might be one of the familiar philosophical disagreements of the modern age: utilitarianism versus some form of rights theory, on the one hand, or the legitimacy of claims made on behalf of animals or future generations, on the other.

THE AGRARIAN MIND

In contrast to the industrial view, an agrarian philosophy takes agriculture to have moral significance that extends well beyond the way that we would think of industries such as transportation, manufacturing or even health care. We might begin with a brief return to ancient Greece. The Greek poet Hesiod (ca. 700 B.C.E.) saw farming as having a religious purpose, but the religious significance of farming for Hesiod is rather different than it might be for contemporary Christians, Muslims, or Jews. His Zeus was one of several immanent gods, fully present in Hesiod's daily life. The depiction of Zeus in Hesiod's poem "Works and Days" is one of a god thoroughly integrated into nature and the source of all natural unity.[14] The seasons, soil, and water are themselves divinities begotten by Zeus that establish a place for human beings. A key message in Hesiod's poetry is that only farmers dependent on seasons, soil, and water can hope to attain piety with respect to these divinities. Farming is the way that human beings justly occupy a place in the divine (i.e., natural) order, and it is the gods' intention that this place be fraught with work, toil, and risk. Warfare, violence, and trickery, in contrast, are unjust in Hesiod's poetry because they short-circuit the gods' intended route to material rewards. These human practices will eventually be repaid with misery and loss. Agriculture is thus the singular practice by which humanity makes its way in the world in a pious and morally just manner. It is, of course, important to Hesiod that agriculture bring forth the food and fiber goods that are the focus of industrial thinking, but this is only the tip of the iceberg for understanding the moral significance of farming.[15]

Hesiod's poetry reveals a religious dimension to the political agrarianism sketched by Victor Davis Hanson. Recall that according to Hanson, Socrates, Plato, and Aristotle lived through an era of radical change in the economic foundations of Athenian society. Once an agrarian city-state like others on the Peloponnesian Peninsula, Athens became a trading state as a result of its ability to dominate the seas. But when this happened, the unique factors in Greek agriculture that created a strong sense of citizenship, loyalty, and solidarity were eroded. Even virtues such as courage and friendship ceased to enjoy the reinforcing support provided by the way that agrarian lifestyles aligned personal and social interests. Of course, neither Hesiod nor Hanson may have the story straight in all its details. As with the complicated moral arithmetic of an industrial philosophy, examining the details in an agrarian philosophy can become intricate.

Throughout history, agrarian philosophies have seen an enormous variety of goods and values stemming from agricultural practice, and they were commonplace in North America until recently. In 1948, political scientist A. Whitney Griswold found it necessary to devote a book-length monograph to refuting the view that democratic societies were inherently agricultural in their economic organization and political structure. Griswold made Thomas Jefferson, third president of the United States and author of the US Declaration of Independence, into the symbolic progenitor of the myth, though it is arguable that other figures of the time were more committed to it.[16] Benjamin Franklin, for example, argued that farming produced a moral personality more inclined toward honest dealing and loyalty to one's fellow citizens than did the city trades (Franklin was a printer and publisher himself). The upshot: only a society of farmers will develop the personal habits and virtues necessary for self-rule.[17]

This kind of argument is still with us. We have already considered Hanson, whose contemporary political writings reflect a conservative point of view. Like Jefferson and Franklin, he has expressed the view that farming is crucial, though in a vein suggesting that the lack of contact present-day Americans have with farming has corrupted their political values. In *The Land Was Everything*, Hanson writes that only farmers have a true understanding of how secure property rights lend support to virtues of patriotism and citizenship.[18] Authors on the left include Brian Donahue, who believes that reconnecting people to the land through gardening and eating patterns that stress both seasonality and local production is essential to the development of a moral personality that appreciates what it takes to support diverse but culturally integrated and unified communities.[19] Donahue believes that "urban agrarianism" is most critical for the type of political mentality that highly integrated and localized eating and farming practices create. A deep sense of mutual interdependence and common purpose emerges in localities where people interact in the production of food.

Wendell Berry is the most articulate and influential advocate of agrarian philosophy in our own time. Berry confronts the claims of specialization directly in his book *The Unsettling of America*, arguing that industrialization has created a way of

life in which people are unable to see the larger wholes in which both human relationships and exchanges with nature acquire their meaning.[20] The fragmentation
of contemporary life corresponds to a vision of human beings as "choice makers"
who move from transaction to transaction, evaluating choice in atomistic terms,
as if choices and the people and places in which people live and work did not form
a larger, more integrated whole. In place of this fragmented consumer lifestyle,
Berry advocates a return, however partial it must be, to practices embedded in
and emanating from a commitment to a given place. For Berry, the communities
that have come closest to achieving true community (and true stewardship of the
environment) are traditional farming communities. Thus Berry advocates, if not
a literal return to agrarian lifestyles, then at least the deliberate cultivation of an
ethical mentality that locates our ideals of polity, community, and environmental
responsibility in agrarian ideals.

AGRARIAN PHILOSOPHY OF AGRICULTURE

Notice how criticisms leveled against industrial agriculture take on a different
meaning when framed within the context of an agrarian mentality. Advocacy of
local food is a particularly salient example. In stressing the energy costs associated
with long-distance transport of foods and the role that this ecologically needless
expenditure of carbon plays in global warming, the force of the criticism is to
suggest that a more comprehensive accounting of environmental costs associated
with industrial farming would produce a different verdict in terms of ethics. This
is a perspective that can accept the claim that low food prices associated with an
industrial food system are ethically good things for all the reasons noted by Jeffrey
Sachs. Yet it also holds that when long-term environmental costs associated with
energy consumption are factored into the equation, we see that the cost-benefit
ratio is not so attractive. Someone inclined to a libertarian way of thinking might
say that these benefits to present-day consumers are being obtained by imposing
costs and risks on future generations, generations that have necessarily been unable
to give or withhold their consent to this "bargain." Either way, we can generate an
ethical critique of industrial food production without abandoning the principles
of an industrial philosophy.

But an agrarian is more concerned with the way that a local food system embeds
people in practices where their commerce with nature and with each other will
create an enduring sense of place. Even people who *buy* most of their food in
farmers' markets or through cooperative arrangements will encounter the same
people repeatedly, week after week. They will build bonds with them, and the need
of honesty and mutual respect is critical in such repeated encounters. Furthermore,
the people they encounter are either the people who are actually growing the food

or they are but one step removed from them. Consumers learn the rhythm of the seasons, and they will know what grows well under local conditions. They can inquire about the condition of the land and animals under the farmer's care. The agrarian hope is that these kinds of localized transactions will gradually develop into an affection for the people and the place in which one lives and that this affection, this sympathy, will in turn mature through the constant repetition of these rhythms into full-fledged habits of character—virtues, if you will.

The overriding moral concern that emerges from the agrarian mind-set is thus one focused on the way that quotidian material practices establish patterns of conduct that are conducive to the formation of certain habits. These habits become "natural" to people who engage in them repeatedly and become the stuff of personal moral character. When such habits are shared throughout a locale, they form the basis for community bonds and become characteristic of people living within that locale. Food production and consumption has been one of the activities most strongly tied to repetitive material practice. Furthermore, these localized practices are shaped by tradition and geography, by soil, water, and climate conditions. It is therefore not surprising that moral philosophies focused primarily on the emergence and stability of virtues, community, and moral character would converge with a mind-set that takes agriculture to have special moral significance.

PHILOSOPHY OF AGRICULTURE:
A NEW CONVERSATION

In point of fact, many of the criticisms noted above as focused on the true costs of food can be reframed in agrarian terms. Concerns about the long-term fertility of soils and for the ecologically adaptive characteristics of plant and animal varieties can be understood as an expression of the stewardship or husbandry that characterizes a well-functioning agrarian economy. To fault industrial systems for paying too little heed to the human practices that safeguard fertility and genetic diversity, as Vandana Shiva does, can be understood as a claim focused not on the *impact* for future generations but on the need to preserve habits or virtues dedicated to land stewardship and animal husbandry. Concerns about the distorting effects of subsidies can be reconfigured as complaints about the way that repetitive material practices (the purchase and consumption of food) have themselves become warped by a dysfunctional economic environment.

It is worth noticing how warnings about the dire consequences straying from agrarian habits and character are wholly consistent with the agrarian mentality. Hesiod's poem "Works and Days" is full of warnings for fools who neglect their farms and engage in "grabbing" or indolence. This was not because Hesiod was encouraging his audience to better calculate the true costs of these vices. The entire concept of a rationally calculating, economizing mind-set was wholly foreign to his outlook. Indeed, it would be more accurate to say that rational calculation amounts to the same thing as "grabbing" for Hesiod. Those who operate outside the place laid for humanity are simply fools. The bad outcomes they experience are evidence of their foolishness, events that confirm the flaws of their character. Impacts and outcomes are signs of an inner virtue for Hesiod, not factors to be counted up and totalized in a rational calculation of costs and benefits. In fact even good farmers can have bad luck—though in their case bad consequences do nothing to controvert their basic righteousness. This proved to Hesiod that calculating costs and benefits has very little to do with morality. Only a grabbing fool would try to outmaneuver the gods! However strange this kind of thinking may sound today, it is important to pay attention to the way that Hesiod associates bad outcomes with bad behavior but without also suggesting that these bad outcomes are the *reason* for thinking that the behavior is bad.

CONCLUSION

The distinction between industrial and agrarian mind-sets is most usefully understood as a heuristic device that helps us orient ourselves to a more extended and careful inquiry into sustainability and its relationship to agriculture. My book *The Agrarian Vision: Sustainability and Environmental Ethics* examines several more episodes in the dialog between industrial and agrarian philosophies of agriculture with the aim of expanding the intellectual underpinnings of each approach by connecting them with some venerable themes in politics and sociability. My strategy there is to allow this initial dichotomy to circle back on itself a number of times, hopefully with growing reach, subtlety, and comprehensiveness. In some iterations of this circle, the debate that seems to be working *within* the basic philosophical commitments of the industrial world is emphasized. This debate tends to see agriculture as having ethical significance in terms of either environmental or social impacts. Consistent with traditional environmental philosophers' emphasis on agriculture's impact *on* nature, participants in this debate emphasize the way that human choices are linked to outcomes, and they tend to understand the ethical acceptability of those outcomes in terms of the way that they affect health, wealth. and well-being, on the one hand, or the way that they affect the freedom or rights of other human beings, on the other. Participants who share a philosophical commitment to this approach are far from agreeing with one another about the ethical acceptability of mainstream agriculture as it is practiced today.

I believe that attention to harmful impacts and to the rights of others must occupy a prominent place in our thinking about the sustainability of our farming systems. But my larger ambition in *The Agrarian Vision* is to create a philosophical space in which those components of sustainability that are so ably being articulated and expressed by others can be augmented by a more ecologically grounded kind of philosophy that I associate with the agrarian tradition. Hence, other cycles in my examination of the contemporary debate over food ethics expand considerably on the range of virtues that agrarians might associate with agriculture or farming. They emphasize the way that thinking about farming in this traditionally agrarian way can influence political philosophy for the better.

The divide between industrial and agrarian philosophies of agriculture is thus offered less as a dichotomy than as a dialectic. Thinking recursively and bouncing back and forth between these two poles has the potential to give us a more critically informed and well-rounded conceptualization of both political and environmental issues that must be faced in contemporary farming practice and food system organization. If I have guessed correctly, our current biases are heavily shifted toward the industrial model. This is so much the case that even when we think of ourselves as being *critical* of industrial farming, we voice our criticisms through philosophical concepts that are actually antithetical to agrarian philosophy and the agrarian mind-set. An agrarian will not see human beings as outside nature in any sense. The dichotomy that frames philosophical questions in terms of human impact *on* nature makes no sense at all to the agrarian mind. While I admit that this mind-set is not adequate to facing every challenge of our age, how wonderful it would be if we could at least think like an agrarian long enough to challenge the unexamined assumptions of the industrial model.

NOTES

1. Michael Pollan, *The Omnivore's Dilemma: A Natural History of Four Meals* (New York: Penguin, 2007).

2. For example, Karl Kautsky, *The Agrarian Question* (Boston: Unwin Hyman, 1988).

3. See, for example, James O'Connor, "The Second Contradiction of Capitalism," in *The Greening of Marxism*, ed. Ted Benton (New York: Guilford Press, 1996), 197–221; and Frederick H. Buttel, August Gijswijt, Peter Dickens, and Riley E. Dunlap, eds., *Sociological Theory and the Environment: Classical Foundations, Contemporary Insights* (Lanham, MD: Rowman and Littlefield, 2002).

4. Aldo Leopold, *A Sand County Almanac* (Oxford: Oxford University Press, 1949), 6.

5. For background on this debate, see, for example, John M. Meyer, "Gifford Pinchot, John Muir, and the Boundaries of Politics in American Thought," Polity 30, no. 2 (1997): 267–84; and Michael B. Smith, "The Value of a Tree: Public Debates of John Muir and Gifford Pinchot," *The Historian* 60, no. 4 (1998): 757–78.

6. Victor Davis Hanson, *The Other Greeks: The Family Farm and the Agrarian Roots of Western Civilization* (Berkeley: University of California Press, 1999).

7. See, for example, Victor Davis Hanson, *Warfare and Agriculture in Classical Greece* (Berkeley: University of California Press, 1983), and *Fields without Dreams: Defending the Agrarian Idea* (New York: Free Press, 1996).

8. Jeffrey Sachs, *The End of Poverty: Economic Possibilities for Our Time* (New York: Penguin, 2005), 137.

9. Ibid., 177.

10. Vandana Shiva, *Monocultures of the Mind: Biodiversity, Biotechnology and Agriculture* (New Delhi: Zed, 1993).

11. Bill McKibben, *Deep Economy: The Wealth of Communities and the Durable Future* (New York: St. Martin's Griffin, 2008).

12. See John Wargo, *Our Children's Toxic Legacy: How Science and Law Fail to Protect Us from Pesticides* (New Haven: Yale University Press, 1998).

13. Gene Baur, *Farm Sanctuary: Changing Hearts and Minds about Animals and Food* (New York: Touchstone, 2008).

14. Hesiod, *Theogeny and Works and Days*, trans. M.L. West (New York: Oxford University Press, 2009).

15. Stephanie Nelson, *God and the Land: The Metaphysics of Farming in Hesiod and Vergil* (Oxford: Oxford University Press. 1998).

16. Paul B. Thompson, *The Agrarian Vision: Agriculture and Environmental Ethics* (Lexington: University Press of Kentucky. 2010), 49.

17. James Campbell, "Franklin Agrarius," in *The Agrarian Roots of Pragmatism,* ed. P. B. Thompson and T. C. Hilde (Nashville, TN: Vanderbilt University Press, 2000), 101–17.

18. Victor Davis Hanson, *The Land Was Everything: Letters from an American Farmer* (New York: Free Press, 2000).

19. See, for example, Brian Donahue, *Reclaiming the Commons: Community Farms and Forests in a New England Town* (New Haven: Yale University Press, 2001).

20. Wendell Berry, *The Unsettling of America: Culture and Agriculture* (San Francisco: Sierra Club Books, 1996).

The Ethics and Sustainability
of Aquaculture

Matthias Kaiser

Seafood is *en vogue*. Modern consumers think of seafood as a healthy supplement to a traditional meat-based diet. Supermarkets offer frozen seafood of great variety and some even fresh seafood. Good restaurants the world over have a variety of seafood on offer, even if they are not located in a coastal area. Typically, a consumer will associate fishermen and fishmongers as suppliers of this food. Yet, chances are that some if not most of what is on offer in restaurants and supermarkets originates from some form of aquaculture. Does that make a difference? And if so, in what respect?

Aquaculture is generally understood to refer to the farming of aquatic organisms, including fish, mollusks, crustaceans, and aquatic plants (see FAO 2009). Such farming usually implies some form of intervention in the rearing process to enhance production, such as regular stocking, feeding, protection from predators, and so on. Farming also implies individual or corporate ownership of the stock being cultivated.

Aquaculture relates to fishery like agriculture relates to hunting and gathering. In other words, aquaculture is the controlled and planned production of aquatic bioproducts for future harvesting rather than going after what we find in nature. As such it is an ancient activity of human culture. Early examples date back more than 4,000 years and are known from China, Egypt, and ancient Rome. Traditional forms of fish farming play an important role in several cultures, largely dependent on resource availability and culturally preferred food customs. In particular, in Asia traditional forms of fish farming are widespread. In Europe, freshwater fish farming of carp and trout has played an increasingly important role since the eighteenth century. During the second half of the twentieth century, fish farming in freshwater and seawater has become increasingly important. This development has shown impressive growth during the last thirty years. The important advantage of aquaculture in comparison with capture fisheries is that the production can be planned and a steady supply of markets is guaranteed.

The rapid growth of aquaculture in recent history is perhaps one marked difference to agriculture: agricultural traditions have evolved slowly and continuously over several thousand years all over the world, while in aquaculture there has been rather limited historical development followed by very rapid technological changes and growth. Thus, aquaculture has developed in quantum leaps, most of them during our time. This fact alone may have a consequence for the professional ethics of aquaculture producers. Thus, it seems necessary to be explicit about both professional ethics and the ethics and sustainability of aquaculture in general.

FACTS ABOUT AQUACULTURE

Aquaculture is the fastest-growing sector in the global food supply. Its development has been breathtaking, and more and more countries now have some form of aquaculture production. Asia is the region with by far the largest production figures, especially China, but other regions have developed impressive activities as well, including Europe, North and Latin America, and Africa. More than 50 percent of aquaculture production is internationally traded, with a net flow from developing to developed countries. Roughly half of global seafood consumption stems from aquaculture. A recent study by the Food and Agriculture Organization of the United Nations (FAO) forecasts that by 2020 aquaculture will contribute 60 percent of food fish (FAO 2009).

Aquaculture involves the production of everything from several species of finfish (carp, tilapia, trout, salmon, etc.), to several varieties of crustaceans (shrimps, crabs, etc.), to mollusks and aquatic plants (oysters, mussels, seaweed, etc.). Thus the term "fish farming" is, strictly speaking, misleading when used as a synonym for aquaculture.

Aquaculture in practice can take many forms. "Extensive" aquaculture production systems are based on fish growing up in sheltered fish ponds where the production of naturally available feed is often stimulated by inorganic and organic fertilizers until the fish are harvested. Sometimes these systems are combined with livestock or crop production, using their by-products to stimulate production. "Intensive" aquaculture production systems, on the other hand, rely on commercial feed for growing of a species in a closed or semiclosed system. "Semi-intensive" production systems add to the naturally available feed by using supplementary feeds that provide extra nutrients in addition to those naturally available and that in themselves are insufficient.

Aquaculture can take place in freshwater (inland), brackish water (coastal area, variable salinity), or in seawater (offshore, constant salinity). Farmed carp, for instance, is typically cultivated in semistatic land-based freshwater systems. Likewise, the farming of freshwater trout has been a tradition in Europe since the eighteenth century. In many countries, such as the United States, varieties of catfish are farmed in ponds or closed containers on land. Brackish waters are in coastal areas, and typical products of aquaculture in such waters are shrimp and crab but also mussels and oysters. The farming of salmon is a typical example of intensive seawater (i.e., offshore) farming, performed in artificial fish cages. The production includes the breeding process, which takes place in land-based, highly controlled fish tanks. Then the fish are transported to sea-based floating fish cages for growing and then finally are transported back to a land-based unit for slaughtering. Tuna aquaculture, on the other hand, is still widely based on fish caught in the wild that are then brought to sea-based fish cages for further fattening; thus the breeding is not (yet) controlled.

Consumers and the media tend to view the more industrialized production in aquaculture with some skepticism. Indeed, in some markets, for example in the European Union, consumer skepticism is seen as the major factor that may impede further growth of the industry or even cause a backlash. Aquaculture is negatively associated with "unnatural" production modes that may cause health and environmental problems. The critical tone toward aquaculture has been dominant in the media, even among the more serious papers, for quite a long time. The German *Die Zeit* stated in a 2001 article that aquaculture "is nothing but the transformation of cheap protein in a form that, given the wrong impression—namely that it is real salmon—flogs it overpriced to the consumer" (Luyken 2001, my translation). The FAO (2009, 95) reports that "concerns about human health and the social and environmental impacts of fisheries and aquaculture show no sign of abating." This critical trend may be on the increase as various forms of so-called political consumerism (see Micheletti 2006) appear to be gaining a foothold in the richer parts of the world. Large parts of the industry are therefore motivated to attend to a wide range of concerns that could be summarized under the label of "good ethics."

DISCUSSING ETHICS

What would it mean to identify ethical problems in aquaculture? What ethical issues are involved when talking about a production system for food?

Here I use the terms "ethics" and "ethical issues" in a nontechnical sense. In particular, these terms do not imply adherence to any specific ethical theory or body of specific ethical principles. The nontechnical meaning of "ethics" refers to issues concerning deeply embedded values and value conflicts. When widely pronounced values like equity, fairness, integrity (of persons or of nature), and so on are at stake, I assume that the issue is of an ethical nature. All ethical issues refer to human choices where different courses of action are possible. Ethics in this sense (partially) subsumes and extends any possible legal aspects. I presuppose that any ethical issue can be made subject of, and can be constrained by, rational argument. Thus I reject the notion that ethics is confined to purely personal and unconditioned preferences and tastes.

I claim that ethical issues are based on values or value conflicts. Some of these values may in themselves be of wider scope than purely ethical. Foremost among these is the concept of sustainability. I use the terms "sustainability" and "sustainable development" in their traditional sense as introduced by the Brundtland Commission in its 1987 UN report, *Our Common Future* (WCED 1987, 81)—"Sustainable development is development that meets the needs of the present without compromising the ability of future generations to meet their own needs"—and as adapted by states in the Rio Declaration on Environment and Development and Agenda 21 in 1992. Thus notions of sustainability comprise environmental, economic, and social factors on a global, regional, and local scale. Sustainability also adheres to some basic values, such as equity among present and future generations. The precautionary principle (see, e.g., Kaiser et al. 2005) is assumed to be part and parcel of sustainable development.

I am well aware of the inherent vagueness and ambiguity of these terms and principles as well as the many attempts to provide more specific meanings for them (see e.g. Kaiser 1997). In this chapter, however, I assume that these terms are sufficient to constrain the discussion.

Among experts there is widespread agreement that some forms of traditional fish farming do not raise significant ethical problems. So-called integrated systems of fish farming where, for example, the production of rice alternates with the production of fish are widely perceived as a sustainable production form in harmony with the environment. Fish-cum-duck or fish-cum-pig systems are used to speed up the recycling of nutrients in the pond and hence enhance the production (Ackefors 1999). These systems are used in many parts of Asia, in particular in China. But these are small-scale production units with a minimum of technology.

Matters become more difficult when we turn to intensive aquaculture. Shrimp farming in particular has been much criticized, and the growing salmon industry has also come under attack (Naylor, Goldburg, Mooney et al. 1998; Naylor, Goldburg, Primavera et al. 2000, 2001). Let us therefore have a closer look at some of these problematic features of aquaculture, even though we need to keep in mind that most of these charges apply only to certain productions and certain management forms.

FIRST ISSUE: WHAT SPECIES TO CULTIVATE AND
HOW TO FEED THEM

The charge here may be that many countries cultivate the wrong species for the wrong reasons, resulting in unsustainable practices in the long run. Predators that are high in the food chain, like salmon, sea trout, cod, or tuna, receive a high market price and are considered high-quality fish. They are often the ingredients for sushi, which is increasingly popular. These species are carnivorous and depend on feed containing a high percentage of fish meal and fish oil. The problem is thus that a significant portion from capture fisheries has to be used for industrial purposes, producing feed. This adds to the already existing use of fish meal and fish oil for feed production in agriculture (cattle, pigs, poultry). The fish used for industrial uses are typically low on the food chain (e.g., capelin) and often (though not always, e.g., anchovy) not considered to be attractive for human consumption. But worries remain that a considerable part of a natural resource from the oceans, already on the brink of overfishing, is used to produce aquaculture products for markets in the rich countries (see Naylor, Goldburg, Mooney et al. 1998; Naylor, Goldburg, Primavera et al. 2000, 2001). Thus, the worry is that this form of aquaculture will contribute to the overexploitation of the seas and will furthermore not improve food security in the poor parts of the world where it is most needed.

What are possible responses to this charge? Can aquaculture with these species be considered an ethical or sustainable production? There are alternatives. We could produce other species that are omnivorous or herbivorous, as is already done, for example, for large parts of the Asian markets. The production of tilapia or pangasius catfish are examples. However, climate conditions do not always favor such production in all parts of the world. In areas where, for example, salmon is common in the wild, it may be a reasonable strategy to build aquaculture using these domestic species. Avoiding the introduction of so-called exotic species may be a part of sustainability.

Aquaculturists also have another response to the charge that they culture the wrong species. They point to the fact that salmon is probably the most effective converter of energy when compared to other livestock. Salmon is nearly twice as efficient as pig and more than twice as efficient as chicken in terms of energy retention. In other words, we need much more feed to grow a kilogram of chicken or pig than a kilogram of salmon. Nowadays, roughly 1 kilogram of dry feed will grow 1 kilogram of salmon, a 1:1 conversion (and sometimes the conversion is less, 0.8:1). For chicken and pigs, however, 1 kilogram of dry feed converts to between 4 and 5 kilograms of biomass (Åsgård and Austreng 1995), comparing energy and protein retention in salmon, poultry, pigs, and sheep, give their digestible energy rate at 34 percent, 17 percent, 20 percent, and 1.3 percent, respectively, while protein retention is given at 30 percent, 18 percent, 13 percent, and 2.1 percent, respectively.

So aquaculture proponents argue that nothing is intrinsically wrong with using resources from capture fisheries as feed, since currently most such resources are used in agriculture anyway and in a much less effective way.

Some people add another argument here. Model calculations seem to indicate that given a wild resource of, say, 10 kilograms of capelin, cultured salmon will transform this into roughly 4.6 kilograms of biomass. Now, if that same resource of 10 kilograms of capelin had remained in the wild and had become the prey of wild cod, it would only result in 2 kilograms of cod (Åsgård and Austreng 1995). Thus, the aquaculture salmon could be seen as a more effective user of natural resources than nature itself.

Proponents of aquaculture thus conclude that the most rational strategy is to fish for low-trophic species and to farm high-trophic species. They also argue that aquaculture use of fish meal is a more rational use than agricultural use. Furthermore, many of them would add that replacement of some of our meat diet with aquaculture products is a recommended strategy for consumers in industrialized countries, since such a shift, they claim, would increase sustainability and improve public health.

SECOND ISSUE: ENVIRONMENTAL SUSTAINABILITY

The questions of feed and the kind of species we culture are not the only ones we need to ask in relation to sustainability and the environment. There are other problems as well.

Pollution from aquaculture is a concern. As in any production system, there are inputs and outputs in aquaculture systems, and most such systems are at least partially open to the environment—releases into the environment are not only possible but are the rule. Sea cages, for instance, are not closed systems; they need to provide for enough water flow to secure near-natural living conditions for the fish. Some discharge of nutrients and organic waste is inevitable in these open-cage systems. Discharges are mainly phosphorus, nitrogen, and organic carbon. Accumulation above critical values may lead to eutrophication (i.e. oxygen depletion) and sediment reduction. Excess fish feed falls through the net in these systems and accumulates on the seafloor if not dispersed by natural water currents. Furthermore, various forms of medication, such as chemotherapeutants and antifoulants, may enter the environment in large quantities, depending on how such medication is administered. We should also note the negative effects of shrimp farming on mangroves and other coastal ecosystems in many tropical countries. Uncontrolled spread of these farms threatens valuable natural resources. Environmental degradation persists in many coastal areas in Asia long after a shrimp farm has moved its production site to better suited places. Some countries, like Thailand, have now introduced strong regulatory measures to counteract this.

These charges are known, and serious aquaculturists show sincere concern. They do not deny that these problems exist. But typically proponents of aquaculture point out that these problems are not inherent to the technology; rather, most of these problems could be significantly reduced if not eliminated by improved management systems. For instance, Norwegian salmon farmers historically placed their fish cages in the interior of a fjord, where water is shallow and the impact of storms is reduced. They overlooked that this practice accumulated discharges at the bottom of the fjord. So they relocated to other sites when they realized that locations in deeper waters would benefit from strong coastal currents. Strongly toxic antifoulants can also be replaced with substances better adapted to the environment.

Industrial fish farming tends to increase the outbreak and spread of disease. This charge is also true of intensive livestock systems. Domesticated animals undergo selective breeding for several generations, which in turn may reduce fitness and genetic variation. The greatest economic threat to any aquaculture producer is not the shifting market but the uncontrollable outbreaks of disease (e.g., the spread of the parasite *Gyrodactylus salaris*). Disease may spread from fish farms to nearby rivers or waters. Many if not most of the traditional salmon rivers in Norway and Scotland are carriers of *Gyrodactylus salaris*. This threatens the wild salmon. Once a river is infected, it is very difficult and costly to perform any effective clean-up operation (if feasible at all).

Again, the problem is real, but the question is whether it can be treated to such an extent that negative effects to the environment and wild stocks can be avoided. There is a lot of research in this field, and the increase of preventative measures to protect the health of cultivated stocks, for example through vaccination, is significant.

Fish escapes from industrial (marine) fish farms threaten the genetic variation of wild stocks. Fish farming in open cages carries with it the danger of fish escapes. This may happen due to faulty gear, weather damage, predator damage, or damages during transport. It is well-documented that escaped farmed fish (salmon) enter nearby rivers and riverlets. The wild stocks of salmon, for instance, occur in genetically distinct populations, with genetic differences between and within rivers. The concern is that cross-breeding between wild and farmed stocks may lead to loss of genetic variation, with negative effects on performance traits (Kaiser 2005, 81–82). Given the number fish that escape each year, chances are that most of the salmon caught as supposedly wild are in fact escaped from farms. Many critics favor a precautionary approach to this problem (Kaiser 1997).

Production sites for fish farms compete for the use of valuable coastal zones.
Coastal zone and catchment areas are already in high demand by other potential
uses, for instance, as human settlements, for agriculture, and for tourism. Conflicts
may arise over water use between aqua- and agriculture, and conflicts may occur
with tourism concerning the use of coastal areas. All of the alternative uses have
economic potential and value. However, decision making about future uses tends
to be influenced by additional values as well, such as maintaining culturally embedded lifestyles in rural districts, human experiences of nature, and aesthetic values.
Counterarguments in favor of sea-cage farming include the creation of employment in rural areas, where job opportunities can be few, and that an alternative
source of protein is produced to meet increasing global needs.

Aquaculture raises the issues of food miles and energy use. Aquaculture
products are mostly traded internationally. It is an important actor in a globalized
economy. A typical cycle of salmon from source to end user may look like this:
Low-trophic fish are caught along the coast of Chile and are then made into fish
meal. This is then exported to a processing country, where other additives are added
and the fish pellets are packed and sold. A salmon producer in a fjord of Norway or
Scotland or British Columbia or New Zealand feeds these pellets to the salmon. The
salmon are slaughtered and frozen, or packed in dry ice, and then transported either
by truck to neighboring countries or by airplane to large markets like Japan or the
United States. There, the salmon are offered unprocessed or are processed into
various other products and then sold on the market. Critics point out that energy
use for the consumption of a salmon compares unfavorably to other products of
a local market and is not truthfully reflected in the price of the final product when
indirect environmental costs are considered.

Again, there is a need to acknowledge the facts, but then we should also consider that food in general, its production and consumption, is now very much part
of such a globalized market. The question then seems to be whether something
is wrong with adjusting to these markets or whether there are real alternatives
available.

THIRD ISSUE: QUALITY AND CONSUMER ISSUES

What does it matter if the fish we consume comes from aquaculture instead of from
capture fisheries? What if the aquaculture fish is produced legally but unsustain-
ably? Other than food safety, what specific features of a product does a consumer
need to know about? Who is to decide what "should" matter to consumers? In
democratic societies, consumers want to be in a position to make informed choices,
and they themselves will then decide what their preferences are.

While experts still argue the wisdom of labeling food products, it seems that
consumers themselves—in the rich consuming countries (the European Union,

the United States, and Japan)—may decide the issue in favor of labeling schemes anyway. There is simply market pressure to improve food labeling and food certification. This applies to aquatic as well as other food products. Political consumerism is an emerging trend, that is, the trend to "vote with your fork" for issues that are essentially political in nature, such as a more sustainable world or more respect for animal welfare or fair conditions of international trade. It is through pressure from retailers and large supermarket chains that such consumer expectations enter into labeling or certification schemes.

Any such system, if it is to be transparent, measurable, consistent, and just, will impose some costs on producers; sometimes these costs can be relatively high, especially for producers in developing countries. There are already a plethora of existing schemes: the UN Conference on Trade and Development estimates the number at four hundred and rising (FAO 2009, 96). The World Wide Fund of Nature in 2007 analyzed standards and certification schemes in aquaculture and found most of them wanting in many respects (FAO 2009, 100). However, given the consumer demand, and in part the consumer skepticism toward aquaculture in general, it seems that the work on better labeling and good certification schemes in this area is set to continue. Let us take a brief look at features that we might expect to constitute adequate consumer information for aquaculture products.

Is the product traceable? This is foremost a matter of assuring quality by tracing an aquaculture product back to its producer. Keywords here are "consumer trust" and "quality assurance" through all links of the food chain. Questions include where and by whom the fish was produced, when it was slaughtered, how it was stored and packed, and so on. Although this has been considered difficult for aquaculture products, we may soon expect that most if not all such products will be traceable back to their original producers.

Is the product from aquaculture or capture fisheries? Until recently, many producers wanted to slip their aquaculture products into the market by giving them names people might associate with wild relatives of the product. Farmed salmon was sometimes marketed as "wild water salmon." It is often difficult to find out where fish is from. Just try to ask in a restaurant whether the fish on the menu is from capture fisheries or from aquaculture. Usually the restaurant will not have an answer, or if it does the answer will be improbable. The market is not yet used to consumers who ask intelligent questions about the origins of their food.

Is the product produced sustainably? To what extent do we get reliable information about the sustainability of an aquaculture product? Given that, for example, one and the same species can be farmed under conditions that may be close to optimal sustainability, or, alternatively, under conditions that violate every aspect of sustainability, how can we know if we are consuming a sustainably produced product? Or, a related issue, how can we know if it is organic or the result of biodynamic production? If labels such as "biodynamic" or "organic" are intended to mark a more "natural" way of production, we may assume that such designations would outlaw use of some chemicals in production, but how about in the feed? If we feed unprocessed fish protein to aquaculture stocks, then we put a larger strain on nature than by using processed feed. Can we accept biodynamic production that is less sustainable than industrialized production? And how about control of diseases? Are preventative measures to protect the health of cultivated stocks "unnatural"?

What animal welfare issues are involved? Animal welfare has become increasingly important as a consumer issue. It is also viewed by many as a consideration that needs to be applied differently to different species. Peter Singer (1990) originally drew a line "somewhere between shrimp and an oyster" when considering the suffering of an animal in the slaughter process. Many people see a difference between fish and mammals in terms of their capacity to suffer. People see fish as "lower" vertebrates from which amphibians and other species evolved a long time ago. But, of course, fish have not been at an evolutionary standstill for 400 million years; they have evolved as well. The scientific reason for denying fish the capacity of pain is mainly the assumed absence of consciousness, that is, the absence of something similar to the human cortex, which operates on the stimuli from nociceptors (see Nordgreen 2009). Yet, several researchers now indicate that fish most likely do feel pain and can suffer more than we would expect given their simple nervous systems (Nordgreen 2009).

This seems to indicate that some animal welfare considerations should indeed apply to aquaculture. And with increased knowledge about these factors, we can expect consumers to demand information about this issue. This has implications for how fish are slaughtered. The various methods of stunning and killing fish are now high on the agenda in several regulatory bodies, and improving these methods is under way (EFSA 2009). In addition to the issue of pain, there is the question of stress. How do fish experience being caged together densely? For some species, overstocking of cages reduces the quality of the final product and makes the fish more prone to disease. Thus some measure of good animal welfare is also in the best interest of the producer.

Again, much depends on the species and the technology. Some varieties of catfish seem not to mind being in close contact with other fish, while salmon require some space and the possibility of swimming in strong currents. Researchers and industry are developing guidelines for best practices concerning these questions. In all of this we can recognize a trend toward incorporating fish into the community of objects of moral concern (Lund et al. 2007).

How can we assess equity, fairness, and good ethics from production to consumer? Aquaculture involves workplaces for a lot of people. In many developing and poor countries, the economic implications of such employment are considerable, with implications for gender policies as well, since many women are typically employed in aquaculture. In Bangladesh, roughly 30,000 workers are employed in processing industries for aquaculture products alone, and roughly 60 percent of them are women; 1.2 million people work in that country's overall aquaculture sector (FAO 2009). People buying shrimp from Bangladesh in one of the industrialized importing countries will typically only have vague ideas about how what they pay for the product relates to the lives of these people. What are the work conditions like for those people? Are they provided with some social security and a stable income? Is child labor involved? These are the type of questions we seek answers to when considering fair trade schemes, corporate social responsibility, or certification for ethical production.

Let us now turn to the consumer issue that is perhaps number one in the minds of most people: the nutritional and health qualities of aquaculture products.

Many people are by now aware that typical diets in industrialized countries are not altogether healthy. Obesity and overconsumption of saturated fats are among the problems. Fish is a rich source of polyunsaturated fatty acids of the n-3 family (PUFAs), such as omega-3 fats. Replacing at least some of the saturated fat in diets with PUFAs is a goal of public health policy. PUFAs have been shown to reduce the risk of coronary heart disease, and there are indications of other beneficial effects relating to arthritis and alzheimer's disease (Ruxton et al. 2007). The UK Scientific Advisory Committee on Nutrition reported in 2004 that "the majority of the UK population does not consume enough fish, particularly oily fish, and should be encouraged to increase consumption" (SACN 2004, 7).

This is the good news for aquaculture. Now to the more worrisome news. In principle, aquaculture products have an important food safety advantage over products from capture fisheries: production is controlled and safeguards against contamination can be built in. Similarly strict regimens cannot apply in capture fisheries, and, ironically, it is through feed composed of wild fish that contaminants enter aquaculture products. Traces of dioxin, PCBs, and mercury can be found in the fish used for feed production. These contaminants are dispersed in the oceans and enter wild fish through food intake. These contaminants remain to some extent in processed feed and thus enter aquaculture production. Maximum levels of these contaminants have been set for fish feed, the assumption being that these levels provide a safe threshold for consumption.

However, what is safe for one consumer is not necessarily safe for another, especially when other health-related aspects come into the picture, such as pregnancy or simply the general differences between men and women and

children. This is why the nutritional advice given to consumers by governmental agencies often differs for different consumer groups. Pregnant women,
for instance, are often advised to consume less fatty fish (such as salmon) than
other people. But perhaps even allowing these contaminants in fish feed might
not be sufficiently precautionary, given the technological possibilities of control.
There are indeed methods available to reduce contaminants in fish feed well
below the threshold levels set by governmental authorities and thus to virtually
eliminate them in aquaculture products. The drawbacks are economic: reducing
contaminants would significantly increase the price of fish feed and thus raise
prices for aquaculture products, making them less competitive in international
markets. But should food safety aspects be traded against economic aspects in
this manner?

These questions are not restricted to aquaculture. They also arise in respect
to other food products, for example, the question of pesticide contamination
of fruit. We may surmise that consumers in rich industrialized countries will
continue to exert pressure to implement stronger standards of food safety, which
will eventually reduce even slight traces of contaminants in aquaculture products.
The question remains, however, how to make an overall assessment of the ethics
and sustainability of aquaculture when pros and cons have to be weighed against
each other.

DISCUSSION: HOW TO EVALUATE AQUACULTURE
FROM AN ETHICAL AND SUSTAINABILITY POINT
OF VIEW

This short overview of issues in modern aquaculture so far has not suggested
any definite judgments. There are still a number of problematic issues in aquaculture production, many of them as yet unresolved. On the other hand, many
problems arise not so much from the nature of the technology itself but rather
from management practices and lack of good regulatory frameworks and
certification standards. Decisions have to be made on the local, regional,
national, and international levels to ensure that aquaculture can fully realize its
positive potential.

In the meantime, there are tools that could guide decision makers toward more
ethically informed decisions and strategies. The so-called ethical matrix is one
such decision tool that includes ethical criteria in decision making (Kaiser 2003,
2005, 2006a; Kaiser, Millar et al. 2007; FAO and WHO 2004). The ethical matrix
approach was first developed by Mepham (1996) and inspired by the principlist
approach in medical research ethics.

Here is how an ethical matrix works: Assume we want to assess the ethical
issues involved in a certain genetic modification of a fish species for aquaculture

TABLE 1   Ethical Matrix for GM fish

	Welfare as Elimination of Negative Utilities	Welfare as Promotion of Positive Utilities	Dignity/ Autonomy	Justice as Fairness
Small producers	Dependence on nature and corporations	Adequate income and employment security	Freedom to adopt or not adopt	Fair treatment in trade
Consumers	Safe food	Nutritional quality	Respect for consumer choice (labeling)	General affordability of product
Treated fish	Proper animal welfare	Improved disease resistance	Behavioral freedom	Respect for natural capacities (telos)
Biota (environment)	Pollution and strain on natural resources	Increasing sustainability	Maintenance of biodiversity	No additional strain on regional natural resources

production. The first step is to identify the relevant stakeholders. This is not necessarily an easy or uncontroversial part of the job. Some people may insist that the
fish itself does not deserve to be ranked as a stakeholder along with consumers
and producers, ascribing only instrumental value to the animal. However, others
feel strongly that animals or even the environment (biota) should be treated with
moral respect, akin to ascribing some degree of inherent value to animals. Instead
of deciding who is right, the ethical matrix approach includes as stakeholders all
those with sufficiently homogenous interests and whom many people believe enjoy
some moral standing. It is one matter to be generous in the inclusion of stakeholders and another to assign sufficient weight to their being affected by the technology.
Once stakeholders are identified, we list them in the matrix grid, one stakeholder
per row (see table 1).

The next step is to establish a set of ethical principles. Ideally, the combination of principles should reflect the variety present in the ethical theory literature. Being too restrictive in choosing principles may result in an incomplete
ethical analysis, while being too generous at worst may complicate the picture
and lead to nonobvious considerations. I suggest that the following combination
of ethical principles works in most settings: welfare as elimination of negative

utilities (nonmaleficence), welfare as promotion of positive utilities (benefi-cence), dignity/autonomy, and justice as fairness. If our only stakeholders were human beings, the principle of autonomy would be sufficient, but since we want to include animals and nature among the stakeholders, it seems more appropri-ate to describe the general moral principle in terms of respecting dignity (or integrity). Once the ethical principles are identified, we list them in the matrix grid, one principle per column.

Having set up the frame of the ethical matrix, we next need to specify what each principle means more specifically when seen from each stakeholder's point of view. Respect for consumer autonomy, for example, means mainly that the consumer's right to choose between alternative and clearly labeled products is respected. We end up with a matrix grid in which all principles are specified in the individual cells correlated to each stakeholder.

The next step is then to investigate how the suggested technology—in this case the GM fish—will affect each and every cell in the matrix. In other words, we start to construct a consequence matrix. For instance, having GM fish in fish farms may provide adequate and stable income for small producers, may increase their dependence on large corporations, may be neutral for consumers with respect to nutritional quality, and may threaten biodiversity or secure biodiversity (depend-ing on the technology). In making these determinations, scientific expertise will be needed to evaluate how a particular case or technology affects all the cells in the matrix.

The final step is to consider what is ethically acceptable, taking all these different implications into account. Typically, the situation may be a little more complex. We may therefore want to ascribe different weight to different cells, thus expressing the view that some harms or some benefits are more important in principle than others. We may also want to differentiate between effects that are certain and others that are merely possible. However we do this, the important point is to make sure that the ethical matrix captures precisely those considerations that people consider morally relevant to an issue.

In principle, the ethical matrix approach can be an exercise that a scholar pursues in isolation from actual stakeholders, on the back of an envelope, so to speak. In that case, the matrix merely serves to clarify issues for that scholar, providing a checklist of relevant considerations. But the matrix may also be used as an instrument in a participatory process, where stakeholders them-selves agree on what the ethically relevant features of an issue are. When used in this way, the ethical matrix typically helps (some) stakeholders recognize that their perspective on an issue is not the only relevant consideration. They may more easily recognize when a controversial issue requires compromise or when the issue involves fundamental conflicts of interest. Advice that comes out of an ethical matrix approach, in particular when generated by a participatory approach, will satisfy demands of transparency and democratic pluralism and will have theoretical support (if the principles are well chosen from a variety of ethical theories).

Using a process like the ethical matrix, we can see that ethical and sustainability considerations can in practice be woven into decision making, thus expanding on existing risk and food-safety assessments. Specific aquaculture products could thus be made more ethical and more sustainable than they currently are.

What are the overall prospects for aquaculture? I believe that its future will be determined based on how we tackle the global problems of food production in general. There is now widespread agreement that existing food production is strained by a variety of factors:

- The world population will continue to grow so that we can expect up to nine to ten billion people by the year 2050. These people will need to have sufficient food supplies.
- Our existing food production is responsible for around 17 percent of the global greenhouse gas emissions, a share that needs to be reduced significantly if we want to tackle climate change.
- Natural resources like fish stocks or arable land are limited and already faced with overuse.
- Human diets in rich countries are indicated in a number of serious health problems such as obesity. A change in diet seems warranted from the point of view of public health policy.
- The global food market does not function satisfactorily, evidenced by the fact that up to one billion people suffer from malnutrition and hunger and that price spikes make basic goods such as rice unaffordable to large parts of the global population. Furthermore, consumer trust in some rich countries is vanishing as a consequence of the opacity of global food production.

These are but some of the main problems that humanity has to deal with, the sooner the better. This is also the background for why many people believe that aquaculture—in some form or other—needs to play an important role in our global food production. Many things are seemingly right in principle about aquaculture, even though practice in many cases falls short of our ideals of ethical and sustainable food production. But given improved technologies and more knowledge, we might reduce or eliminate some of the worrisome issues in aquaculture. Given a wider public discussion of these issues, we might also hope for informed consumer attitudes and even changed and more healthy dietary habits. Thus it could be that aquaculture is an important test case for our ability to move toward a more sustainable future.

REFERENCES

Ackefors, H. 1999. "Environmental Impact of Different Farming Technologies." In *Sustainable Aquaculture—Food for the Future?*, ed. N. Svennevig, H. Reinertsen, and M. New, 145–69. Rotterdam: A. A. Balkema Publishers.

Åsgård, T., and E. Austreng. 1995. "Optimal Utilization of Marine Proteins and Lipids for Human Interest." In *Sustainable Fish Farming*, ed. H. Reinertsen and H. Haaland, 79–87. Rotterdam: A. A. Balkema.

EFSA (European Food Safety Authority). 2009. "Species-Specific Welfare Aspects of the Main Systems of Stunning and Killing of Farmed Atlantic Salmon." *The EFSA Journal* 2012: 1–77.

FAO (Food and Agriculture Organization of the United Nations). 2009. *The State of World Fisheries and Aquaculture 2008*. Rome: FAO. www.fao.org/docrep/011/i0250e/i0250e00 .HTM. Accessed April 4, 2009.

FAO and WHO (Food and Agriculture Organization of the United Nations and World Health Organization). 2004. *FAO/WHO Expert Consultation on the Safety Assessment of Foods Derived from Genetically Modified Animals, Including Fish, Rome, 17–21 November 2003*. Rome: FAO. ftp://ftp.fao.org/docrep/fao/006/y5316E/y5316E00.pdf.

Kaiser, M. 1997. "Fish-Farming and the Precautionary Principle: Context and Values in Environmental Science for Policy." *Foundations of Science* 2:307–41.

———. 2000. "Fish Farming and Biotechnology: Ethical Considerations for Future Applications." In *International Conference of the Council of Europe on Ethical Issues Arising from the Application of Biotechnology, Proceedings, Oviedo (Spain), 16–19 May, 1999*, vol. 2. Strasbourg, France: Council of Europe Publications, 2000.

———. 2003. "Ethical Issues Surrounding the GM-Animals/GM-Fish Production." Paper presented at the FAO/WHO Expert Consultation on the Safety Assessment of Foods Derived from Genetically Modified Animals, Including Fish, Rome, November 17–21.

———. 2005. "Assessing Ethics and Animal Welfare in Animal Biotechnology for Farm Production." *OiE, Scientific and Technical Review of the World Organisation for Animal Health* 24 (1): 75–87.

———. 2006a. "Practical Ethics in Search of a Toolbox: Ethics of Science and Technology at the Crossroads." In *Ethics, Law and Society*, vol. 2, ed. J. Gunning and S. Holm, 35–44. Cardiff, UK: Ashgate Publishing.

———. 2006b. "Turning Cheap Fish into Expensive Fish? The Ethical Examination of an Argument about Feed Conversion Rates." In *Ethics and the Politics of Food*, ed. M. Kaiser and M. E. Lien, 431–36. Wageningen, the Netherlands: Wageningen Academic Publishers.

Kaiser, M., K. Millar, E. Thorstensen, and S. Tomkins. 2007. "Developing the Ethical Matrix as a Decision Support Framework: GM Fish as a Case Study." *Journal of Agricultural and Environmental Ethics* 20:65–80.

Kaiser, M., J.P. Van der Sluijs, S. Beder, V. Hösle, A. Kemelmajer de Calucci, and A. Kinzig (from COMEST) and H.T. Have, S. Scholze, and E. Kuok (from UNESCO). 2005. *The Precautionary Principle*. Paris: UNESCO. http://unesdoc.unesco.org/images/0013/001395/139578e.pdf. Accessed April 4, 2009.

Lund, V., C.M. Mejdell, H. Röcklinsberg, R. Anthony, and T. Håstein. 2007. "Expanding the Moral Circle: Farmed Fish as Objects of Moral Concern." *Diseases of Aquatic Organisms* 75:109–18.

Luyken, R. 2001. "Aus kleinen Fischen grosse zaubern." *Die Zeit Online*, September 6. www.zeit.de/2001/37/Aus_kleinen_Fischen_grosse_zaubern. Accessed April 4, 2009.

Mepham, T.B. 1996. "Ethical Analysis of Food Biotechnologies: An Evaluative Framework." In *Food Ethics*, ed. T.B. Mepham, 101–19. London: Routledge.

Micheletti, M. 2006. "Political Consumerism: Why the Market Is an Arena for Politics." In *Ethics and the Politics of Food*, ed. M. Kaiser and M.E. Lien, 23–27. Wageningen, the Netherlands: Wageningen Academic Publishers.

Naylor, R.L., R.J. Goldburg, H. Mooney, M. Beveridge, J. Clay, C. Folke, N. Kautsky, J. Lubchenco, J. Primavera, and M. Williams. 1998. "Nature's Subsidies to Shrimp and Salmon Farming." *Science*, 282, 883–884.

Naylor, R.L., R.J. Goldburg, J.H. Primavera, N. Kautsky, M.C.M. Beveridge, J. Clay, C. Folke, J. Lubchenco, H. Mooney, and M. Troell. 2000. "Effect of Aquaculture on World Fish Supplies." *Nature* 405 (June 29): 1017–24.

———. 2001. "Effects of Aquaculture on World Fish Supplies." *Issues in Ecology* 8 (Winter): 1–14.

Nordgreen, J. 2009. "Nociception and Pain in Teleost Fish." PhD thesis, Norwegian School of Veterinary Science, Oslo.

Ruxton, C.H.S., S.C. Reed, M.J.A. Simpson, and K.J. Millington. 2007. "The Health Benefits of Omega-3 Polyunsaturated Fatty Acids: A Review of the Evidence." *Commentary: Journal of Human Nutrition and Dietetics* 20 (3): 275–87.

SACN (Scientific Advisory Council on Nutrition). 2004. *Advice on Fish Consumption: Benefits and Risks*. Norwich, UK: Food Standards Agency and the Department of Health.

Singer, P. 1990. *Animal Liberation*. Revised ed. New York: New York Review/Random House. First published 1975.

WCED (World Commission on Environment and Development). 1987. *Our Common Future*. Oxford: Oxford University Press.

Scenarios for Food Security

David Castle, Keith Culver, and William Hannah

Food insecurity is a devastating reality for people around the world despite ongoing development and aid programs. There remain those idealists who believe that the global food security problem is no more than a matter food distribution, a perspective based on a misguided extrapolation to global scale of Amartya Sen's analysis of food distribution in India. Such idealism takes the total caloric content of food produced around the world, divides it by the number of people, and—*presto!*—food security with appropriate redistribution. This view is, on the face of it, too optimistic, and it is increasingly contradicted by evidence about the drivers of change in food production, distribution, and demand. Global redistribution schemes cannot alone address current or future global food insecurity. In the current context, regional and global gridlocks persist between the three Fs: food, fuel, and fiber. These gridlocks will deepen in the future with the impact of global population increase on ecosystems (Lovelock 2009), the worsening water situation (Brown 2009), the balance of humanity now living in cities (UN Habitat 2009), fuel shortages making distribution of food more difficult, and the aggravating cofactor of global warming (World Bank 2009). Some of the most-feared shortages of water and energy may come sooner than initially anticipated, as growing populations stretch the coping capacity of energy-hungry urban areas. UK chief scientist John Beddington has famously predicted a "perfect storm" of shortages versus demands by 2030 (Sample 2009).

These factors are among the major causes of the global food security problem. Manifested as acute or chronic food shortages, or persistent malnutrition, the basic problem of food security is one of scarcity of food. Proposed solutions to scarcity beyond redistribution include changing consumption patterns, lowering overall demand, and attenuating severe trade-offs between food, fuel, and fiber. Other approaches seek to lessen environmental impacts of agriculture, better use water resources, resettle rural areas, and lessen the impact of agricultural practices on global warming by preventing deforestation and lessening fossil fuel inputs. If these approaches can be collectively construed as attempts to mitigate the causes and consequences of food insecurity, they can be contrasted with efforts focused on reducing scarcity through gains in productivity and nutritional quality.

Productivity gains, particularly in crops, have improved food security. Crop-rotation techniques, soil-management techniques, high-yielding and hybrid crops, crop mutagenesis, genetic modification, marker-assisted selection, fertilizers, and pesticides have contributed to agricultural productivity. Gains in dairy, fiber, and meat production have also been achieved in terrestrial animal husbandry, mostly through careful breeding programs, husbandry, and better veterinary practices. Yet animal productivity and crop yields often reach a point where they are in competition with one another, particularly as animal production changes land use and diverts crop production from human to animal production systems (IFPRI 1999). With dwindling availability of arable land, only incremental gains in productivity can be expected from terrestrial systems.

One particularly important dimension of the food security challenge is to sustainably deliver dietary protein as terrestrial systems become locally optimized to produce crops or livestock. Many observers have suggested that we might look to aquaculture as a major contributor, growing aquatic plants, shellfish, and finfish for food. There is little difficulty in making the case for the potential to increase aquaculture's contribution to food security in general and protein production more specifically. Aquaculture exists in some form in nearly every place in the world and is associated with many of the oldest and most enduring civilizations. Most of the world's population lives near water; capture fisheries have all but collapsed (Worm et al. 2006); and aquaculture productivity gains have tripled gains in terrestrial production (FAO 2004). Increasing the number of aquaculture operations around the world, and improving their productivity, also holds the potential for alleviating pressures on terrestrial agriculture, particularly with respect to the production of protein sources. Yet productivity gains in aquaculture have mostly benefited industrialized countries producing high-value fish such as salmon. Developing-country aquaculture is, however, lagging. The technologies developed in industrialized countries tend to remain there, and relatively little aquaculture R & D is conducted for the direct benefit of developing countries.

The gap between aquaculture's potential and its current contribution to food security is important in global terms. One of the United Nations' celebrated Millennium Development Goals is to address "extreme poverty and hunger" by halving, between 1990 and 2015, the number of people living on less than one dollar a day and, in the same period, halving the proportion of people who suffer from hunger (United Nations 2000). Given that there is a moral obligation to achieve global food security, focusing on developing countries most at risk of food insecurity, the main challenge in achieving this goal is how, not why. How can the science and technology of industrialized countries benefit global aquaculture productivity? This question raises a complicated problem whose resolution requires knowledge of existing industrialized science and technology, its potential role in other countries, opportunities for research and development of developing country–specific technology, and the application conditions of the technology. Synthesizing these elements into a strategy for aquaculture development requires knowledge of multiple scientific disciplines, technology developers and industry people, those who create and manage development programs, and end users of technologies. Good governance of aquaculture is equally crucial to address potential concerns that aquaculture is another technofix, doomed to fail as other technofixes have. Some claim that aquaculture will not alleviate food insecurity, arguing that it will instead simply further entrench corporate or developed-world control, leading to further ecological destruction and perpetual food insecurity.

Our view is decidedly more optimistic: we argue that there is mounting evidence in support of the proposition that aquaculture can play an increasingly important role in alleviating food insecurity. While acknowledging the seriousness of food distribution problems, we note at the same time a set of equally pressing problems whose resolution could contribute a great deal to food security. Those problems include persistent scarcity, threats to the stability of food supply, variable food quality, and the need for local production of culturally relevant food. Aquaculture has the capacity to alleviate hunger and address each of these aspects of sustainable food security. The impact of aquaculture will depend on the appropriate understanding of food insecurity, in particular regulatory, legal, social, and technical contexts. Because aquaculture is technology-intensive, especially when productivity gains are expected, the developing world will benefit in many cases from industrialized technology transfer (North-South) in addition to transfer of technology within regional innovation systems (South-South). Technology transfer is not, however, a simple task. At the very least, successful technology transfer requires knowing what to transfer, how, to whom, and when. Development of a comprehensive approach to technology transfer may arguably benefit from a broad, long-term understanding of the challenges and opportunities facing potential recipients or cocreators of technology.

Here we explore a foresight exercise conducted to develop scenarios regarding aquaculture's potential to contribute to global food security via technology transfer. Scenario building can be used to develop plausible stories about the possible futures for the planet and for global food security in which aquaculture might play a variety of roles. These scenarios reveal that, for aquaculture to achieve its potential impact on food insecurity, aquaculture requires good governance to manage the inevitable social transformation caused by new technology use. We explore the scenario method further in due course; but first, it is helpful to have a broader understanding of the context of food insecurity past, present, and future.

PUTTING THE PROBLEM OF FOOD INSECURITY IN CONTEXT

Over one billion of our fellow humans are at serious risk of starvation—a risk explained technically and diplomatically as "food insecurity." The Food and Agriculture Organization of the United Nations (FAO) estimates that 854 million people are undernourished and, worse, that this situation has changed little since the early 1990s (FAO 2006a). From 1990 to 1992, the number of malnourished people fell by 26 million but grew by 23 million after that until 2003. The FAO estimates are not self-interested, exaggerated reports: Canadian and American agencies offer much higher estimates of the number of persons who are food insecure. Most of the undernourished, and nearly all of those who are severely undernourished, are in developing countries: 820 million, according to the FAO. Of the remaining 34 million, FAO puts 25 million of those in so-called transition countries (Belarus, Hungary, Poland, and eleven others) and 9 million undernourished in developed countries (FAO 2006a).[1]

The FAO's most recent projection suggests the number of undernourished people will drop to 582 million in developing countries by 2015, amounting to 10.1 percent of the developing world's population (FAO 2006a). This situation arguably amounts to change without a difference. In the late 1960s there were over 900 million undernourished according to the FAO, yet by the late 1990s there were 777 million, rising to the current estimate of 854 million (Southgate, Graham, and Tweeten 2007). At most, a hollow victory might be seen in the fact that undernourishment in developing countries was halved between the late 1960s and late 1990s, from 35 to 17 percent (Southgate, Graham, and Tweeten 2007). Behind this apparent victory a stubborn fact remains: even as efforts to reduce food insecurity have reduced the proportion of people experiencing food security in developing countries, there is little change to the *absolute number* of food insecure people. We have far to go before we reach what the 1996 Rome World Food Summit identified as the ideal and practice of food security: "when all people, at all times, have physical and economic access to sufficient, safe and nutritious food to meet their dietary needs and food preferences for an active and healthy life" (FAO 2006a).

THE SIGNIFICANCE OF FOOD INSECURITY

Food insecurity causes a vast array of problems for individuals, communities, and entire societies in the developing world and beyond. Nutritionally incomplete diets and chronic and infectious disease are causes of malnutrition, defined as a shortage of both macronutrients (carbohydrates, protein, and fat) and micronutrients, which are needed in very small quantities yet are nonetheless essential to development and growth (Maxwell and Frankenberger 1992). Poor maternal nutrition leading to intrauterine developmental problems is a serious and widespread result of food insecurity, and there is evidence that nutritional regimens of mothers can adversely affect their children through life. Blindness, stunting of growth, and anemia all result from the impacts food insecurity has on iodine, iron, and vitamin A deficiency (FAO 2002). The Center on Hunger and Poverty documents other effects, including illness, infection, aggression, anxiety, antisocial behavior, and impaired cognitive functioning (Center on Hunger and Poverty 2002).

Although the effects of undernourishment need the most urgent attention, food insecurity's role in overeating is also reaching pandemic proportions. Food insecurity in developed countries is purportedly a risk factor for obesity—now a very serious health problem for much of the developed world (Martin and Ferris 2007) and a growing problem for countries with rapidly expanding economies. The FAO identifies several causes of this situation, including prominently a correlation between increases in income and higher-fat diets low in key micronutrients, a transition to a sedentary lifestyle associated with urbanization, and a reduction in the diversity of domestically produced foods as farmers produce single crops best suited to export demands (FAO 2006a). The metabolic syndrome often characterized as the "four horsemen of the apocalypse" because of the joint increased incidence of insulin resistance, hypertension, dyslipidemia, and abdominal obesity is ravaging industrialized countries with increasingly poor diets (Lutsey, Steffen, and Stevens 2008).

CAUSES OF FOOD INSECURITY

The social impact of food insecurity is clear, yet its causes are complex and poorly understood. Food insecurity and poverty, for example, are clearly connected, but the precise relationship has yet to be elucidated. The FAO observes that labor (the only resource of many people in developing countries) is severely affected by hunger. Nobel laureate Robert Fogel estimates that 50 percent of the economic growth in the United Kingdom and France between 1700 and 1900 was due to improvements in food security, and this led to improvements in nutrition and overall health. But the inverse relationship also holds: production, output, and wages all suffer in times of food insecurity (FAO 2002). Food insecurity is also implicated in breakdowns of domestic and civil society. Conflict increases when food insecurity is high (FAO 2002); and since women are more often affected by food insecurity, they suffer disproportionately more than men (Quisumbing, Meinzen-Dick, and IFPRI 2001; Isis-WICCE 2004).

Food insecurity results from diverse and often localized causes of scarcity. Population growth and household incomes are cited as demand-side changes that affect food insecurity (Southgate, Graham, and Tweeten 2007). Supply-side issues remain a contributing albeit minor cause of food insecurity, since most of the countries that have high food insecurity also have a net food surplus in terms of total supply (Smith, Obeid, and Jensen 2000). Of all regions in the world, only Sub-Saharan Africa has a persistent and nearly ubiquitous food shortage.

Nobel prize–winner Amartya Sen has convinced many, on the basis of an analysis of India, that food insecurity is fundamentally an issue of buying power, not only of production or total supply of food within the borders of a country. Food insecure people suffering poverty cannot afford to purchase available food (Maxwell and Frankenberger 1992; Tong 1993; Thompson 1997; Sen and Dráeze 1999; van Wijk 2002; Runge 2003; Bhatt 2004; Heintzman and Solomon 2004; GRAIN 2005; Espíndola, UN Economic Commission for Latin America and the Caribbean, and World Food Program 2005). One way of framing this problem is in terms of entitlement to a package of resources that enable purchase of food: entitlement to what is inherited, what is produced, what is given, what can be traded (Dráeze and Sen 1990). A breakdown in entitlements is associated with the rise of food insecurity; and just as food insecurity can occur at levels of social organization from individual to state, so a breakdown in entitlements can occur from national down to individual levels.

It should be emphasized that "entitlement" is used in a special, diagnostic sense here. Sen is known for a "capabilities" approach to understanding development, which understands "entitlements" as "the set of alternative commodity bundles a person can command" enabled by a legal structure structuring the command of those commodity bundles (Sen and Hunger Project 1990). Entitlements are the means to capabilities that, if arranged in the right sort of network, allow the holder to work toward self-sufficiency. A legal framework enabling property claims, for example, enables fish farmers to acquire entitlements to fish, which can be exchanged for entitlement to cash, in turn enabling entitlement to dietary export income enabling purchases of dietary items that form part of fish farmers' food security. In this influential yet controversial approach, food insecurity is viewed as part of a broader absence of a network of capabilities that enable individuals in a country to make and exchange entitlements to reach relative self-sufficiency.

A collapse in a nation's entitlements may be due to such troubles as sanctions, debt, or resource depletion (Smith, Obeid, and Jensen 2000). Individual citizens may encounter loss of entitlements in labor, land rights, gendered distribution, and conflict. Low wages, unemployment, and intermittent employment have a major impact on food security in all countries (Kruger et al. 2006). Even access to affordable food may be insufficient to overcome social practices that cause food security. Where cultural practices privilege men over women, women may suffer food insecurity (Quisumbing, Meinzen-Dick, and IFPRI 2001; Isis-WICCE 2004; Kruger et al. 2006). Further distributional breakdown occurs when adequate, accessible food supplies are not used efficiently, as food storage and preparation are associated with waste. Issues of efficient use of food are, however, of less importance than its variety and nutrient content. Most of the cheapest food is also the food that is the least nutritious (Allen 1994), and nutritious foods of diverse kinds are required for health and associated social and economic growth (Cunningham 2005).

It should also be noted that illness, allergy, and cultural needs may influence dietary needs associated with food insecurity (FAO 2006a). Some states have struggled with food security since their inception. Bangladesh, for example, has suffered food insecurity since its creation in 1971, and while it has transitioned from aid dependence to near self-sufficiency in food production, food insecurity is still evident as distributional issues associated with legal frameworks, corruption, and gender issues persist (European Commission 2007). Food security for Bangladesh is accordingly a matter of establishing entitlements, not restoring them.

Finally, conflict and corruption contribute to food insecurity. Southgate, Graham, and Tweeten (2007, 328) argue that African food insecurity is comparatively worse than the rest of the world because the continent "suffers from a long history of acute ethnic divisions, a colonial legacy of borders that neglected these division and of poor preparation for nationhood, as well as the emergence of repressive regimes after independence." Critics of this widely accepted view argue against a strong connection between corrupt governments and the impact of food aid, for example, suggesting that enduring food insecurity has other more significant causes (Goldsmith 2001).

SOLVING FOOD INSECURITY

Solutions to food insecurity can be found in aid and development, but the challenge is to identify and implement local solutions to local causes of food insecurity. Aquaculture, because it is largely underdeployed and shows promising productivity gains, holds significant potential to reduce food insecurity. A compelling track record is emerging, for example in the World Fish Centre's work on the genetically improved farmed tilapia in East Africa and Southeast Asia (IDRC 2004). A successful track record for aquaculture could dispel fears that it is a replacement or mere substitute for other, failed methods of food production. Aquaculture would need to expand while remaining a sustainable means of food production, part of reliable systems of production and available to the world's most food insecure people.

In many food insecure countries in Asia, Oceania, and Africa, fish is already a major contributor to dietary protein. Twenty-four African countries have a per capita protein ratio made up of higher than 20 percent fish (FAO 2006b). The contribution of aquaculture is already rapidly increasing. In Africa and the Near East, aquaculture has added to the food supply from 4.5 percent of fish production in 1994 to 18.7 percent in 2003 (FAO 2006b). The prospects for positive reception of increased aquaculture production and novel aquaculture technologies are thus very good in some countries most threatened by food insecurity, where aquaculture has already made a socially acceptable contribution to diets.

According to FAO statistics, the contribution of aquaculture to global supplies of fish, crustaceans, and mollusks continues to grow, increasing from 3.9 percent of total production by weight in 1970 to 29.9 percent in 2002. Aquaculture continues to grow more rapidly than all other animal food–producing sectors. Worldwide, the sector has grown at an average rate of 8.9 percent per year since 1970, compared with only 1.2 percent for capture fisheries and 2.8 percent for terrestrial farmed meat-production systems over the same period. Production from aquaculture has greatly outpaced population growth, with the world average per capita supply of fish from aquaculture increasing from 0.7 kilogram in 1970 to 6.4 kilograms in 2002, representing an average annual growth rate of 7.2 percent, based largely on China-reported growth (FAO 2004).

The extent to which aquaculture can contribute to further mitigation of food security is uncertain, yet the basic relations between aquaculture and food security show that aquaculture deserves further consideration as an underrated contributor. As noted, solutions to food insecurity involve an interconnected web of supply and access. Aquaculture is a local producer of food and a provider of local jobs. Diversification of food production methods, including adoption of aquaculture, consistently results in fish for food, higher income for farmers, and more employment opportunities (Sununtar 1997a, 1997b; FAO 2006b). Wealth creation attributed to aquaculture is noted by the FAO in projects in Bangladesh, the Philippines, and Thailand. The Asian Development Bank claims aquaculture has improved "overall food and fish consumption" and "cash incomes from fish farming" (FAO 2006b).

FORESIGHT METHODOLOGY AND SCENARIOS

Aquaculture's current growth trajectory is hampered to some extent because it is widely perceived as a new and unproven method of producing food. It may therefore be useful to consider aquaculture in a way that removes its current context and the preoccupations of actors in that context. In other words, it may help aquaculture's present and future to engage in foresight activities concerning aquaculture's context. In general terms, foresight is an activity that attempts to make sense of future technological developments for current circumstances (Georghiou 2006). Foresight is sometimes conflated with forecasting, particularly economic variants of forecasting, in which predictions about the future are based on the assumption that the past, present, and future will be essentially the same (Eriksson and Weber 2008). When time and events are construed this way, it is logically consistent to assume that trends from the past will continue to exist in the future following a constant pattern. Foresight, by contrast, does not assume that the future can be extrapolated from the past as trend analysis and therefore does not presume a model of continuous change. Foresight is based on the belief that there are new and evolving drivers of change and acknowledges that a multitude of factors could alter future outcomes (UNIDO 2005). Foresight methodology stresses our collective ability to imagine and to shape the future.

Industrialized countries are increasingly adding scenario methods to their planning processes for projects and programs that support innovation. In general, the scenario method consists of a multiday workshop in which expert participants identify drivers of change that may lead to desirable or undesirable outcomes within a delimited time horizon. With those future states in mind, participants are asked to "backcast" to the present to develop courses of action that will shape desirable futures. Scenario development is participatory and is qualitative and creative, but this should not be viewed as a limiting characteristic: the method also has the virtue of being able to incorporate other methods such as trend analysis, brainstorming, road mapping, bibliometrics, and survey results. Further, once a scenario is created, it can feed into other processes, such as strategic planning exercises, or it can be evaluated by nonexperts or stakeholders in subsequent workshops.

To evaluate the potential of aquaculture to alleviate food insecurity, a scenario workshop was held in March 2008 at the James Martin Institute for Science and Civilization, Saïd School of Business, Oxford University. The workshop goal was to understand the role of industrialized countries with respect to transferring technology and providing expertise and guidance for sustainable aquaculture in order to achieve the first of the eight UN Millennium Development Goals: to eradicate extreme poverty and hunger. Achieving this goal has implications both for the quality and quantity of protein and nutrient supply in the twenty-first century.

The workshop consisted of fourteen participants involved in a variety of aquaculture and other food production systems, technology transfer, governance, ethics, and international development. The workshop was a collaborative event, professionally facilitated by two experts in scenario methods. The workshop participants were reminded of the FAO definition of food security: "when all people at all times have physical, social, and economic access to sufficient, safe, and nutritious food that meets their dietary needs and food preferences for an active and healthy life." They were also alerted to the fact that, "globally, fish provides more than 2.8 billion people with almost 20% of their average per capita intake of animal protein; exceeding 50% in the Pacific Island States, as well as in some developing countries" (FAO 2006b).

The generic question motivating the scenario exercise was, "What role could aquaculture play in global food security in the next 10 years? 20 years? 50 years?" The more focused question motivating the scenario was, "What can developed countries such as Canada do to contribute their aquaculture capacity to global food security?" Although Canada is a small player in global aquaculture, it nevertheless has been a developer and exporter of aquaculture expertise in the private sector. Additionally, institutions such as the International Development Research Centre and the Canadian International Development Agency are well known internationally for their work in poverty and hunger reduction. Workshop participants were reminded that "scenarios are not projections, predictions, or preferences. . . . They are coherent and credible stories about the future" (Cornelius 2005). Thus, the workshop was not developing a road map for Canada alone but for the role of industrialized countries with relevant aquaculture innovation.

SCENARIOS FOR FOOD SECURITY

The workshop commenced with an overview of the goals for the scenarios before developing the PESTLE analysis (politics, economics, social, technology, legal, and environment) in which the context of the problem was articulated. Following the articulation of the context, the key contextual forces, actors, and transactions were identified. From a long list of drivers of change, those forces that have the greatest potential for impact and whose impact is most uncertain were selected to make the poles of the scenario matrices. The four-celled matrices that emerged are diagrammed in figure 1, from which the workshop participants eventually "backcast" policy options.

For our purposes here, in a volume concerned with the philosophical dimensions of food, it will be most instructive to focus on two scenarios built to explore

Matrix 1

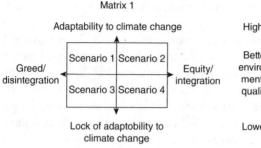

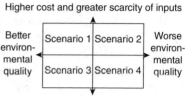

Matrix 2

FIGURE 1. Scenario matrices for food security.

futures with similar environmental challenges but quite different moral contexts. These scenarios explore cells 3 and 4 of matrix 1, the continuum between greed and equity on a global scale, in a world in which the effects of climate change are severe. In the first scenario discussed below, participants explored a possible future they titled "chaos," referring both to the effects of successive environmental catastrophes and the protectionist, isolationist attitudes foreseen to prevail in a relatively nonaltruistic world in which supernational moral communities have diminished in size and influence. The second scenario took up the perhaps unduly optimistic, yet still possible future world in which increasingly frequent environmental disasters are faced by a highly altruistic, open, and integrated community of states and international bodies.

SCENARIO 1: CHAOS

If catastrophic events such as Hurricane Katrina and the 2004 and 2011 tsunami disasters occur more frequently, and we are nationally and globally oriented in law and policy to the state and private commercial actors, we will face a range of consequences arising from lack of integrated policy and action. Human populations in the midst of catastrophe will be dispersed from coastal and affected areas, and those able to migrate will do so en masse. The worst off will become environmental refugees in shattered states unable to cope with uncoordinated offers of aid from better-off states. Massive food insecurity will ensue, as net productivity collapses and net global wealth declines. The collapse in global wealth will be accompanied by a gradual failure of social institutions—whether government or civil society. Our ability to respond effectively to environmental catastrophes will be accordingly reduced, along with our capacity to implement any plans we do have, since our distribution mechanisms—harbors, docks, and travel infrastructure—will be damaged or ruined. State responses to this situation will include reduced trade, protectionism, and mobilization against the danger of terrorism; and citizens will react to what they view as ineffective government by migrating wealth, technology, and human resources during what will likely be a global recession.

This is a story of disintegration, as regions stay regional. Protectionist states and regions will engage in less collaborative R & D, and existing food insecurity will worsen because relatively isolated states will lack the means to find and implement comprehensive solutions. Value chains dependent on global communications and transport will be slowed. Key international organizations will be ineffective or weakened, as nationality issues and national control over capital and natural resources will inhibit global commerce. Isolationism will be the norm in this new world. While some collaborative R & D may continue, barriers to new collaborations will be high, and the character of R & D may change from fundamental to largely applied research. Some states will serve as temporary havens, likely to be overwhelmed by the challenges of managing the finances, technology, and persons that might arrive in them. Still other countries may be effective safe havens that will nonetheless face difficulties in coping with short-term change.

Large aquaculture operations may migrate along with other financially powerful industries to more suitable operating environments and markets, or they will adapt their species and methods in their markets, whether as a survival mechanism or a choice to stay and adapt despite having the means to leave. Some may close, their owners' capital will be invested elsewhere, or they will be reduced to subsistence farming. Small-scale aquaculture will be periodically wiped out, as we have seen in Bangladesh, and rebuilding will depend on access to some part of the largely unorganized financial structures that continue. Lack of coordination between state-based and uncoordinated civil society aid organizations will persistently hamper the redevelopment of small-scale aquaculture.

Key defining characteristics of this scenario:

- Protection of economic borders, protectionist policies driven by lack of integration and the need to preserve national industries.
- Some thriving states, surprisingly; their populations will change as wealth enables migration to those states.
- Diversion of funds to rebuilding and maintaining infrastructure destroyed by catastrophes.
- Reduced net wealth, as it is spent rebuilding funds; reduced job security, family and national wealth, and government resource spending.
- Less innovation as less risk-tolerant entrepreneurs cease participation.
- Changes in recreation and tourism.
- Exacerbated gaps between rich and poor; the wealthy can purchase more health care or move to less dangerous areas, the poor cannot.
- Increasingly costly access to high-tech equipment.
- Regional inequality because of the regional nature of catastrophes.

Implications of these characteristics:

Strengths
· Relatively resilient aquaculture sector (particularly shellfish) in relatively resilient communities.
· Large natural capital base (land, clean water).

Weaknesses
· Transportation (long distances).
· Collaborative R & D relations between university and industry.
· Uncertainty regarding the ability of aquaculture facilities to survive.
· Support for disease management.

Threats
· Trade barriers rising.
· Mismatch between current technologies and unpredictable threats.

Opportunities
· When disasters strike others, Canada may suddenly have new markets.
· If Canada is relatively "safe," we may at least temporarily benefit from inflow of capital and people.
· Severely disrupted capture fisheries may open the way for aquaculture to replace the supply of fish.
· If hit hard in a particular region, we may be able to trade our large natural capital base for technology to rebuild rapidly and to regain competitiveness rapidly.

SCENARIO 2: LOVE IN A TIME OF CHAOS

Nationally and globally integrated systems of response from a blend of government and civil society institutions may, by comparison with scenario 1, mitigate the social and economic costs of disaster. Shared communications standards and practices will enable more efficient operation of disaster response. Increased accommodation of minority communities may be evident as an integrated approach does away with historical practices of preference for former colonies or "client" states, regions, or peoples. Coordinated R & D efforts will focus expertise and resources on new ways of doing business, support pioneering approaches in largely publicly funded research, and support inclusion of social research into thinking about catastrophe response.

While this new world of unpredictable natural disasters will require levels of taxation and standardization that may stifle individual initiative for lack of incentive, willing participation in this globally integrated society will be desired by those who take the equality of persons seriously and take equally seriously the importance of preserving all humans from misery. Food security will be an ongoing issue, but swings to extreme food insecurity will be mitigated.

Aquaculture will be a blend of large-firm operations and some small-scale aquaculture preserved for economic or noneconomic policy reasons as a kind of buffer against dangerous concentration of production in any one species, area, or firms, or to preserve certain species or to contribute specially to a particular region's food security. In some situations, disaster will be a crucial opportunity to diversify, as in Aceh (after the tsunami) shrimp farming, which was destroyed, but that destruction offered an opportunity—taken up by some—to take up other aquaculture activities. Opportunities arising out of catastrophic destruction of prior production and distribution capacity may include offshore aquaculture; use of other species. including plants; rebuilding of facilities to be more efficient; or rebuilding of transportation networks to enable faster shipping, reduction of spoilage, or access to new markets.

Key defining characteristics of this scenario:

- Ongoing global trade, minimal trade protections.
- Diversion of funds to rebuilding and maintenance of infrastructure internationally.
- More concern about other parts of the world, exchanging lessons.
- Policies and funds enabling NGOs.
- High degree of job mobility.
- Increased government revenues from either taxes or economic activity more broadly.
- Increased interregional resource flow.

Implications of these characteristics:

Strengths
- Experience in practical federalism helps regional difficulties.
- Experience in international aid programs.
- Positive perception of Canada as a global citizen.

Weaknesses
- Less net funds in public and private sectors.
- Possibility of diminished entrepreneurship.
- Need for bold choices, may be divisive.
- Testing of commitment to assisting others.
- Lack of large firms able to work globally (small- and medium-sized firms only).
- Atrophied international development capacity in aquaculture.

Threats
- Cash outflow to other states whose large firms have taken over Canadian small- and medium-sized firms.
- Rent capture by foreign interests.
- Aid strategies that create entities that outcompete us.
- Lack of governance focus on growing aquaculture.

Opportunities

· Coastal communities dependent on capture fisheries may be converted to highly adaptive aquaculture.
· Industry may be better able to lobby governments low on cash, full of problems, and needing solutions.
· Economics of scale may be to our advantage if we develop and export technology used initially to help us adapt to changing circumstances.
· We may be able to focus on being a center of expertise in research and knowledge transfer, trading on our reputation as good global partners.

Both scenarios, as can be seen, suppose that aquaculture expansion can be pursued even under conditions of significant climate change. Progress slowed, however, once participants were encouraged to backcast policy options from the developed scenarios. It is one thing, it turns out, to imagine a plausible future 50 years from now and a quite different thing to conceive of what that future would be like just 49 years from now, what would have changed between years 48 and 49, years 49 and 50, and so on. In fact, it seemed not to matter to some aspects of both scenarios whether altruism was local or international. Instead, it seemed that many of the problems likely to face both open and protectionist responses to food insecurity and climate change were matters of complex interaction between technologies and societies—whether, in the chaos scenario, for example, it seemed more likely that chaos would get worse or better at some point, or whether we might instead see a cycle of booms and busts following waves of optimism and risk taking, pessimism and risk aversion.

In other words, much of participants' exploration of the chains of events that would precede the imagined 40- to 50-year scenario tended to depend on judgments regarding human psychological responses to unfamiliar challenges, and to make judgments regarding the length of time in which particular responses might dominate, without reference to evidence, before evidence and the weight of reasons prompted a more reflective understanding and practice in response to challenges. Participants were hesitant to make those judgments, even while they were relatively quick to grasp the moral importance of facing the challenge of food security—perhaps, in their hesitation, under-scoring the sheer difficulty of moving from principle to action. In the end, in the case of the scenarios we have reproduced here, participants were unable to generate specific policy options for countries such as Canada that would refocus their R & D and broader innovation systems and would focus simultaneously on national benefit and support of food insecure countries. The reasons for this situation are complex yet worth exploring in our concluding remarks below.

CONCLUSION

Participants in the scenario building we have described chose scenario topics that required participants to make judgments regarding obligations to future generations and to engage in practical reasoning regarding the kinds of norms likely to support pursuit of general obligations to future generations. Our experience shows that it is extraordinarily difficult to bring together a group of experts, whose expertise does not extend to techniques of moral reasoning, and to ask them to stretch individually and as a group to engage in unfamiliar reasoning whose importance they recognize even as they shy away from engaging in it—or perhaps worse, a few participants attempt to bring the needed moral reasoning to a closure through force of rhetoric or appeals to dubious standards such as common sense. And yet, these are exactly the experts whose scientific, social, and technical knowledge are essential to considering practical options for preparation of national R & D systems to make better contributions to food security.

Even though the original scenario builders' intentions were not fully borne out with practical policy recommendations for change starting today, there were some important lessons learned about aquaculture and deliberation regarding aquaculture. One crucial lesson is the participants' perhaps surprising convergence on the importance of preparing for the effects of *climate change*. In that context, participants from private, public, and university sectors were keenly aware of the *limits to solutions from a single, production-oriented developed state*. Canada was viewed as an important actor only when its efforts were combined with the efforts of others—and the same judgment was made regarding other aquaculture nations. Recognition of the limits of individual actors was amplified by *skepticism regarding the readiness and ability of Canada to change* its aquaculture focus from production to production *and* service, and transfer of knowledge and technology.

Our participants' skepticism may be further evidence of the gap between knowing and being able to apply sound moral judgments: skepticism regarding readiness to change was not disagreement with the importance of changing. It was simply doubt that the diverse parts of Canadian society are sufficiently knowledgeable about and committed to addressing food insecurity. These lessons left participants and organizers very soberly aware of the distance between current practice and practical realization of UN Millennium Development Goals for food security. And, above all, participants and organizers produced these scenarios with the knowledge that interdisciplinary deliberation and action are necessary to face the problem of food security—no one discipline or actor is sufficient. Yet deliberation of this kind takes time and patience and a willingness to engage seriously with the distant and unpredictable future using plausible stories about it.

NOTES

1. Even wealthy developed countries suffer the problems of food insecurity: America's Second Harvest and the Institute for Food and Development Policy put American food insecurity numbers around 25 million (Cohen, Kim, and Ohls 2006) or 35 million (Ahmadi and Ahn 2004). A report prepared for ConAgra by the Center on Hunger and Poverty claims that 13 million children alone were food insecure in the United States in 2002 (Center on Hunger and Poverty 2002). The US Department of Agriculture measure for 2006 was 11 percent of households—12.6 million food insecure households (Nord, Andrews, and Carlson 2007). In Canada, HungerCount counted 753,458 people as food bank users (Tsering 2006). A new dimension appearing in industrialized countries is the food insecurity of those who have poor nutrition but excessive caloric intake; the *New England Journal of Medicine* has reported that this generation of children in industrialized countries has *lower* predicted life expectancy than the last (Olshansky et al. 2005).

REFERENCES

Ahmadi, B., and C. Ahn. 2004. "Beyond the Food Bank." *Food First Backgrounder* 10 (4).

Allen, L. H. 1994. "Nutritional Influences on Linear Growth: A General Review." *Journal of Clinical Nutrition* 48:S75–S89

Bhatt, M. S. 2004. *Poverty and Food Security in India: Problems and Policies.* Delhi: Aakar Books.

Brown, L. R. 2009. *Plan B 4.0: Mobilizing to Save Civilization.* New York: W. W. Norton.

Center on Hunger and Poverty. 2002. *The Consequences of Hunger and Food Insecurity for Children.* Boston: Heller School for Social Policy and Management Brandeis University.

Cohen, R., M. Kim, and J. Ohls. 2006. *Hunger in America.* Chicago: America's Second Harvest—the Nation's Food Bank Network.

Cornelius, P. 2005. "Three Decades of Scenario Planning in Shell." *Management Review* 48 (1): 92–109.

Cunningham, L. 2005. *Assessing the Contribution of Aquaculture to Food Security: A Survey of Methodologies.* Rome: Food and Agriculture Organization of the United Nations.

Dráeze, J., and A. K. Sen. 1990. *The Political Economy of Hunger.* 3 vols. WIDER Studies in Development Economics. Oxford: Oxford University Press.

Eriksson, E. A., and K. M. Weber. 2008. "Adaptive Foresight: Navigating the Complex Landscape of Policy Strategies." *Technological Forecasting and Social Change* 75 (4): 462–82.

Espíndola, E., UN Economic Commission for Latin America and the Caribbean, and World Food Programme. 2005. *Poverty, Hunger and Food Security in Central America and Panama.* Serie Políticas Sociales 88. Santiago de Chile: Naciones Unidas CEPAL Social Development Division.

European Commission. 2007. *Bangladesh: European Community Country Strategy Paper for the Period 2007–2013.* www.eeas.europa.eu/bangladesh/csp/csp_07_13_en.pdf.

FAO (Food and Agriculture Organization of the United Nations). 2002. "Reducing Poverty and Hunger." Paper presented at the International Conference on Financing for Development, Monterrey, Mexico, March 18–22.

————. 2004. *The State of World Fisheries and Aquaculture*. Rome: FAO.

————. 2006a. *The State of Food Insecurity in the World*. Rome: FAO.

————. 2006b. *The State World Aquaculture*. Rome: FAO.

Georghiou, L., and M. Keenan. 2006. "Evaluation of National Foresight Activities: Assessing Rationale, Process and Impact." *Technological Forecasting and Social Change* 73 (7): 761–77.

Goldsmith, A. 2001. "Donors, Dictators and Democrats in Africa." *Journal of Modern African Studies* 39 (3): 411–36.

GRAIN. 2005. "Food Sovereignty: Turning the Global Food System Upside Down." *Seedling* (April): 1–4.

Heintzman, A., and E. Solomon, eds. 2004. *Feeding the Future*. Toronto: House of Anansi Press.

IDRC (International Development Research Council). 2004. *Genetic Improvement of Farmed Tilapia: Lessons from the GIFT Project*. Ottawa: IDRC.

IFPRI (International Food Policy Research Institute). 1999. *Livestock to 2020: The Next Food Revolution*. Washington, DC: IFPRI/FAO/ILRI.

Isis-WICCE. 2004. *Women, Armed Conflict, and Food Security in Uganda: An Exploratory Study of Four Districts*. Isis-WICCE Research Report. Kampala: Isis-WICCE.

Kruger, A., S. Lemke, M. Phometsi, H. Van't Riet, A. Pienaar, and G. Kotze. 2006. "Poverty and Household Food Security of Black South African Farm Workers: The Legacy of Social Inequalities." *Public Health Nutrition* 9 (7): 830–36.

Lovelock, J. 2009. *The Vanishing Face of Gaia: A Final Warning*. New York: Basic Books.

Lutsey, P. L., L. M. Steffen, and J. Stevens. 2008. "Dietary Intake and the Development of the Metabolic Syndrome: The Atherosclerosis Risk in Communities Study." *Circulation* 117 (6): 754–61.

Martin, K. S., and A. M. Ferris. 2007. Food Insecurity and Gender Are Risk Factors for Obesity. *Journal of Nutrition Education and Behavior* 39 (1): 31–36.

Maxwell, S., and T. Frankenberger. 1992. Household Food Security: Concepts, Indicators, Measurements; A Technical Review. New York: IFAD and UNICEF.

Nord, M., M. Andrews, and S. Carlson. 2007. *Household Food Security in the United States, 2006*. Economic Research Report No. 49. Washington, DC: USDA Economic Research Service, November.

Olshansky, S. J. Jay, D. J. Passaro, R. C. Hershow, J. Layden, B. A. Carnes, J. Brody, L. Hayflick, R. N. Butler, D. B. Allison, and D. S. Ludwig. 2005. "A Potential Decline in Life Expectancy in the United States in the 21st Century." *New England Journal of Medicine* 352 (11): 1138–45.

Quisumbing, M. A. R., R. S. Meinzen-Dick, and IFPRI (International Food Policy Research Institute). 2001. *Empowering Women to Achieve Food Security*. Washington, DC: IFPRI.

Runge, C. F. 2003. *Ending Hunger in Our Lifetime: Food Security and Globalization*. Baltimore: Johns Hopkins University Press.

Sample, I. 2009. "World Faces 'Perfect Storm' of Problems by 2030, Chief Scientist to Warn." *Guardian*, March 18.

Sen, A. K., and J. Dráeze. 1999. *The Amartya Sen and Jean Dráeze Omnibus: Comprising Poverty and Famines, Hunger and Public Action; India: Economic Development and Social Opportunity*. New Delhi: Oxford University Press.

Sen, A. K., and Hunger Project. 1990. *Public Action to Remedy Hunger*. New York: Hunger Project.

Smith, L., A. E. Obeid, and H. Jensen. 2000. "The Geography and Causes of Food Insecurity in Developing Countries." *Agricultural Economics* 22 (2): 199–215.

Southgate, D. D., D. H. Graham, and L. G. Tweeten. 2007. *The World Food Economy*. Malden, MA: Blackwell.

Sununtar, S. 1997a. "Environmental and Health Impacts of Integrated Fish Farming in Northeast Thailand." *Aquaculture Asia* 3 (1): 8–10.

———. 1997b. "Total Economic Valuation of Integrated Farming Practices: A Case Study in Northeast Thailand." *Aquaculture Asia* 3 (1): 10.

Thompson, P. B. 1997. *Food Biotechnology in Ethical Perspective*. Ed. S. Hill. Techniques and Perspectives in Food Biotechnology Series. London: Blackie Academic and Professional.

Tong, Z. 1993. "Poverty, Food Insecurity and Commercialization in Rural China." Thesis, University of Guelph.

Tsering, C. 2006. *Hunger Count 2006*. Toronto: Canadian Association of Food Banks.

UN Habitat. 2009. *Global Report on Human Settlements 2009*. www.unhabitat.org/categories.asp?catid=555.

UNIDO (UN Industrial Development Organization). 2005. *UNIDO Technology Foresight Manual*. Vienna: UNIDO.

United Nations. 2000. *55/2. United Nations Millennium Declaration*. New York: United Nations.

van Wijk, J. 2002. "Food Insecurity: Prevalence, Causes, and the Potential of Transgenic 'Golden Rice.'" *Phytochemistry Reviews* 1:141–51.

World Bank. 2009. *World Development Report 2010: Development and Climate Change*. Washington, DC: World Bank.

Worm, B., E. B. Barbier, N. Beaumont, J. E. Duffy, C. Folke, B. S. Halpern, J. B. C. Jackson et al. 2006. "Impacts of Biodiversity Loss on Ocean Ecosystem Services." *Science* 314 (5800): 787–90.

Nutritionism and Functional Foods

Gyorgy Scrinis

From the 1960s through the 1990s, dietary guidelines and nutritional advice were dominated by negative messages regarding the dangers of consuming too much of the wrong types of nutrients and foods. Nutrients were divided into "good" and "bad" types, and the main aim was to reduce consumption of bad nutrients and of the dangerous foods that contained them. Fat in particular was vilified, and low-fat diets were universally promoted as a means of minimizing the risks of a range of chronic diseases. The food industry eventually adapted and responded to these nutritional guidelines with a flood of reduced-fat and reduced-calorie foods. Such nutritionally "reduced" or "lesser evil" foods remain popular today and continue to tap into the negative messages and fears of that earlier nutritional era.

Over the past decade, however, a range of novel food products carrying more positive health messages have appeared. A new set of nutrients and food components now compete for attention on food labels, such as omega-3 fats, plant sterols, probiotics, and antioxidants. These foods and nutrients also claim to deliver a broader range of health benefits related to weight management, joint and bone health, immunity, digestive health, cardiovascular health, mental performance, and physical energy. Probiotic ice-cream, heart-healthy chocolate-chip muffins, satiety smoothies, calorie-burning green teas, fiber-rich snack bars, omega-3-fortified baby foods for brain and eye development, and low-glycemic-index meal replacements exemplify this new generation of so-called functional food products.[1] In this contemporary nutritional era, the new imperatives are to achieve an *enhanced* state of health, to *target* particular bodily functions and health conditions, to *optimize* nutritional and dietary intake, and to *personalize* foods and diets to one's specific bodily requirements.

The marketing focus on the nutrient composition of these foods and their claimed health benefits is a key feature of what I call the *ideology of nutritionism,* which is characterized by a reductive understanding of nutrients and their relationship to bodily health. Nutritionism has been the dominant paradigm within nutrition science over the past century and has increasingly framed popular dietary advice and dietary guidelines, food and nutrition policies, food manufacturing and marketing practices, food labeling regulations, and the public understanding of food and dietary health. Nutritionism not only underpins the scientific knowledge informing the production of nutritionally modified foods, but has also shaped the consumer demand for and acceptance of these products and their associated health claims through the construction of nutricentric persons who understand and engage with food in these ways.

In the contemporary period—which I refer to as the era of *functional nutritionism*—the rise of a functional approach to food and the body has created the conditions for the emergence of the functional foods concept and frames the scientific knowledge, technological practices, marketing strategies, and consumer demand for these products.

This chapter outlines the general characteristics of the ideology of nutritionism, including a number of forms of reductionism with respect to food, nutrients, and the body. I identify three distinct forms and historical eras of nutritionism—quantifying nutritionism, good and bad nutritionism, and functional nutritionism and the dominant characteristics of each of these eras. I then consider the ways in which nutritionally reductive scientific knowledge has been translated into nutritionally reductive technological practices and marketing strategies, including the production of nutritionally engineered foods and the use of nutrient claims and health claims to market these products. I also examine the limitations of the common definitions of functional foods and the role of the functional foods concept in legitimating the nutritionism paradigm and the commercial interests of the food industry.

THE IDEOLOGY OF NUTRITIONISM

In understanding the relationship between food and bodily health, at least three levels of engagement with food can be distinguished: the dietary level, the level of food or the food product, and the nutrient level.[2] The scientific engagement with food at the nutrient level has revealed important and useful knowledge about the nutrients and other components in foods and their role in bodily functioning and maintaining bodily health. However, the dominant paradigm within nutrition science over the past century has been characterized by a distinctly reductive approach to studying nutrients and interpreting and applying this nutrient-level knowledge.[3]

Nutritionism—or *nutritional reductionism*—can be defined as where the nutrient level becomes the *dominant* level and mode of understanding food, such that it does not merely inform and complement but instead tends to undermine, displace, and even contradict other levels and ways of understanding and contextualizing the relationship between food and the body.[4] Two forms, or orders, of nutritional reductionism can be distinguished, which otherwise tend to be conflated or confused in critical discussions of nutrition science: a first-order reduction *to* the nutrient level, or *nutrient-level reductionism;* and a second-order reduction *within* the nutrient level, which typically takes the form of *single-nutrient reductionism.*[5]

Nutrient-level reductionism refers to the reduction *from* the level of food, or the level of dietary patterns, *to* a dominant and often exclusive focus on this nutrient level. The assumption is that the healthfulness of a food can be adequately studied—and translated into dietary advice—on the basis of the quantities of some of its nutrient components. Nutrients are decontextualized, in the sense that they are taken out of the context of the foods and dietary patterns in which they are consumed. We then overlook other approaches, including evaluating foods in terms of the quality of the food and its ingredients, particularly in terms of its level of processing; the broader dietary patterns and cultural and ecological contexts within which food is consumed; traditional and culturally specific understandings of the healthfulness of foods; and the use of the senses for understanding food quality.[6]

An enduring example of this nutrient-level reductionism is the attempt to characterize not only foods but also entire cuisines and dietary patterns on the basis of their macronutrient profiles—that is, the relative ratios of fats, carbohydrates, and proteins. The search for the optimal macronutrient profile is a feature of many popular weight-loss diets, from the standard low-fat/high-carb diet, to the Atkins-style low-carb/high-fat diet, as well as the more recent high-protein diets and low-glycemic-index, or good-carb, diets.[7] The guiding assumption has been that such an optimal nutrient profile can be discovered for the purposes of effective weight loss or for reducing the risk of chronic diseases, and that it does not really matter what foods are eaten as long as the optimal macronutrient criteria are met.

Within the terms of nutrient-level reductionism, nutrition scientists' understanding of nutrients may involve a detailed analysis of the composition and interaction of nutrients within foods and between nutrients and the body. However, nutritional reductionism also commonly involves a simplified understanding of the role of nutrients *within* the nutrient level.[8] This typically takes the form of single-nutrient reductionism—a reductive focus on single nutrients—whereby individual nutrients are abstracted out of the context of, and analyzed in isolation from, other nutrients and food components, as well as from foods and dietary patterns. This single-nutrient reductionism also commonly carries the assumption that these single nutrients can be extracted or synthesized and then consumed in isolation from particular foods, such as in the form of nutritional supplements or nutritionally fortified foods. Nutritional epidemiologist David Jacobs argues that this reductive focus on single nutrients ignores the synergies and interactions that occur between nutrients in whole foods.[9]

An example of single-nutrient reductionism is the low-fat campaign that dominated mainstream dietary advice throughout the 1980s and 1990s. The advice to reduce overall fat intake and to eat low-fat foods was promoted by government authorities and nutrition experts as a means to reduce the risk of chronic diseases, such as heart disease and cancer, as well as to prevent weight gain. The low-fat message was to an extent a deliberate simplification of the slightly more nuanced—though still nutricentric—advice to decrease consumption of saturated fats and overall calorie intake.[10] This low-fat advice was not contextualized or qualified in terms of the types of foods one was meant to consume to achieve these fat reductions, such as whether people should eat less of, or reduced-fat versions of, particular types of foods; or whether the reductions were to be achieved from adjusting the consumption of processed foods or whole foods. Instead, all that mattered was the reduction in total fat consumption and/or reducing the proportion of fats in the diet to less than 30 percent. One of the consequences of this simplified and decontextualized single-nutrient advice was that any foods perceived or marketed as "low-fat" or "reduced fat" came to be understood as "healthy" in some respect, regardless of the quality of the food, the level of processing or additives it contained, or the overall nutrient profile of the food.

The distinction between nutrient-level reductionism and single-nutrient reductionism can be illustrated with the types of nutrition labeling commonly found on the back and front of food packaging, respectively. The nutrient information panel on the back of food packaging listing the quantities of a range of nutrients is a symbol of nutrient-level reductionism, particularly when it appears above and in much larger type than the ingredients list.[11] Single-nutrient reductionism, on the other hand, is represented by the inflated nutrient-content claims on the front of packaged foods that focus on the presence or absence of single nutrients, such as "high in omega-3s" or "cholesterol-free." These front-of-pack nutrient-content claims effectively promote both forms of reductionism: they shift attention from the ingredients list to the quantified nutrient information, and they also reduce the focus from the overall nutrient profile to the presence or absence of particular nutrients.

The promotion of margarine as a healthier alternative to butter based on their respective proportions of saturated and unsaturated fats is a classic illustration of how nutritionism can undermine and contradict the evaluation of foods.

Margarine is a processed reconstituted food that was until recently manufactured with partially hydrogenated vegetable oils; it also incorporates a range of other highly processed ingredients and chemical additives. The hydrogenation process solidifies the liquid vegetable oils by chemically transforming the unsaturated fats into novel types of trans-fatty acids. From the 1960s until the 1990s, margarine was thought to have a healthier fat profile than butter, as it was produced with oils high in polyunsaturated and monounsaturated fats. By contrast butter was vilified for containing higher ratios of the supposedly harmful and artery-clogging saturated fats. However, by the early 1990s nutrition scientists had come to the conclusion that the high levels of transfats in margarine are even more harmful than saturated fats, particularly in terms of their effects on blood cholesterol levels. Since then, margarine manufacturers have either replaced or combined the hydrogenation process with other techniques for chemically reconstituting—and thereby solidifying—the vegetable oils, such as the "interesterification" and "fractionation" processes.[12] The end products are no less highly processed and chemically transformed, though they may contain low levels of transfats. Yet by continuing to focus on the fat composition of these "virtually transfat free" margarines, rather than on the quality of the ingredients and additives used in their production, margarine's reputation as a heart-healthy spread has been saved.[13]

The "mistake" of inadvertently promoting transfat-laden margarine is one of several mistakes, revisions, and backflips in scientific knowledge and dietary advice over the past century. Other cases include advice regarding dietary cholesterol, eggs, low-fat diets, and vitamin B.[14] Yet these revisions do not seem to have tempered the sustained and confident discourse of precision and control that continues to pervade nutrition science, nor the willingness to translate limited and partial scientific insights into definitive population-wide dietary advice. I refer to this nutritional hubris as the *myth of nutritional precision*, as it involves an exaggerated representation of scientists' understanding of the relationship between nutrients, foods, and the body and a failure to acknowledge the limits of the nutrient-level perspective. At the same time, the disagreements and uncertainties that exist within the scientific community with respect to particular nutritional theories tend to be concealed from, or misrepresented to, the lay public.

Regardless of the precision or otherwise of nutricentric scientific knowledge, the limitations of nutritionism are accentuated when this knowledge is translated into nutricentric dietary advice.[15] This is in part due to the difficulties involved in incorporating decontextualized nutricentric dietary advice into everyday food-level choices and eating patterns,[16] such as expecting individuals to monitor and count calories or to make sense of the ratio of fats and carbs in their diets.

The other side of this nutritionally reductive approach to food is an equally reductive approach to understanding the body and bodily health, particularly in terms of a narrow range of quantifiable biomarkers and biochemical and genetic processes. This often takes the form of what I call *biomarker reductionism,* characterized by a reductive and decontextualized understanding of particular nutritional biomarkers, such as HDL and LDL (or "good" and "bad") blood cholesterol levels, the GI (glycemic index), and the BMI (body mass index). Biomarkers such as these have been interpreted as directly representing—and even as determining—one's bodily health. Biomarker reductionism shares many of the characteristics of nutritional reductionism, such as the claims to a precise understanding of how foods and nutrients affect biochemical processes; the simplification of the understanding of these biomarkers and their relationship to bodily health; the differentiation of biomarkers into "good" and "bad" types; and the tendency to undermine and erase the distinctions between types of foods in terms of food quality.

The GI, for example, is now used to differentiate "good" and "bad" carbs based on how foods affect blood sugar levels. GI scores seem to broadly correlate with levels of processing, such that highly refined and processed foods tend to have higher GI scores than whole foods. Yet GI scores also cut across and undermine the distinction between minimally and highly processed foods. For example, many high-sugar foods have moderate GIs (Coke: GI = 58; Snickers chocolate bar: GI = 55), yet some vegetables have a high GI (mashed potatoes: GI = 90), and whole wheat and brown rice often have similar GIs to refined, white versions of these grains.[17] Another case of biomarker reductionism is BMI reductionism. Within the dominant "obesity epidemic" discourse, the BMI is assumed to represent and determine a person's state of health and susceptibility to a range of chronic diseases, regardless of, for instance, a person's dietary and exercise patterns.[18]

QUANTIFYING, GOOD AND BAD, AND FUNCTIONAL FORMS OF NUTRITIONISM

Since the mid-nineteenth century, at least three forms of nutritionism can be identified, each of which has been dominant within three distinct eras: *quantifying nutritionism, good and bad nutritionism,* and *functional nutritionism.* These forms of nutritionism have framed scientific research, dietary advice, food manufacturing and marketing practices, and food and nutrition policies.[19] They have also shaped forms of identity and ways of experiencing food and the body. Each of these forms of nutritionism coexist in the contemporary era, with functional nutritionism emerging as the new dominant form that overlays, intersects with, and reconstitutes the quantifying and the good and bad forms of nutritionism.

Quantifying nutritionism refers to the logic of quantification and the calculating approach to food, nutrients, and the body that pervades scientific research, dietary advice, and food-labeling practices.[20] The era of quantifying nutritionism dates from the late nineteenth century through to the mid-twentieth century. It was characterized by a concern with the consumption of "adequate" quantities of nutrients in order to promote bodily growth and avoid nutrient-deficiency diseases, with a particular focus on the role and quantification of calories, protein, and vitamins.[21] The nutrient composition of foods and the nutrient requirements of bodies were calculated, and the body was conceived of and manipulated, in terms of mechanistic input-output equations, thereby constituting what I refer to as the *quantified-mechanized body*.[22]

Wilbur Atwater's work in measuring and quantifying the caloric content of foods and human caloric requirements can be described as a form of caloric reductionism.[23] Caloric measurements were used to determine the most cost-effective diet for workers and could be used to override cultural or culinary preferences for particular types of foods, thereby shaping dietary choices.[24] The idea of food as fuel fits precisely with the mechanistic view of the body and the attempt to quantify its energy requirements. Protein—and animal protein in particular—was prized during this period as a growth-promoting macronutrient, and used to legitimate government policies supporting meat and milk production and consumption.[25]

The discovery of vitamins highlighted the importance of fruit and vegetable consumption but also led to vitamin fortification of the food supply. The enrichment of white flour with some of the nutrients lost in the refining of whole grains was essentially a technological fix—or more specifically a nutri-technological fix—for the shift to a diet of refined grains.[26] Food manufacturers exploited the new fascination with vitamins through a range of fortified foods. But vitamins were also enthusiastically embraced by many consumers,[27] signaling the beginnings of a popular nutritional consciousness in this era and the rise of what I call the *nutricentric person* or the *nutricentric self*—a person who would come to view and to engage with foods primarily in terms of their nutrient composition.

Beginning in the 1960s, the era of *good-and-bad nutritionism* was defined by the emergence of "good" and "bad" nutrients—and of bad or dangerous nutrients in particular—as well as by a concern with the excess consumption of foods and nutrients in general. Fats and carbs were the focus of much scientific research and dietary advice, with cholesterol, fat, saturated fat, and calories singled out as the bad nutrients or food components to be avoided in excessive quantities, while carbs, fiber, and unsaturated fats featured on the list of good nutrients. The focus also shifted from nutrient-deficiency diseases to reducing the risk of chronic diseases and to the identification and measurement of biomarkers of these diseases. Good and bad nutrients, as well as good and bad biomarkers, were now subject to quantification and scientific management, including the ratio and quantities of types of fats and types of macronutrients, HDL and LDL blood cholesterol levels, and calories. The mechanical body of the quantifying nutritionism era was reframed as what I call the *at-risk body* of the good and bad era—a body at risk of chronic diseases and obesity and having to avoid the dangerous nutrients and foods that were flooding the food supply. Warren Belasco has referred to the idea of "negative nutrition" that emerged and pervaded American food culture in the 1970s and 1980s.[28] Marion Nestle has also characterized this new era in terms of a shift from "eat more" to "eat less" dietary messages.[29]

During the good-and-bad era, nutritionism shifted from the margins to the center of mainstream public consciousness and discourses around food. This was particularly due to the shift toward nutricentric dietary guidelines issued by government authorities and public health institutions, as well as the nutricentric marketing practices of the food industry. Concerns regarding high levels of consumption of animal products (largely due to their saturated fat content), and about the growing consumption of highly processed and refined foods, were translated into nutrient-level recommendations to reduce fat, saturated fat, or calorie intake rather than to directly reduce the consumption of these foods.[30] The shift to nutricentric discourses around food was also reflected in the use of nutrient-level terms to represent types of foods and to thereby replace food-level terminology and categories. For example, the term "refined carbohydrates" came to be used to refer to refined grains and flours; the term "empty calories" to refer to high-calorie, nutrient-poor processed foods.

However, this shift to nutrient-level language and dietary advice arguably favored the interests of the food industry over the dietary advice of nutrition experts and enabled food manufacturers to selectively appropriate and exploit these dominant nutrient messages. The reductive focus on fat was relatively easy for food manufacturers to deal with, as it allowed for the substitution of fat with other—often highly processed and reconstituted—ingredients. It also enabled the lay public to interpret their consumption patterns in these nutricentric terms and to seek out nutritionally engineered versions of what they were already eating. Rather than consuming less meat or dairy products, individuals could select "lean" meats and low-fat milk or switch from red meat to white meat. Similarly, they could switch to nutritionally modified versions of processed and fast foods rather than consuming less of these products.

Since the mid-1990s there has been a further shift in the dominant form of nutritionism to *functional nutritionism,* which is characterized by a heightened focus on the relationship between foods and nutrients, on the one hand, and specific bodily functions, health conditions, and biomarkers on the other. There has also been a shift from a concern with minimizing the risk of chronic diseases to the idea of achieving an "enhanced" state of health and of "optimizing" bodily performance. Whether nutrition scientists have been able to define and deliver dietary recommendations capable of achieving such an enhanced state of health is, however, open to question.

The era of functional nutritionism has seen a proliferation of categories and subcategories of nutrients, but with each nutrient now more precisely targeted to particular bodily functions and health outcomes. There has been a return to the good and bad fats discourse, with transfats having joined saturated fats in the bad fats category and omega-3 fats the good fats category. But there has also been a reemphasis on the positive and beneficial attributes of nutrients, particularly on a new range of "wonder nutrients" and food components, including the omega-3 fats, phytochemicals, and plant sterols. These "functional nutrients"—and the "functional foods" in which they are contained—are now attributed with medicinal and therapeutic qualities and the power to prevent or overcome diseases and other health conditions.[31]

Rather than simply seeking to maximize or minimize the consumption of particular nutrients, the new imperative is to optimize the quantities and ratios of nutrients consumed or to identify new nutrient components and nutrient combinations in order to achieve similar or novel outcomes. For example, instead of simply eating less or seeking out reduced-calorie or reduced-fat foods to address the health or weight issues associated with overconsumption, consumers can select foods with added plant sterols claiming to block cholesterol absorption, or high-protein and low-GI foods and diets claiming to increase "satiety" levels and thereby increase the time between meals or snacks.[32] Similarly, while nutrition experts recommend the increased consumption of omega-3 fats, the importance of lowering the *ratio* of omega-6 to omega-3 fats is also emphasized, in order to restore the balance of these fats to a more optimal level.[33] From being told to eat more in the quantifying era and to eat less in the good and bad era, we are now expected to eat smarter.

In terms of functional approaches to the body, there has been a new focus on, and explicit references to, internal bodily processes within public education campaigns and commercial marketing strategies.[34] The concept of the glycemic index, for example, encourages the lay public to imagine the speed at which sugars are released into the bloodstream and the effects this has on energy levels. In targeting specific bodily functions and conditions, there has also been a shift away from the idea of a universal, one-size-fits-all healthy diet—typified by the low-fat/high-carb diet of the good-and-bad era that claimed to address multiple health conditions—toward a more personalized and targeted diet for individuals and their unique bodily requirements and health concerns. Individuals now have a wider range of nutritional concepts and packaged products from which to choose and to combine in order to address their specific needs, such as for heart health, sporting performance, or weight loss. The science of nutritional genomics (or nutrigenomics) also promises to extend our understanding of the relationship between food and nutrients to the genetic level of the body, with claims that we may one day be able to tailor diets to each individual's unique genetic profile.[35]

Functional nutritionism not only gives rise to new types of foods but also to new types of nutricentric individuals and embodied identities that demand and require these food products and their associated health claims. We would not be manufacturing and purchasing so-called functional foods if we did not already have a corresponding view and experience of our own bodies in these functional terms. This *functional body* now coexists with and overlays the quantified mechanical body and the at-risk body of earlier periods.[36]

The fate of the egg has mirrored some of these broad shifts in the form of nutritionism over the past century. During the first half of the twentieth century, eggs were prized as a protective food and a cheap, compact, and convenient source of many desirable nutrients, such as protein. Following the vilification of dietary cholesterol in the 1960s, eggs too were vilified because of their cholesterol content, with recommendations to limit egg consumption to a maximum of three per week.[37] However, by the late 1990s, nutrition experts had largely exonerated eggs due to the waning concerns over dietary cholesterol, and eggs could once again be celebrated for their protein content, favorable fatty-acid profile, and other valued food components. The emergence of "designer" eggs with enriched omega-3 fats—via the engineering of chicken feed—has also enabled the repositioning of eggs as a functional food that supposedly delivers additional and enhanced health benefits.[38]

NUTRITIONALLY REDUCTIVE TECHNOLOGICAL PRACTICES: NUTRITIONALLY ENGINEERED AND TRANSNUTRIC FOODS

Nutrient-level scientific knowledge can be used to guide our food choices, such as for choosing between different types of whole foods or for avoiding particular processed foods, in order to achieve specific nutritional goals. However, the food industry has increasingly drawn on this nutricentric knowledge over the past century as the basis for more direct nutrient-level interventions in the design of food products.

Nutritionally engineered foods are foods that have had their nutrient profile deliberately modified, usually through the addition or reduction of quantities of particular nutrients or ingredients. These engineered foods may be whole foods bred or produced in a way that modifies their nutrient profile, such as genetically engineered Golden Rice, with enhanced beta-carotene, or omega-3 enhanced eggs.[39] They may also be minimally processed or refined foods nutritionally modified during processing, such as reduced-fat milk and dairy products or probiotic yogurts produced with specific cultures. However, in many cases nutritionally engineered foods are highly processed and reconstituted foods produced using poor-quality and processed ingredients, a range of chemical additives, and high levels of added fats, salt, and sugar. In these cases, the claimed or implied health benefits of these foods are especially dubious, given that they focus on one or two ingredients added to or subtracted from the foods rather than the food's overall quality or nutritional profile.

Nutritional engineering may involve the addition of nutrients already present in a particular food in its unprocessed form. This includes vitamin C–enhanced orange juice or white flour fortified with the vitamins and minerals removed from the whole grain during the refining process. However, nutritional engineering often entails the introduction of nutrients not otherwise found in or associated with a particular food, such as the addition of plant sterols in margarine, calcium-enriched orange juice, fiber in drinks, fish oil in bread, and vitamins in water.[40] I refer to these latter foods as *transnutritionally engineered foods*—or simply *transnutric foods*—as they involve the transfer of nutrients across recognized food categories and boundaries. Transnutric foods tend to blur the distinction between types of foods and food categories and may thereby undermine dietary advice based on traditional food groups and food types.[41]

A range of new technologies are also being developed for nutritionally engineering foods, such as the genetic engineering of crops or nanotechnologies for adding nanoscale-encapsulated nutrients into foods in order to enhance the bioavailability and stability of these nutrients.[42] At the same time, these nutritional-engineering applications are being used to promote the benefits of the technologies themselves and to thereby overcome consumer and social-movement opposition to these technologies and their products. Genetically modified Golden Rice, for example, has been touted as a technological solution to vitamin A deficiency for the world's poor; and it is used to counter arguments that genetically modified crops are undermining the food security of poor farmers and communities and that they facilitate the corporate control of seeds and farmers.[43]

The nutritional engineering of a food can be described as a nutritionally reductive technological practice both in the sense that it involves the materialization—or technological embodiment—of nutritionally reductive scientific knowledge, and also in the sense that it involves reductive and narrowly framed technological solutions to perceived problems of dietary health. Nutritional engineering tends to be guided by nutritionally reductive scientific knowledge, either in the form of nutrient-level reductionism, single-nutrient reductionism, or biomarker reductionism. The claimed health benefits of these nutritionally engineered foods not only rely on the accuracy of the scientific knowledge upon which these nutritional modifications are based—such as the claimed benefits of enhanced omega-3 consumption in the case of omega-3-fortified foods. In many cases the health claims also assume that these single nutrients will directly impart health effects regardless of the particular types of foods, or the food "matrix," in which they are embedded.[44]

These foods may well deliver a substantial dose of extracted or synthesized nutrients and food components. However, this dose is only a simplified and narrow range of valued, popularly recognized, and easily attainable nutrients that are usually added to food products, rather than the much wider range of known and unknown components in foods. The ways in which the body metabolizes these nutrients may also be compromised if they are not consumed together with the nutrients and food components with which they are otherwise combined in whole foods. Similarly, it is assumed that a food's health benefits are enhanced through the removal of so-called bad nutrients, such as reduced-fat milk and dairy products. Yet the absence of these nutrients may also disrupt the nutrient balance of these foods and diminish their health benefits.

Nutritional engineering thereby represents a one-dimensional strategy of maximizing or minimizing the quantities of particular nutrients and food components, at the expense of a more multidimensional approach to food and dietary health. At the same time, by transferring particular nutrients to a range of food products, this one-dimensional rationality is also overlayed by what I refer to as a *logic of interchangeability,* whereby foods come to be viewed as interchangeable sources of a set of standardized and generic nutrients.[45]

NUTRITIONALLY MARKETED AND FUNCTIONALLY MARKETED FOODS

The marketing of foods on the basis of their nutrient profile has a long history. But its rise as a dominant marketing strategy has followed the shift to nutricentric dietary advice since the 1970s, when the food industry realized that this nutricentric focus created opportunities and not just threats to the markets for their products. Foods marketed on the basis of their nutrient content can be considered *nutritionally marketed foods.* Nutritional marketing typically focuses on the presence or absence of one or two nutrient components of a food, such as the presence of vitamins C, calcium, or omega-3 fats or reduced quantities of fat, cholesterol, or calories. Nutritionally marketed products may be whole foods or minimally processed foods, but they are often highly processed and packaged convenience foods nutritionally engineered in order to advertise the corresponding nutritional marketing claims.

These nutritional marketing practices are reductive in a number of ways. First, the reductive focus on nutrient composition—that is, nutrient-level reductionism—tends to conceal the quality of a food and its ingredients. This is particularly the case with highly processed foods such as many children's breakfast cereals, products that typically contain highly refined grains, sugars, and chemical additives but are marketed based on an extensive list of added vitamins and minerals. At the same time, the nutrient-content claims on the front of the pack, or on the nutrition information panel, do not distinguish between nutrients intrinsic to a food product and its ingredients, on the one hand, and those added to a food during processing on the other.[46] Second, the reductive focus on the quantities or ratios of one or two nutrients—that is, single-nutrient reductionism—tends to distract from the overall nutrient profile of a food product. Having been convinced by nutrition experts of the health effects of single nutrients outside of any other nutritional, food, and dietary context, the lay public is understandably accepting of these single-nutrient marketing claims. It is the very simplicity of most nutritional-marketing messages that probably accounts for their power and success in influencing consumer choice. Consumer research also suggests that people tend to eat more servings of a food product if they perceive it to be healthy—such as low-fat biscuits—and therefore such nutritional marketing may increase consumption of otherwise poor-quality foods.[47]

Since the 1990s, food regulators in the United States and a number of other countries have permitted a range of direct health claims on food labels and in advertisements.[48] These health claims make explicit links between foods, nutrients, and other food components, on the one hand, and specific health outcomes on the other. I refer to foods marketed with health claims as *functionally marketed foods,* since these claims refer directly to the effect on bodily functions and health conditions. While nutrient-content claims rely on consumers making their own connections between nutrient claims and perceived health outcomes—and are therefore limited by such commonly recognizable nutrient-health associations—functionally marketed foods open up a wider range of marketing possibilities for the food industry. Health claims may therefore be particularly effective for reaching and influencing consumers with lower levels of nutritional knowledge.[49] Like nutrient-content claims, however, health claims tend to decontextualize foods from broader dietary contexts, and they tend to exaggerate the potential health benefits of consuming single foods or single nutrients.[50]

The US Food and Drug Administration (FDA) distinguishes between three types of health-related claims on food labels: health claims, qualified health claims, and structure/function claims.[51] Health claims are those that refer directly to the relationship between food components and the risk of disease or other health-related conditions, particularly chronic diseases. These require the highest level of scientific substantiation and regulatory approval. FDA-approved health claims include the link between calcium and osteoporosis; soy protein and the risk of coronary heart disease; saturated fats, transfats, dietary cholesterol, and heart-disease risk; and folic acid and neural tube defects.

Qualified health claims are a relatively new category introduced in 2003 and are essentially claims that have not yet met the FDA's scientific substantiation criteria required for health claims.[52] Nevertheless they are permitted to advance similar types of claimed health benefits—such as the link between omega-3 fats and the reduction of heart-disease risk—along with an accompanying statement that "conclusive" evidence does not exist for such claims. Some whole foods or whole-food extracts have also received approval for health claims or qualified claims, such as whole oats or oat flour, nuts, tomatoes or tomato sauce, and green tea.

Structure/function claims are generally those that link nutrients or foods to normal bodily functioning and growth—such as "calcium builds strong bones" and "fiber maintains bowel regularity." These claims are largely unregulated and do not require preapproval by the FDA.[53] Yet these structure/function claims are essentially health claims, as they refer directly to the effects of foods and nutrients on bodily health and may be equally effective as marketing tools. The US General Accounting Office has acknowledged that "the differences between health claims and structure/function claims are not apparent to consumers and can lead to misuse."[54] That a distinction is even made between health claims and structure/function claims for regulatory purposes—as is the case in a number of countries— seems designed to give food companies an easy and relatively unregulated avenue for advertising claimed health benefits. The introduction of qualified health claims is similarly a means for permitting a wider range of disease-risk claims but with a lower level of substantiation requirements.

The era of functional nutritionism has opened up a range of new possibilities for designing, promoting, and adding value to foods. This includes a proliferation of nutrients, food components, and whole foods considered as health enhancing; new types of direct health claims on food labels; and a wider range of bodily processes and health conditions being explicitly targeted by food companies.[55] A distinct feature of this functional marketing has been the more explicit reference to internal bodily processes in food-marketing campaigns. Advertisements for cholesterol-lowering margarines, for example, explicitly describe how plant sterols enter the intestines and block the absorption of cholesterol into the blood, while probiotic yogurts are advertised with reference to "good microorganisms" in the stomach. The maturing of the market for nutritionally engineered and functionally marketed foods has also created spaces for higher-quality "premium" food products that target wealthier consumers—such as foods produced largely from good-quality whole-food ingredients, perhaps with an added food component—in contrast with the "lesser evil" versions of relatively cheap, highly processed foods aimed at a mass market.

The commercial application of nutritional engineering and marketing practices can be understood as contributing to the process of nutricommodification, whereby nutrients become a means for commodifying the knowledge, practices, and products of food production and consumption.[56] Nutrients that are otherwise readily available in the everyday foods we consume are isolated or synthesized to form objects for direct consumption and are transformed into products with a monetary exchange value, either in the form of nutritionally engineered foods or nutritional supplements. Similarly, the knowledge of what constitutes nutritious and healthful foods is commodified in the form of nutritional and functional marketing claims and used as a means for creating a demand for particular products, such as weight-loss diet plans framed in terms of their macronutrient profile. Nutricentric consumers thereby become trapped within the nutrient treadmill, compelled to keep up with the latest scientific studies and nutrient fetishes in order to maintain and enhance their health or to minimize their disease risks.[57] It is primarily the larger, global food corporations that have the resources and capacity to develop and patent the technologies and products of nutritional engineering and to produce any scientific evidence required for health claims. Nutritionally engineered and functionally marketed foods are therefore also likely to facilitate the further concentration of corporate ownership and control within and across the various sectors of the agri-food system.[58]

THE IDEOLOGICAL ROLE OF THE FUNCTIONAL FOODS CONCEPT

The concept of functional foods has been notoriously hard to define.[59] Since the 1990s, nutrition experts and the food industry have increasingly used this term to refer to foods that have been nutritionally engineered in some way or to foods that are marketed with nutrient-content or health claims.[60] Nutrition scientist Martijn Katan, for example, defines functional foods simply as "a branded food that claims explicitly or implicitly to improve health and wellbeing."[61] Marion Nestle has similarly defined functional foods as "products created just so that they can be marketed using health claims."[62]

However, most definitions of functional foods provided by nutrition experts and the food industry go further, asserting that such foods not only *claim* to but also *deliver* precisely targeted and enhanced health benefits. Indeed the term "functional foods" itself proclaims that these foods *are* functional and that by default "conventional" foods are not. Functional foods are said to provide health benefits "beyond" the "basic nutrients" contained in conventional foods or to provide "targeted health benefits."

The American Dietetic Association (ADA), for example, in its position paper on functional foods, "classifies all foods as functional at some physiological level because they provide nutrients or other substances that furnish energy, sustain growth, or maintain/repair vital processes. However, functional foods move beyond necessity to provide additional health benefits that may reduce disease risk and/or promote optimal health."[63] The ADA begins by admitting that all foods are functional in some way, yet still goes on to suggest that functional foods are a separate class of especially healthful foods. The examples of functional foods given by the ADA include both "conventional" or "unmodified whole foods" as well as "modified foods." Most fruits, vegetables, and nuts seem to qualify as conventional foods (or whole foods). The ADA identifies the beneficial properties of citrus fruits for stomach cancer, tree nuts for sudden cardiac death, cruciferous vegetables and lycopene (found in tomatoes) for various cancers, and fermented dairy products for irritable bowel syndrome. The modified foods (or nutritionally engineered foods) identified include calcium-fortified orange juice, folate-enriched breads, plant sterol–enriched margarines, "energy-promoting" beverages enhanced with ginseng and guarana, and genetically engineered oil seeds that have been omega-3 enhanced or that are transfat free.

Another definition of functional foods is the widely quoted European consensus document prepared by the International Life Sciences Institute, which states that "a food can be regarded as 'functional' if it is satisfactorily demonstrated to affect beneficially one or more target functions in the body, beyond adequate nutritional effects, in a way that is relevant to either an improved state of health and well-being and/or reduction of risk of disease."[64] More recently, Maurice Doyon and JoAnne Labrecque consulted a team of experts and reviewed the literature on functional foods before formulating what they considered to be a precise definition: "A functional food is, or appears similar to, a conventional food. It is part of a standard diet and is consumed on a regular basis, in normal quantities. It has proven health benefits that reduce the risk of specific chronic diseases or beneficially affect target functions beyond its basic nutritional functions."[65]

Doyon and Labrecque consider the distinction between different of types of "physiological effects" as an important aspect of their definition. Functional foods are those that "reduce the risk of disease, enhance function and contribute to restore health," but they specifically exclude foods that merely "improve nutritional equilibrium" or prevent nutritional deficiencies. The examples given that meet their definition of functional foods include all-bran cereals, 2 percent milk with added vitamin D, omega-3-enriched milk, and orange juice fortified with calcium. Foods they exclude from their definition include Oreo cookies low in fat and high in sugar; energy drinks high in sugar, caffeine, and guarana; and even apples. They classify apples as merely a healthy food that maintains "basic nutritional functions," although apples could be recategorized as functional food if scientific studies prove that apples reduce the risk of chronic diseases or "beneficially affect target functions."[66]

There are a number of limitations, questionable assumptions, and even contradictions within these and most other definitions of functional foods, particularly with respect to the types of foods and health effects included in the category. While unmodified whole foods are frequently given as examples of functional foods, most definitions tend to be biased toward nutritionally engineered or fortified processed foods. By excluding foods that merely provide "basic" and "adequate" nutrients— presumably those nutrients that are readily obtainable in a balanced whole-foods diet, and in quantities required to merely avoid nutritional-deficiency diseases— functional foods are invariably foods that have been nutritionally engineered in some way, such as those with concentrated doses of particular nutrients. Nutritionally engineered processed foods can thereby be positioned as being healthier—or more health enhancing—than most whole foods.

The meaning of "basic nutrients" and "beyond basic nutrients" is particularly confusing. Many so-called functional foods seem to have been fortified with beneficial nutrients and food components that are readily available in sufficient quantities in other foods or in a generally well-balanced diet, so it is unclear how such functional foods provide more than basic nutrients. The claimed benefits of any small differences in the quantities or ratios of particular nutrients in these functional foods also seem greatly exaggerated if not simply erroneous. These nutritionally engineered foods may well partially compensate for some nutrient deficiencies or excesses in those individuals consuming an otherwise poor diet. But it is questionable whether such fortified foods in themselves provide a more optimal range of nutrients, or additional health benefits, to those attainable from conventional, good-quality foods and diets. As many public health nutritionists have emphasized, health outcomes such as reducing the risk of chronic diseases are primarily shaped by broader dietary patterns rather than the consumption of individual foods or nutrients.[67] At the same time, there may also be direct health *hazards* associated with the excess consumption of particular nutrients and ingredients added to a range of foods.[68]

Another general problem with these definitions is the distinction they set up between some sort of "basic" state of health and bodily functioning, on the one hand, and an "enhanced" state of health on the other. Most definitions suggest that nonfunctional or conventional foods merely provide the adequate nutrients required for normal growth and bodily functioning and to avoid nutrient-deficiency diseases. In this sense, conventional foods are said to only address the concerns associated with the era of quantifying nutritionism. Functional foods, by contrast, are positioned as optimizing the consumption of "good" nutrients, reducing the consumption of "bad" nutrients, reducing the risk of chronic diseases, and enhancing specific bodily functions—that is, they address the concerns of both the good and bad and the functional eras of nutritionism. This seems an arbitrary way of differentiating functional from nonfunctional foods.

The functional foods concept is also defined in such a way as to cut across and blur the boundary between food and medicine.[69] As with terms like "nutraceuticals" and "pharmafoods," functional foods are perceived and marketed as having druglike qualities. The idea of food as medicine is not new of course.[70] However, the more traditional or premodern approaches to food as medicine involved recognizing the medicinal properties of whole foods and utilizing them in their received, whole, or unprocessed form. The modern era has been characterized by a fragmentation of food and medicine at the biochemical level and the development of distinct industries producing processed industrial foods, on the one hand, and chemically synthesized medicines and pharmaceuticals on the other. In the contemporary era, the emergence of the functional foods concept does not herald a simple return to traditional approaches to food as medicine. Rather, functional foods can be understood as a postmodern food category that represents the reintegration of industrial foods and chemical medicines *at the biochemical level,* to the extent that this involves inserting nutrients, food components, and other chemical compounds into processed reconstituted foods.

The functional foods concept essentially performs an important ideological role both for nutrition experts and for the food industry. First, it serves to legitimate the functional nutritionism paradigm by demonstrating nutrition experts' knowledge of precisely which foods and nutrients affect and enhance bodily health and specific bodily functions. For the food industry, on the other hand, the functional foods category legitimates the promotion and marketing of some highly processed foods as health enhancing, while also undermining the idea that whole foods are necessarily more healthful than highly processed foods. The term "functional foods" is ultimately a misnomer or is defined so broadly as to render it meaningless. The term could instead be substituted with more specific categories that accurately describe the types of foods being referred to. Some of the alternative categories I have suggested here are nutritionally engineered foods, transnutric foods, nutritionally marketed foods, and functionally marketed foods.

Given that the functional foods concept—along with the nutritionism paradigm in general—also tends to blur the distinction between processed and unprocessed foods, a broader range of categories are also required for more clearly identifying types of foods in terms of levels of processing, techniques of production, and other indicators of food quality.[71] For example, at least three broad categories of foods could be distinguished relating to processing methods: unprocessed or minimally processed whole foods; refined processed foods; and processed reconstituted foods. I define *processed reconstituted foods* as those foods with little if any direct relation to any particular whole foods but that have been reconstructed—from the ground up—out of the deconstituted components of whole foods and other technoscientifically engineered ingredients and additives.[72] In terms of technologies of food production and processing, descriptions such as manually processed foods, mechanically processed foods, chemically processed or chemically engineered foods, and nanoprocessed or nanoengineered foods, would also give a sense of the methods used to process and transform foods and their ingredients.

These food categories can contribute to the development of what I refer to as a *food quality paradigm,* in which the quality of a food and its ingredients are considered paramount and are evaluated in terms of the types of agricultural and processing techniques used in their production.[73] A food quality paradigm would provide one possible alternative to the nutritionism paradigm, both as an alternative to nutricentric ways of evaluating the healthfulness of foods and also as a framework for contextualizing and qualifying nutrient-level knowledge.

NOTES

1. L. M. Ohr, "The Best of Functional Foods 2009," *Food Technology* 63, no. 5 (2009): 93–107; E. Sloan, "The Top 10 Functional Food Trends," *Food Technology* 62, no. 5 (2008): 25–44.

2. The nutrient level can be described as a more abstract and disembodied level or mode of engaging with food, in the sense that it abstracts from direct sensory perception of food. On the concept of material levels of abstraction, including in relation to forms of scientific knowledge, see G. Sharp, "Constitutive Abstraction and Social Practice," *Arena* 70 (1985): 48–82; G. Sharp, "Intellectual Interchange and Social Practice," *Arena* 99–100 (1992): 188–216.

3. G. Scrinis, "Sorry Marge," *Meanjin* 61, no. 4 (2002): 108–16, and "On the Ideology of Nutritionism," *Gastronomica* 8, no. 1 (2008): 39–48. For other critical perspectives on different aspects of nutritionism, see R. H. Hall, *Food for Nought: The Decline in Nutrition* (Hagerstown, MD: Harper and Row, 1974); D. Jacobs and L. Tapsell, "Food, Not Nutrients, Is the Fundamental Unit in Nutrition," *Nutrition Reviews* 65, no. 10 (2007): 439–50; G. Cannon, *The Fate of Nations: Food and Nutrition Policy in the New World*, Caroline Walker Lecture (London: Caroline Walker Trust, 2003); T. C. Campbell, *The China Study: The Most Comprehensive Study of Nutrition Ever Conducted and the Startling Implications for Diet, Weight Loss and Long-Term Health* (Dallas: Bendella, 2005); and M. Pollan, *In Defense of Food: The Myth of Nutrition and the Pleasures of Eating* (New York: Allen Lane, 2008). On the exploitation of nutritional knowledge for food marketing, see M. Nestle, *Food Politics: How the Food Industry Influences Nutrition and Health* (Berkeley: University of California Press, 2007); J. D. Gussow and S. Akabas, "Are We Really Fixing Up the Food Supply?" *Journal of the American Dietetic Association* 93, no. 11 (1993): 1300–1304; and J. Dixon and C. Banwell, "Re-embedding Trust: Unravelling the Construction of Modern Diets," *Critical Public Health* 14, no. 2 (2004): 117–31. On

the cultural history of nutricentrism in the United States, see W. J. Belasco, *Appetite for Change: How the Counterculture Took on the Food Industry* (New York: Cornell University Press, 2007); and H. Levenstein, *Paradox of Plenty: A Social History of Eating in Modern America* (Berkeley: University of California Press, 2003).

4. In identifying nutritionism as an ideology, this is not to suggest that nutritionism represents a distortion of otherwise objective nutrition science research. Rather, all scientific knowledge and technological practices are produced, interpreted, and applied within particular paradigms.

5. Nutrient-level reductionism is a form of *inter*level reductionism, while single-nutrient reductionism is an example of *intra*level reductionism. Similar forms of reductionism can be observed in other branches of science, such as biology and genetics.

6. Ross Hume Hall argues that the technological system has undermined the role of the senses in understanding food quality. Hall, *Food for Nought.*

7. For an example of a high-protein weight-loss diet, see M. Noakes and P. Clifton, *The C.S.I.R.O. Total Wellbeing Diet* (Camberwell, UK: Penguin, 2005).

8. The characterization of naturally occurring nutrients in foods as "good" and "bad"—as in the case of "good and bad fats"—is another example of this simplification of nutritional knowledge, as it exaggerates and distorts scientific understanding of the role of these nutrients.

9. Jacobs and Tapsell, "Food, Not Nutrients"; D. R. Jacobs, M. Gross et al., "Food Synergy: An Operational Concept for Understanding Nutrition," suppl. *American Journal of Clinical Nutrition* 89: 1543S–48S; D. R. Jacobs and L. M. Steffen, "Nutrients, Foods, and Dietary Patterns as Exposures in Research: A Framework for Food Synergy," suppl. *American Journal of Clinical Nutrition* 78 (2003): 508S–13S.

10. P. R. Marantz, E. D. Bird et al., "A Call for Higher Standards of Evidence for Dietary Guidelines," *American Journal of Preventative Medicine* 34, no. 3 (2008): 234–66; G. Taubes, "The Soft Science of Dietary Fat," *Science* 291 (March 30, 2001): 2536–45.

11. For a critique of the nutrient information panel, see Cannon, *Fate of Nations.*

12. L. Unnevehr and E. Jagmanaite, "Getting Rid of Trans Fats in the US Diet: Policies, Incentives and Progress," *Food Policy* 33 (2008): 497–503.

13. G. Scrinis, "The Artificial Taming of the Fat Scare," *Sydney Morning Herald,* May 11, 2007.

14. Jacobs and Tapsell, "Food, Not Nutrients"; B. Trivedi, "The Good, the Fad and the Unhealthy," *New Scientist* 191 (2006): 42–49.

15. John Coveney uses the term "nutricentric" in *Food, Morals and Meanings: The Pleasure and Anxiety of Eating* (London: Routledge, 2006).

16. L. Holm, "Food Health Policies and Ethics: Lay Perspectives on Functional Foods," *Journal of Agricultural and Environmental Ethics* 16 (2003): 531–44.

17. M. Franz, "The Glycemic Index of High-Sugar Foods," *American Journal of Clinical Nutrition* 107, no. 4 (2007): 564; K. Foster-Powell, S. H. Holt et al., "International Table of Glycemic Index and Glycemic Load Values," *American Journal of Clinical Nutrition* 76 (2002): 5–56.

18. For a critique of the use of the BMI, see, for example, M. Gard and J. Wright *The Obesity Epidemic: Science, Morality and Ideology* (Abingdon: Routledge, 2005); E. Oliver, *Fat Politics: The Real Story Behind America's Obesity Epidemic* (New York: Oxford University Press, 2006); and J. Guthman and M. DuPuis, "Embodying Neoliberalism: Economy, Culture and the Politics of Fat," *Environment and Planning D: Society and Space* 24, no. 3 (2006): 427–48.

19. For other ways of periodizing the history of nutrition science, and in particular for some of the characteristics of the first two of these three eras, see Cannon, *Fate of Nations;* and B. Santich, "Paradigm Shifts in the History of Dietary Advice in Australia," *Nutrition and Dietetics* 62, no. 4 (2005): 152–57.

20. On the history and analysis of quantification in US dietary guidelines and nutrition policy, see J. Mudry, *Measured Meals: Nutrition in America* (New York: State University of New York, 2009); and

S. B. Austin, "Fat, Loathing and Public Health: The Complicity of Science in a Culture of Disordered Eating," *Culture, Medicine and Psychiatry* 23 (1999): 245–68.

21. B. Santich, *What the Doctor Ordered: 150 Years of Dietary Advice in Australia* (Melbourne: Hyland House, 1995).

22. On mechanistic metaphors of the body with regard to dietary discourses in the early modern era, see B. Turner, "The Government of the Body: Medical Regimens and the Rationalization of the Diet," *British Journal of Sociology* 33, no. 2 (1982): 254–69.

23. Caloric reductionism is a specific case of nutrient-level and single-nutrient reductionism.

24. H. Levenstein, *Revolution at the Table: The Transformation of the American Diet* (Berkeley: University of California Press, 1988); Mudry, *Measured Meals;* M. DuPuis, "Angels and Vegetables: A Brief History of Food Advice in America," *Gastronomica* 7, no. 3 (2007): 34–44.

25. Cannon, *Fate of Nations.*

26. On the technological fix of flour fortification, see M. Ackerman, "The Nutritional Enrichment of Flour and Bread: Technological Fix or Half-Baked Solution," in *The Technological Fix: How People Use Technology to Create and Solve Problems,* ed. L. Rosner (New York: Routledge, 2004), 75–92.

27. R. Apple, *Vitamania: Vitamins in American Culture* (New Brunswick, NJ: Rutgers University Press, 1996).

28. W. J. Belasco, *Appetite for Change: How the Counterculture Took on the Food Industry* (New York: Cornell University Press, 2007).

29. Nestle, *Food Politics.*

30. Ibid.

31. M. Lawrence and J. Germov, "Functional Foods and Public Health Nutrition Policy," in *A Sociology of Food and Nutrition,* ed. J. Germov and L. Williams (South Melbourne: Oxford University Press, 2008), 147–75.

32. J. Dixon, S. Hinde, and C. L. Banwell. , "Obesity, Convenience and 'Phood,'" *British Food Journal* 108, no. 8 (2006): 634–45.

33. S. Allport, *The Queen of Fats: Why Omega-3s Were Removed from the Western Diet and What We Can Do to Replace Them* (Berkeley: University of California Press, 2006).

34. D. Lupton, *Food, the Body and the Self* (London: Sage, 1996).

35. When applied within the nutritionism paradigm, nutrigenomics can be understood as a form of genetic nutritionism.

36. G. Scrinis, "On the Ideology of Nutritionism," *Gastronomica* 8, no. 1 (2008): 39–48.

37. P. Crotty, *Good Nutrition? Fact and Fashion in Dietary Advice* (Sydney: Allen and Unwin, 1995).

38. P. F. Surai and N. H. C. Sparks, "Designer Eggs: From Improvement of Egg Composition to Functional Food," *Trends in Food Science and Technology* 12 (2001): 7–16.

39. G. Scrinis, "Engineering the Food Chain," *Arena Magazine,* June-July, 2005, 37–39.

40. Holm, "Food Health Policies and Ethics"; Jacobs and Tapsell, "Food, Not Nutrients."

41. Gussow and Akabas, "Are We Really Fixing Up the Food Supply?"

42. G. Scrinis and K. Lyons, "Nanotechnology and the Techno-Corporate Agri-Food Paradigm," in *Food Security, Nutrition and Sustainability,* ed. G. Lawrence, K. Lyons, and T. Wallington (London: Earthscan, 2009), 252–70.

43. M. Nestle, *Safe Food: Bacteria, Biotechnology, and Bioterrorism* (Berkeley: University of California Press, 2003); H. Paul and R. Steinbrecher, *Hungry Corporations: Transnational Companies Colonize the Food Chain* (London: Zed Books, 2003).

44. T. Wilson and D. Jacobs, "Functional Foods: A Critical Appraisal," in *Nutritional Health: Strategies for Disease Prevention,* 2nd ed., ed. N. Temple, T. Wilson, and D. Jacobs (Totowa, NJ: Humana Press Inc., 2006), 363–72; Nestle, *Food Politics,* 297; D. M. Kaplan, "What's Wrong with

Functional Foods?," in *Readings in the Philosophy of Technology*, 2nd ed., ed. D. M. Kaplan (Lanham, MD: Rowman and Littlefield, 2009), 498–505.

45. On the logic of interchangeability, see Scrinis and Lyons, "Nanotechnology and the Techno-Corporate Agri-Food Paradigm." This logic of interchangeability can also be understood as a form of transdimensionality, in the sense that a particular dimension of a food's composition is transferred to other foods and across food categories.

46. Cannon, *Fate of Nations*.

47. Gussow and Akabas, "Are We Really Fixing Up the Food Supply?"; B. Wansick, *Mindless Eating: Why We Eat More Than We Think* (New York: Bantam Books, 2006); A. F. La Berge, "How the Ideology of Low Fat Conquered America," *Journal of the History of Medicine and Allied Sciences* 63, no. 2 (2008): 139–77; V. Provencher, J. Polivy et al. "Perceived Healthfulness of Food. If It's Healthy, You Can Eat More!" *Appetite* 52 (2009): 340–44.

48. C. Hawkes, *Nutrition Labels and Health Claims: The Global Regulatory Environment* (Geneva: World Health Organization, 2004).

49. G. Ares et al., "Influence of Nutritional Knowledge on Perceived Healthiness and Willingness to Try Functional Foods," *Appetite* 51 (2008): 663–68.

50. Lawrence and Germov, "Functional Foods and Public Health."

51. American Dietetic Association, "Position of the American Dietetic Association: Functional Foods," *Journal of the American Dietetic Association* 109, no. 4 (2009): 735–46; USDA food-labeling website, www.fda.gov/Food/LabelingNutrition/default.htm (accessed December 9, 2009).

52. American Dietetic Association "Position of the American Dietetic Association: Total Diet Approach to Communicating Food and Nutrition Information," *Journal of the American Dietetic Association* 107, no. 7 (2007): 1224–32.

53. M. B. Katan and N. De Roos, "Promises and Problems of Functional Foods," *Critical Reviews in Food Science and Nutrition* 44 (2004): 369–77.

54. Quoted in ibid., 372. See also American Dietetic Association, "Position of the American Dietetic Association: Functional Foods."

55. See, for example, Ohr, "Best of Functional Foods 2009."

56. Nutricommodification is in this sense a specific case of the more general process of techno-commodification—the technological mediation of commodification practices across the food system and in the broader economy. G. Scrinis and K. Lyons, "The Emerging Nano-Corporate Paradigm: Nanotechnology and the Transformation of Nature, Food, and Agri-Food Systems," *International Journal of Sociology of Agriculture and Food* 15, no. 2 (2007): 22–44.

57. Scrinis and Lyons, "Nanotechnology and the Techno-Corporate Agri-Food Paradigm."

58. Ibid.

59. G. Scrinis, "Functional Foods or Functionally-Marketed Foods: A Critique of, and Alternatives to, the Category of Functional Foods," *Public Health Nutrition* 11, no. 5 (2008): 541–45.

60. Ibid.

61. M. B. Katan, "Functional Foods," in *Essentials of Human Nutrition*, ed. J. Mann and S. Truswell (Oxford: Oxford University Press, 2007), 397.

62. Nestle, *Food Politics*, 316. See also Wilson and Jacobs, "Functional Foods."

63. American Dietetic Association, "Position of the American Dietetic Association: Functional Foods," 736.

64. A. T. Diplock, et al., "Scientific Concepts of Functional Foods in Europe: Consensus Document," *British Journal of Nutrition* 81, suppl. 1 (1999): S6.

65. M. Doyon and J. Labrecque, "Functional Foods: A Conceptual Definition," *British Food Journal* 110, no. 11 (2008): 1144.

66. Ibid., 1145.

67. Nestle, *Food Politics;* Lawrence and Germov, "Functional Foods and Public Health."

68. A. Sibbel, "The Sustainability of Functional Foods," *Social Science and Medicine* 64 (2007): 554–61; Wilson and Jacobs, "Functional Foods."

69. J. Lehenraki, "On the Borderline of Food and Drug: Constructing Credibility and Markets for a Functional Food Product," *Science as Culture* 12, no. 4 (2003): 499–525.

70. N. Chen, *Food, Medicine and the Quest for Good Health* (New York: Columbia University Press, 2008).

71. Even food-based dietary guidelines—such as food pyramids and the basic food groups—almost exclusively refer to types of whole foods (grains, dairy, meat, fruit and vegetables). In this respect they bear little resemblance to the actual form in which many of these foods are typically consumed, and in this sense these guidelines have remained silent on the increasingly processed character of the foods in many people's diets over the past forty years. Scrinis, "Sorry Marge"; R. H. Hall, *The Unofficial Guide to Smart Nutrition* (Foster City, CA: IDG Books, 2000).

72. G. Scrinis, "On the Ideology of Nutritionism," *Gastronomica* 8, no. 1 (2008): 39–48.

73. See also Hall, *Unofficial Guide to Smart Nutrition.* Hall distinguishes between whole foods in terms of four categories of food quality based on types and degrees of processing.

16

In Vitro Meat

What Are the Moral Issues?

Stellan Welin, Julie Gold, and Johanna Berlin

Looking back in human history, there was a time when hunting was the most common method for getting meat to eat. Gradually, agriculture was established and with this the domestication of animals. Hunting was no longer necessary in agricultural areas but could be used as a complementary way of obtaining meat. Of course, in populated and industrialized areas, there are no longer many wild animals to hunt. Where there are big animals, like the moose in Sweden, hunting is strictly regulated to keep the stock sustainable and to hinder overpopulation. Even if it is popular to hunt moose in the northern part of Sweden, the meat gleaned from this activity is a very small part of Swedish meat consumption.

In fisheries, we are now witnessing the first steps toward something similar to the human use of domestic animals. Still, "hunting" is the predominant mode of obtaining fish, and ever more effective fishing fleets threaten to wipe out many of the most popular fish stocks.

If hunting animals for meat was the first stage, and slaughtering domestic animals the second, it is now time to move on to the third stage in meat production. With progress in tissue engineering and cell culturing, it is now possible to grow animal cells and tissues in bioreactors. Although the technology is at a very early stage and there are many hurdles to overcome, such technology for large-scale production is on its way. Producing meat in this way will constitute a radically new version of meat production, namely meat produced in vitro without any animals being slaughtered.

A living animal does many more things than just grow—at least that is how we wish to see the lives of domestic animals. But from a food-production point of view, much of the energy that goes into a living animal is "wasted." The inputs include not just the feed but also fossil fuel and other resources (Horrigan, Lawrence, and Walker 2002). Even though there is no full-scale in vitro meat bioreactor in operation today, it is an acceptable guess that the output-to-input energy ratio will be more favorable than in conventional meat production (a guess that must of course be verified). If this guess comes true, the result will be less impact on the environment.

In this chapter, we discuss ethical issues related to in vitro meat technology. We contrast this with the "old" meat technology, claiming that the new technology may actually contribute to solving some pressing problems caused by conventional meat technology. We end by briefly outlining the new problems that emerge with the application of in vitro meat technology. But before we turn to these and other issues, let's make a short visit to the future.

SCHOOL TRIP TO THE MEAT PLANT OF THE FUTURE

It is a gray and chilly day, someday in the future. A school bus stops in front of a low building on the outskirts of the city, and children get out to tour a meat plant—this is one of the educational activities for schoolchildren sponsored by the in vitro meat company. The ten-year-olds have learned some basic cooking in school, and now it is time to see where their food comes from. On this day, meat is the topic. Inside the building, the director of the meat plant greets them in front of a large metallic container.

"Welcome to the city's meat plant," the director begins. "What you see here is the very heart of the process, namely, our bioreactor. We have no animals here. This is meat without animals."

A schoolchild raises his hand: "Is it really true that once upon a time they made meat from dead animals? That's what mother says. When she was young she never wanted to eat meat."

"Yes, but that was a long time ago," says the director. "At that time there was something called slaughterhouses, where animals were killed. But that does not exist any longer. Instead, we take tiny cells from animals and these are cultured and grow in the bioreactor." The director points to the container. "In the old days, animals were kept inside big buildings before they were brought to slaughter. We had to import food for them and the animals emitted large amounts of greenhouse gases."

The director tells the children that there were many reasons to start in vitro meat production. "One problem was the environmental impact of all the animals kept for meat production. Vast resources were needed to breed the animals indoors. Our animal cells here do not need so much. As meat production increased around the world when formerly poor countries grew more affluent, it would have required enormous numbers of animals kept indoors to supply all that meat; or many forests would have been cut down to obtain more pasture. Advances in medicine are another reason why in vitro meat production took off. Scientists learned how to grow human organs from human cells. If you can grow a human organ, a muscle for example, to be implanted and function in the human body, it was easy to make the leap to growing animal organs for eating. The muscle to be implanted must function; it must be connected to tendons, blood vessels, and nerves. A muscle for eating does not need to be able to contract. It is much easier to produce."

The schoolchildren move on to an exhibition hall where they see advertisements from the beginning of in vitro meat production. "It was difficult in the beginning," the director explains. "People were very skeptical and regarded in vitro meat as unnatural. At the start, it was also about the same price as natural meat. It was not like today, when in vitro meat is cheap. Shops were afraid to sell the new meat. But then we came up with an idea of a campaign that changed everything. We called our product 'meat without suffering' and made a promotional movie showing pictures from slaughterhouses. We also described the process as good for the climate. Now there is only in vitro meat: And it tastes good too! All the indoor meat production has gone.

FOOD MATTERS

This future snapshot provides the context for discussing various issues that arise when considering in vitro meat. First, most broadly, we turn to food ethics, a field that has grown out of the sphere of traditional ethics. Early on, medical ethics appeared. More recently, we have seen bioethics, animal ethics, research ethics, and even space ethics (Williamson 2003). Now we have an upsurge of interest in what is often called food ethics.

Food ethics has a long history, mostly connected to religion. Many religions have explicit dietary rules that believers must follow. Some foods are deemed unclean and not fit for eating; there are rules for how food should be prepared and sometimes also for when eating various kinds of food is appropriate. These kinds of rules continue to play a large role for many people today.

From a secular perspective, there is what may be called a lifestyle kind of food ethics, perhaps best summarized as "you are what you eat." In this view, food needs to be compatible with a person's basic values and life plans. Even people who do not reflect very much on food refuse to eat some kinds of food. In the Western world, we do not like to eat dogs and cats and other pet animals. Aspects of food production also play a role. Animal ethics has for a long time been at the center of the discussion of meat production. Other considerations in this kind of lifestyle food ethics are that food products be produced in a fair and just manner and traded in a nonexploitative way.

The present interest in food ethics can also be understood in relation to concerns about food safety and food quality. Since the outbreak of BSE—or mad cow disease—these issues have been in the forefront of public interest. There is intense public discussion about food quality and about supplements added to food. Much of this is related to health, but some groups focus on other issues. Such issues range from organic or natural farming in food production, concern over long-distance transportation, questions of waste, and also fair trade and justice for food producers. The recent increase in prices for basic food has also triggered a concern about food security: how will we feed the world and avoid famine and undernourishment?

Concern about climate change has also moved to the forefront of public attention. There is also competition for land with the recently booming demand for, and production of, biofuel from cultivated crops. This has triggered more discussion of food security and the morality of using valuable land to produce fuel for cars—mostly in the rich Western world—instead of food for a starving world population. In general, there is a need to produce enough food for a growing population on a diminishing amount of land.

In vitro meat is not only about technology and science. Will people eat in vitro meat? Will in vitro meat be considered "unnatural" and run into the same problems as genetically modified crops? The naturalness/unnaturalness issue will perhaps be rendered more difficult if animal cells used in bioreactors need to be genetically modified in some way to make them grow faster. Other important issues are the environmental impact of in vitro production compared to conventional meat production and, of course, the question of price.

In vitro meat is a technology that changes the moral landscape. This has happened before and will happen again.

TECHNOLOGY CREATES MORAL PROBLEMS . . .

It is no mystery why new technologies force us to increase our moral responsibilities. In the old days, when it was impossible to send food around the world to relieve famine in distant areas, there was no moral obligation to come forward with such support. It was simply impossible to do. There *was* a moral obligation to come forward and help your neighbors if you were in the lucky position of having excess food. Then, as now, it was not clear exactly how much you were obliged to do for your neighbors. However, before the advent of transport technology, there was no moral obligation to send food to distant countries. Such technology has since vastly widened our moral responsibility to distant persons, while the obligation to people in our neighborhoods has been there all the time.

Another example is organ transplantation. In former times, it was not possible to move one kidney from a living person to another. This is possible today. Hence, a new moral question has emerged: should I give my kidney to someone in desperate need of one? As most of us have two functioning kidneys, we have the possibility of giving one of our two kidneys to someone with end-stage kidney disease. This is a moral question created by the development of modern medicine. It is a question too seldom asked. Most of us tend to shy away from the fact that modern medical technology has expanded what we can do for our fellow beings. It is not just time and property that may be shared with others; even parts of our bodies may be of value for others in distress. Organ transplantation, especially from living donors, generates further moral problems formerly unknown. Should human organs always be given freely with no financial reward? Or can there be a scheme for paying volunteers who are willing to part with one kidney (Omar et al. 2008)? Whatever your view on these issues, the questions are all created by a new technology.

Another example involves human embryos. With the advent of in vitro fertilization, and in particular of human embryonic stem cell technologies, human embryos can be used as a resource to produce potentially medically valuable stem cell lines. This immediately prompted a moral issue: is it right to destroy human embryos in order to produce human embryonic stem cell lines? Whatever your position, the very question did not exist before the technology did. Technology can create moral problems.

. . . BUT IT MAY ALSO SOLVE OLD MORAL PROBLEMS—AND CREATE NEW ONES

Sometimes technological development may partly solve some moral problems. For example, recent development of induced pluripotent stem cells seems to do away with the issue of harvesting stem cells from human embryos. If differentiated adult stem cells can be reversed and turned into more primitive stem cells, ultimately the embryo may no longer be necessary (Persson and Welin 2008, 137).

Let's return to the question of kidney donation: should I volunteer to give my kidney to someone in need? If tissue engineering can produce human organs for transplantation, there will no longer be any need for me to volunteer. If organs can be grown outside the human body from donated cells or from stem cells, then the issue of giving my kidney is no longer pressing. There may be better alternatives.

Such a development is not without drawbacks. First of all, the possibility of engineering organs will in the long run likely be quite expensive. Today, organs are free—except on the black market and a few other places—but the surgery is expensive. The volume of organ transplantation is restricted because of lack of organs. This is particularly true of organs that cannot be obtained from living donors. If organs can be grown in laboratories, the sheer amount of possible transplantation would be astonishing. Why wait until you have a serious heart failure? Better to get a new heart in time. Savings would result in such a case because there would be no need for expensive advanced heart surgery. But the increase in transplantation that would come with increased supply would probably be quite expensive to society overall. National health care systems—such as in Sweden and most of Europe—would likely need to ration transplant procedures.

Similar problems would appear if regenerative medicine succeeds. Such procedures will likely prolong life. It is difficult to know how much the average life span might be extended, but it will come with costs: the actual cost of supporting an ageing population and the less tangible cost of what a changing proportion of old people to young will mean for our societies. Shifting age demographics are already a global issue, though seldom discussed. In the affluent world there is a (slightly diminishing) ageing population with vast resources at their disposal, while in the developing countries we find a much younger population with far fewer resources.

IN VITRO MEAT: THE TECHNOLOGY

What is the present status of in vitro meat technology and what can we expect in the near future?

The main idea is to select suitable cells from animals and make them proliferate in vitro with the help of a growth medium and a bioreactor. Stem cells are the only cell type that can naturally give rise to the large numbers of cells needed to generate sufficient quantities of meat to make this a viable process. The source of the stem cells remains open at the moment. While embryonic stem cells were first thought to be the only alternative, these have been superceded by the use of skeletal muscle progenitor cells and mesenchymal stem cells: cells that are easier to isolate from animals and that still maintain high proliferation rates. Attention has now turned to induced pluripotent stem cells, in which a mature animal's skin cell can be transformed to an embryonic stem cell simply by turning on only three or four genes (Holden and Vogel 2008). This can be done without genetically modifying the cells themselves (Zhou et al. 2009), and although additional verification from the scientific community is needed, the process paves the way for non-genetically modified in vitro meat.

The energy needed to produce in vitro meat consists mainly of nutrients to grow the cells plus what it takes to operate the bioreactor at controlled levels of temperature, humidity, gas atmosphere, and sterility. Stimulation (electrical, mechanical, physical, and biochemical) will likely be needed to get cells to grow into something that resembles muscle tissue as rapidly as possible (Dennis et al. 2009). There will be emissions and waste products from the cells to deal with, but the gases that result can rather easily be captured and controlled. Sterile, deionized water is a key component in this process, which is important to keep in mind when considering future scenarios of climate change and water shortage.

The first successful in vitro meat will likely be in the form of minced meat, which could be further processed into hamburgers, sausages, and so on. Cells grown on porous microbeads suspended in the growth liquid in large bioreactors are expected to offer higher cell yields, and cells plus microbeads could easily be harvested and processed further as a minced meat equivalent. This is not a new concept—microcarriers are used for culturing animal cells to produce insulin and vaccines—and this has already been applied to skeletal muscle cells, although not with meat in mind (Bardouille et al. 2001).

Later on, the idea is to produce the "real" thing: meat filets comparable to their natural counterparts. Today we can grow skeletal muscle tissue in vitro having dimensions up to only a few millimeters (Dennis et al. 2009; Powell et al. 2002), mainly because current approaches lack the internal plumbing system we have in our bodies, namely blood vessels. Cells need fresh oxygen and nutrients continuously, and the waste products need to be removed. Currently, cells are grown on three-dimensional porous structures (e.g., fibers, gels, foams) (Beier et al. 2009), often in the presence of flowing growth media, to allow for transport of nutrients and waste, especially for the cells located at the interior of the structures. Interestingly, the shape of these porous structures will dictate the shape of the cultured in vitro meat filet. There is still a long way to go, but we believe that in vitro meat technology will profit from the intense interest in developing medical-tissue-engineering applications to produce vascularized human tissues and organs for transplantation (see, e.g., Scime, Caron, and Grenier 2009). Such organs for transplantation need to be fully functional. In that sense, in vitro meat has a simpler task. Such an animal organ need not be functional; it is enough if it is edible.

Benjaminson and colleagues (2002) were the first to report successfully cultured in vitro meat using skeletal muscle explants from goldfish. Their study is one of only a few scientific publications on in vitro meat to date (see also Edelman et al. 2005), and unfortunately their approach yielded insufficient quantities of newly generated meat mass. NASA, in the United States, supported this and other research in the interest of developing a sustainable food source for long-distance space travel. New Harvest (www.new-harvest.org), a nonprofit research organization founded 2004, also supports the development of competitive in vitro meat products. Furthermore, in 2008 PETA (People for the Ethical Treatment of Animals) announced a prize for the first research group able to produce a commercially available in vitro meat product.

The ultimate goal is to produce all varieties of meat now obtainable from animals. It is not yet clear precisely how in vitro meat will compare to conventional meat production in terms of environmental costs, though the thought is that in vitro meat will have a lighter environmental load. The picture will become increasingly clear as bioreactor design improves, the right cell source is found, the most effective nutrition is established, and appropriate methods for handling the culturing process are determined.

Because we do not need to kill animals to produce in vitro meat, and if in vitro meat diminishes environmental impact, then this technology may indeed solve a moral problem. We may be able to enjoy meat eating while being good (or at least better) to the environment and reducing animal suffering.

ENVIRONMENTAL, BIODIVERSITY, AND LAND-USE ISSUES IN CONVENTIONAL MEAT PRODUCTION

There is wide consensus that human activity is affecting the global climate and our ecosystems. This includes activities such as burning fossil fuels and also agricultural production. It is not just that we may run out of coal and oil in the future, but use of fossil fuels also produces greenhouse gases that tend to increase global temperature. The system of meat production based on grain and soybeans—especially if they are grown on open, newly deforested land—emits a considerable amount greenhouse gases. Studies of the environmental impact of the life cycle of conventional meat production (i.e., agriculture, slaughter, retailing, household use, waste management, and transport at all stages) suggest that the greatest impact comes from the agricultural portion of meat production. The Food and Agriculture Organization of the United Nations reported in 2006 that worldwide livestock activities contribute approximately 18 percent of the anthropogenically emitted greenhouse gases and 65 percent of anthropogenic nitrous oxide (Steinfeld et al. 2006). Moreover, a slaughtered animal contains many more parts than just the edible ones and needs energy input just to live. A conservative estimate is that about 80 percent of the energy input in animal farming is lost. The edible parts of a pig or chicken amount to 70 percent of the animal, while for a cow the amount is 50 percent (LivsmedelsSverige 2009). The rest is used as fodder or is considered waste, which requires waste management. One way to reduce greenhouse gas emissions is by reducing agriculture-related emissions. Using the European Commission's integrated product policy framework, Eder and colleagues (2008) showed that the aggregate environmental impact of meat and dairy product production can be reduced by only 20 percent. For associated greenhouse gases, the improvement potential is about 25 percent. For further reductions, a totally new kind of production is required; maybe that will be in vitro meat production.

Conventional intensive meat production, as all agriculture, puts pressure on land use, whether production is indoors or free range. When animals are raised indoors, substantial input of food is needed. This demand for food for animals (but also for direct consumption) has led to an increase in soybean production. Indoor meat production in combination with free-range meat production exerts additional pressure. For example, in Latin America pastures for cattle grazing have been converted to soybean fields and the cattle have been moved deep into the Amazon (Rother 2003). This threatens biodiversity and also diminishes the rain forest's capacity to absorb carbon dioxide.

Another worldwide problem is the growth of cities, which often takes place on good and fertile land and which may affect the global food supply (Ananthaswamy 2002). The increase in human population and the expansion of agricultural land for growing plants and for pasture will also involve more and more of the planet's land. There is simply no free space left.

ANIMAL ETHICS

There is general consensus that animal suffering is an evil thing and should be avoided as much as possible (DeGrazia 1996). In particular, present-day slaughterhouse practices evoke negative reactions among the public (Eisnitz 2006). There is also a discussion in the European Union about reducing the transportation of animals to be slaughtered. This can be seen as an attempt to avoid (unnecessary) animal suffering.

The views among philosophers and ethicists are divided when it comes to animal slaughter. Painful killing is generally considered unacceptable, but there is intense debate about (painless) killing of (merely sentient) animals who do not have clear sense of a future (McMahan 2002). An important distinction is made by some between persons (human beings and sometimes higher apes) and "mere" sentient animals (Cavalieri and Singer 1994). For persons, we have stricter ethics. Most people find it morally acceptable to kill an intensely suffering animal "for it owns sake," while this is considered morally outrageous if applied to persons.

Not all ethicists concur with this distinction between an ethics for persons and another ethics for merely sentient beings. For a dissenting view, see Regan (1983), who claims that most animals should be treated as persons and be viewed as having rights akin to those that humans have. This is also an idea held by many animal rights groups.

Animal suffering in instances other than slaughter is also an issue. As discussed above, animal husbandry and meat production cause large emissions of greenhouse gases. The easiest way to control these emissions would be to keep animals indoors and capture the gases before they escape into the atmosphere. However, many consider that such lives indoors are not good for animals. Modern factory-like animal production has serious drawbacks regarding animal welfare and animal suffering (Singer 1979). Most animal ethicists believe that an animal life outdoors, grazing freely, is much preferable. This would also give animals the possibility of a more natural life. But the outdoor grazing makes it impossible to control the emission of greenhouse gases.

WHY NOT GO VEGETARIAN?

Some studies indicate that it is environmentally friendly to reduce meat consumption and switch to eating vegetables and plants (Marlow et al. 2009). Why, then, should we be interested in introducing in vitro meat? The simple answer is that most people like to eat meat and will probably resist switching. It is already a disturbing fact that meat consumption increases with economic development (Worldwatch Institute 2006). While global meat production has more than doubled since 1970, the rate of increase in developing countries is higher; and the type of meat production that is increasing consists of confined and intensive meat production (Worldwatch Institute 2006).

That the public, to a large extent, prefers to remain meat eaters instead of turning to a vegetarian diet is a statement of fact. This does not answer normative questions, such as should we become vegetarians for the sake of the environment and animals? A simple answer would be perhaps that we should stop (or reduce) eating meat if this were the only way to avoid serious adverse effects to the environment and to animals. But in vitro meat offers an interesting way out of this problem. In vitro meat may "save animals and satisfy meat eaters" (Hopkins and Dacey 2008). Meat produced by in vitro technology does not involve animal suffering or the killing of animals. There is at least one source animal for the cells in the bioreactor, but the cells can in principle be obtained without killing the animal.

HOW TO CLASSIFY IN VITRO MEAT: IS IT NATURAL?

Will the consumer accept in vitro meat? There is to our knowledge no discussion of consumer preferences, with the exception of the Eurobarometer, the public opinion analysis arm of the European Commission (Eurobarometer 2006). Any public skepticism may partly be attributed to lack of knowledge—and at present there is very little knowledge about in vitro meat as a consumer product. However, it is far from certain that skepticism will melt away with more information. It is popular to claim that public skepticism is due to lack of knowledge, but this general thesis of knowledge deficit and the associated claim that the public would be more favorable if they were better informed does not hold up well in other technology areas (Persson and Welin 2008, 193).

The main issue for consumers concerning in vitro meat may very well be, is it natural or artificial? One answer is that in vitro meat is both natural (produced from real cells) and also artificial (grown and cultured through a tightly controlled technological process). However, exactly the same can be said of much present-day intensive meat production: it is both natural and artificial. The really natural thing seems to be free-grazing animals living out in the countryside. Given the distinction between animal suffering (always bad) and the killing of animals (perhaps not always bad), free-grazing animals may be an acceptable source of meat for many consumers. But slaughterhouse practices seem to be a problem for much of the public. Most people (today) seem to want to eat meat from animals living as naturally as possible, but they do not like the way the animals are killed. In vitro meat does have a competitive edge, then, in avoiding the killing of animals.

Will people actually prefer to eat meat from animals that were once alive? Can we envisage a situation where the quality of in vitro meat is as good as ordinary meat and where people still prefer to have animals killed to get meat that was once alive? Even if we personally believe that it is pure superstition to believe that "once alive" confers some extra benefits to the eater, we cannot rule out that such an idea may take root.

Another question that may emerge connects to religious food ethics. Some religions have strict ideas about how animals for meat should be slaughtered. Only animals slaughtered in the appropriate way are allowed for meat consumption. How will these rules apply to in vitro meat? Will it be considered something other than meat in this religious sense, or will it be ruled out as not appropriately slaughtered? We are eagerly awaiting the first pronouncements from religious leaders.

That we can expect conceptual issues on how to classify in vitro meat to emerge illustrates how important classifications are to humans (Douglas 1996). This has been seen already in the debate around genetically modified food, where opponents claim that this is something radically new and unnatural, while proponents claim that genetic modifications are just a small extension of what nature does already.

CONCLUDING REMARKS

Are we moving into the third era of meat production? From hunting wild animals, to slaughtering domestic animals, and finally to producing in vitro meat? Our belief is that we are. It will take some time to get there, and it will take people quite some time to adjust. The main factor pushing development forward is the medical interest in tissue engineering. We also think that the emerging awareness of the earth's vulnerability and of the dreadful lives of the many animals kept for human consumption will move us in the direction of in vitro meat.

REFERENCES

Ananthaswamy, A. 2002. "Cities Eat Away at Earth's Best Land." *New Scientist* 176 (2374–2375): 9–12.

Bardouille, C., J. Lehmann, P. Heimann, and H. Jockusch. 2001. "Growth and Differentiation of Permanent and Secondary Mouse Myogenic Cell Lines on Microcarriers. *Applied Microbiology* and Biotechnology 55:556–562.

Beier, J. P., D. Klumpp, M. Rudisile, R. Dersch, J. H. Wendorff, O. Bleiziffer, A. Arkudas, E. Polykandriotis, R. E. Horch, and U. Kneser. 2009. "Collagen Matrices From Sponge to Nano: New Perspectives for Tissue Engineering of Skeletal Muscle." *BMC Biotechnology* 9:34.

Benjaminson, M., J. A. Gilchriest, and M. Lorenz. 2002. "In Vitro Edible Muscle Protein Production System (MPPS): Stage 1, Fish." *Acta Astronaut* 51 (12): 879–89.

Cavalieri, P., and P. Singer,. eds. 1994. *The Great Ape Project: Equality beyond Humanity.* New York: St Martin's Press.

DeGrazia, D. 1996. *Taking Animals Seriously: Moral Life and Moral Status.* Cambridge: Cambridge University Press.

Dennis, R. G., B. Smith, A. Philp, K. Donnelly, and K. Baar. 2009. "Bioreactors for Guiding Muscle Tissue Growth and Development." In *Bioreactor Systems for Tissue Engineering: Advances in Biochemical Engineering Biotechnology Series* vol. 112, ed. C. Kasper, M. van Griensven, and R. Pörtner, 39–79. Berlin: Springer.

Douglas, M. 1996. *Purity and Danger: An Analysis of the Concepts of Pollution and Taboo.* London: Routledge

Edelman, P. D., D. C. McFarland, V. A. Mironov, and J. G. Matheny. 2005. "In Vitro-Cultured Meat Production." *Tissue Engineering* 11 (5–6): 659–62.

Eder, P., and L. Delgado, eds. 2008. *Environmental Improvement Potentials of Meat and Dairy Products.* Seville, Spain: European Commission Joint Research Centre and Institute for Prospective Technological Studies.

Eisnitz, G. A. 2006. *Slaughterhouse: The Shocking Story of Greed, Neglect, and Inhumane Treatment inside the U.S. Meat Industry.* Amherst, NY: Prometheus Books.

Eurobarometer. 2006. *Risk Issues.* Special Eurobarometer 238/Wave 64.1: TNS Opinion and Social. http://ec.europa.eu/public_opinion/archives/ebs/ebs_238_en.pdf. Accessed June 2011.

Holden, C., and G. Vogel 2008. "A Seismic Shift for Stem Cell Research." *Science* 319: 560–63.

Hopkins, P. D., and A. Dacey, A. 2008. "Vegetarian Meat: Could Technology Save Animals and Satisfy Meat Eaters?" *Journal of Agricultural and Environmental Ethics* 21:579–96.

Horrigan, L., R. S. Lawrence, and P. Walker. 2002. "How Sustainable Agriculture Can Address the Environmental and Human Health Harms of Industrial Agriculture." *Environmental Health Perspectives* 110 (5): 445–56.

LivsmedelsSverige. 2009. "Förädling av kött" [Meat processing]. www.livsmedelssverige.org/livsmedel/animalier/kott/foradling.htm. Accessed on August 28, 2009.

Marlow, H. J., W. K. Hayes, S. Soret, R. L. Carter, E. R. Schwab, and J. Sabaté. 2009. "Diet and the Environment: Does What You Eat Matter?" *American Journal of Clinical Nutrition* 89:1699S–1703S.

McMahan, J. 2002. *The Ethics of Killing.* Oxford: Oxford University Press.

Omar, F., G. Tufveson, and S. Welin. 2009. "Compensated Living Kidney Donation: A Plea for Pragmatism." *Health Care Analysis.*

Persson, A., and S. Welin. 2008. *Contested Technologies: Xenotransplantation and Human Embryonic Stem Cells.* Lund, Sweden: Nordic Academic Press.

PETA. 2008. "PETA Offers $1 Million Reward to First to Make In Vitro Meat." www.peta .org/features/In-Vitro-Meat-Contest.aspx. Accessed April 2008.

Powell, C. P., B. L. Smiley, J. Mills, and H. H. Vandenburgh. 2002. "Mechanical Stimulation Improves Tissue Engineered Human Skeletal Muscle." *American Journal of Physiology, Cell Physiology* 283:1557–65.

Regan, T. 1983. *The Case for Animal Rights.* Berkeley: University of California Press.

Rother, L. 2003. "Relentless Foe of the Amazon Jungle: Soybeans." *New York Times,* September 17.

Scime, A., A. Z. Caron, and G. Grenier. 2009. "Advances in Myogenic Cell Transplantation and Skeletal Muscle Tissue Engineering." *Frontiers in Bioscience* 14:3012–23.

Steinfeld, H., P. Gerber, T. Wassenaar, V. Castel, M. Rosales, and C. de Haan. 2006. *Livestock's Long Shadow: Environmental Issues and Options.* Rome: Food and Agriculture Organization of the United Nations.

Williamson, M. 2003. "Space Ethics and the Protection of the Space Environment." *Science Policy* 19 (1): 47–52.

Worldwatch Institute. 2006. www.worldwatch.org/node/3893. Accessed on November 22, 2006.

Zhou, H., S. Wu, J. Y. Joo, S. Zhu, D. W. Han, T. Lin, S. Trauger et al. 2009. "Generation of Induced Pluripotent Stem Cells Using Recombinant Proteins." *Cell Stem Cell* 4:381–84.

CONTRIBUTORS

JOHANNA BERLIN is Senior Researcher at The Swedish Institute for Food and Biotechnology and co-editor of *Environmental Assessment and Management in the Food Industry*.

EMILY BRADY is Senior Lecturer in Human Geography at Edinburgh University. Among her books is *Aesthetics of the Natural Environment*.

JEFFREY BURKHARDT is Professor of Agriculture and Natural Resource Ethics and Policy at the Institute of Food and Agricultural Sciences, University of Florida. His books include *Making Nature, Shaping Culture*.

DAVID CASTLE is Associate Professor of Philosophy, University of Guelph. His books include *Science, Society, and the Supermarket: Opportunities and Challenges for Nutrigenomics*.

GARY COMSTOCK is Professor of Philosophy at North Carolina State University. His books include *Vexing Nature*.

KEITH CULVER is Professor of Philosophy and Econoving Chair at UniverSud Paris and Université de Versailles Saint-Quentin-en-Yvelines and is author of *Legality's Borders*.

GARY L. FRANCIONE is Distinguished Professor of Law and Nicholas deB. Katzenbach Scholar of Law and Philosophy, Rutgers School of Law. His many books include *Animals as Persons*.

DAVID FRASER is Professor in the Animal Welfare Program, University of British Columbia and has published over 200 papers on animal behavior and animal ethics.

JULIE GOLD is Associate Professor of Biological Physics at Chalmers University of Technology.

WILLIAM HANNAH is a research assistant at the Institute for Food and Agricultural Standards and member of the Nanoscale Interdisciplinary Research Team at Michigan State University.

RICHARD HAYNES is Professor Emeritus of philosophy at the University of Florida and the author of *Competing Conceptions of Animal Welfare.*

LISA HELDKE is Sponberg Chair of Ethics and Professor of Philosophy at Gustavus Adolphus College. She is the author of *Exotic Appetites: Ruminations of a Food Adventurer.*

MATTHIAS KAISER is Director of the National Committee for Research Ethics in Science and Technology in Norway, and Senior Researcher at the Centre for the Study of the Sciences and the Humanities at the University of Bergen.

CAROLYN KORSMEYER is Professor of Philosophy, State University of New York at Buffalo and is the author of *Savoring Disgust: The Foul and the Fair in Aesthetics.*

MICHIEL KORTHALS is Professor and Chair of Applied Philosophy at Wageningen University. His publications include *Voor het eten* (Before Dinner).

GYORGY SCRINIS is a Senior Tutor in the Office for Environmental Programs, Honorary Fellow in the School of Philosophy, Anthropology, and Social Inquiry at the University of Melborne, and author of *Nutritionism.*

ROGER SCRUTON is currently a visiting professor at Oxford University, St. Andrews, and the American Enterprise Institute in Washington, DC. His publications include *I Drink Therefore I Am: A Philosopher's Guide to Wine.*

KEVIN W. SWEENEY is Professor of Philosophy at the University of Tampa and the editor of *Buster Keaton: Interviews.*

PAUL THOMPSON is W. K. Kellogg Chair in Agriculture, Food, and Community Ethics at Michigan State University. His books include *The Agrarian Vision: Sustainability in Environmental Ethics.*

STELLAN WELIN is Professor of Bioethics in the Department of Health and Medical sciences, Linköping University. He is author of *Contested Technologies* (2008) and *Från nytta till rättigheter* (From Utilities to Rights) and numerous article on ethical and social issues in emerging biomedical technologies including, xenotransplantation, human embryonic stem cells research, tissue engineering, and in vitro meat.

INDEX

COVER DESIGNER
Claudia Smelser

TEXT
10/12.5 Minion Pro

DISPLAY
Minion Pro (Open Type)

COMPOSITOR
Toppan Best-set Premedia Limited

PRINTER AND BINDER
Maple-Vail Book Manufacturing Group

COVER PRINTER
Brady Palmer